# Be It Ever
# So Humble

# Be It Ever So Humble

*Poverty, Fiction, and the Invention*

*of the Middle-Class Home*

## SCOTT R. MacKENZIE

University of Virginia Press    Charlottesville and London

University of Virginia Press
© 2013 by the Rector and Visitors of the University of Virginia
Printed in the United States of America on acid-free paper

*First published 2013*

1 3 5 7 9 8 6 4 2

Library of Congress Cataloging-in-Publication Data
MacKenzie, Scott R., 1969–
Be it ever so humble : poverty, fiction, and the invention of
the middle-class home / Scott R. MacKenzie.
p.     cm. — (Winner of the Walker Cowen Memorial Prize)
Includes bibliographical references and index.
ISBN 978-0-8139-3341-2 (cloth : alk. paper) — ISBN 978-0-8139-3342-9 (e-book)
1. Home in literature.  2. English fiction—18th century—History and criticism.
3. Middle class in literature.  4. Nationalism in literature.  5. Social structure—England—
History—18th century.  6. Poverty—Government policy—England.
7. English literature—Scottish authors—History and criticism.
8. Literature and society—History—18th century.
I. Title.  II. Title: Poverty, fiction, and the invention of the middle-class home.
PR858.H65.M33 2013
823'.6093564—dc23

2012022706

*For my mother and father*

# Contents

# Acknowledgments

This book takes issue with home and its ideals, but my critiques don't imply that I have been deprived personally of the benefits and comforts of home. In fact, the generosity of many people and quite a few institutions has allowed me to make myself at home, to feel at home, to be at home in more than my share of situations. That this book is one of the consequences of all the bounty I have received, then, does not mean I'm not endlessly grateful. So the effort I have put into this work (not the attitude it takes to its subject) is affectionately consecrated to all of my homes and all of my homebodies and homegirls and homeboys and homies.

My dissertation committee was Laura Brown, Harry Shaw, and Mary Jacobus. They got me started and recommended me to others at peril to their own reputations. I have found other guides, guardians, colleagues, mentors, and sponsors—who have helped me carry on with my vagrant wanderings—at the University of Canterbury, Cornell University, Texas Christian University, Keene State College, the University of Alabama, Davidson College, the University of British Columbia and elsewhere, and these good folks include Denis Walker, Alan Shepard, Salli Davis, Randy Ingram, Annie Ingram, Deidre Lynch, Miranda Burgess, Patsy Badir, Tina Lupton, Mary Chapman, Sîan Echard, Stephen Guy-Bray, Dennis Danielson, Gernot Wieland, Jessica De Villiers, Alex Dick, Liz Hodgson, Laura Moss, Jeff Severs, and Mike Zeitlin.

The road crew overseeing my research and publication career so far has included the staffs of the Newberry Library, the British Library, Cornell University's libraries, the Lewis-Walpole Library, and the libraries of Harvard University. The Newberry also provided me a short-term fellowship in December 2000 that was the germinal moment for this book. At PMLA, Adam Potkay, Patricia Yeager, and Vicky Unruh were very supportive and helpful readers, and I am grateful for permission to reproduce here the portion of chapter 1 that appeared in the May 2010 issue. Thanks also to *ELH* for permission to reproduce part of chapter 2, which appeared in the Fall 2007 issue. My readers at the University of Virginia Press have been wonderful to work with, and Angie Hogan has made this process very easy. Thanks also to my Research Assistant at UBC, Alissa McArthur.

Other folks who have read and commented on (and saved and deserve more credit than I do for) parts of this book include: Deanna Kreisel, Vivien Dietz, Patricia Tilburg, the participants in the 2007 Eighteenth-Century Summer Institute at the Newberry Library, Greg Mackie, Vin Nardizzi, Robert Rouse, Sandy Tomc, and Deanna Kreisel.

And then there are the friends who have sustained and supported and instructed me, and paid out money on my behalf: Adam Schnitzer, Dan Brayton, Antonia Losano, Bethany Schneider, Katie Louise Thomas, Jen Hill, Steven Nightingale, Pam Thurschwell, Sam Newton, Eva and Claire Ajdukiewicz, the Hills of Muswell Hill, Heather White, Randy Fowler, Burkhard Henke, Keyne Cheshire, Alyssa Wood, Dory Nason, Quinton Lowry Shaw, Jeff Toward, Louise Mâsse, Vin Nardizzi, Greg Mackie. Thank you, awesome people.

As befits one who has more than one home, I have more than one family. I have my Alabama/beach family: Harold Weber, Petra Schuler, Wendy Rawlings, Joel Brouwer, Elizabeth Meese, and Sandy Huss. RMFTR. I have my Carolina/Paris Family: Trish Tilburg and Thomas Ricard. Make new memories! I have my family of origin: Meredith, Hamish, Callum, Bill, and Lyn MacKenzie, and Ra McBeth, and my grandmother, Joyce Murray. Keep NZ beautiful. And I have my immediate family: Beans & Lou & Hattie & Alice and the one about whom it's all about, Deanna Kreisel—I belong to you and, with you, I am home.

# Introduction
## There's No Case Like Home

Thou art the thing itself: unaccommodated man is no more but such a poor bare, forked animal as thou art.
—William Shakespeare, *King Lear*

Nouns in English, as a rule, do not have full-fledged declensions and equally seldom have distinct cases. Certainly English has no case as specialized as the locative, the case that subsumes prepositional markers indicating location, *at, in, on*. Languages that do feature locative cases include Latin, Sanskrit, and Old English, though lexicographers of English agree that the language lost its declensions long ago. There is one modern English noun that behaves as though it has retained its locative case from the Old English—*home*. Every other locational noun requires an orienting preposition. I may *be* home, but I must be *at* school, *in* Auckland, *on* the moon. *Home* also appears to have a lative case, a very rare one found in languages of the Finno-Ugric group, expressing movement *to* or *into*. I may choose to go home, but I cannot go the Getty Center. Without prepositional orientation the verb *to be* typically precedes appositive nouns (I am boss) or adjectives (I am hot or dismayed), while *to go* requires adjectives or adverbials (I go mad, or blue in the face). *Home*'s special cases also require another implicit orienting term, a possessive noun or pronoun. When the home concerned is not that of the subject, the locative and lative functions of the word do not obtain: I cannot say, "I am Adeline's home," nor can I say, "Adeline is going my home." *Home* always carries with it this implicit possessive. The concept and the syntax of *home* mandate a proprietary subject; every home is somebody's home. The syntactic eccentricity of *home*, then, suggests that its place-ness is complicated by its subjective-ness; it modifies, doubles, or even constitutes the self it syntactically incorporates.

*Home*'s eccentricity among English words is matched by its uniqueness to English; no other language has a term that equates precisely to it. Mihaly

Csikszentmihalyi and Eugene Rochberg-Halton have made a careful search: "In Italian, for instance, *casa* is the nearest equivalent, yet it is much closer in meaning to 'house' than to 'home.' The same is even truer of the French *maison*, and by the time one gets to the Hungarian *haz*, the references are almost exclusively to the physical structure rather than to the emotional space" (121). Robert Southey's caricature Spaniard, Don Manuel Espriella, noticed the singularity of the word in 1807: "There are two words in [English] on which these people pride themselves and which they say cannot be translated. *Home* is the one, by which an Englishman means his house" (*Letters from England* 1: 107). The second untranslatable term is "comfort," and for Don Manuel, that second term explains the peculiarity of the first: "it means all the enjoyment and privileges of *home*, or which, when abroad make no want of *home*; and here I must confess that these proud islanders have a reason for their pride" (108). Home seems to be composed by its own penumbra of syntactic and semantic supplements.

I am unable to say authoritatively when *home* (re)acquired what I have called its locative and lative usages. A content search in the Gale *Eighteenth-Century Collections Online* shows that what I am calling the lative form was in use throughout the eighteenth century: to *go home* was a standard expression.[1] *Home* may never have lost its lative case. I found only one example of what might be a locative usage in the entire Gale collection; it would appear that in the eighteenth century one could not be at home without a preposition. Johnson's *Dictionary* assigns a separate entry to *home* in its lative case, but designates it an adverb: "1. To one's own habitation. 2. To one's own country. 3. Close to one's own breast or affairs. 4. To the point designed; to the utmost; closely; fully. 5. United to a substantive, it implies force and efficacy [a 'home thrust']." In Johnson's estimation, to speak of going home, hitting home, or bringing home to one's heart are all more or less figural variants of the same adverbial function. There are, by the same token, no examples of locative usage (or an adjectival substitute) in Johnson. His definition of *home*'s noun form is: "1. His own house; the private dwelling. 2. His own country. 3. The place of constant residence. 4. *Home*, united to a substantive, figures domestick, or of the same country."

The *Oxford English Dictionary* has a much longer list of entries, including many that register semantic shifts late in or after the eighteenth century. The *OED* acknowledges a lative function for *home*, assigning it to a residual accusative: "10. The accusative retains its original use after a verb of motion, as in *to go* or *come home* (= L. *ire, venire domum*); but as this construction is otherwise obsolete in the language, *home* so used is treated practically as an adverb, and has developed purely adverbial uses" (7: 323). A separate entry is accorded to the adverbial *home,* but the third subcategory in section A of the noun entry militates against the practicality of treating lative and locative cases of *home* as adverbials: "(Without qualifying word or plural.) The place of one's dwelling or nurturing, with the conditions, circumstances, and feelings which naturally and properly attach to it . . . The absence of the article is prob[ably] connected historically with the constructions *at home, to go home . . . from* home . . . but it appears also to be connected with the generalized or partly abstract sense, which includes not merely 'place' but also 'state,' and is thus constructed like *youth, wedlock, health,* and other nouns of state" (7: 322). We may also illuminate the merging of place and state in the locative case of *home* if we consider other examples of place that take *at* rather than *in* for a locative preposition: one may, for instance, be *at* the bank, *at* the Hoover Dam, *at* the show. Such places are defined by a combination of specificity (either personal or public) and institutionality, and like home places that do not command, proper nouns generally imply some sort of proprietorship—my bank, the show I am attending.

The *OED*'s treatment of the locative case is also ambivalent, acknowledging a "locative, in sense 'at home,'" but only as a modifier in compound constructions: "with ppl. adjs., vbl. ns., nouns of action, agent-nouns, as *home-baked, -based, -built, -consumed, -cooked, -cured*" (7: 324). In effect, the editors of the *OED* refuse to recognize a locative sense of *home* as a nominal usage. The closest they will allow is (in the entry for *home* as adverb) that "it sometimes expresses the result of motion," with examples that include, "My son will be home soon," and "people who have been home from Europe three years" (7: 326). Any other expression indicating at-homeness must, presumably, make use of the preposition in order to receive *OED* sanction. But having *been home* from Europe three years seems to me little more a "result of motion" than having *stayed home* from Europe altogether would be a result of no motion. These contortions are perplexing enough to suggest that acceptance of a locative case would be a better solution. While an implied preposition very clearly *allows* us to construe these usages of *home* as adverbial modifiers, the equally intractable claim of the appositional ("constructed like *youth*"), along with the implied possessive, make the nominal function hard to relinquish because, implied or otherwise, *home* is not an adverbial *phrase* and adverbs do not have possessive cases. Perhaps we should say that *home* is a word remarkable for its capacity to occupy more than one part of speech at the same time.

Along with the syntactic heterogeneity of *home* there is a crucial semantic doubling that will inform all of my analysis: besides place of personal dwelling, *home* can of course also mean one's own nation of origin and/or residence, the collective dwelling place. That additional meaning is pivotal to my claim that this study is something other than simply a literary history of private domesticity. Indisputably, dwelling and nation did share a common title long before the Romantic era;[2] Csikszentmihalyi and Rochberg-Halton trace the etymology of *home* as far back as "the Old Norse and Teutonic origins of the word, which originally connoted both a safe place and the whole world" (121). *Home*'s main antecedent in Old English, *ham,* means "homestead, village, manor, estate" (Mills 381). Nation as home was a figure available to, and used by, Shakespeare, but a remarkable shift occurs in the double signification of *home* during the later eighteenth century. At around the same time that the middle-class private home drove out all competing models and meanings of personal dwelling, the national sense of *home* began to privilege its reference to Britain/England over any other nation of origin or residence. The *OED* recognizes this sense, "used by Britons abroad, by inhabitants of (former) British colonies and territories, and by those of British descent in the U.S., for Great Britain = the mother-country, the 'old country'" (7: 322). At around the same time, according to Anne Janowitz, "the sense of 'country' as a rural terrain and 'country' as nation . . . began to melt one into the other . . . the myth of the homogeneous coherence of the nation" was born (4). I will argue that home is a kind of two-bodies metaphor, one that was supplementary to the original, but that replaced the body natural/body politic analogy during the eighteenth century with its "home private"/"home national" revision.

The curious custom by which subjects of British ancestry, but not necessarily native British birth, would refer to Britain (or England) as *home* emerged not just in the United States, but throughout the former empire—in fact more so in territories other than the United States that had large British settler cultures (Australia, New Zealand, India, Canada, South Africa). The example concocted for the 1892 *Australian National Dictionary* is a little deranged, but illustrative: "All good Australians hope to go to England when they die. Not only does everybody, now-a-days, go 'home' when able to do so, but many stay there" (qtd. in Woollacott 1004 n. 6). This usage of the word *home* is intrinsic to the "paradox" described by Bill Schwartz: "England claiming exaggerated subjective affiliation overseas, in the white communities of distant colonies far beyond the home shores of geographical England, was a familiar trope in the narrative of Empire" (95). According to the *Times English Dictionary,* New

Zealand is the origin of that paradoxical usage. Whether or not that is the case, it also took hold in India: "Although Anglo-Indians were 'country-born' and domiciled in India, many imagined Britain as a home and identified with British life even as they were largely excluded from it" (Blunt, *Domicile and Diaspora* 2).[3]

The capacity of home to exert its discriminations on a colonial scale provides material for satire in Christopher Hope's 1996 novel *Darkest England,* in which a South African Bushman, David Mungo Booi, relates his expedition to England: "'Home,' I fell to reflecting, is a terrible word in the mouths of others and worst of all in the mouths of the English, who are the only people in the world whose very country is called Home and for whom the homeliness of other peoples' homes is hatefully foreign where it is not absolutely incomprehensible" (200). Home's synonymy with England coincides roughly with the imperial century and is now disappearing, along with living memory of the British Empire.[4] The oldest example in the *OED* of this semantic detour comes from a 1755 letter by George Washington ("My command was reduced, under a pretence of an order from home" [7: 323]), a resonant source: only after the American War of Independence is there another independent, English-speaking nation-state in the world competing with Britain for the title of home to its citizens. Just as the middle-class private home is preparing to contest the right to call itself the only kind of home there is, England must dispute its title as the singular, original home nation. In 1782, the two principal secretaries of state were renamed the home and foreign secretaries, and hence the Home Office became one of the most powerful agencies of British domestic governance. The implied analogy between a nation in pursuit of imperial domination and a social class in pursuit of hegemony is by no means simply contingent. Private home and home nation were, and are, intimately connected in the development, articulation, and maintenance of their respective bourgeois-universalist forms.[5]

Between 1790 and 1830, the modern meanings of *home* sharpened and grew more rhetorically dense, particularly in the relationship between its private and national senses. *Home* became a keyword marshalling class and political alliances, then reorganizing national order and sentiment, and then asserting hegemonic totality. During this period, what we now think of as proverbs of home—"home sweet home," "there's no place like home,"[6] "home is home"[7]—proliferated, not as comforting platitudes, but as openly politicized slogans. Such slogans ranged from the conservatism of Samuel Jackson Pratt—"give to each that balm of life—a *Home!*" (83)—to the radical—"All things have a home but one— / Thou, Oh, Englishman, hast none" (Shelley, "The Mask of Anarchy," *Major Works* 406, lines 203–4).[8] This study aims to locate and define the crucial rhetorical characteristics of the polemics of home and to trace the processes by which their particular and oppositional meanings transform from limited, factional appeals into a broadly consensual, depoliticized, and dehistoricized bourgeois nature—the accomplishment of hegemony. From an indeterminate designator of dwelling, region, or nation, the term and concept of home shifted to become the constitutive figure and sociopolitical embodiment of domicile *and* nationality, domicile *as* nationality. In his 1803 advertisement for *Cottage Pictures; or, The Poor*, Pratt identifies "what, nationally or individually, is always of the greatest importance—PEACE AT HOME."[9] Citing the philosopher Suzanne Langer, Mary Douglas calls "the idea of home" a "virtual ethnic domain" (293). My private home is both English and a figure for England, while England is the cozy and familial sphere of my nurturance (or would be, were I English—my home anglicizes me).[10]

We hardly need syntactic and etymological evidence to establish home's hegemonic significance. In the English-speaking world, certainly in those nations that retain a popular identification with England as a mother country or ancestral home (I include the United States in this category), home as term, concept, and social practice has an insuperable grasp on the forms, discourses, and orders of social and psychic life. There is no selfhood or identity in these English-speaking nations that subsists wholly outside the systems of home.[11] Modern social life offers no refuge from our place of refuge. We are born into it. One may, of course, be homeless, but the distinction between "homed" and homeless is much more complex than that between, say, hairy and hairless or lively and lifeless. Consider that, even though English has myriad parts of speech for the word *home,* it does not actually have a discrete adjectival form meaning the opposite of *homeless.* One is not simply either "homed" or homeless. To be homeless is to embody an unspeakable exteriority, one that the very syntax of English refuses to accommodate. Homelessness is a calamitous state, abjected by civil order and consequently threatening to the legitimacy of that order. It generates fierce social anxiety and the most urgent collective demands for remedy or removal.

The homeless subject in an important sense does not exist, has no stable place in the social order, and is therefore an enemy to civil society, able (and motivated) to carry out insurgencies undetected. The homeless person threatens to bring civilization to an end and hence is in many respects pivotal to its continued existence; her continual erasure produces and reproduces home-bounded society. There are institutions of homelessness, but they tend to be confined (like the homeless) to such acute liminality as to cluster perpetually at the brink of extinction.[12] One of the sourest ironies of home's convoluted development is its nineteenth-century adaptation as a name for institutions whose purpose is to stand in for the absence of home itself, "providing refuge or rest for the destitute, the afflicted, the infirm, etc., or for those who either have no home of their own, or are obliged by their vocation to live at a distance from the home of their family . . . Sailor's Home . . . Home for Confirmed Invalids . . . Dr. Barnado's Homes for Orphan Waifs" (*OED* 7: 323). The realtor's slogan "if you lived here, you'd be home now" enforces home's tyranny: you do not live here and you are not home now. You are menaced by homelessness even as you make your way home.

Homelessness, then, is not only supplemental to the conceptual life of home, but constitutive of it.[13] The unspeakable opposition between homeless and "homed" is key to the mystification and naturalization of home. The term and concept of homelessness as a particular category of poverty did not come into use until the late eighteenth century, when, arguably, William Wordsworth provides its first full articulation (indeed, I will argue in chapter 3 that Wordsworth has worked out the major conditions and relations of homelessness before those of home have been as clearly defined). The nearest equivalents in prior usage were *unhoused* and the taxonomy of vagrancy: *vagrant, vagabond, wanderer, rogue*.[14] *Homeless* does not appear in Johnson's dictionary and the terminology of vagrancy designates not one who lacks a home, but one who has strayed from the parish in which she is legally settled, the only place in which she is entitled to reside if she cannot afford to pay at least ten pounds per year in rent. The conventional (though not universal) resort for the unhoused during this period was the poorhouse or workhouse, and the parish was the primary unit of administration for poverty.[15] An entirely different set of oppositions comprised the "old poor-law" system (vagrant/settled, unhoused/parish ward, sturdy beggar/invalid) from the "homed"/homeless distinction that organizes modern social welfare. This historical shift is central to the argument of my book: the middle-class private home—as an epistemological construct, an affective complex, and an administrative instrument—was first invented by, but not *for,* the emergent middle classes; it was invented for the poor.

## OUTDOOR RELIEF

The territory through which this study will pursue the origins of the modern middle-class home is the vastly polymodal set of discourses concerned with poverty in Britain between the first half of the eighteenth century and the omnibus Poor-Law Reform Bill of 1834. Among the discursive fields I visit will be philosophical, legal, parliamentary, religious, economic, and aesthetic tracts, all of which bump up against and often spill over into literary productions. Home does not have its own archive; there are no self-aggregated collections of home's early documents, no blueprints for hegemonic innovation, and no feasibility studies devoted to its functions and effects. It came to conceptual life as a disparate array of strategic objects and objectives formulated within discussions whose purposes were other than the invention of home itself. From our perspective, the invention of home takes place in a trace work of symptomatic articulations and strategic affiliations scattered through these other archives. From the eighteenth-century perspective, no such teleological process can be discerned.

My research has led me to conclude that the closest thing to a discrete archive of home's etiology is the body of texts that confront poverty in the late eighteenth century. In that arena we are more likely than anywhere else to find enumeration and testing of home's attributes and the discursive contests that culminate in important kinds of consensus on the shape and value of home. Such is the case in part because, as I have noted, formation of a strong concept of homelessness and its attendant reorganization of geographic, institutional, sociopolitical, and affective coordinates and relations was crucial to the epistemological and ideological grounding of home, but discourse about poverty is also the richest archive I have found of positive delineations and explorations of the categories and qualities that accumulated remarkably quickly around the emergent reconception of home.

Allusions to, debates over, praise for, and polemics on home crop up regularly after around 1780 in texts that deal with poverty and the management of the poor. The basic narrative that underlies this argument is as follows: over the course of the eighteenth century, participants in debates about English poverty management realize that the parish workhouse system and the vagrancy laws are one or more of the following: hopelessly inconsistent, unjust, and costly. In more than one sense, they cannot sustain themselves, and for a few years at century's end the dominant school of thought holds that private family dwellings can turn England's indigent, unemployed, and discontent into a self-sufficient, productive, and patriotic labor force. Happy homes make a happy homeland. Writers and thinkers involved in these debates (and few writers or thinkers managed to neglect the poverty crises altogether) produced copious descriptions and representations of what a private home was and how it fitted into the collective national home. Understandably, novelists and poets were heavily invested in these representational interchanges between poverty and domesticity.

Sandra Sherman's claim that there are no "vivid portraits of the poor" (1) in late eighteenth-century fiction notwithstanding, novelists and poets throughout the eighteenth century dwelt intently upon the en-homing and dis-enhoming of the poor, refracting economic vulnerability through genre topoi such as sentimentality, criminality, the pastoral, the devotional, polemic, satire, familiar correspondence, the comic-epic poem in prose, and often enough the economic.[16] From *Robinson Crusoe* (1719) and *Moll Flanders* (1722) through *Pamela* (1740) and *Joseph Andrews* (1742), what we often call the origins of the English novel are rife with struggles not just for food and shelter, but for private, independent, comfortable, and respectable food and shelter. Henry Fielding is the novelist most intimate with the actual apparatus of poverty management in England, but hardly any novelists in the period ignore poverty altogether. Later in the century, Laurence Sterne, Oliver Goldsmith, and Henry MacKenzie make encounters with suffering poverty a characteristic scene of sentimental fiction. Goldsmith's *The Deserted Village* (1770) helps provoke a broad adaptation of English pastoral and georgic for polemical analyses of rural poverty, which George Crabbe takes up in *The Village* (1783), followed by extensive modifications of those forms in Cowper's *The Task* (1785) and the early verse of Wordsworth. I will also argue in this study that anxiety over the poor and homeless resonates very clearly in the Radcliffean and "Jacobin" gothic fiction of the 1790s, the same decade when the poorhouse is most often painted as a dreadful castle from which paupers flee, seeking shelter in safe and cozy cottages.

Readers may see an awkward parallel between my thesis that home was first tested on the poor and Michel Foucault's assertion that bourgeois sexuality was not: "One must suppose that sexual controls were the more intense and meticulous as they were directed at the poorer classes . . . But this does not appear to be the way things actually happened. On the contrary, the most rigorous techniques were formed and, more particularly, applied first, with the greatest intensity, in the economically privileged and politically dominant classes" (*History of Sexuality* 120).

The same is finally true of home. The poverty debates from which I will derive much of my evidence were much more a set of exercises in codification than actual social practice, hence my qualification that home was invented as an epistemological construct, an affective complex, and an administrative instrument. The ideological, rhetorical, and material application of home was packed up and moved over to middle-class quarters soon after its invention in philosophical romances of an arcadia for laborers. The prevalence of what was paradoxically (to our eyes) termed "outdoor relief" was only short-lived, and it would be a mistake to assume that provision of modest, cozy cottages was accomplished in any comprehensive way in the last years of the eighteenth century.[17] A universal homeliness did not blossom in the English countryside, and certainly not in the English cities. This period was, after all, also the climax of enclosure: "the evidence, between 1790 and 1820, would appear to be unambiguous. 'Whoever travels through the Midland Counties,' wrote Lord Winchilsea in 1796, 'and will take the trouble of enquiring, will generally receive for answer, that formerly there were a great many cottagers who kept cows, but that the land is now thrown to the farmers' and this, not only because the latter preferred to use the land but also because 'they rather wish to have the laborers more dependent upon them'" (E. P. Thompson 217).

There was and remains a general sense that cottage stocks dwindled rather than increased as a consequence of agricultural reforms and the vogue for immense picturesque estate gardens, such as that of the heartless English Baron Lord Langlands, in Elizabeth Hamilton's 1808 novel *The Cottagers of Glenburnie,* who "had resolved against having any cottages on his estate, and was to have them all destroyed" (111–12). In *Northanger Abbey,* the "sweet little cottage" visible from the drawing room at Woodston has its condemnation stayed as long as General Tilney values Catherine Morland's tastes (200), but the narrator does not have occasion to tell us whether it survives the general's disillusionment.

Some direct efforts to support paupers in their own domestic circumstances did occur, among county magistrates, for instance, who at petty sessions frequently enforced outdoor relief, as happened in Maidstone, Kent, in 1797, where the justices affirmed the desirability of letting laborers and their families "feel the enjoyment of domestic comfort" in preference to workhouse confinement (qtd. in Melling 156). Magistrates in Berkshire established the famous Speenhamland system in 1795, which pegged relief subsidies to the price of bread,[18] and a small succession of parliamentary acts between 1782 and

1796 sought to facilitate provision of outdoor relief.[19] Other, private, efforts included Hannah More's *Cheap Repository Tracts* project and Sir Thomas Bernard's Society for Bettering the Condition and Improving the Comforts of the Poor (SBC).

These efforts were, whatever their intent, uniformly beneficial, if not directly subordinate, to modernization and capitalization of labor and property. Consider this excerpt from what might as well be the manifesto of the homes-for-paupers movement, Sir William Young's *Considerations on the Subject of Poor-Houses and Work-Houses* (1796):

> The industrious father of a cottage family leading forth his industrious sons to their morning work, forms a picture as gratifying to the statesman as to the moralist. Such a father of such a family is the most valuable of citizens: his labours, his morals, his affections, all interwoven and implicated, form a character on which the British Constitution may securely rest, and its statesmen well depend, for returns of profitable labour, and for happy and zealous defense of the country, he who hath *no home* to defend, hath *no country!* ... Let the word HOME be appropriated to as many as the lot of life can admit to it, under human institution. (17–18)[20]

This passage is florid, but not unusual in its concern with making home a representational matrix. The production of domestic imagery and figuration seems to have outpaced the production of actual domiciles for the poor so emphatically that it is hard not to feel that generating representations was the primary purpose of the homes-for-paupers movement. This study will focus on the rhetorical and thematic history of home rather than on material histories of poverty management because, ultimately, the textual career of home is a great deal more influential and consequential than the brief abatement in carceral poverty supervision that took place around the end of the eighteenth century.

The vogue for home among the guardians of the poor, as I have implied, did not last long. Poverty-management theory, legislation, and practice stumbled through increasingly disordered and unsettled reforms and breakdowns until the 1834 Poor Law decisively reestablished the workhouse within a severe and homogenized, county-based system that essentially ended the parish's role in English social administration.[21] More than thirty years earlier, even as the cottage home was enjoying its greatest popularity, some economists had already begun to call for a return to workhouse/poorhouse systems; in fact, Jeremy Bentham was stridently assaulting outdoor relief as early as 1797.[22] The pauper cottage, having had its cultural image transformed from a dirty and ramshackle hovel to a comfortable and self-sufficient haven, found itself changing yet again into a hideout for fraudsters imposing on the public weal and engaging in imprudent reproductive activity. By 1833, the Royal Commission investigating the state of poor laws was receiving reports that "the most injurious portion of the poor-law system is the outdoor relief . . . [I]t is utterly impossible to prevent considerable fraud, whatever vigilance is exercised" (Chadwick 11). The repudiation of *populationniste* economic theory, receding fears of French invasion or French-inspired insurrection, and urbanization of labor rendered the 1790s cottage/agrarian ideal of home less and less valuable as a source of ideologically charged representations and as a policy objective.[23]

Having tested the social, moral, and aesthetic components of home on the poor, the middle classes found it very adaptable to their own wants and so appropriated it to themselves. What began as the evangelical (in many cases quite literally) work of groups formulating their own common interests gradually became a repository of the aspirations and values that defined those very common interests and of the collective identity of the coalescing social class. Along the way, the disciplinary mechanisms and functions of homes for the laboring poor turned into "natural," familial, and sentimental attributes that helped define and promote the universal benevolence, virtue, and naturalness of bourgeois values.

Waller Rodwell Wright's Prologue to *Not at Home,* an 1809 "dramatic entertainment" by Robert Charles Dallas, exemplifies the universality and naturalness that home has acquired by the early nineteenth century:

> HOME! 'tis the name of all that sweetens life;
> It speaks the warm affection of a wife,
> The lisping babe that prattles on the knee
> In all the playful grace of infancy,
> The spot where fond parental love may trace
> The growing virtues of a blooming race:
> Oh! 'tis a word of more than magic spell,
> Whose sacred power the wanderer best can tell;
> He who, long distant from his native land,
> Feels at her name his eager soul expand:
> Whether as Patriot, Husband, Father, Friend;

To that dear point his thoughts, his wishes bend;
And still he owns, where'er his footsteps roam,
Life's choicest blessings centre all—*AT HOME.*

Wright folds into his syrupy concoction many crucial virtues of the modern home: the name that evokes a taxonomy of wholesome desires; the combination of place and familial bonds; their extension to a larger kinship group ("race" and "native land"); the vague mystery of magic and sanctity veiled by privacy; the telos of venture, both literal ("where'er his footsteps roam") and aspirational ("life's choicest blessings"); and the hint of a constitutive lack or loss that means "the wanderer best can tell" home's "sacred power."

Another motivation for my focus on rhetoric and representation is recent revisions in social history, which show that the emergence of middle-class domesticity was not, as had been assumed, a sociohistorical transition from standard household forms that were large, suprafamilial, multigenerational, and bound by feudal obligation to new kinds of households based presumptively on the nuclear family and companionate marriage: "The wish to believe in the large and extended household as the ordinary institution of an earlier England and an earlier Europe, or as a standard feature of an earlier nonindustrial world, is indeed a matter of ideology"; "there is no sign of the large, extended, coresidential family group of the traditional peasant world giving way to the small, nuclear, conjugal household of modern industrial society" (Laslett 73, 126). Radical changes to the material circumstances of households and families do not coincide with or explain the emergence of the modern home. Indeed, the historian Karen Harvey asserts that during the later eighteenth and early nineteenth centuries, "'home' was increasingly distinguishable from related terms such as 'house,' 'household' and 'family.' Contemporary meanings of home, particularly in the later eighteenth century, suggest something other than a collection of social relationships (family), an economic unit (household), a physical construction (house or domestic interior), or a co-resident unit bounded by household management (household-family). Instead, 'home' encompassed all these meanings and more, connoting emotional states and serving imaginative or representational functions" (525–26). One of the modern home's crucial attributes is its capacity to comprehend and mediate many other institutions and social formations without being reducible to any one, or several, of them.

A distinguished body of literary-historical work that precedes my own authorizes me to insist that literature is among the most important of the archives from which I can build my historical and rhetorical analysis. Mary Poovey, for instance, begins *Uneven Developments* with what has become an accepted historiographic technique (despite her own recent, unconvincing renunciation): "The object of my study is neither the individual text (of whatever kind) nor literary history, but something extrapolated from texts and reconstructed as the conditions of possibility for those texts—what I have called the symbolic economy or, more generally, the internal structure of ideology" (15).[24] Eve Tavor Bannet endorses that technique, arguing that "the popular novel was where different ideas about the polity, different models of domestic life, and different forms of conduct were presented, contrasted, and contested" (57). Literary reading "will permit us to understand the extremes of imagined possibility in a particular cultural environment" (Bannet 10), though not anything like the full range of negotiations between those extremes. Bannet settles on exemplarity as the foundation of her interpretations: "If, as James Thompson has pointed out, 'novels are a kind of cultural laboratory or imaginary in which various forms of social evaluation can be modeled and tested,' then understanding better how eighteenth-century women deployed exemplarity is key to understanding the ways in which eighteenth-century women's novels 'offer models of choice and expectation'" (12). My own approach is strongly informed by Bannet's example.

The kind of knowledge a study like this one can generate is modeled, in part, by the etymological development I trace at the beginning of this introduction; while I cannot locate conclusively the motivations, negotiations, and utterances that created the middle-class home, I can pick out discursive signs that the epistemic conditions and elements that characterize home are emerging, developing, and operating at discrete moments across the historical period of my study. It may be difficult to demonstrate convincingly where and when home is absent, unthought, or not-yet-conceived, but it is certainly possible to pinpoint discursive evidence that its conception and articulation is taking place. Anxieties about poverty and emerging ideas about home were too culturally prominent in the period for writers not to feel them pressing. Eighteenth-century and Romantic literature regularly appropriates and contests both the rhetorics and thematics of those looming fears and swelling hopes.[25]

## THEORY AND PRACTICE

The historiographic and philosophical premises of this study are drawn from two theoretical sociologies: that of Michel Foucault and that of Gramscian Marxism. Foucault's term *dispositif,* most often translated as "apparatus," is a useful categorical descriptor for the complex and elusive attributes and functions of home. A *dispositif* is "a thoroughly heterogeneous ensemble consisting of discourses, institutions, architectural forms, regulatory decisions, laws, administrative measures, scientific statements, philosophical, moral, and philanthropic propositions" and "the system of relations that can be established between these elements" (*Power/Knowledge* 194). A *dispositif* "has as its major function at a given historical moment that of responding to an *urgent need,*" such as "the assimilation of a floating population found to be burdensome for an essentially mercantilist economy" (195). My argument begins with the assertion that the modern home emerges as a solution to the perceived problem of laboring classes whose productivity is not adequately fostered by the workhouse system. Foucault's framework for historical and critical analysis of social systems has tremendous value for my study because it emphasizes the distributedness of power relations, their reciprocal constitution, and the specificity of every particular articulation of power. Foucault provides a rich vocabulary for discussing social formations like home in terms of the horizontally distributed networks that link individual homes together and the "regimes of truth" (collective and autonomous) that substantiate home's general ascendency. Home is not a hierarchical or centralized apparatus for domination; its individual manifestations are only tangentially shaped by the way other homes look and operate, but home is, nonetheless, a hegemonic cultural object—it serves and helps to maintain modes of governance, class supremacy, and capitalist production.

The terminology of hegemony, class, and production is not itself Foucauldian in the first instance. As has been widely observed, Foucault resists making comprehensive interpretive connections between particular/local examples and abstract/general principles.[26] Because my study proposes some kinds of broad generality and because it asserts the historical operation of class formation, I will also use Gramscian Marxism to refine parts of my analysis. I will insist at the same time that my resort to Gramsci is not incommensurable with the Foucauldian components of my analysis. Writers in the Marxist tradition have sought diligently to account for the emergence and efficacy of powerful cultural formations such as home, and they have generated working theses that readily parallel Foucault's *dispositif.* Marx himself devised the simple abstraction (*einfache Abstraktion*), an instrumental concept that can "arise only in the midst of the richest possible concrete development, where one thing appears as common to many, to all. Then it ceases to be thinkable in a particular form alone" (*Grundrisse* 104).[27] The simple abstraction enables its patrons to "smudge over all historical differences and see bourgeois relations in all forms of society" (105). In Louis Althusser's formulation, "there is no longer any original essence, only an ever pre-givenness, however far knowledge delves into its past" (qtd. in McKeon, *Origins* 19).[28] It provides means to think away contradictions and exclusions, to erase the particular historical circumstances of its formation, and to reconceive prior historical conditions in relation to itself.

Antonio Gramsci's conception of hegemony totalizes the simple abstraction in order to describe the achievement and exertion of sociopolitical dominance by a corporate group that universalizes its own interests. His model of hegemonic process is basically compatible with Foucault's description of the formation and operation of a *dispositif.*[29] The key distinction between Gramsci and Foucault is that the former's frame of reference tends to be collective action and class definition, rather than particular tropes or cultural formations. Gramsci—loosely—explicates historical events in terms of their sociopolitical influences and consequences: preliminary affiliations and strategies in social groups working toward self-definition and self-assertion become "hegemonic activity even before the rise to power" (Gramsci 59). Foucault, by comparison, disavows any priority of event over consequence or vice versa: his *dispositif* begins in "a first moment which is the prevalent interest of a strategic objective" (*Power/Knowledge* 195), but it consists only in "the system of relations that can be established between these elements" (194).[30] Gramsci argues that significant historical transformations develop out of growing confluences among emerging corporate groups, producing what he calls *transformism:* "the gradual but continuous absorption, achieved by methods which varied in their effectiveness, of the active elements produced by allied groups—and even those which came from the antagonistic groups" (59), leading to a hegemonic moment, "in which one becomes aware that one's own corporate interests, in their present and future development, transcend the corporate limits of the purely economic class, and can and must become the interests of other subordinate groups too" (181). In Foucault, the equivalent "moment" is the entry of the *dispositif* into "a perpetual process of strategic elaboration" (*Power/Knowledge* 195) and "functional overdetermination," where "each effect . . . enters into resonance or contradiction with the others and thereby calls for a readjustment or a re-working of the heterogeneous elements that surface at various points" (195). Gramsci expounds upon the "intellectual and moral leadership" of a ruling class (qtd. in Femia 24), while Foucault concentrates on an "ensemble of discourses," eschewing hierarchical topographies of power and any imperative to totalize local instances as general principles.[31]

More than one scholar working in the Gramscian tradition has sought to rearticulate Gramsci's general principles of hegemony in ways that describe discrete instances of hegemonic activity. Jacob Torfing, for instance, argues that "the political as well as moral-intellectual leadership of a hegemonic force (state, class, movement, or other) hinges on the construction of a discursive formation that provides a surface of inscription for a wide range of demands, views, and attitudes" (118).[32] That figuration is eminently suited to the apprehension of home that I will pursue. It is precisely as an ensemble of discourses and relations, which has acquired the social prestige of a natural thing (upon which other discursive contests can be inscribed or projected), that home can exert its coercions and its accommodations.[33] Two of Gramsci's most prominent interpreters, Ernesto Laclau and Chantal Mouffe, construe hegemony in a way that accords with Foucault's distaste for hierarchical schematics. They see hegemony in operation where "a particular social force assumes the representation of a totality" (x), a "contaminated universality" that "lives in this unresolvable tension between universality and particularity" (xiii): consider the way in which home sutures singular, originary, and personal privacy to total, sanctioned, and homogeneous collectivity.[34]

The modern middle-class home is a lavish demonstration of Gramscian hegemony. It may be hard to imagine a more successful one. Home has been a key base of operations in the bourgeois/capitalist conquest of the world. Its institutions and representations have obscured its historical determination, the grounds of its modern emergence, its political affiliations, and its powerful mechanisms of exclusion. After its initial spectacular irruption, home merged into the English landscape as though it had been there all along: "The economics disappear when 'home' reappears as a natural formation" (George 23). It is successful enough as an instrument (or symptom) of middle-class self-assertion that it seems to justify the strongest terms that Marxian historicism can apply to it. The danger, therefore, that home's pervasiveness presents to my study is its hospitality to an orthodox, and potentially teleological, dialectic. The continually posed and resolved contradiction between home as national collective and home as autonomous exemption is so thoroughly implicated in Western cultural life that it is tempting to propose home as *the* salient fact of Anglophone modernity. Home also follows the dialectical prescription that predicts it will rise as the expression of coalescing class spirit and settle into the encompassing ideological structure that is the new middle-class version of Nature. This way of theorizing home has a perfect facility, but I do not claim that the dialectics of home are also those of a total historical process. Without taking a strong position regarding dialectical historical method, I will cite John Grant's summation of Foucault's objections: "'The dialectic' forces events into a predetermined conceptual architecture, domesticating what is otherwise aleatory and reducing a hazardous reality to nothing more than a formula or a 'Hegelian skeleton'" (221–22). Grant's use of "domesticate," meaning to confine within a facile dialectical frame, is apropos. To undomesticate the history of home requires, first of all, dismantling its image as the reified aspirations of *avant-la-lettre* middle-class subjects.

Not only was home first formulated in strategies and fantasies that were by no means directly oriented toward bourgeois domestic idylls, but its accession to that status, to hegemonic prestige, resulted immediately in its fragmentation into a perpetually troubled region of social practice. The tensions between its collective dictates and its particular eccentricities turn home into the "contaminated universality" identified by Laclau and Mouffe, which "lives in this unresolvable tension between universality and particularity" (xiii). Foucault's term "strategic elaboration" describes what I take to be the same fundamental historical transition: each of the hegemonic discourse's elements enters into "resonance or contradiction with the others and thereby calls for a readjustment or a re-working of the heterogeneous elements that surface at various points" (*Power/Knowledge* 195). In my estimation, the "heterogeneous ensemble" of discourses and alliances that first defined home gradually lost their character as overt tactical groupings after about 1800, and from that point forward its tensions and contradictions made themselves felt in ways that look like disaffection with home, especially when compared to the unambiguous rhapsody of 1790s tributes.

A key distinction between discourse about home in the 1790s and after 1800 is that in the later period there is essentially no one writing against home, just as there is no one writing against Nature, only against other writers' representations of home/Nature. In the prior decade home was an instrument for managing poverty, not the social fabric to which poverty was a threat. Hence some writers of the 1790s were proposing home and praising it unequivocally, while others were advocating distinct approaches to superintending the poor. Jeremy Bentham, in his 1797 *Observations,* explicitly opposes home-making policies in poor relief, complaining that legislation providing relief without confinement to workhouses allows laborers to "go on for an indefinite time, receiving whatsoever may be thought proper to allow them under the name of maintenance, although what they do shall continue to be worth nothing; and this without so much the inconvenience of quitting their own homes" (38). After around 1800, the relief of insufficiency and abjection loses its appeal as a means of promoting home's virtues, which no longer require a lot of promotion. Home is, in any case, coming to be understood primarily as the condition that prevails where indigence and privation have already been overcome. As a dominant cultural formation, home does better at excluding and erasing poverty than easing its pangs. The intensity of the revolution decade's fixation on self-sustaining, encompassing, and fiercely guarded domestic spheres (at both the private and national levels) comes to be viewed as solipsistic, confining, and paranoid.

Hegemony can tolerate neither the particular application of its principles in social practice—actual homes cannot adequately embody home itself—nor the residual legibility of its own historicity—the social changes that brought it into being. Hence, writers in the early nineteenth century set about the task of forgetting the specific historical conditions of home's development, redefining what might appear to be historical change as minor deteriorations in and renovations of an edifice that has stood since time immemorial. The 1790s are revised so they were no longer the moment of home's invention, but nothing more than a disruptive moment in the longer history of the great English home, whose actual roots lie in British antiquity. The grand metaphors of Edmund Burke's *Reflections* seem to anticipate this development: "It is with infinite caution that any man ought to venture upon pulling down an edifice which has answered in any tolerable degree for ages the common purposes of society, or on building it up again without having models and patterns of approved utility before his eyes" (152).

Poets played an important part in overwriting the historical conditions of the middle-class home. Lyric verse in particular (but by no means in isolation) provided representational modes that could lift home out of historical-progressive time and resituate it in pastoral, folkloric, and eternizing time schemes. Felicia Hemans, for instance, is an assiduous naturalizer. In 1812, she published a volume of verse titled *The Domestic Affections,* which includes "The Emigrant," in which a nameless speaker laments that "oft will memory . . . /

Recal [*sic*] the dear, regretted charms of home!" (13), and her later poem "The Homes of England" (1827) is a classic of retrospective antiquation: the first four of its five stanzas trace a hierarchy of opulence, from "The Stately Homes of England, / . . . Amidst their tall ancestral trees," to "The Cottage Homes of England! / By thousands on her plains" (392), while the last stanza draws all together:

> The free, fair Homes of England!
> Long, long, in hut and hall,
> May hearts of native proof be rear'd
> To guard each hallow'd wall!
> And green for ever be the groves,
> And bright the flowery sod,
> Where first the child's glad spirit loves
> Its country and its God! (392)

Hemans lyricizes the sense of what William Wordsworth had called a "unity entire" between homes of all varieties, the nation they adorn, its enduring traditions, and its very landscape.

Wordsworth's phrase comes from a poem that seems politically transitional, both for Wordsworth himself and for the English home, *Home at Grasmere*. Written between 1800 and 1806, the poem conceives of home much the way Hemans does, adoring its

> sense
> Of majesty and beauty and repose,
> A blended holiness of earth and sky,
> Something that makes this individual Spot,
> This small abiding place of many men.
> (46–47, lines 161–65)

The effect of these kinds of effusion is, oddly, home's disappearance beyond the horizon of its vanished historicity, the unnamable "something that makes this individual Spot." No longer the advance guard of improvement and reform, home very rapidly turns into an object of nostalgia, a lost origin and a place of return to be yearned for and mourned.

Absence and mystery have haunted the cultural image of home ever since, even during what we tend to think of as the high-water mark of the English middle-class home, the Victorian era. For instance, Coventry Patmore's *The Angel in the House*, one of home's greatest literary monstrosities, celebrates "yonder English home," where the poet Felix Vaughan and his wife, Honoria, "thrive on mortal food and sleep" (1.7), but do so "in these last days, the dregs of time" (1.4), where the only "undiscover'd ground" left for verse to explore, "the first of themes sung last of all," is the wife herself, the angel in the house (1.5). In the concluding verses of the fourth and final part ("The Victories of Love"), Felix finds another means of praising Honoria:

> meeting so my lovely Wife
> A passing pang, to think that life
> Was mortal, when I saw her laugh,
> Shaped in my mind this epitaph:
> "Faults had she, child of Adam's stem,
> "But only Heaven knew of them." (2.226)

The very heart of Victorian domestic bliss is the ecstatic anticipation of bereavement and mourning.

Another of the poem's voices, Frederick Graham, chafing at his naval service and his thwarted love for Honoria, indicts the effusive chauvinism of Hemans's "Homes of England" and the burden those homes set on the backs of the laboring classes:

> "The stately homes of England," lo,
> "How beautiful they stand!" They owe
> How much to nameless things like me
> Their beauty of security!
> But who can long a low toil mend
> By looking to a lofty end? (2.39)

Discontents are, of course, all smoothed over, and the last word is much more affirmative:

> But read this Poet, and say if home
> And private love did e'er so smile
> As in that ancient English Isle! (2.233)

Still, even in this "epic of the hearth" (2.224), home feels more tenuous and elusive than it generally does in the quests for and hymns to domesticity of the Romantic era. Just a page before the concluding benediction, Felix asks, "How read from such a homely page / In the ear of this unhomely age[?]" (2.232).

Victorian writers seem just as likely to chafe at the confinement of home as to celebrate its plenitude, and they regularly insist on turning outward, looking beyond its bounds.[35] Deanna Kreisel cites a particularly striking example from an essay by Robert Louis Stevenson: "Our race has not been strained for all these ages through that sieve of dangers that we call Natural Selection, to sit down with patience in the tedium of safety; the voices of its fathers call it forth. Already in our society as it exists, the bourgeois is too much cottoned about for any zest in living; he sits in his parlour out of reach of any danger, often out of reach of any vicissitudes but one of health; and there he yawns" (qtd. in Kreisel, "Wolf Children" 24). A "retrenchment in the cultural status of home" happens, Kreisel argues, when Victorians decide that too much of a good thing results in "a kind of atavistic regression to a dumb and primitive state, one in which the comforts of domesticity and the fireside render human subjects almost animal-like" (25).[36] Fifty years earlier, the modern home had been firmly established as an ideological formation, a structure and figuration doubled in dialectical opposition between absolute free heterogeneity and totalized collective homology, with the effect that no actual home can ever adequately actualize the intricate conditions of its metaphysic. All homes are more or less inferior to home itself, but at the same time the hegemonic figure of home is perpetually subordinated to particular homes that confute any governing metaphysic.

As I have indicated, I wish to distinguish this study from other scholarly analyses by its attendance specifically to what is named and implied by the word *home* (as distinct from related but not identical terms like *domesticity, privacy,* and *family*), its historical developments within my chosen period, my attendance to the inextricably national dimensions of home, and my insistence on finding many of home's inventors among writers about poverty, both literary and nonliterary. The connections between prose fiction and emergent bourgeois domesticity are already very well and widely examined in critical scholarship. I will survey that field of study in the following section of this introduction and, I hope, establish my grounds for offering a study with these particular dimensions. I do not seek to rewrite the broader history of privacy, which was a firmly established sociopolitical category in Britain well before the end of the eighteenth century. Jürgen Habermas's foundational study *The Structural Transformation of the Public Sphere* has established that the separation of public and private spheres was largely accomplished in England by the early eighteenth century. Disaggregating public from private life is a necessary but not sufficient condition for the emergence of the middle-class home. There are, in Karen Harvey's view, "a number of different levels" of development in "the unstable, varying and intertwined meanings of the concept," in particular a secondary "conflation of public and private" (528). That second stage, a reaggregation of public and private in the double figuration of home nation and private home, continues through the early nineteenth century, transforming—it has been argued—the institutional and collective into subordinate functions of the personal.[37]

## HOUSE + *x*

The home bequeathed to us by the hegemonic struggles of the Romantic era is an origin, whether it is the site, region, or nation of nativity; the dwelling of earliest memory; or simply the threshold one crosses to enter public life. Home is also a destination: the retreat from public life; the prison of marital confinement; a repository for the fruits of private aspiration, professional striving, and domestic collaboration; the end of welfare and charity; the vehicle of personal autonomy and independence; or the location at which the state and my creditors know to find me. My development, my *bildung,* carries me from home to home, letting me choose, as Wordsworth says, to "fix my habitation where I will" (*Prelude* 1: 107) but never letting me choose to renounce home altogether.[38] "It is always a localizable space," Mary Douglas observes, "but it is not necessarily a fixed space," and "it also has some structure in time" (289). We might call home the institution of bourgeois subjectivity. If we define as dialectical the relationship between the unlegislated, notionally autonomous, heterogeneous private home and the total, collective, and homologous home nation, it may make sense to think of the modern middle-class subject as the *aufhebung* continually resolving itself out of that dialectic.

Despite the compulsory inclusiveness of home, the intuitive certainty with which all its subjects understand what it is, it is shrouded in mystery. Even very recent studies by sociologists, geographers, anthropologists, and scholars of built environments have faltered because "what goes on inside a house is home life, . . . is something about which relatively little is known" (Allan and Crow 1); "what really goes on in most people's homes remains a mystery, an intriguing and frustrating mystery" (Hunt 66). Lorna Fox provides this equation: "On the basis that *home* = house + *x,* it is the '*x* factor' elements of *home* that are identified as being of primary significance when the home interest is threatened. Yet the '*x* factor' element—the meanings associated with social, psychological, emotional and cultural attachments to home—are not generally recognised or protected in the context of legal disputes, such as possession actions, where the risk of losing one's home becomes a reality" (139). Home,

Fox concludes, is "an intangible and subjective phenomenon" (145). Alison Blunt and Robyn Dowling encounter the same dilemma: "Whilst house and household are components of home, on their own they do not capture the complex socio-spatial relations that define home" (3). It is, they suggest, "*both* a place/physical location *and* a set of feelings" (22). Home would appear to be a problem of affect, and hence a problem *like* affect: what happens inside is stubbornly resistant to exposure, systematization, and especially to historicization: its "abstract, subjective factors," David N. Benjamin writes, "are very human but hard to grasp and work with in conventional positivistic research" (7); "even though we recognize [home], and 'know' it, it will always defy a rational deconstruction and complete explication of its meaning content" (3). In the same volume, Amos Rapoport concludes that social science should give up and look elsewhere: "the serious problems with the term *home,* which I have discussed, make its use so problematical that there does not seem to be enough potential in the term to persevere with attempts to improve it" (44). None of his fellow contributors seem to agree.

Empirical and quantitative disciplines cannot find their way across the threshold. Those disciplines seem still to be bound by the logic that formed home originally as the sphere where politics, economics, and public discourse end.[39] Home does not simply resist disciplinary investigation; it retains the epistemic prestige of having helped first define the boundaries of the Enlightenment disciplines. "New strategies of representation not only revised the way in which an individual's identity could be understood," Nancy Armstrong proposes, "but in presuming to discover what was only natural in the self, they also removed subjective experience and sexual practices from their place in history" (*Desire and Domestic Fiction* 9)—and their utility to the social sciences. The systematizing and positivist knowledge of the social sciences is precisely the kind of knowledge one cannot have about home. The private threshold is a barrier stern enough to render social-scientific methods ineffective.

Where they do cross the threshold, quantifying and scientistic analytics tend to destroy the delicate atmosphere and poetic symbology of private domesticity. Home ceases to be itself if one invites a vampire inside.[40] We should perhaps assume that only literary representation, with its (by implication) feminized, irrational, intuitive methods, can shine light on the secrets of home life without reducing them to dust and ashes.[41] And surely the novel, with what Frances Burney called its "stationary standard of insignificance" is best suited to the task and least likely to damage the precious objects it studies: "[The novel] is, or it ought to be, a picture of supposed, but natural and probable human existence. It holds, therefore, in its hands our best affections; it exercises our imaginations; it points out the path of honour; and gives to juvenile credulity knowledge of the world, without ruin or repentance; and the lessons of experience, without its tears" (*The Wanderer* 7). William Godwin makes the claim more boldly in the preface to *Things as They Are; or, The Adventures of Caleb Williams:* no "refined and abstract speculation," the novel (or at least this novel) is "a study and delineation of things passing in the moral world," which can provide "a general review of the modes of domestic and unrecorded despotism" (3). The moral truth without factual truth of realist fiction may be the best means of representing the identity without sameness of home.[42]

The descendants of eighteenth- and nineteenth-century political economists are apparently still struggling to unlock the doors that their predecessors first bolted against themselves ("It is high time we directed a flashlight into this hitherto black box" [de Vries 117]). But home seems to reveal an insufficiency in the vocabularies and conceptual reach of the disciplines. With the torch of Enlightenment-categorical analytics flickering and dimming as its bearers advance deeper into the castle, home's social-scientific investigators tend to get lost chasing troves of secrets hidden in deep recesses where they are guarded by the conscious modesty and unconscious mendacity of the modern Western subject. The studies I have cited, in other words, place upon themselves the burden of a repressive hypothesis, "by formulating the matter in the most explicit terms, by trying to reveal it in its most naked reality, by affirming it in the positivity of its power and effects" (Foucault, *History of Sexuality* 9).[43] The impulse to find and expose the naked reality of home has helped generate the mystery itself, the conditioning belief that something must be hidden within the empirically evident "exterior." This kind of inquiry presumes that during the nineteenth century, "sexuality was carefully confined; it moved into the home" (Foucault, *History of Sexuality* 3), and so, following this logic, home will be understood as a kind of closet, built by the "Victorians" to conceal truths that they believed had to be secret in order to be socially productive. The disciplines aiming to locate and/or liberate these truths have not only accepted this exterior/interior conception of the private home, but actively enforced it with the assumption that their object of inquiry disappears without it. Consequently the science of home has wandered for two centuries in a discursive labyrinth that has much in common with gothic romance. Our intrepid researchers are always closing in on the truth and a language in which to express it; they simply have not found it yet.

Home's opacity to the disciplines may help explain its durability. It has had sufficient vitality and adaptability to survive, transformed and yet uncannily the same, since its emergence in the last years of the eighteenth century. Every challenge to the fundamental conditions of home's universality and natural-ness has, to date, been absorbed without irreparable damage to the façade of domestic refuge. The nineteenth-century transplanting of home to the fields of empire, for instance, preserved and elaborated its essentially English char-acter. Urbanization, the growth of suburbs, and new urbanism have likewise been shaped in their developments to accommodate and indeed reinforce the hegemony of home.

Other social institutions and other figurations of home predate the middle-class version. I do not wish to imply that the entire formation of the middle-class home took place between 1780 and 1815. Don E. Wayne insists that "the conception of home involved [in Ben Jonson's "To Penshurst"] can be traced back at least as far as the seventeenth century in English literature . . . [T]he idea of an essential ground of Being is situated in the image of property, fam-ily, and home" (171). Jonson's conception of home is, for Wayne, "the product of emergent forms of social praxis which will eventually replace a decaying social order that is no longer sanctioned by viable structures of belief and expression" (169).[44] But the developments of the late eighteenth century are pivotal, and manifest home in recognizably modern cultural forms that can-not be found in earlier literary or nonliterary discourse. I will, in this study, seek to explore these pivotal movements in the historical determination of the middle-class home, distinguishing it from prior forms and identifying its par-ticular attributes. While I will not pretend to expose the whole historical deri-vation of the middle-class home, let alone unsettle its hegemonic monopoly, I hope this study can participate usefully in effective critique of the totalizing and mystifying powers of the *sanctum sanctorum* of private life.

The sociologist Ray Oldenburg has, since 1989, worked to promote a social-territorial concept that might contest some part of home's hegemonic dominance, his "third place," which he suggests is "often more homelike than home" (39). The third place is "a generic designation for a great variety of pub-lic places that host the regular, voluntary, informal, and happily anticipated gatherings of individuals beyond the realms of home and work" (16). Such places consist mainly of dining and drinking establishments and other small

businesses that nurture "informal public gathering," and some nonpropri-
etary spaces such as the piazzas of Florence and the vanished main streets of
"America in prewar days" (xxx). "In cities blessed with their own characteristic
form of these Great Good Places," Oldenburg suggests, "the stranger feels at
home—nay, *is* at home—whereas in cities without them, even the native does
not feel at home" (xxviii). Home is conceptually rich enough and syntactically
lithe enough that one can be *at home,* and at the same time not at home.[45]
Oldenburg stresses that the voluntaristic sociability of these informal public
spaces offers the possibility of refuge from the narrower selection of company
and surroundings available in one's actual home.

Oldenburg should, perhaps, be applauded for resisting a simplistic public/
private distinction and also for refusing to sanctify the private home. But the
third place is hardly a challenge to existing hegemonic systems. While it does
not sanctify the private home, its greatest virtue is "at homeness." Like the
bourgeois home, it presents itself as natural rather than historically determined: "the eternal sameness of the third place overshadows the variations in
its outward appearance and seems unaffected by the wide differences toward
the typical gathering places of informal public life" (20). Along with Florentine
piazzas and eighteenth-century coffeehouses, Oldenburg counts the Forum
and the Agora as ancient examples of informal public space. All of these examples are odd, especially the last two, because the third place is not only informal, but resolutely apolitical; its schematic takes no account of the possibility
that genuine political discourse might occur in or be enabled by such spaces,
nor that they are structured and determined by political asymmetries.[46]

Certainly the purpose of dialogue or dispute within a third place cannot be
revolutionary, cannot change or undermine its basic nature or its relationship
to other places. The superior experience of *at homeness* it offers only enforces
the sanctity of home itself, which was already premised on the deficiency of
actual homes. Oldenburg's separation of at homeness from actual homes is
the same separation that divides actual homes from the conceptual plenitude
of home itself, but by other means. While Oldenburg acknowledges the failure of homes to adequately realize the paradigm of home, his analysis shies
away from genuine critique, such as Adorno mounts in *Minima Moralia:* "The
traditional residences that we grew up in have grown intolerable: each trait of
comfort in them is paid for with a betrayal of knowledge, each vestige of shelter with the musty pact of family interests" (38). If anything, the third place
reinforces the naturalness and determinacy of home by offering purely voluntary affinal relations that allow an escape from the suffocating compulsory

relations of family, which is essentially what middle-class domesticity offered to begin with, as Margaret Cullen explained in her 1802 novel *Home:* "The improper influence of consanguinity may gradually diminish, till it shall at length be destroyed . . . and Home, instead of being a prison in which the Virtuous are condemned to associate with the Vicious, will become a secure refuge from the wicked, and the most delightful asylum of Man" (5: 363)

Oldenburg's model has been adapted by the Starbucks Corporation, whose website proclaims: "Starbucks has long been dedicated to creating a unique 'third place' between home and work. We also draw on the centuries-old tradition of the coffeehouse as a place to gather, share ideas, and enjoy delicious beverages. We see this program as an extension of the coffeehouse culture—a way to promote open, respectful conversation among a wide variety of individuals." The third place, as may be clear, sounds like an attenuation of Jürgen Habermas's rational public sphere. Indeed, I think *The Great Good Place*—not to mention the Starbucks website—appropriates elements of *Structural Transformation of the Public Sphere* (without ever citing Habermas), but shows little interest in moving beyond an uncritical humanism.

Lastly, the third place effectively maintains the abjection of other spaces that it does not incorporate: transitional, unapportioned, and expropriated spaces where homelessness and other kinds of social exclusion tend to concentrate. An influential article by Chandra Talpade Mohanty and Biddy Martin ("What's Home Got to Do with It?") examines that kind of space. Mohanty and Martin analyze portions of Minnie Bruce Pratt's memoir "Identity: Skin, Blood, Heart," including a description of Pratt's residence on H Street North East in Washington, D.C., "a place that does not exist as a legitimate possibility for home on a white people's map . . . 'the jungle,' 'the H Street corridor as in something to be passed through quickly, going from your place to elsewhere'" (91). Mohanty and Martin observe that for Pratt, "walking down the street and speaking to various people . . . are all rendered acutely complex and contradictory in terms of actual speakings, imagined speakings, and actual and imagined motivations, responses, and implications—there is no possibility of a coherent self with a continuity of responses across these different 'speaking-to's.' History intervenes" (93–94). Home is a hegemonic figure precisely because it overwrites the H Street corridor and other spaces like it, expelling them from bourgeois discourses of civil order and social justice. The hegemony of home is reinforced, not undermined, by the supposed unhomeliness, virtual homelessness, of high-density, poverty-stricken, and typically minority-occupied residential precincts with names like tenement, ghetto, or slum.

Of course I have no intention of implying that there has been no resistance to or critique of the natural and sanctified image of home. Mohanty and Martin's article is at the forefront of this critique, the largest and most sophisticated portion of which has emerged from feminist and postcolonial analyses.[47] Among Mohanty and Martin's main tactics is a refusal to reject home out of hand: "Both leftists and feminists have realized the importance of not handing over our notions of home and community to the right" (85). They advocate strategic appropriation, which Mohanty exemplifies in a later article from the same volume, "Genealogies of Community, Home, and Nation": "Political solidarity and a sense of family could be melded together imaginatively to create a strategic space I could call 'home'" (128). The same kind of indeterminacy informs bell hooks's often-cited dictum: "At times, home is nowhere. At times, one knows only extreme estrangement and alienation. Then, home is no longer just one place. It is locations. Home is that place which enables and promotes varied and ever changing perspectives, a place where one discovers new ways of seeing reality, frontiers of difference" (148). But Mohanty and Martin always stress the recognition that "there is an irreconcilable tension between the search for a secure place from which to speak, within which to act, and the awareness of the price at which secure places are bought, the awareness of the exclusions, the denials, the blindnesses on which they are predicated" (101). They call for "new forms of community not based on 'home'" (103) that renounce "the desire for the kind of home where the suppression of positive differences underwrites familial identity" (99).

The intimate connections between feminist thought and domesticity predate modern forms of domestic life (and indeed feminism strictly defined). Mary Astell, in 1700, suggests that a woman "has no reason to be fond of being a wife, or to reckon it a piece of preferment when she is taken to be a man's upper-servant; it is no advantage to her in this world, if rightly manag'd it may prove one as to the next. For she who marries purely to do good, to educate souls for heaven . . . does certainly perform a more heroic action than all the famous masculine heroes can boast of" (78). When the modern home does begin to coalesce, advocates for women and women's rights are prominent among those who articulate its conditions; Mary Wollstonecraft, for instance, promotes the companionate marriage: "The woman who strengthens her body and exercises her mind will, by managing her family and practicing various virtues, become the friend, and not the humble dependent of her husband" (29). Recent critics have located in women's writing of the eighteenth century a strong tactical valuation of domestic privacy as a space of limited self-determination.[48] For Wollstonecraft and others, the middle-class home was a least potentially a liberatory development.

Other critics have sought to "contest the seamless account of the triumph of domestic ideology in England between 1750 and 1850" that they associate with the major feminist studies of the 1980s (Mellor 83). Eve Tavor Bannet divides Enlightenment women writers into Matriarchs and Egalitarians where domestic order is concerned (3).[49] "While retaining a firm belief in domestic, social, and political hierarchy," she writes, "Matriarchs taught ladies how to obtain and deploy the ascendancy over men, over their families, and over their inferiors, which they thought were the ladies' due. Egalitarians, on the other hand, preached independence from all subordination, both at home and abroad, and sought to level hierarchies both in the family and in the state" (3). Bannet's Matriarchs include Mary Astell, Jane West, and Hannah More, and her Egalitarians include Judith Drake, Charlotte Smith, Mary Hays, and Mary Wollstonecraft (3). Whatever their differences, feminist and antifeminist, conservative and radical, Tory and Whig women writers of the late eighteenth and early nineteenth centuries most often champion domesticity as a sphere for some form of natural feminine authority. Few, if any, voices object to the general domesticating tendency that we now recognize as the emergence of home.[50] It is, nevertheless, not hard to see that home was subject to intense ideological struggle at this time because it was so instrumental to the formation of bourgeois class alliances, but also to the liberties women could enjoy, to self-formation, to subjection, and to property rights.

At the same time, recent critical analysts rarely underestimate the severe limitations to the self-determination women acquire in middle-class homes. Bannet, for instance, observes that "'feminization,' marginalization, and disempowerment of the family, and of the eighteenth-century women's novels that had debated and transformed it, almost immediately accompanied implementation of this particular domestic revolution as its shadow" (218). Although pre-1800 women's writing (even that of Wollstonecraft) seldom represents private domesticity as anything other than a liberatory invention, once domesticity has done its liberating it quickly begins to seem much more prison-like. Compare, for instance, Margaret Cullen's triumphant prediction that home "will become a secure refuge from the wicked, and the most delightful asylum of Man" (5: 363), with the gloomy sentiments expressed by the narrator of Maria Edgeworth's 1809 *Ennui*: "My home was disagreeable to me" (167), and "unless roused by external stimulus, I sank into that kind of apathy, and vacancy of ideas, vulgarly known by the name of *a brown study*" (144).

Britain's period of most fervent and unequivocal home-worship was over before the Victorian era began.[51] I do not mean to downplay the centrality of
the private home in British Victorian culture. I have already suggested that the
sense of home as a lost horizon, an object of nostalgic longing, or a rallying
point for aspiration is key to the Victorian cult of domesticity, and although I
will not discuss much that happened after 1834, I hope to offer at least a partial
explanation for that state of affairs.

At the very end of the Victorian period and on the other side of the At-
lantic, Charlotte Perkins Gilman published *The Home: Its Work and Influence*
(1903), a remarkable polemic that sets out much of what has since become the
standard prosecution against the institutions of domesticity. The book embraces its iconoclasm, "offering [itself] to a public accustomed only to the unquestionable acceptance of the home as something perfect, holy, quite above
discussion" (3). Gilman's book frames its analytical object in the same way
that I wish to: home is to be understood as institution, as ideal, as ideological
formation, as disciplinary mechanism, as an arcane compound of actual lived
reality and rich figural topology. Like later feminists, Gilman emphasizes the
historical determination of domesticity: "We have constantly believed that
this was the true way to live, the natural way, the only way" (6). "The two
main errors," she finds, "in the right adjustment of the home to our present
life are these: the maintenance of primitive industries in a modern industrial
community, and the confinement of women to these industries and their limited area of expression" (10). Also like later feminists, she does not wish to tear
the whole edifice down: "The home need be neither a prison, a workhouse,
nor a consuming fire" (13). For Gilman, the memory of home's originary relationship to carceral institutions is apparently still perceptible. I propose that
home is not only not a workhouse but that its etiology is determined by that
antithesis; home arises as a new jurisdiction for management of, care for, and
discipline of the poor—all of the functions belonging to the workhouse—but
precisely not a workhouse.

## THE HOME'S TWO BODIES

It may be objected that my study equivocates its object: I risk failing to distinguish literary representations, particularly fiction, from nonliterary representations or, worse, from lived reality. Homes represented in novels have no
necessary relationship to actual homes. But the home in which I am interested
is a representation more than a material reality, and an instrumental figuration

more than a set of actual social practices. For Rosemary Marangoly George, realist novels "have situated themselves in the gap between the realities and the idealizations that have made 'home' such an auratic term" (1–2). I will make no broad claims about the actual lived practice and experience of dwelling at home in this period.[52] Indeed, a considerable portion of my evidence is at marked variance from "reality," very often avowedly so. The object of my study is a figure from the English/British cultural imaginary and as such is frequently presented in terms that are nostalgic, aspirational, or hortatory—we tend to find home represented as it was or will be or ought to be.

While I will avoid strong assertions about actual homes in the eighteenth and nineteenth centuries, this limitation does not amount to an implicit concession that literary representations have no effect on actual social practice. The figure and figurations of home demonstrate powerfully that there is no clean and stable division between representation and material culture.[53] I take this same principle to be a clear premise of much or all of the large body of literary criticism relating to eighteenth- and nineteenth-century British domesticity that I cite as precedent for my study. Such an approach to the relationship between literature and the world has a strong heritage. One of its most famous expressions is Benedict Anderson's request that we "consider the basic structure of two forms of imagining which first flowered in Europe in the eighteenth century: the novel and the newspaper. For these forms provided the technical means for 're-presenting' the *kind* of imagined community that is the nation" (30). The special and multivalent relationship that the modern middle-class home organizes between nation and private dwelling had and still has a formative influence on the imagined communities of English-speaking countries.

Home, as distinct from domesticity in general, develops a special capacity to intermediate and yoke together the private and the national spheres of personal, civic, and cultural life. The private home's relation to nationality is governed by the capacity of the term *home* to name both. Every use of the word is charged with a certain equivocality. The private home is presumptively English, while England consists of all its homes, "hut and hall," "Where first the child's glad spirit loves / Its country and its God!" (Hemans, "Homes" 392).[54] Each figures the other in a dynamic range of tropes and relations: the private home can be a synecdoche or metaphor for the nation or its opposite, its counterpart or its exception; the home nation can be a metonymy or metaphor for its constituent dwellings, or it can generalize them, abstract them, or suspend the limitations of their particularity.[55] Private and national home can each be more like the other than like itself.

The relation between personal and collective figured by home sublates the primary political metaphor that did the same duty in the early modern period: the king's two bodies are replaced by the body's two homes. The body natural is atomized—every civic subject acquires one—and it, along with its activities, is hidden from view in England's numberless private kingdoms.[56] The body politic remains one of the names for the national collective, but only as an acknowledged metaphor for sums and averages of wealth, aspiration, sentiment, and health that no longer belong to a single, naturally embodied proprietor.[57] Body natural and body politic can no longer meet in person, let alone stand before the nation in the particular person of the sovereign.[58] Edmund Burke's reframing of the Filmerian god-king-father system is an important example of the new social figuration: "We have given to our frame of polity the image of a relation in blood; binding up the constitution of our country with our dearest domestic ties; adopting our fundamental laws into the bosom of our family affections; keeping inseparable, and cherishing with the warmth of all their combined and mutually reflected charities, our state, our hearths, our sepulchres, and our altars" (*Reflections* 120). Instead of a top-down hierarchy of obligations, Burke imagines a bottom-up compact of personal affective bonds in which domestic ties form and naturalize the orders of authority and governance.

Home mediates all contact between the state and the civic subject. The private home makes citizens "free" to shepherd their moral, social, and enterprising energies in a replete, self-realizing environment, and the state acts only to safeguard that freedom and to sanction its aspirations. Without a system of that kind, there can be no sense to Adam Smith's claim that, "by pursuing his own interest [the merchant] frequently promotes that of the society more effectually than when he really intends to promote it" (*Wealth of Nations* 399): for this economy to work, there must be a set of *oikoi* whose interests are simultaneously intermutual (alike and shared) and wholly independent, best served when mutuality is expressly neglected.[59] The prosperity of all is most effectively promoted when all presume that their own prosperity is distinct from and incompatible with that of all others and pursue no prosperity but their own. Home answers precisely to this paradox: it is absolutely singular, unlegislated, experienced in every case as though it were the first and only one of its kind, and at the same time a homogeneous norm and a homologized set of aspirations, linked to all other private homes and to the national collective. So not only does home mediate between the subject and the state, it also mediates between subjects within the state.

In order to sustain this contradictory system of common and mutual wealth that is simultaneously a patchwork of incongruent and autonomous monads, home nullifies the system of commodity exchange that serves it and for which it is a primary telos. Although it is the end and beneficiary of economic striving, home's purpose is the negation of economics per se. Within the home, monetary economies and the rule of the commodity are suspended. While financial prosperity is a necessary and ongoing condition for home, its systems and values are negated at the moment of entry and displaced by prosperity that is measured in affective and "natural" values: comfort, happiness, devotion, self-actualization, and so forth.[60] Consequently home must be imagined as immune to the temptations and depredations of the marketplace, but not frozen in a stasis that cannot register prosperity, growth, and improvement. Home is independence and self-sufficiency generalized as a principle of communion and mutuality.[61] It is the legitimating purpose for labors and desires, the accumulated fruit of our strivings. It provides the solution to problems, the object of aspirations, the end of struggles, and the heart of a stable and decent social order. So the national home assembles, and has little existence apart from, a congregation of scattered institutions that (because they have repudiated patriarchal obligation) would otherwise have no interest in one another and no particular solidarity. There is thus no center to home, nor hierarchy of rank, and power can operate in a distributive network without needing to flow from the top down through an opposition between ruler and ruled.[62]

The strands and fibers of home's network did not spontaneously knit themselves together and blanket the nation in brand-new cloth. The new fabric of national communion was woven largely from threads that had made up, and continued to make up, other fabrics. I will argue that the most important of these older social networks is the parish system, whose decline and transformation I examine in chapter 1, "Stock the Parish with Beauties." Henry Fielding's journalism, social treatises, criticism, and fiction (especially *Joseph Andrews*) meticulously chronicle the parish's role as the basic unit of social administration in England. *Joseph Andrews* is heavily inflected by the laws of settlement and vagrancy, contemporary patterns of enforcement, and relations between the landed gentry, parish officials, and the poor. Indeed, this novel can be read as a subjection of the motifs and themes of romance to the conditions of poverty management. The parish's command over the allocation and distribution of punitive and relief measures to the poor was dismantled over the course of the eighteenth century. Its statutory processes were gradually assumed by county bureaucracies, and its more intimate functions, as well as its shaping of the topography of England, were taken over by the middle-class home. I emphasize the parish in contradistinction to the manor and the great house, whose position as center of social and political influence had faded more than a century earlier, and which middle-class polemicists had little interest in reviving as a model of domestic values.

My analysis traces Fielding's consistent efforts to halt the decline of the parish system by reforming and reinvigorating parochial care within a comprehensive system of judicial oversight that resuscitates a modified form of manorial paternalism. The means of detecting affectation that Fielding outlines in his preface to *Joseph Andrews* closely parallel his explanation of social emulation in the treatises of the 1750s. His critique of affectation in *Joseph Andrews* also incorporates ridicule as a test of truth, a heuristic formulated from Shaftesbury's *Characteristicks* and debated for decades in the eighteenth century by a range of writers and thinkers. Fielding establishes a basic measure of the ridiculous on the boundary drawn by poverty: the pauper lacks the means of assuming convincing forms of affectation and so the poor become the stabilizing measure in a comparative rhetoric of the ridiculous that anchors a general ethic of representation and social justice. He tests that ethic on the characters in the novel, modeling readerly modes of judgment akin to those of the wise magistrate and the benevolent parish cleric. The test of truth is also, for Fielding, a weapon against chivalric romance and the kind of romantic temperament (exemplified by Lady Booby) that has brought paternalism to a point of crisis and turned fiction into an enemy of social justice. In the novel and in his schematic for reformed poverty management, then, Fielding envisions a divided topography where the poor and their immediate (clerical) guardians dwell in confined parochial territories of intimate care and oversight, while the national system is maintained by a landholding magistracy eager to ensure correct and homogeneous organization of the system as a whole.

Fielding's efforts to coordinate private and collective, intimate and disciplinary social relations may, ultimately, have done as much to hurry the decline of the parish system and the rise of private domesticity as to arrest those transitions. By the last decade of the century, the centerpiece of the old poor-management institutions, the poorhouse/workhouse/house of correction, was under constant assault for its perceived failure as a self-sustaining, or even just sustainable, apparatus for relieving and disciplining the indigent poor.

Chapter 2, "An Englishwoman's Workhouse Is Her Castle," offers the hypothesis that gothic fiction transfigures the workhouse into the nightmare image of the gothic castle. The turn away from workhouse solutions and toward "outdoor relief" coincides with the rise of evangelical political economists, the cresting wave of sentimentalism, and wild upheaval in wage-price-supply structures. This chapter interrogates a large sample of material from the poor-law debates of the period, identifying several important rhetorical and philosophical themes that contribute to the formation of the modern concept of home. Among those themes is the turn away from *populationniste* theory toward Malthusian calls for the shepherding of labor supplies; the movement to design and build cottages for the poor; and the focusing of disciplinary mechanisms on poor women who are picked out as the managers of, as well as rewards for, orderly and temperate laboring lives.

Gothic fiction—Ann Radcliffe's *The Romance of the Forest* is my primary example—performs crucial cultural work, translating the anxieties and strategies of poverty management into therapeutic narratives that symbolically resolve the calamities perceived to be rising in the English countryside and leaking out of the French Republic. Radcliffe's ever-lurking banditti figure the population of paupers whose dissatisfaction and undirected reserves of labor power might turn into a civil insurgency. The protagonist of *The Romance of the Forest,* Adeline, is an orphan cast on the stewardship of a family who are themselves virtually indigent. She encounters a variety of "overseers" ranging from an aristocratic seducer to a benevolent clergyman, and the narration of her experiences recurs with striking regularity to terms that feature prominently in poverty debates: *removal, relief,* and *settlement.* In the gothic milieu, the statutory functions of those terms become private literalizations: Adeline is removed from one place of confinement or refuge to another and another; her suspense (and ours) is relieved by narrative *eclaircissements,* or her overwrought feelings are relieved by sighs, tears, and swoons; and at last she finds settlement in a lavishly modest home, demonstrating in the process a virtuous self-sufficiency that draws poor and bourgeois subjects together in a compact of domestic harmony, generous provision, and guaranteed fair remuneration.

After the heyday of Radcliffean gothic fiction, anti-French paranoia, and the cottage-building boom that never was, writers began to query the conception of home as fully self-sufficient and impermeable to the foreign. Chapter 3, "Home and Away," examines this shift in attitudes and finds it indicative of home's rise to hegemony. Paradoxically, as a cultural figure rises to hegemonic status, it becomes less and less accessible to actual social practice. Homes as such cannot adequately embody the ideological repletion of home. The home-ness of other homes undermines the home-ness of the subject's own home because, for everyone else, it is not home. In other words, the nationalization of home alienates the inhabitant from her own private home. I locate in a variety of texts, including Maria Edgeworth's *Ennui,* a disaffection with the previous decade's domesticating rhetoric. Critical attacks on gothic fiction echo and bolster this turn against home, deeming gothic themes, motifs, and narratological features airless and solipsistic. I read John Galt's story "The Buried Alive" as an attempt to revivify the gothic that thematizes the very problem of domestic confinement and excessive inwardness. It does so by evoking a dilemma from poverty management over the disjunction between relieving the suffering body and making the idle body productive, which Galt refigures as a confusion in materialist life sciences between systems that sustain affective communion and systems that sustain organic life.

Chapter 3 then turns to Wordsworth's treatments of poverty and home, particularly the *Salisbury Plain* poems and *Home at Grasmere.* The well-studied changes in Wordsworth's political sympathies between the early 1790s and the early 1800s coincide with the shift I am identifying in the cultural position of home from vigorously political rallying cry to naturalized social form, from instrument of activism to object of contention. The earliest versions of *Salisbury Plain* show Wordsworth's clear understanding of the capacity of a national home figuration to render social exclusion invisible in an apparently prosperous and fertile land. The poet imagines Stonehenge as an emblem of imperialist exploitation and then as a monument to the overthrow of bloodthirsty civil regimes. The later *Salisbury Plain* poems seem to presume the success of that overthrow and embrace the kind of idealized home figurations I have outlined. *Home at Grasmere* celebrates the poet's settlement at Dove Cottage with a contentment that implies that the homeless have made their own misery. Stonehenge recurs in the final text I discuss in chapter 3, Frances Burney's *The Wanderer.* It appears in the conclusion of the novel as a figure for the topographic ordering of England into a circulatory network of homes linked to other homes by open channels of affectionate exchange. Burney's vision of a home nation in happy communion unrestrained by residual antirevolutionary paranoia rests upon another emerging hegemonic figure, the postal service, which is invoked by the heroine's persistent resemblance to a letter caught in a system of distribution that she herself finally calls into orderly and comprehensive shape.

My final chapter, "There's No Home-Like Place," looks to Scotland and an early, local case of home's application to the British imperial project. The term *home* seems much less widely used in Scottish fiction of the early nineteenth century than in its English counterpart. That diffidence is perhaps not surprising given the nagging sense that the Scottish wing is always an alien element in the British home nation. Persistent memory of the 1707 Act of Union recalls a historically specific renunciation that fits uncomfortably with the ahistorical naturalness associated with home. Romantic-era Scottish writers follow the English pattern of treating the self-sufficient private home as more prison-like than pleasant. But more than that, I argue that in early nineteenth-century Scottish fiction and verse there is a pattern of departures. The relation of Scottish literary characters to home is very often diasporic, looking backward to a lost origin or forward in hope of a new settlement. The national tale and the bardic verse of the Romantic era are filled with exiles. Literary characters very frequently experience the national interior as a menacing outdoors where flight and concealment are the primary imperatives. James Hogg and John Galt dwell intently on this kind of experience. Hogg especially indexes the formal and structural fragmentation of his literary works to the failures and injustices of national domestication.

Walter Scott shows a stronger interest than Hogg in reconciling Scotland's subordinate national position with a British national home-figuration. My discussion of Scott focuses mostly on *The Tale of Old Mortality,* which is notable for its lack of anything resembling the modern middle-class home. That absence, I argue, is not contingent, but constitutive. The novel is full of domesticities that the text identifies as archaic and flawed. The manorial household is too much a microcosm of the state, and the private one is too hermetic. Both sides of the civil conflict that dominates the events of *Old Mortality* are hostile to the private home. The state finds it dangerously secretive, a hideout for political intrigue and insurgency. The Covenanters see it as, like the state, an institution that competes with the Kirk for the subject's spiritual devotion. The Covenanters are, consequently, homeless. They have renounced domestic refuge and become dwellers in the wilderness. Both sides also visit destruction on the existing domestic realms that they encounter, but Scott's protagonist, Henry Morton, joins the Covenanters anyway because he finds himself disaffected with all private connections, especially his aspirations in love, which he believes have been spurned. By the conclusion of the war, every domestic sphere in the novel needs some kind of reconstruction, perhaps most significantly at the level of property systems. Morton returns from exile to a country embracing peace and refreshed private relations under the new regime of William and Mary. By focusing on the Glorious Revolution instead of the Act of Union as the key historical event of the period, Scott ascribes the founding of the home nation not to a renunciation, but to a "revolution" that Edmund Burke famously defined as a reestablishment of the natural constitutional order rather than a rupture with the past. The British home nation coalesced, according to this narrative, not when Scotland lost its political independence, but when feudal relations gave way to private property. The narrator's express failure to present a happy middle-class home in the concluding pages of *Old Mortality* betokens Scott's tactically intricate effort to give a history of the rise of middle-class domesticity in Scotland, without actually historicizing and hence denaturalizing the institution of home itself.

# "Stock the Parish with Beauties"
## Henry Fielding's Parochial Vision

A parish where the minister and the parochial officers did their duties with activity and zeal, might be almost as well ordered as a private family.

—Robert Southey, *Quarterly Review*, 1820

While no British Parliament of the eighteenth century ever met to outlaw chivalric romance, the nation's unacknowledged legislators certainly did. Poets and reviewers subjected the motifs and themes of romance to derision and made its characteristic sensibilities vehicles for satire. In *The Rape of the Lock,* the Baron "to Love an altar built, / Of twelve vast French Romances, neatly gilt" (161, lines 37–38) and set the whole lot on fire. Classicism, Cervantes, and the trading interest combined to declare chivalric romance childish, foolish, deluded, and Frenchified. Charles Gildon, a regular object of scorn for Pope and Swift, finds common ground with them in sneering at the "Heroes in *French* Romance, who do nothing but love and fight and never eat" (303). Many English examples of romance from the early part of the century, such as Delarivier Manley's *The New Atalantis* and Eliza Haywood's *The Adventures of Eovaai,* are complicated by their status as satire, but Haywood's more conventional romances of the 1720s (such as *Love in Excess*) made her subject to attacks from Pope and others for hackery and undisciplined femininity. The decline of courtly virtues in literature, we tend to say, accompanied the decay of aristocratic paternalism, the end of feudalism, and, of course, the rise of the novel.

Had Parliament written its bill against romance, it might well have sounded, in part, like this:

> All common players of interludes; ... all minstrels; jugglers; persons pretending to be gypsies, or wandering in the habit or form of Egyp-

tians, or pretending to have skill in physiognomy, palmestry, or like crafty science, or pretending to tell fortunes, or using any subtil craft to deceive and impose on any of His Majesty's subjects, or playing or betting at any unlawful games; . . . all persons wandering abroad, and lodging in alehouses, barns, outhouses, or in the open air, not giving a good account of themselves; all persons wandering abroad . . . pretending to be soldiers, mariners, seafaring men, or pretending to go to work in harvest; and all other persons wandering abroad and begging shall be deemed rogues and vagabonds. (*Statutes at Large* 101)

The passage actually comes from the vagrancy law of the thirteenth session of the reign of George II (1741). This law, one of a series passed in the early to midcentury, all saying essentially the same thing, belongs to the body of legislation and administrative practices that would eventually be known as the old poor law. The main effects of vagrancy laws were their maintenance of the parish as the primary administrative unit of poverty management and their restriction of movement (both geographical and social) for the laboring classes. The Settlement Act of 1662 had codified the principle that entitlement to poor relief was founded on the pauper's settlement in a parish, a qualification established at birth by the settlement of one's parents and difficult to change thereafter if one could not afford a ten-pound tenancy.[1] One who had no employer and no particular employment was not permitted to move about the countryside in search of either.[2] In effect, the English poor laws outlaw the knight errant of romance and his quest, not to mention the wandering minstrel and his song.

A state of unwilled errantry is the predicament that Joseph Andrews faces when he finds himself in London, far from his parish of settlement, cast out of employment, and stripped of his livery. I will suggest in this chapter that vagrancy law helps define the "hitherto unattempted" species of writing that Fielding proclaims in his preface to *Joseph Andrews* (8): he subjects the conventions of romance to the conditions of poor law and poverty management.[3] Fielding was an eager participant in the poor-law debates of midcentury. His "Social Pamphlets"—*An Enquiry into the Causes of the Late Increase of Robbers,* and *A Proposal for Making Effectual Provision for the Poor*—published in the 1750s, are important contributions to the literature of the debates. In them he argues that social aspiration and its attendant emulation are the root cause of the sufferings of, and dangers posed by, the poor:

Thus while the nobleman will emulate the grandeur of a prince, and the gentleman will aspire to the proper state of the nobleman, the tradesman steps from behind his counter into the vacant place of the gentleman. Nor doth the confusion end here; it reaches the very dregs of the people, who aspiring still to a degree beyond that which belongs to them, and not being able by the fruits of honest labour to support the state which they affect . . . the more simple and poor-spirited betake themselves to a state of starving and beggary, while those of more art and courage become thieves, sharpers and robbers. (*Enquiry* 3 [1751 ed.])

Fielding's social polemics and his fiction share with the vagrancy laws a policy of figuring patriarchal hierarchies of status and condition in topographic and geographic terms: the tradesman steps "into the vacant place of the gentleman."[4] Restraint of social movement means restraint of physical movement, and so the knight errant must put aside his lance and be content with his laborer's implements.[5]

Aspiring "beyond" one's station, we will see, tends to manifest in quite literal departures from one's proper place within a geography whose foundational unit is the parish and whose constitutive administrative practice is the confinement and supervision of the parish poor. The register of high and low is clearly not abandoned altogether—as the term "dregs" attests—but its mystification is implied, for instance, in Fielding's satirically skeptical "Dissertation concerning high People and low People" midway through volume 2 of *Joseph Andrews*. By high people, the narrator informs us, he means "no other than people of fashion"; low people are "those of no fashion" (136), and their segregation is geographic: "Whilst the people of fashion seized several places to their own use, such as courts, assemblies, operas, balls &c. the people of no fashion . . . have been in constant possession of all hops, fairs, revels, &c." (136–37). In the *Enquiry*, Fielding reasserts these territorial divisions without structural irony: "let them [the 'great'] have their plays, operas, and oratorios, their masquerades and ridottos; their assemblies, drums, routs, riots, and hurricanes, their Ranelagh and Vauxhall; their Bath, Tunbridge, Bristol, Scarborough, and Cheltenham" (8–9). While Fielding may affect a distaste for vertical hierarchies of social rank, his geographic partitioning of national space maintains their fundamental distinctions.

The social pamphlets were authorized by Fielding's prominence as a lawyer and magistrate, and were taken seriously by his fellow pamphleteers. His contemporary Charles Gray, M.P. for Colchester, praised the "excellent piece" in which Fielding "has shown himself a most worthy labourer in the vineyards of the public" (6); the legal scholar Richard Burn includes a summation of Fielding's pamphlet in his 1764 compendium *The History of the Poor Laws* (196ff.); and the polemicist clergyman Joseph Townsend quotes from the proposal in his 1786 *Dissertation on the Poor Laws* (63). The pamphlets were also written nine and eleven years respectively after *Joseph Andrews*. Hence I will not be able to take an uncomplicated stance toward the literary example; *Joseph Andrews* is not a simple redaction of Fielding's thinking about poverty management to a satiric fiction. That novel's engagement with the poor laws and the poor is at a remove from actual social practice, though not such a great one: Fielding's pre-1742 essays in the *Champion* and elsewhere abound with social and political admonition.[6] Notably also, the legal career that led Fielding to his social pamphlets began before he read *Pamela* for the first time: by July 1740, he had completed his legal studies at the Middle Temple, had been called to the bar, and was riding the Western Circuit "looking for cases to plead" (Paulson, *Life* 98–118). I will not take a strong position in the scholarly debate over the extent to which Fielding's politics and moral principles changed between the end of the Walpole administration in 1742 and his entering the magistracy in 1749, although I will cite Bertrand Goldgar's suggestion that, while Fielding may have been willing to sell his pen to the highest bidder, there is little reason to see a radical break between the Fielding of the *Champion* and *Joseph Andrews* and the Fielding of the *Covent Garden Journal* and *Amelia* ("Fielding, Politics, and 'Men of Genius'" 258–59).

Fielding's social project aims to revive the patriarchal social bonds embodied by the parish in the face of a general decline in landed paternalism.[7] The parish was, in eighteenth-century England, the primary unit of social administration. For Fielding it is also the defining instance of the local and of the convergence of intimate, personal relations with relations of governance and civic management. To a considerable extent that is true of the parish's role in English life and social imagination generally. K. D. M. Snell goes so far as to argue that "the old poor law provides the key to a social understanding of the eighteenth century. Parochial organization ensured a face to face connection of administrators and the poor; while generous terms of relief and often humble officers facilitated agreement and mutual respect between the ranks and orders of parish society" (104). Over the course of the century, however, the

hierarchical, consanguineal, and obligational social ties that organized Filmerian patriarchy and paternalistic community gave way to conjugal and affinal
bonds whose primary sphere of manifestation was domesticity.[8]

I will argue here that the middle-class home rises from the ruins of the
parish more than it does from those of the great house. The crises that condition the decline of parochial orders are in many cases the same crises from
which private domesticity emerges. The parish is, in other words, one of the
private home's most significant antecedent institutions. Hence, my account
will resist a plain analogy between the transformations of familial structures
and those of the domestic setting. I do not imagine the aristocratic household metamorphosing into the middle-class family while the manorial hall
dissolves around them into the bourgeois parlor. Nor do I want to imply that
such a conflation is a significant feature of historical or literary scholarship.
Scholars have long recognized the parallel, mutually influential, but distinct
developments of family and domesticity. Thomas Sokoll reports that "by the
mid 1970s, research into the social history of household and family had made
it clear that the traditional notion of the large and complex households of pre-
industrial time was a romantic myth and that . . . in England . . . the nuclear
family had been the predominant household form since the sixteenth century" (xix). Without question the hegemonic imagery of the modern domestic sphere overwhelms that of the great house, and indeed an effect of the
modern home's rise is the thorough naturalization and commingling of family, household, house, and home in popular representation. But the structures,
bonds, functions, and jurisdictions that belong to the parish are absorbed by
and translated to the features of familial, social, and national life for which the
private home acquires responsibility by the early nineteenth century, while
the structures characteristic of manorial households become functions of
public ritual, museum exhibits, and nostalgic pastiche.[9]

Among my objectives in this chapter is an examination of the prominence
in *Joseph Andrews* of the parish and the social systems it sustains, both as a
contribution to analyses of Fielding's fiction and social theory and as a provocation for broader consideration of the parish as topos in eighteenth-century
fiction generally. I will argue that Fielding's parochial vision, formulated across
the range of his literary, critical, and juridical writings, constitutes an intricate
scheme of surveillance, discipline, and care that Fielding hoped to see applied
homogeneously and universally throughout the nation. What I am calling his
parochial vision combines a plan for reforming oversight of the poor (from
the intimate confines of parish management through the supervisory offices

of the county and the magistracy) with a heuristics of judgment and discrimination, based on the visible authenticity of poverty and verified by the ridiculousness of affectation, which he exemplifies in *Joseph Andrews*. But *Joseph Andrews* does not simply provide literary examples of, or thematic figurations for, this improved parochial system. The reformation of romance is a central component of Fielding's social polemics, providing, it seems to me, much of the initial formulation as well as the governing logics of his projects.

Romance, in Fielding's schematic, is visibly inauthentic. His use of the term denominates forms of representation (both literary representation and self-presentation) that have no authorizing connection to substance or precedent, no verifiable truth value. It is important to note that his condemnation falls most emphatically on the "voluminous works commonly called *Romances,* namely, *Clelia, Cleopatra, Astraea, Cassandra, The Grand Cyrus,* and innumerable others which contain, as I apprehend, very little instruction or entertainment" (3)—French seventeenth- and eighteenth-century chivalric/nostalgic narrative and its English imitations.[10] As will become clear, the romantic mode typifies, for Fielding, more than a group of exemplary works; it originates in and defines an epistemology of delusion, distortion, and insolent pretension—the quixotism that Fielding associates with "modern" ways of defining property relations, social ambition, and personal merit.[11] Romance is empty, depicting what is not to be found in nature, or it is a fraudulent affectation of what is not in one's own nature. It is, in other words, the vulgar masquerade produced by transgressive emulation, a kind of imitation that abjures "the just imitation of nature" for a burlesque "exhibition of what is monstrous and unnatural" (*JA* 4). The romantic/quixotic subject abandons his natural place in favor of emulative ambition just as the authors of romances discard Nature in favor of "the confused heap of matter in their own brains" (*JA* 163). The generic characteristics of literary romance are of a piece with the corrupting influences spreading decay through the manor-parish system. Each has lost its grounding in "natural" traditional orders.

The imitation of nothing—or nothing natural—that constitutes romance makes it subject to ridicule, an elaboration of Cervantean travesty that Fielding develops into a mechanism of judgment for readers of *Joseph Andrews*. In his "Author's Preface," he explains the function of the ridiculous, with which "life everywhere furnishes an accurate observer" (4): its recognition, "which always strikes the reader with surprize and pleasure," enables us to detect affectation: "The only source of the true ridiculous is affectation" (6), and affectation, like romance, is a product of improper social emulation. "Now affectation," Fielding continues, "proceeds from one of these two causes, vanity, or hypocrisy" (6), a definition that he revisits, and modifies, ten years later in his account of the emulation responsible for "the late increase of robbers": "Now the two great motives to luxury, in the mind of men, are vanity and voluptuousness" (*Enquiry* 23). Here and elsewhere, the resonances between Fielding's literary work and his social analytics are striking enough to justify the parallel investigation that I propose and that other critics have also employed.[12]

The structuring logics shared by Fielding's fiction and his social pamphlets are these: first, the neoclassicist edict that legitimate form must mediate proper substance and/or authorizing precedent; second, an ethics of judgment that applies the first edict to examination of person/character; and third, an attempt to bring the mechanisms of private and intimate relations into congruous and homogeneous communication with those of collectivity and the state. All three edicts devolve from a demand for congruity between signifier and signified (between word and idea or thing) and for modes of policing that congruity, and all three are worked out on exemplary cases involving poverty. Fielding's governing assumptions are: that the pauper has no capacity (no means) to assume any outward form distinct from the poverty that is his effective substance; that a capable judge can easily tell when anyone affects what he is not; and that adequate provision for and discipline of the poor is key to personal virtue and harmonious civic order—for the poor as well as for those doing the providing and disciplining. The test by which one judges affectation is based on a heuristic (in this case a rule of judgment that assesses *a* in terms of *b*) borrowed and adapted from Shaftesbury's *Characteristicks* that became known as "the test of truth," which asserts that a sense of the ridiculous is an intuitive and reliable means of judging when a person's outward appearance is incongruous with his natural self.

According to Fielding's promulgation of this rule, the unadorned pauper becomes a stable, authentic signified upon which to anchor expressions of ethical truth and a kind of sumptuary code of self-display. In the *Covent Garden Journal* number 27, Fielding asks: "Where . . . shall we look for an example of temperance? In the stinking kitchins of the rich, or under the humble roofs of the poor? Where for prudence but among those who have the fewest desires? Where for fortitude, but among those who have every natural evil to struggle with?" (172). Literary representations of poverty and systems of poverty management, then, share a relation to ethical and political truth that Fielding sees as foundational for comprehensive models of representation and civil order.[13] Hence, the poor and their oversight occupy a central place in

Fielding's reform scheme. The persistent image of the honest pauper ridicules and rebukes the indolent vagabond, the tradesman with ideas above his station, and the neglectful estate holder alike.

## SEPARATE SPHERES

Before the conclusion of the medieval period, according to N. J. G. Pounds, the parish had achieved "almost complete coverage of the country" and become "the chief vehicle of public administration at the local level" (4). Sidney and Beatrice Webb emphasize that "the relief of destitution was inextricably entangled with the constitution and activities of the ecclesiastical parish," which they see as having been, in about the fourteenth century, the site of the "spontaneous creation of a local governing body, consisting of the whole of the householders periodically meeting in the parish church" (*English Poor Law* 1: 5) and afterwards the means of keeping local government "most commonly in the hands of a parish oligarchy" (*Parish* 43). But parish governance had, according to Pounds, "by the end of the eighteenth century run its course" (498), though parishes officially remained a key sector of poverty management until the comprehensive "new poor law" of 1834. In the decades leading up to 1834 cooperative parish unions, hostility to settlement regulations, and increasingly assertive county-appointed justices of the peace undermined the autonomy (and heterogeneity) of parish relief activities.[14] The centrality of the parish to poverty management was already in dispute when Fielding joined the debate. Richard Burn, for instance, declared the system unsustainable: "Every parish is in a state of expensive war with all the rest of the nation; regards the poor of all other places as aliens and cares not what becomes of them, if it can but banish them from its own society; no good therefore is ever to be expected till parochial interest is destroyed" (*History of the Poor Laws* 185–86). Charles Gray, by comparison, argued that "the divisions are at present *too large* not too small" (5).

Parish administration, as it functioned in the 1740s, had been set down initially by the Elizabethan Poor Law of 1601 and extensively refined thereafter. Most, but not all, seventeenth- and eighteenth-century commentators tend to see the 1601 law as the codification of a relief system that had already existed in practice, but that required, after the reformation, at least a provisional legislative definition. Joseph Townsend, for example, laments that "at the dissolution of the monasteries, the lazy and the indigent, who were deprived of their accustomed food, became clamorous" (18). Richard Burn, on the other hand, attacks the "vulgar error" of "affirming, that the poor, during the times of popery, were maintained chiefly by the religious houses. Their hospitality was to the rich . . . the poor received scraps at their gates" (*History of the Poor Laws* 106). The various legislative developments subsequent to 1601 established, as I have already noted, the principles of settlement and vagrancy, as well as an increasingly complex system of overseers, court procedures, workhouse tests, and rate assessments. The Webbs tell us that "the number and variety of regulative and administrative functions [of] the eighteenth-century parish simply bewilder the modern student" (*English Poor Law* 1: 4). The clergyman was in some respects a peripheral figure in this process, but his office was entangled with those of the clerks, vestrymen, overseers, and constables who carried out the duties of relief, removal, and confinement, and he was, finally, the locus of parish authority.[15] Fielding's writings from around 1740 on emphasize the clergyman's duty to exemplify charitable care, providing the other functions of poverty management with their ethical standard.

The magistracy, which originated in the fourteenth century with the creation of the office of justice of the peace, served as the principal supervisory arm of the county, a much broader administrative territory that grew in prominence and influence as the parish declined.[16] During the eighteenth century, justices of the peace, who were most often landholding gentry but might also be ranking church officials or aristocrats, were responsible for a wide range of judicial and administrative functions. They oversaw criminal and civil proceedings in private sessions, petty sessions, and quarter sessions. They fixed wage rates and issued licenses for alehouses. Most significantly for the purposes of this chapter, they "appointed officials such as parish overseers of the poor, they scrutinized Poor Law accounts, they approved parish poor rates, they adjudicated in disputes and they heard appeals against overseers' decisions" (Briggs et al. 47). In the middle of the eighteenth century, justices of the peace combined capacities that, to our eyes, seem to confuse the private, intimate, local, and amateur with the public, statutory, national, and professional. Most historians see such a distinction taking shape during the period, though it was far from fully developed in the 1740s.[17]

It is important to note that Fielding and other commentators see the parish and the magistracy as decisive spheres of action in contradistinction to the manor (the patrilineal estate): "the vestry or parish meeting stood as the unit of administration, transformed from a medieval ecclesiastical usage to an amateur agent of civil administration, the most important local government outside the city of London and the boroughs" (G. Taylor 15). Originally, manors were largely coterminous with parishes, which originated as "the religious expression of the manor" (Pounds 4), but parishes had, over manors, the advantage of not being subject to the solvent effects of hereditament and marriage settlement.[18] Parishes retained "precise and generally accepted boundaries" (Pounds xiii); the annual tradition of "beating the bounds"—walking around the boundaries of the parish—was an important secular and religious ceremony that persisted into the nineteenth century (Pounds 70–71, 76–77). Manorial boundaries, meanwhile, shifted and changed rapidly, so "before the end of the middle ages the pattern of parishes had ceased to bear any close similarity to that of landholding" (Pounds 4). While a manorial interest remains a key component of what I am calling the parochial vision, what is left of the manorial system by the 1740s lacks the comprehensiveness and the (potential) homogeneity that Fielding identifies with the parish system.[19]

The influence of gentry and aristocracy over parochial affairs did endure in the form of advowsons—exclusive right to nominate the holder of a parish living. In many, though certainly not all cases, landowning families held one or more parish advowsons. The patron often also "received, administered and distributed the several sources of income which arose within the benefice" (Pounds 49). The English Reformation and the dissolution of the monasteries actually bolstered this species of influence; "the laity reacquired the majority of the rights of presentation" (Pounds 49), and private ownership of advowsons remained widespread into the twentieth century. That customary right helps account for the frequency with which English novelists allocate property settlements by means of beneficed livings from *Joseph Andrews* through *Mansfield Park* and beyond. Anthea Jones reports that "when Jane Austen was writing, rather more than half the livings of the Church of England were 'family' livings" (231). In *Joseph Andrews,* as we will see, advowsons and other patronal rights, real or perceived, arise at several important junctures.

What remained of the manorial interest was by no means inevitably the controlling one in parish politics despite the tendency of novels to represent them as such. In *Tom Jones,* for instance, Squire Allworthy's prestige is certainly indexed to his status as manorial gentleman, but Fielding makes perfectly clear that Allworthy's instrumental authority resides mostly in his position as county official.[20] From *Joseph Andrews* on, Fielding's fiction thematizes the extent to which sway over the clergy and other aspects of parish business enables landowning patrons to influence, interfere with, or abuse the processes of poverty management, and the manner in which patrons *ought* to involve themselves.

The treatment of poverty in *Joseph Andrews* is divided into two main segments, each of which refracts one of the major morphologies of chivalric romance.[21] The first of these morphologies is the quest—Joseph's journey home—which takes up three of the four volumes, and exposes Joseph and his companions to the hazards of vagrancy law. The second romance morphology is the courtship, here transformed into Joseph and Fanny's struggle to prove a settlement in Lady Booby's parish and get themselves married. I will discuss the "courtship" in the final section of this chapter. Joseph's quest begins with his expulsion from Lady Booby's service. He leaves London immediately, despite the fall of night, because he has "inducements which the reader, without being a conjurer, cannot possibly guess" (41). The reason for Joseph's hurry, we are told, is his desire to see Fanny, who "was a poor girl, who had been formerly bred up in Sir John's Family; whence a little before the journey to London, she had been discarded by Mrs. Slipslop on account of her extraordinary beauty, for I never could find any other reason" (42). Both of these mysteries seem to relate to problems of poverty: Joseph's need to travel at night would most likely be spurred also by the fact that he has "stript off his livery" (41) and will not, therefore, be able to "give a good account of himself," as the vagrancy law requires; and Fanny's expulsion from service proves later to be a pretext for Lady Booby to deny her a settlement in the parish.

We also find, in the passages I am discussing, a pair of inconsistencies in the narrative; Fanny has been bred up in Sir Thomas Booby's family; there is no Sir John; and when Joseph breaks his journey after just a few miles to shelter from a storm, the proprietor of the inn where Joseph takes shelter, "observing his livery, began to condole the loss of his late Master" (43). Fielding corrected the first error in his second edition of *Joseph Andrews* and repairs the second in the following chapter when Joseph is attacked by robbers, beaten, and stripped naked. Rescued thereafter by a coachload of unwilling good Samaritans, Joseph finds himself at the inn owned by the Tow-wouses, where his recovery is not expected. Mrs. Tow-wouse takes little pleasure in helping Joseph: she calls her husband "a pretty sort of man to take in naked vagabonds and clothe them with his own clothes . . . I shall have no such doings . . . [W]hat the devil have we to do with poor wretches? The law makes us provide for too many already. We shall have thirty or forty poor wretches in red coats shortly" (48–49). Mrs. Tow-wouse's complaint is the first in a series of expressions of anxiety over swelling populations of paupers and the possibility that those populations might organize. In this instance, she refers to forced billeting of soldiers, whose status as servants of the state does not keep them from seeming like a marauding gang and rapacious consumers of resources—a common image of standing armies in the period.[22]

Growing fears that the poor would form insurgent populations and corporations color a significant portion of the eighteenth-century debates on poverty and crime.[23] Fielding plays on such fears in his *Enquiry into the Causes of the Late Increase of Robbers:* "What indeed may not the public apprehend, when they are informed as an unquestionable fact, that there are at this time a great gang of rogues, whose number falls little short of a hundred, who are incorporated in one body, have officers and a treasury, and have reduced theft and robbery into a regular system" (2). Had Fielding written this sentence ten years earlier, we would assume he was referring to Walpole's Whig administration, and of course in *Jonathan Wild* he sketches a more elaborate version of the same picture, portraying Walpole and the parliamentary Whigs as a gang of thieves through a redaction of the story of an actual notorious criminal. The poor figure the potential of a kind of anti-nation, or an outlaw corporation that may take (and in the case of the Whig ministry had taken) command of the nation. "I make no doubt," Fielding warns in the *Enquiry*, "but that the streets of [London], and the roads leading to it, will shortly be impassable without the utmost hazard" (1).

As Joseph makes his way home, his party also multiplies, first by the addition of the parson Abraham Adams, who finds Joseph at the Tow-wouses' Inn, then with Fanny, who has embarked on her own quest to find Joseph. The threesome become a kind of gang, damaging property, disturbing the peace, and causing bodily harm as they make their way across the countryside. Their inability to pay their way forces them to beg for charity and to disguise their vagrancy behind Parson Adams's cloth, though not everyone sees the ragged preacher as a primitive-church worthy. Adams's "Brother in the Parish," Parson Trulliber, for instance, wishes "the Tithing-Man was here . . . I would have thee punished as a vagabond for thy impudence" (145). To Adams's protests, Trulliber responds, "I know what charity is, better than to give to vagabonds," and Mrs. Trulliber adds, "Besides, if we were inclined, the Poors Rate obliges us to give so much charity" (146). Parson Trulliber is a portrait of the reprobate overseer. If we have attended to Fielding's preface, we should detect hypocrisy in Trulliber's protestations: charity can only be charity when it is its own imperative and not otherwise enforced. In a 1740 two-part "Apology for the Clergy" in the *Champion*, Fielding defines charity as "the relieving the wants and sufferings of one another to the utmost of our abilities. It is to be limited by our power, I say, only" (267). Adams calls that principle to his own

support, a little self-servingly: "Suppose I am not a clergyman," he tells Trulliber, "I am nevertheless thy brother; and thou, as a Christian, much more as a
clergyman, art obliged to relieve my distress" (145–46).

Strictly speaking, Adams and company are vagabonds and not entitled to
relief under the poor statutes. Parson Trulliber might be justified in heeding
advice offered by Fielding in the *Enquiry:* "Every beggar who can but moder-
ately well personate misery is sure to find relief and encouragement; and this
though the giver must have great reason to doubt the reality of the distress,
and when he can scarce be ignorant that his bounty is illegal, and that he is
encouraging a nuisance" (36). But Adams is not personating his distress, and
Trulliber would be better guided by the *Champion* "Apology" essay, which reminds him that a clergyman is "a successor to Christ's disciples . . . he must
be humble, charitable, benevolent, void of envy, void of pride, void of vanity," and "live in daily communication with his flock, and chiefly with those
who want him most (as the poor and distress'd)" (283). Indeed, "this virtue
of charity . . . comprehends almost the whole particular duty of a Christian"
(270). It is my contention that Fielding uses the concept of charity to define
the local, personal, and intimate relations of parish life, over against the secular and juridical relations by which the magistracy and county officialdom in
general operate. His charity is not supposed to be wholly indiscriminate; per-
sonated misery should be discovered, but by means of intimate, even familial,
character judgment, rather than abstract statutory tests. Parson Adams refers
to Joseph and Fanny as "his children; a term he explained to mean no more
than his parishioners; saying, He looked on all those whom God had intrusted
to his care to stand to him in that relation" (*JA* 150). Indeed all parochial activities should be conducted in this prestatutory, private manner.

The unmediated (though mediating) "natural" bonds of parish care will
ideally subsume the legal mandates of clerical duty, ensuring that economic
and social justice is nurtured by affective and kindred bonds.[24] Fielding envisions that paternalism within the parish can be reinvigorated on this familial model, while providing also points of contact with the external (county
and national) juridical and managerial systems that hold supervisory authority over parochial spheres but do not exercise their management directly and
openly within the parish. It is confusion of parish offices with those belonging to more comprehensive administrative jurisdictions that Fielding hopes
to repair. I will discuss the magistrate's role as intermediary between parochial
and statutory spheres later in this chapter. First, however, I will sketch out the
model of judgment that *Joseph Andrews* exemplifies, its basis in contemporary

theories of representation and ridicule, and its instrumentality to both management of the poor and broader conceptions of social justice.

## DARKNESS RISIBLE

The importance of *Joseph Andrews* to my argument consists not only in its literary exemplarity. That is to say, while it does present manifest examples of the kinds of parochial method that Fielding advocates and illustrate the ruinous state of parish administration as he sees it, it also teaches an epistemic regime that draws together a theory of representation with a heuristic that is instrumental to the formation of judgment and the self-governance required for effective reform. The heuristic at issue is an adaptation of the "test of truth" derived, by contemporary disputants, from Shaftesbury's meditations on ridicule in the *Characteristicks*. Its satiric function in *Joseph Andrews*, censuring misrepresentations of the poor and their supervisors, is supplemented by (or supplementary to) its fostering of sound supervisory judgment and practice. And its evaluative logic resonates through much of Fielding's thought on justice, governance, and social relations. The test of truth emerges from and refines contemporary accounts of the relation between signifier and signified— between surface and substance or between word and idea/thing—and an assessment of Fielding's participation in that area of aesthetics is preliminary to my discussion of the mechanics of ridicule.

His reformation of romance begins in a thoroughly conventional claim to "the just imitation of nature," and a warning against burlesque "exhibition of what is monstrous and unnatural" (*JA* 4). Burlesque, like *caricatura* in painting, aims "to exhibit monsters, not men; and all distortions and exaggerations whatever are within its proper province" (5). Although "we have sometimes admitted this in our diction, we have carefully excluded it from our sentiments and characters," Fielding notes, claiming for *Joseph Andrews* instead the comic style, which "should of all others be the least excused for deviating from Nature" (4).[25] Romance and the burlesque, then, are empty forms, imitations of nothing: at the beginning of book 3, Fielding reiterates his condemnation of "the authors of immense Romances, or the modern Novel and *Atalantis* writers; who without any assistance from Nature or History, record persons who never were, or will be, and facts which never did nor possibly can happen: Whose heroes are of their own creation, and their brains the chaos whence all their materials are collected" (163). The proximate example of this kind of romancer is, of course, Samuel Richardson. Ronald Paulson observes that the

Nature and history to which Fielding proclaims his fidelity constitute a "reality" that "means moral or factual truth apprehended by the reader, whereas he sees in *Pamela* the accurately reported workings of a character's mind, without any concern for the truth or falseness in relation to the external world" (*Life* 146). The Pamela of Richardson's novel is Fielding's prototypical case of romantic delusion fostered by debauched modern ideals of personal virtue and social worth.

To distinguish his own fiction from the vaporous prodigies of romance, he evokes typology; his characters are not singular, self-generating anomalies, but compounds of generality and particularity: "I describe not men, but manners: not an individual, but a species. Perhaps it will be answered, are not the characters then taken from life? To which I answer in the affirmative . . . I have writ little more than I have seen" (*JA* 164). That passage and the following are drawn from the first chapter of volume 3, "Matter Prefatory in Praise of Biography": "Truth is only to be found in the works of those who celebrate the lives of great men, and are commonly called biographers . . . The facts we deliver may be relied on, tho' we often mistake the age and country wherein they happened: for tho' it may be worth the examination of critics whether the shepherd Chrysostom, who, as Cervantes informs us, died for the love of the fair Marcella, who hated him, was ever in *Spain,* will anyone doubt but that such a silly fellow hath really existed?" (162–63). Oddly it is the historian's specificities that distort facts, interpose themselves between us and imitable nature: "Is not such a book as that which records the atchievements [*sic*] of the renowned *Don Quixote,* more worthy the name of a history than even *Mariana's;* for whereas the latter is confined to a particular period of time, and to a particular nation; the former is a history of the world in general" (163–64). *Pamela,* we should not be surprised to learn, then, "is communicated to us by an historian who borrows his lights, as the common method is, from authentic papers and records" (16). The attentive reader will catch the resonant irony of this notional authentic paper. (Fielding's ironies always exhort us, train us, to be attentive readers.) The dismissal of *Pamela,* and romance generally, as a variety of paper currency helps Fielding to disavow the logical inference that all fiction is no better than paper credit. Bolstering that disavowal is a constant labor of his novelistic career.

The paper-currency innuendo testifies that Fielding's antiromance is founded in the privileging, pervasive in both British neoclassicism and Addisonian commercial humanism,[26] of bound form (that is, form bound to substantial precedent, content, or referent) over autonomous, self-constitutive form. Erin Mackie notes, for instance, that Joseph Addison often expresses "a distaste for forms of verbal manipulation that call attention to the body of language, to the material word, to the autonomy of the signifier," seeing in them "a disregard for sense and a cultivation of features of language that have little to do with verbal stability, permanence, reason, and easy communication" (226). The dichotomy between bound and autonomous form has an immensely important role in neoclassical poetics and the ethical and political values of the emergent public sphere in the first half of the eighteenth century, lending its logic to (and borrowing its logic from) the oppositions between nature and art, true and false wit, gold and paper credit, and fixed and mobile property. Autonomous form is the empty wit of Thomas Shadwell/Mac Flecknoe's "genuine night," his "rising fogs," tautology, anagrams, and acrostics ("What share have we in nature or in art?") (Dryden 99–105); it is the pedantry of Scriblerus *pere et fils* and all the dullness that stands opposed to—and helps define—true wit.

The bound/autonomous form dichotomy is also implicated in the genesis of what economic historians call substance theories of value: "Starting with [William] Petty and Richard Cantillon, it became common to postulate a distinction between intrinsic value, naturally determined and fundamentally stable, and market price, an epiphenomenon of the myriad conjunctures of the historically specific market"; "balance-of-trade mercantilists drew their sustenance from this nexus, comparing value with substance, gold with the lifeblood of the polity, economic prosperity with bodily health, and trade with motion" (Mirowski 154, 150). From these theories arise popular perceptions that market prices, paper credit, and stocks, as paperized forms representing gold and fixed property, pose a threat where they cease to bind to the substantial value they are supposed to stand for—where they are exposed as empty promises and vanish in bubbles.[27] The best-known case, the South Sea Company, was "a company erected upon a bad foundation, a false title, for we have no trade to the South-Sea" (Baston, preface). Gold, landed estates, and the person of the king, on the other hand, embody value, authority, and continuity intrinsically, substantially, and much less frangibly.

The bound form/autonomous form binary provides constitutive oppositions for contested cultural categories like ornamentation and dress, proportion, the Longinian sublime, and the (then) recently revived Aristotelian distinction between the possible/impossible and the probable/improbable.[28] In virtually all areas of social, economic, and aesthetic enterprise, it is possible to find variations on what Carolyn Steedman calls "the mission of written language in the eighteenth century, that is, the effacement of difference between event and representation" (333). That this mission was pursued so vigorously alerts us to the assumption motivating it: unfettered symbologies were not without appeal, even utility.[29] However widely they were disparaged, paper credit, stocks, masquerade, fashion, and the Grub Street presses all thrived. And it was often the case that these "modern" symbolic systems referred themselves to stabilizing reserves of substantial value—most famously the gold standard. In addition, calling one's antagonists names like *hack, gamester, projector,* and *coquette* was a key means of disavowing autonomous form. "Mac Flecknoe," the Swift-Montagu quarrel, Fielding's stage farces, and any number of pamphlet wars are propelled by energetic rhetorical variations on this principle: one's opponent is a friend to signs that do not signify.[30]

Like libertinism, with which it was frequently associated, autonomous form was often viewed as licentious, even voluptuary: Richardson's Lovelace, for example, "helps to undo the matrix of truth and value through which Clarissa would have us see, know and judge"; he "empties the self . . . makes it a surface, a mask, a series of folds" (Warner 30, 32). Inconstancy, wantonness, duplicity, casuistry, and punning are some of the dangers—and pleasures—of form that defies the authority of substance and precedent. Joseph Addison, on the other hand, writes in cautious defense of what he calls the "fairy way of writing," "wherein the poet quite loses sight of nature, and entertains his reader's imagination with the characters and actions of such persons as have many of them no existence, but what he bestows on them" (3: 570). Among the successful practitioners of this kind of writing Addison ranks Shakespeare and Milton, though he warns that fiction "that depends on the poet's fancy, because he has no pattern to follow in it" (3: 570), may breed quixotic error in readers who "are prepossest with such false opinions, as dispose them to believe these particular delusions" (3: 571).[31] Fielding is willing to allow that such works may "be as an example of the wonderful extent of human genius" (*JA* 163), but enlists Milton to help disparage "authors of an inferior class" who "carry the genius far off . . . beyond the realm of Chaos and old Night" (*JA* 163). Romance authorship, then, affronts nature with "shape, / If shape it might be called that shape hath none / . . . / Or substance might be call'd that shadow seem'd" (Milton 51, lines 666–69), born out of the "wide womb of uncreated Night" (37, line 150) as the offspring of profane demiurges whose works are "their own creation, and their brains the chaos whence all their materials are collected" (*JA* 163).[32]

In one of the prefatory chapters of *Tom Jones,* Fielding invokes probability and possibility to explain how his own fiction provides readers reasonable grounds for accepting that it has more substantial sources than the chaos of his own brain. The judgment of "every reader in the world" (346n) falls somewhere between "very different extremes": one exemplified by the French commentator on Aristotle, André Dacier, whom Fielding's narrator calls "ready to allow that the same thing which is impossible may yet be probable" (346),[33] and the other exemplified by those who "believe nothing to be either possible or probable, the like to which hath not occurred to their own observation" (346). Dacier's probable impossible belongs to representations of the supernatural, which are to be avoided altogether among "us moderns" in works for which "a horse-laugh in the reader would be any great prejudice or mortification" (347–48). Novelists/biographers, on the other hand, who record "scenes of private life" and "deal in private character, who search into the most retired recesses, and draw forth examples of virtue and vice from holes and corners of the world," cannot call upon the "public notoriety," "concurrent testimony," or "records to support and corroborate" their descriptions that historians of national events enjoy (348). The novelist is "obliged to record matters as he finds them though they may be of so extraordinary a nature as will require no small degree of historical faith to swallow them" (348)—he trades, in other words, in improbable possibility, which is the defining condition of private life.[34]

The novel, or at any rate the comic epic-poem in prose, establishes a new epistemology of credibility.[35] The standard by which its substantiality, plausibility, and fidelity to nature can be tested is neither the internal coherence of neoclassical propriety ("the same thing which is impossible may yet be probable") nor the external confirmation of radical empiricism (the strict evidence of one's "own observation"), but their mutual negation in the process of readerly judgment. In the terms proposed by Michael McKeon, "naïve empiricism negates the idealist epistemology of romance, and is in turn negated by extreme skepticism and a more circumspect approach to truth" (*Origins* 267). The double negation is, for McKeon, Fielding's characteristic narrative gesture. It generates "instrumental belief"—paradoxically, "a fiction so palpable, so 'evident to the senses,' that its power to deceive even a 'willing' audience becomes neutralized" (*Origins* 393). The inhabitants of Fielding's version of private life are not simply avatars of ancient and immutable principles, nor heteroclite eccentricities who must be seen to be conceived; they are the dialectical interplay of the two extremes. Fielding's notion of private character and private life, then, seems compatible with the dialectic of home that I outline in the introduction to this book: home is at once a homogeneous norm and a homologized set of aspirations, linked to other private homes and to the national collective, but it is also singular, unlegislated, experienced in every case as though it were the first and only one of its kind.

McKeon's account of the double negation that generates instrumental belief is compelling, and I want to retain in particular his thesis that Fielding accomplishes a "subsumption of questions of virtue by questions of truth" (*Origins* 408), but the negative comparison McKeon describes is supplementary to a positive comparison—the ridicule test. A debate over the heuristic principle that ridicule could provide a test of truth bubbled along from the early years of the century until after Fielding's death. Its forgotten role in *Joseph Andrews* is a codification of narrative veracity, establishing a stable locus for Fielding's negations and linking the ethics of poverty management to the epistemology of fiction.

Here is what I mean: according to Fielding, the delight we draw from the comic epic-poem in prose proceeds from recognition of the ridiculous, examples of which "life every where furnishes an accurate observer" (*JA* 4). Those examples, he argues, arise always in the exposure of some variety of affectation (either vanity or hypocrisy), an exposure whose fairness, whose justice any right-thinking person will intuitively recognize. In doing so, Fielding adapts a part of the moral philosophy outlined by the third Earl of Shaftesbury in his 1711 *Characteristicks*: "Truth, 'tis supposed, may bear all lights: and one of those principal lights, or natural mediums, by which things are to be view'd, in order to a thorow recognition, is Ridicule" (1: 61); "nothing is ridiculous but what is deform'd: nor is anything proof against raillery, but what is handsome and just" (1: 128).[36]

Shaftesbury's postulate on ridicule, which subsequent discussants came to call the test of truth, was hotly disputed until at least the mid-1750s.[37] The poet Mark Akenside, for example, declares:

> To ask then whether ridicule be a test of truth, is, in other words, to ask whether that which is ridiculous can be morally true, can be just and becoming . . . [I]t is most evident, that as in a metaphysical proposition offer'd to the understanding for its assent, the faculty of reason examines the terms of the proposition and finding one idea which was suppos'd equal to another to be in fact unequal, of consequence rejects the proposition as a falsehood . . . thus a double advantage is gained; for we both detect the moral falsehood sooner than in the way of specu-

lative inquiry, and impress the minds of men with a stronger sense of
the vanity and error of its authors. (120–21)

For its defenders, the test of truth is an intuitive propositional logic, a kind
of prerational reasoning; it works faster than "speculative inquiry" and produces a "stronger sense" of vanity and error. The test of truth works as though
the observer were generating and affirming or declining syllogistic truth statements, but instantly, feelingly, and without painstaking ratiocination: Akenside's friend and defender Jeremiah Dyson writes, "The ridicule generally
strikes you at first view, and always without the intervention of any other
means" (11).

"No proposition can ever appear ridiculous to us," Dyson continues, "till
we have first seen it to be false, whether by its inconsistence with itself, or
with some known truth" (11). That which is ridiculous is incongruous with
itself (resembles what it is not), while that which is proper, just, or correct is
self-congruous and will throw ridicule back upon the railer: "Whenever . . .
ridicule is unjust, instead of wounding the object its [sic] directed against, like
a gun over-charg'd, it always recoils on the author . . . [L]et any man, the most
perfect master of banter, or jest, try if he can ridicule a noble, humane, generous, publick-spirited, or friendly action, gratitude to the deity, or love to a free
country, this is impossible, for what makes any man, or character, ridiculous
is an affectation of good qualities he doth not possess" (Weekly Oracle, 1737,
qtd. in Gilmore 14). That the famous preface to Joseph Andrews participates in
this debate seems to have been neglected in recent discussions of this novel,[38]
but Fielding was certainly aware of the debate—he cites Shaftesbury's postulate in an attack on Bolingbroke ("Fragment" 234–35). As he does so, he acknowledges that "there may be some justice" in allegations that "truth may by
such a trial be subjected to misrepresentation, and become a more easy prey
to the malice of its enemies; a flagrant instance of which we have in the case
of Socrates" (235). William Warburton's client John Brown develops the case
against ridicule, which he calls "no more than the application of that particular
species of poetry called wit, to . . . persuasion. It tends to excite contempt, in
the same manner as the other modes of eloquence raise love, pity, terror,
rage, or hatred, in the heart of man" (42). But Fielding quite clearly has a use
for ridicule: "Whatever objection there may be against trying truth by ridicule, there can be none, I apprehend, of making use of its assistance in expelling and banishing all falshood and imposture, when once fairly convicted";
indeed "this method . . . is the most efficacious that can be invented" ("Frag-

ment" 235). Despite this apparent concession, *Joseph Andrews* in particular and Fielding's doctrines of inquiry and judgment generally do, nonetheless, mandate a test of truth that incorporates the fundamental mechanism of the ridicule test.

The trial by which Fielding would have "falshood and imposture . . . fairly convicted" still asks whether the object of examination is congruent "with itself, or with some known truth" (Dyson 11), but the known truth concerned is determined by conditions meant to stabilize its reliability. It is not merely a contingent fact or specificity like those of the empirical historian "confined to a particular period of time, and to a particular nation" (*JA* 163), nor is it a mere probability beholden only to abstract proprieties. Fielding's test of truth is a workhouse test—the demarcation and policing of a binary opposition that has a settled place in the "natural" hierarchy of things, but that requires in every instance the attentive discrimination of the magistrate combined with the charitable care of the cleric: "What would give a greater shock to humanity, than an attempt to expose the miseries of poverty and distress to ridicule?" (*JA* 6). True poverty rebuffs ridicule: "Surely he hath a very ill-framed mind, who can look on ugliness, infirmity, or poverty as ridiculous in themselves: nor do I believe any man living who meets a dirty fellow riding through the streets in a cart, is struck with an idea of the ridiculous from it . . . In the same manner, were we to enter a poor house, and behold a wretched family shivering with cold and languishing with hunger, it would not incline us to laughter" (7). Where Charles Gray complains that "it is difficult in many cases to determine, who are real paupers, or proper objects of parish charity. It is so easy to personate misery, and feign distress" (8), Fielding argues that a capable observer will never be fooled: "Should we discover [in a poorhouse] flowers, empty plate, or china dishes on the side-board, or any other affectation of riches or finery either on [the paupers'] persons or in their furniture; we might then indeed be excused for ridiculing so fantastical an appearance" (*JA* 7).[39] From the poor, and the charitable attitude that this novel mandates, we derive a standard of justice and propriety: in the *Proposal*, Fielding asks, "What indeed must be his composition who could see whole families in want of every necessary of life, oppressed with hunger, cold, nakedness, and filth . . . who could look into such a scene as this, and be affected only in his nostrils?" (9). Poverty is a paradoxically valorized category, which authorizes ridicule by marking the limit at which it stops: "The affectation of high life appears more glaring and ridiculous from the simplicity of the low" (*Tom Jones* 426).

In his *Enquiry into the Causes of the Late Increase in Robbers,* Fielding declares that "the two great motives to luxury, in the mind of men, are Vanity and Voluptuousness" (4); but crucially, "the former of these two operates but little in this regard with the lower order of people. I do not mean that they have less of this passion than their betters; but the apparent impossibility of gratifying it in this way deters them" (4). Poverty restrains affectation and therefore transgressive social emulation: the poor have no means of putting on the trappings of their betters and so cannot effectively develop any effective vanity. Affectation always signifies negatively. It displays what one is not, and it does so visibly.[40] Poverty signifies positively, embodying itself. The face of poverty is a bound form while affectation is autonomous. Hence genuine poverty, contrasting with any pretense to unmerited status, unmasks such pretense.[41] Affectation in *Joseph Andrews* is routinely undone by poverty, usually the virtuous poverty of Joseph, Fanny, and Abraham Adams, whose honesty, naïveté, and constancy get them in scrapes but also expose the vanity and hypocrisy of their various antagonists.[42] Judith Frank contends that Fielding generates "a kind of ethics of representation of the poor" (31). I would go further and argue that this mode of judgment, which takes the honest pauper as a measure of truth, founds a general ethics of representation and of civic relations. Poverty authorizes satire and provides a fund of unadorned human nature, nature that is indeed unable to adorn itself.

Fielding's poor are objects of analysis and comparison, the stable figure in portable dyads that substantiate judgments about virtue and vice.[43] Michel de Certeau terms this representational strategy "discourse authorized by the other" (68)—the temporary inversion of a single opposition in a binary hierarchy where a term normally consigned to otherness, or supplementarity, changes places with its opposite, becoming privileged and aligned with other privileged values, especially truth. So, in Certeau's example, Michel de Montaigne allies his cannibals with Nature: "The savage body obeys a law, the law of faithful and verifiable speech" (Certeau 75). The naked cannibal cannot be other than what he appears to be, and for Fielding the same is true of the pauper clad only in rags and filth. In its usual operation, the supplement functions to absorb or compensate for a lack, a failure of self-sufficiency, in the privileged term to which it stands opposed.[44] In the case of Montaigne and Fielding, the substitutive action of the supplement, usually covert, becomes explicit and thereby exposes the lack in the term it displaces: for Montaigne, civilized man's lack of civilization and, for Fielding, the lack of virtue, condition, or means in a vain or hypocritical person. The inversion Certeau describes does remain contingent; it is not permitted to destabilize the whole binary hierarchy. It merely provides a test or figure of comparison that finally sanctions the system it seems to unsettle. Joseph and Fanny's defiance of the poor laws and of the authority of their superiors, justified or otherwise, is thoroughly recuperated by the end of the novel. Fielding has invented what we might call the noble pauper, who exposes the self-division of affectation; the pauper's visible self is reliably bound to the nature it represents.

Further, this mode of judgment does not only propose reliable grounds for distinguishing between honesty and affectation in others, but encourages good nature in the subject who judges. In one of his *Champion* essays, for instance, Fielding asks: "Can [an honest clergyman] be the object of contempt? . . . Perhaps indeed boys and devils, and madmen, and rakes, and fools, and villains, may laugh at this sacred person" (283). In another number of the same journal, he asserts that "good nature requires a distinguishing faculty, which is another word for judgment, and is perhaps the sole boundary between wisdom and folly" (*Champion* 253).[45] According to Fielding's contemporary Francis Hutcheson, Professor of Moral Philosophy at Glasgow, "ridicule gives our minds as it were a bend to the contrary side; so that upon reflection they may be more capable of settling in a just conformity to nature" (29); "nothing is so properly applied to the false grandeur, either of good or of evil, as ridicule" (33). Thus the comic mode is designed not simply to encourage the well-off to exercise astute and benevolent supervision over their laboring charges, but to restrain their own affected impulses and romantic notions. In the following section, I will examine how Fielding's epistemology of judgment informs the institutional structures and practices he advocated for England's parishes and counties.

The hierarchical and segregated social relations that he envisions will sustain his parochial vision are, finally, also enforced by the comedy of ridicule. Carolyn Steedman's excellent discussion of jokes about servants in eighteenth-century England helps clarify what I mean: the comic mode shapes discourse on the dependent poor, Steedman argues, because

> if it's funny . . . then it's not uncanny; if it's funny, it is so because you know where it came from . . . The servants in the (unfunny) eighteenth-century joke come from a social unconscious that knows them to be phantom limbs, dispossessed and alienated body parts; prostheses, indeed. Do the employing classes tell these jokes in order to retrieve something that has been lost? . . . something that . . . fictional and real authors . . . employers and their readers, all dimly, anxiously,

discerned: that once, we were all on a foot, each a part of each other, in that lost realm of imagined community that the eighteenth century invented and that served it as a real Political Unconscious. (349–50)

Ridicule, then, staves off regression and the collapse of social divisions, because it insists that genuine, natural laughter springs from an intuitive, even visceral recognition of the truth, stability, and rightness of social difference.[46] Comic laughter affirms the divided and reciprocally obligated social order of Fielding's parochial imaginary. It seizes on those who abscond from or counterfeit their proper social stations. Hence the comic epic-poem in prose, paradoxically, tills the fertile soil of romance to cultivate a right sense of humor. Far from simply abolishing the works and deeds of those who form "originals from the confused heap of matter in their own brains" (*JA* 163), Fielding's new species of writing preserves romance as a defining essence, the ground upon which the comic novel bases its credibility.

## MOB AND MOBILITY

The English manorial system in the eighteenth century, I have noted, was not a simple landholding analogue to the administrative system of the parish. Manorial authority was becoming ever more abstract and, in Fielding's estimation, disaggregated from the parochial care it ought to superintend. Indeed, the power of the manor at the local level transforms into that of the magistracy. Fiction in the period works hard to maintain a masquerade of traditional landholding around what were actually mechanisms of county bureaucracy, "to project a communal pattern in which these two aspects seem to belong together naturally, even while they are no longer organically linked" (Schmidgen, *Eighteenth-Century Fiction* 79). Fielding is, if anything, more frank about the façade than most of his contemporaries, but he advocates judicial practice that methodizes the values of the manor. In his social treatises he sought to reinvigorate manorial supervision, and in *Joseph Andrews* he models the manorial/judicial vision in the subjection of character to readerly judgment. I propose that the benevolent and malevolent landholders in Fielding's fiction, and perhaps in most eighteenth-century fiction, are overdetermined by their figural embodiment of judicial authority. They are magistrates who discharge their offices (well or badly) in the guise of country gentlemen superintending estates.

The parochial benevolence of the good clergyman operates in a more confined sphere than that of the magistrate. Parson Adams is "a standing lesson to all his acquaintance," but, as is often the case, "the best men are but little known, and consequently cannot extend the usefulness of their examples a great way" (*JA* 15). Nor does the good parson see far beyond that narrow sphere he inhabits (Adams does not, for instance, have any notion of the value that a bookseller is likely to place on his sermons [69]). The readerly subject position, on the other hand, is more privileged, having the benefit of the authorial perspective, which, "by communicating such valuable patterns [as Adams] to the world . . . may perhaps do a more extensive service to mankind than the person whose life originally afforded the pattern" (*JA* 15). That broader view aligns also with that of the manorial interest and the judicial perspective as Fielding conceives it. Ronald Paulson was the first scholar to identify Fielding's reader function as a judicial surrogate.[47] Revisiting the thesis in his 2000 biography of Fielding, Paulson sees him, as his legal career develops, adopting "a modified definition of the satirist . . . a transition from a prosecuting attorney to an impartial judge . . . who often acquits or forgives. The metaphor that makes the satirist, and, later, the reader, a magistrate and every character or action a case for judgment" (107). The moral and economic judgment for which the tests of truth in *Joseph Andrews* train us is an integral component of Fielding's paternalism. In the essay "Characters of Men," Fielding declares that his rules for interpreting action and expression "are of no use but to an observer of much penetration" (197). The reader should read and interpret like a magistrate, and the magistracy should form judgments the way a reader of Fielding's fiction does.

The authority of judgment, for Fielding then, is vested not in narratorial or character surrogates, but in the heuristics and taxonomies that his texts define. They train the reader to enact the reformed judicial and patronal superintendence that his scheme requires, to position themselves as notional members of a landed magistracy.[48] In his "Letter on Enthusiasm," Shaftesbury makes an explicit analogy between judicial process and epistemological continence: "If men are vicious, petulant, or abusive; the magistrate may correct them: but if they reason ill, 'tis reason still must teach 'em to do better" (10). Readers should think like the estate holders who occupy the magistrates' chairs. Although the manor had lost much of its sway as a unit of direct social administration, landed patronage exerted a continuing influence, especially in Fielding's fiction, in the form of advowsons, administration of parochial stocks and endowments, and domination of the county offices of justice of the peace. Justices were effectively the final authority in parish poverty cases, and the conduct of parish officers "was subject only to the surveillance of the justices of the peace" (G. Taylor 15). The social status of rural magistrates on average actually rose in the decades preceding 1834. Carl Zangerl cites K. B. Smellie "expressing a widely-held viewpoint [that] describes the county magistracy in the nineteenth century as the 'rear guard of an agrarian oligarchy,' the 'most aristocratic feature of English government,'" and goes on to affirm Smellie's thesis, while emphasizing that gentry rather than aristocrats still held a considerable majority in these posts (113). Zangerl also notes that in 1745 "the qualification of a £100 per year landed income" was instituted for magistrates (117). Fielding himself needed help from the Duke of Bedford to fulfill that qualification before entering the magistracy (Zirker xix).

The condensation of readerly and juridical roles in Fielding's fiction receives its fullest analysis from John Bender in *Imagining the Penitentiary*. The narrator of *Tom Jones*, for Bender, "amalgamates traits of the untrammeled judge at the traditional Old Bailey trial with those of the investigative Justice of the Peace" (178). Bender sees Fielding's fiction developing along a trajectory toward increasing abstraction of authority ("the constitutive impersonality of written rules, regulations, and procedures . . . shaped the emergent order" [165–66]), transparency (176), and delegation of authority to instruments of civil order (the Bow Street Runners, the information gathering of judicial offices). This transformation Bender sees developing concurrently in "the realist conventions of transparent narration" (178) and in the private subject's identification with the "disinterested, objective, and transparent" rules by which the state safeguards civil order (176).[49]

For Bender, the goal of Fielding's reforms is a transparent and fully centralized system of surveillance and distribution of redress, whose counterpart in the fiction is the "omniscient, enquiring authority" of his narrators and their embodiment of "authoritative moral control" (145). Bender's analysis of the abstraction and reincorporation of authority is valuable, but the problem in his account is its resort to the concept of omniscience: "[Fielding] takes the step from consciousness contrived as a narrative of the material world to the inclusion of omniscient, inquiring authority in that world" (145). Omniscience does not inquire; it reveals. Fielding's narrators are never distinguished by strong claims to omniscience, and their authority is continually subject to ironic circumscription. The partiality of Fielding's narrators cannot constitute a partial omniscience; omniscience is by definition total: as Jonathan Culler says, "you can't have selective omniscience, only selective communicativeness" (24). The figural omniscience of the panopticon does not emerge in

England until Bentham codifies it and Godwin's Caleb Williams identifies it with aristocratic tyranny. While Fielding certainly contributed to its formation, there is too much teleology in the argument that Fielding's scheme genuinely anticipates panoptic surveillance. There is considerable difference between the aspiration for a comprehensive system of investigation and that for an all-seeing, all-knowing disciplinary center.

I argue that Fielding's narratives and pamphlets aim much more at inculcating effective and accurate readerly judgment whose abstract universality is mediated by the parochial function. The order of vision that my chapter title evokes is quite specifically limited—divided between a broad administrative vision (associated with the county and magistracy), and a confined, intimate, and pastoral vision (associated with the clerical function). The first chapter of *Joseph Andrews,* "Of Writing Lives in General," explains the role of literary representation in this two-order system: "A good man . . . is a standing lesson to all his acquaintance, and of far greater use in that narrow circle than a good book. But as it often happens that the best men are but little known, and consequently cannot extend the usefulness of their examples a great way; the writer may be called in aid to spread their history farther, and to present the amiable pictures to those who have not the happiness of knowing the originals" (15). Despite this claim that the novel serves to publicize private lives, the narrator is not himself an intimate participant in those lives, as he reminds us occasionally—the report on the roasting of Adams, for instance, has been reconstructed from more than one source: "Mr. Adams, from whom we had most of this relation, could not recollect all the jests of this kind practised on him, which the inoffensive disposition of his own heart made him slow in discovering; and indeed, had it not been for the information which we received from a servant of the family, this part of our history, which we take to be none of the least curious, must have been deplorably imperfect" (213). The narratorial perspective, then, is analogous to that of the magistrate, relying on report that mediates intimate knowledge and experience. While Fielding's reader function offers privileged access to both orders of vision, they remain distinct and depend upon separate agencies and spheres of practice. The mediation of narrative in *Joseph Andrews* models, by analogy, a close partnership between broad managerial oversight and intimate surveillance; supervisors and magistrates at the county and national level must attend to the firsthand knowledge of parochial guardians, who must in turn follow the synoptic guidance of their superiors.

Fielding adopts the view, ever more widely held in the eighteenth century, that where the lower orders inhabit restricted realms of knowledge, experience, and vision, their desires and ambitions, their emulation, will be equally limited: "All temptations . . . are to be carefully removed out of the way" (*Enquiry* 95). At the end of the century, Jeremy Bentham will echo Fielding's thesis that close confines for the poor can be epistemic as well as geographic, envisioning a poorhouse that generates "no unsatisfied longings, no repinings, nothing within knowledge that is not within reach" (quoted in Himmelfarb 83). Proponents of home will take essentially the same position regarding their favored institution. As I have already noted, failure of such restraint accompanied by uncontrolled movement and commingling of the poor is, for Fielding, the essential cause of England's crisis in civic order. In two numbers of the *Covent Garden Journal,* he decries the power of the mob, for whom he coins the honorific the "mobility" (272).[50] The mob functions essentially by negation, particularly negation of law, for "tho' this estate have not AS YET claimed that right which was insisted on by the people or mob in old Rome, of giving a negative voice in the enacting laws, they have clearly exercised this power in controlling their execution" (268). They interfere with river traffic, particularly "whenever they meet any persons in a boat, whose dress declares them to be of a different order from themselves" (270); they obstruct foot traffic in the streets (270); and they claim the "right of excluding all women of fashion out of St. James's Park on a Sunday evening" (271). Indeed, it is only by the good offices of justices of the peace and soldiers that "they have not long since rooted all the other orders out of the commonwealth" (273).

Prominent among the causes of the formation and "elevation" of the mobility, for Fielding, is the Elizabethan Poor Law of 1601 because of its compromise, which "stipulated, that the Fourth Estate should annually receive out of the possessions of the others, a certain large proportion yearly, upon an implied condition (for no such was exprest) that they should suffer the other estates to enjoy the rest of their property without loss or molestation" (272).[51] The mobility's power of negation, or power in the form of negation, aligns it with the realm of Chaos and Old Night invoked in the preface to *Joseph Andrews* and locates their threat in the extinguishing of social order and hierarchy that would result should they take command of the nation's thoroughfares—of both geographic and social movement. The concentric topography of status and its parallel geography of administration constitute and bolster one another.

The "great" are entitled to luxurious and idle pursuits: "Let them have their plays, operas, and oratorios, their masquerades and ridottos; their assemblies, drums, routs, riots, and hurricanes, their Ranelagh and Vauxhall; their Bath, Tunbridge, Bristol, Scarborough, and Cheltenham" (*Enquiry* 8–9). But they must also keep those pleasures to themselves: it is "the business of the politician . . . to prevent the contagion from spreading to the useful part of mankind . . . and this is the business of persons of fashion and fortune too," and "it becomes the legislature, as much as possible, to suppress all temptations" (*Enquiry* 9). The political and paternalistic resources of the ruling classes should be devoted to confining such pleasures to those who "have any title to spend their time in this idle, though otherwise innocent way," in places "as are totally set apart for the use of the great world" (9). The wealthy and well-heeled, not the mob, must control the figural and literal boundaries and thoroughfares of England.[52]

The requisite boundaries are not being maintained, as Fielding sees it, and the levees have failed: "The vast torrent of luxury, which of late years hath poured itself into this nation," Fielding claims, "hath greatly contributed to . . . the mischief I here complain of" (*Enquiry* 3). Although luxury is "rather a moral than a political evil" among the great, its effect, where the great leave their stations vacant for its sake, is a pernicious and contagious spirit of emulation—"the gentleman will aspire to the proper state of the nobleman, the tradesman steps from behind his counter into the vacant place of the gentleman. Nor doth the confusion end here" (*Enquiry* 3). The poor become vagrants or active criminals when they emulate the appetites and pursue the means to gratification of the wealthy: "The more simple and poor-spirited betake themselves to a state of starving and beggary, while those of more art and courage become thieves, sharpers and robbers" (*Enquiry* 3). That passage does, interestingly, seem to catch Fielding in the act of holding thieves, with their superior wit and bravery, in greater esteem than mere beggars, perhaps because thieves are hypocrites, whose vice "strikes the reader with surprize and pleasure . . . in a higher and stronger degree" than vanity (*JA* 7). Hypocrites, then, make better subjects for the novelist's pen and perhaps more satisfying objects for the magistrate's dispensations.

They may also make fatter lambs for the pastor's crook. Fielding, however, admits that "there is some difficulty in distinguishing" vanity and hypocrisy (*JA* 6). "Hypocrisy sets us on an endeavour to avoid censure by concealing our vices under an appearance of their opposite virtues," while "vanity puts us on affecting false characters, in order to purchase applause" (*JA* 6). The two vices proceed "from very different motives"; "the affectation which arises from vanity is nearer to truth than the other; as it hath not that violent repugnancy of Nature to struggle with, which that of the hypocrite hath" (6). But purchase of applause and avoidance of censure are both accomplished by the same means—masquerading virtues—whose foremost purpose is concealment of vicious motives. Both vanity and hypocrisy seem perfectly repugnant to truth and Nature; the most stable opposition that Fielding's ethic allows is between what one is and what one is not. At best, we can grant that hypocrisy is a category of vanity, but by no means a clearly separated one.

In the *Enquiry*, Fielding drops the distinction between vanity and hypocrisy, opting instead (as I have noted) for one between vanity and voluptuousness. Voluptuousness is, in itself, not an affectation. It has its ill effects when it is aroused to emulation and therefore social aspiration, by the operation of vanity in the higher orders. Though the poor have not the means to carry off affectation, their voluptuary impulses will lead them astray when those who do possess means leave their own stations unoccupied and duties neglected. Affectation has the form of imitation (as I noted earlier, emulation can also be a motivation to virtue—"in what is amiable and praiseworthy . . . emulation most effectually operates upon us, and inspires our imitation" [*JA* 15]), but affectation takes a negation as its object and thus belongs to the self creation of romantic authorship that Fielding assaults. Affected persons become characters "of their own creation . . . their brains the chaos whence all their materials are collected" (*JA* 163) in defiance of Nature. The Pamela who appears in *Joseph Andrews*, for instance, turns the romancer's negation on herself: "I am no longer Pamela Andrews, I am now this gentleman's lady, and as such am above [Fanny]" (264).

Hence, despite the appeal Fielding finds in the outlaw wanderings of the principal characters in his fiction, his disquisition against the "mobility" in the *Champion* and his social pamphlets show him very much in favor of restricting the poor to their parishes.[53] In the *Enquiry*, he argues for tighter vagrancy laws: "If we cannot discover, or will not encourage any cure for idleness, we shall at least compel the poor to starve or beg at home; for there it will be impossible for them to steal or rob without being presently hanged or transported out of the way" (72),[54] it being "impossible for any thief to carry on his trade long with impunity among his neighbours, and where not only his person, but his way of life must be well known" (65). Richardson's Pamela imagines herself transfixed by the gaze of an extensive conspiratorial network of surveillance and control exerted by the manorial landholder, incorporating his servants, the neighboring gentry, the local thieves (208), and even the "horrid bull" guarding the pasture beyond the back gate (192).[55] But Fielding's fiction and treatises do not presume such an open relay of information from all social strata up to the patronal eye and ear, nor the patron's boundless capacity to make every subordinate an agent of his will. His supervisory class relies on statutory instruments and quasi- and nonstatutory institutions, particularly the offices of minor parish officials, to mediate relations at the local and intimate level. If the poor are kept at home, their transgressions will come to the attention of the authorities through local intermediaries.[56]

Fielding's proposed administrative system certainly does retain elements of feudal paternalism, but hybridized with a modern large-scale carceral system.[57] The *ancien* paternalism is exemplified in the *Enquiry:* "Where is now that power of the sheriff... Where is that *posse comitatus,* which attended at his beck? What is become of the constitutions of *Alfred* ...? What of the antient conservators of the peace? Have the Justices, on whom this whole power devolves, an authority sufficient for the purpose?" (xiii). The modernizing reforms we can readily find in the *Proposal:* "There shall be erected, for the County of Middlesex... a large building consisting of three several courts ... [S]aid County-house shall be large enough to contain five thousand persons, and upwards" (17), where "the keepers and under keepers ... shall by turns constantly attend and supervise the labourers, and shall take an account of any neglect of work, or other misbehaviour" (34). Traditionary kindred relations and fealty bonds combine with surveillance and standardized bureaucracy in the Fielding scheme.

Justices, which means of course the landed classes, must provide careful supervision of Fielding's system: "Those duties, however, which fall to the higher ranks of men... are by no means of the lightest or easiest kind. The watchings and fatigues, the anxieties and cares which attend the highest stations, render their possessors, in real truth, no proper objects of envy to those of the lowest" (*Proposal* 5). Current levels and methods of supervision, he finds, vest too much supervisory authority in minor officials: "The trust is too great for the persons on whom it devolves; and tho' [work] houses are, in some measure under the inspection of the Justices of the Peace, yet this in the statute is recommended in too general a manner to their care, to expect any good fruits from it" (*Enquiry* 50).[58] The parish official can consult only the immediate advantage of his own little fiefdom: "it can be no wonder that parishes are not very forward to put [vagrancy law] in execution. Indeed in all cases of removal, the good of the parish, and not of the public is consulted" (*Enquiry* 68). That narrow vision must be combined with the more comprehensive one of the patron.[59] Both the law and the noblesse, though, need reformation: "There will be some among the rich whose indolence is superior to the love of wealth and honour, and who will therefore avoid these public duties" (*Proposal* 5). There is little that is particularly new in the practical features of Fielding's proposals, and they did not have any marked impact on the national systems of legislation and administration, but they illustrate what I am calling his hybrid regime; he seeks to combine a broad and homogeneous managerial superstructure with self-contained parochial divisions under the watchful guidance of a compassionate landowning class.[60]

*Joseph Andrews,* then, is not a satire on the institutions of parish authority, but on dereliction of just and merciful stewardship by vain, idle, and voluptuous gentry and aristocracy.[61] Lady Booby is the main offender, while her son, Squire Booby, turns out to exemplify something like the kind of benevolent manorial interest that can set things right. He intervenes to prevent Joseph and Fanny from being committed to Bridewell for theft of Lawyer Scout's "own proper twig" (*JA* 252) and presents Parson Adams, in the novel's conclusion, "with a living of one hundred and thirty pounds a year" (303). Squire Allworthy, of course, is the virtuous parish steward incarnate, and Dr. Harrison fills the role in *Amelia,* though none of these figures—like the narrators—is infallible in his judgment. I must emphasize that the literal kinds of paternalistic and parochial care presented in the fiction have a more broadly figural application in Fielding's later pamphleteering and judicial practice. The abstraction of paternalism is necessitated particularly by the urban milieu of his magistracy. Hence, in *Amelia,* Dr. Harrison combines the paternalistic and clerical functions. The popularity in eighteenth-century fiction generally of the country patron who manages the parish and populace has a wishf[...] convenient element to it. The manorial system in this era was irretriev[...] partial and under continual renegotiation. Feudal title had been extingui[...] by act of Parliament in 1646, enclosure was in full swing, estates had lost t[...] political coherence over centuries of inheritance and donation, and b[...] means were all advowsons in the hands of private landowners. The parish [...] the only unit of local governance in eighteenth-century England whose co[...] age was anything like comprehensive, but its very comprehensiveness was [...] gated, for Fielding's purposes, by the self-enclosed and heterogeneous nat[...] of each constituent unit.[62]

The idle rich who neglect their parish and county duties, Fielding observes in his *Proposal,* are not an absolute blight on the nation: "Whilst they dispose

what is their own for the purposes of idleness . . . they may be well called useful members of trading commonwealths, and truly said to contribute to the
good of the public" (138). At the beginning of book 4, Lady Booby

> entered the parish amidst the ringing of bells and the acclamations of
> the poor, who were rejoiced to see their patroness returned after so
> long an absence, during which time all her rents had been drafted to
> London, without a shilling being spent among them, which tended not
> a little to their utter impoverishing; for, if the court would be severely
> missed in such a city as London, how much more must the absence of
> a person of great fortune be felt in a little country village, for whose
> inhabitants such a family finds a constant employment and supply;
> and with the offals of whose table the infirm, aged, and infant poor are
> abundantly fed, with a generosity which hath scarce a visible effect on
> their benefactors' pockets? (*JA* 241)

Lady Booby does not add corrupt magistrate to her list of delinquencies; her
gender precludes the possibility. But she can call on the corruptible services
of a local gentleman (Justice Frolick), and her agent, Lawyer Scout, does
so in arranging the attempt to imprison Joseph and Fanny for twig stealing
(248–52).

Lady Booby is also holder of the advowson that controls Parson Adams's
living, though he is merely a curate, appointed at the behest of Sir Oliver
Hearty, the previous owner of the Booby estate, and is regarded by Lady
Booby "as a kind of domestic only, belonging to the Parson of the parish"
(21).[63] Adams explains his position in a discourse to the "patriotic" gentleman, lamenting that he might have been granted the full living by Sir Thomas:

> He promised me a living, poor man! and I believe I should have had
> it, but an accident happened, which was, that my lady had promised
> it before, unknown to him. This, indeed, I never heard till afterwards;
> for my nephew, who died about a month before the incumbent, always
> told me I might be assured of it. Since that time, Sir Thomas, poor man,
> had always so much business, that he never could find leisure to see me.
> I believe it was partly my lady's fault too, who did not think my dress
> good enough for the gentry at her table. (116–17)

The unnamed "Doctor" who holds the position in Adams's stead is clearly
an absentee and exploiter of Adams's labor; Adams reports, "I preach at four
churches" (117), in the hope of seeing fulfilled the word of "Sir Thomas, and

the other honest gentlemen my neighbours, who have all promised me these five years, to procure an ordination for a son of mine" (117). His situation exemplifies the inequities of the clerical profession and the degradations that Fielding blames on voluptuary estate holders who wield the prerogatives of county officials.

The poverty of Adams's circumstances is reinforced in book 4, when Lady Booby brings a company of onlookers to his home and offers to "divert them with one of the most ridiculous sights they had ever seen, which was an old foolish parson, who, she said, laughing, kept a wife and six brats on a salary of about twenty pounds a year; adding, that there was not such another ragged family in the parish" (273). Although Lady Booby is not directly responsible for Adams's pitiful salary, she makes it clear that she commands the encumbent who is: when Adams publishes banns for Joseph and Fanny, she warns him to cease: "And if you dare, I will recommend it to your master, the doctor, to discard you from his service" (246). Adams's master is likely one of what N. J. G. Pounds calls "the 'fat cats' of the clerical profession" (500), living on tithe and benefice money and paying a salary to one or more curates. This practice was widespread; Pounds reports that in the York diocese in 1743, for example, 47 percent of parishes "had no resident encumbent" (500). Anthea Jones quotes Bishop William Nicolson, in notes from his visitations to Carlisle Diocese between 1704 and 1713, lamenting the case of a parsonage house, "in that neglected state, as is usual where the parson is either too rich or too poor" (201)—a sentence Fielding himself might have written.

Lady Booby's reprobate patronage enables and encourages the abuses and emulation of churchmen like Adams's master and Parson Trulliber, who unabashedly tells Adams, "I believe I am as warm as the vicar himself, or perhaps the rector of the next parish too; I believe I could buy them both" (144). In fact, despite his subordinate status, Trulliber is "a parson on Sundays, but all the other six might more properly be called a farmer" (141) and so takes his place among what Pounds calls "well-to-do Rectors" who "were among the chief beneficiaries of the agricultural advances of the eighteenth century. They . . . were becoming assimilated to the landowning gentry class" (501). Fielding's corrective models of a benevolent patronal class—Joseph himself, and his rediscovered father, Mr. Wilson—begin in virtuous poverty, but their assimilation to the ruling classes is distinguished from other cases. Joseph's elevation countermands Pamela's. Where her assertion, "I am no longer Pamela Andrews" is fraudulent and affected, Joseph's elevation is not, because it does not result from transgressive emulation. The concluding page of the novel details Joseph, Fanny, and Wilson's modest settlement in idyllic familial and parochial bliss and Lady Booby's departure to London, where her idle life may presumably contribute to the commerce of England and do no further harm.

The providential conclusion is ironized, like all of the romance morphologies in *Joseph Andrews,* by the logic of poverty management, so that it becomes something like the merging of Joseph's and his father's personal virtues with the institutions of landed paternalism. In the *Enquiry,* Fielding exhorts us to wait patiently "till great men become wiser or better; till the prevalence of some laudable taste shall teach them a worthier manner of employing their time; till they have sense enough to be reasoned, modesty enough to be laughed, or conscience enough to be frightened out of a silly, a shameful and a sinful profligacy, attended with horrid waste of time, and the cruel destruction of the families of others, or of their own" (18).

Fielding offers his reformation of romance and his epistemology of fiction (not to say his fiction itself) as a repository of such taste, employment, sense, modesty, laughter, and conscience. Fiction may work to discipline the excesses of the great—at least the nobility and gentry of the countryside. Suppressing the delirious ecstasies of romance may serve to clarify the primacy of the parish and the imperative of paternalistic care for parishioners. McKeon asserts that "Fielding's subsumption of questions of virtue by questions of truth transfers the major challenge of utopian projection from the substantive to the formal realm" (*Origins* 408). The social and the literary very often meet, in Fielding, where form becomes an object of reflection. "Formal innovation in the novel," Bender suggests, is "a mode of action" in a broader sociocultural sphere (139). Comic convention, for instance, decrees that the resolution of *Joseph Andrews* is restorative, reinvigorating an existing, if decayed, order. Fielding's "hitherto unattempted" species of writing has been unattempted only "in our language" (*JA* 8). Its novelty is by no means an endorsement of the wholly new. Just as Joseph and Fanny incarnate a new ruling class that is actually the original and proper model of a ruling class adapted to modern circumstances, so the comic epic-poem in prose restores to the literary tradition a form that "Homer . . . gave us a pattern of"—the *Margites* identified by Aristotle—but that had been "entirely lost" (*JA* 3). Fielding manages at once to innovate and to keep faith with classical precedent.

## "A Small Circle Described upon the Circle of the Great World"

At the beginning of book 4, Joseph, Fanny, and Adams have returned to their home parish, and so has Lady Booby, still intent on interfering with Joseph's chastity and consequently also intent on preventing Joseph and Fanny's marriage. What I have called the courtship portion of this exploded romance narrative is not really a courtship at all. It is a struggle to overcome a series of pitfalls standing in the way of a properly ratified marriage contract. Those pitfalls are for the most part legal ones that Lady Booby interposes. Of Joseph, she says, "he is a vagabond, and he shall not settle here," disregarding what Adams correctly asserts, that "any person who serves a year, gains a settlement in the parish where he serves" (246).[64] Her agent, Lawyer Scout, devises a suit to remove Fanny from the parish, and a second, already noted above, to have Joseph and Fanny committed to a house of correction for poaching a twig. "And so this wench," Lady Booby laments, "is to stock the parish with beauties . . .—but sir, our poor is numerous enough already; I will have no more vagabonds settled here" (245–46). She rephrases her sexual rivalry with Fanny in terms of her responsibilities as steward of the parish. Fanny's obstruction of Lady Booby's voluptuary impulses can be circumvented under the guise of patronal duty. Lady Booby's desire for Joseph drives her to distraction: she "loved, hated, pitied, scorned, admired, despised the same person by fits" (250). She is possessed by the sensibilities of the Petrarchan lover and his Laura all at once.

Her romantic temperament makes a mockery of her stewardship. And the instability of Lady Booby's personality finds a parallel in Lawyer Scout's unqualified, nonsensical interpretations of the law: "Now there is a material difference between being settled in law and settled in fact; and as I affirmed generally [Joseph] was settled, and law, is preferable to fact, my settlement must be understood in law, and not in Fact! . . . He is not settled in fact; and if he be not settled in fact, he is not an inhabitant; and if he is not an inhabitant, he is not of this Parish" (248). Lawyer Scout is "one of those fellows who, without any knowledge of the law, or being bred to it, take upon them, in defiance of an act of Parliament, to act as lawyers in the country, and are called so" (249).[65] His unauthorized impersonation of a lawyer is another example of the false imitation that Fielding attacks in writers of romance and a figure for Fielding's disgruntled conviction that "a space has opened up between the prescriptive authority of the law and the sum of social practices . . . that is supposed to exemplify it" (J. Lamb 102). The suppression of romance functions here, as elsewhere, as a metonymic code for banishing Lawyer Scout and eliminating disjunctions between the proceedings of law and intimate fact and justice.

Lawyer Scout's solipsistic self-authorization, which is equivalent to the self-authorization of romance writing, of Pamela's assumed gentility, and of Lady Booby's impersonation of an ingénue at the mercy of Joseph's manhood, appears also in Mrs. Slipslop's malapropisms, the "patriotic" sportsman's bellicose vows (bk. 2, chap. 6), the "charitable" gentleman's extravagant promises (bk. 2, chap. 16), and in all the other affectations we encounter. They make up a considerable catalogue, just as the Vagrancy Act cited at the beginning of this chapter does, but a taxonomic list will not suffice: "*Wandering* is of itself made no offence: so that unless such wanderer be either a petty chapman, or a beggar or lodger in ale-houses, &c. he is not within the act of parliament" (Fielding, *Enquiry* 70). The existing Vagrancy Act lacks the kind of generally applicable test that Fielding's fiction demonstrates. A typology of sturdy beggars, idle wanderers, and disguised criminals cannot account for all of the improbable possibilities of roguery and vagabondage. What is needed is intimate acquaintance: it will be "impossible for any thief to carry on his trade long with impunity among his neighbours, and where not only his person, but his way of life must be well known" (*Enquiry* 65). This kind of surveillance in the form of kindred and communal familiarity characterizes Fielding's version of the parish and its chief exemplar is the humble cleric.

The parish, then, must be sequestered from the world of public and statutory relations so that its affective communion can thrive, but also so that the laboring classes can be confined to these little realms of privacy. Hence I am determined to argue, against John Bender's account, that Fielding is not intent on promulgating "the modern conception of a self at once isolated and transparent to view" under the gaze of a national omniscience (Bender 201).[66] The conspicuous and secure boundaries against geographic movement and social contagion that Fielding prescribes are also opaque, confining intimate social visibility within the kind of narrow sphere that the parish best exemplifies. The poor, as I noted earlier, should not see, let alone wander, beyond their parish bounds, and the great must keep their idle pursuits within their Vauxhalls and their Ranelaghs, but Fielding's scheme presumes also that the supervisory gaze of the magistrate and other supraparochial officials will not penetrate into the recesses of parochial life. Accurate judgment of character requires an observer able "carefully to observe the actions of men with others, and especially with those to whom they are allied in blood, marriage, friendship, profession, neighbourhood, or any other connection" ("Characters of Men" 220), which is a privilege conditioned by parochial seclusion.

Fielding defends the status of the parish as what Pounds calls "a little, self-contained world, a microcosm of national life" (268). It is a self-contained, but not self-sufficient regulatory body. While Fielding sees parishes nurturing and defending personal interests, he does not consider them adequate instruments for the distribution and administration of collective or national interests. Their economic, legal, and political functions need supervision from a magistracy cured of romantic habits and competent to make judgments based on mediated evidence, which is to say the magistrate must appoint trustworthy officials, direct them wisely, and interpret the reports of officials and parishioners astutely. Squire Allworthy's "natural love of justice," for example, "joined to his coolness of temper, made him always a most patient magistrate in hearing all the witnesses which an accused person could produce in his defence" (*Tom Jones* 87). There is no doubt that the partnership between parish and county envisioned by Fielding looks in hindsight like a step along the way toward the society of surveillance and impersonal public institutions described by Bender. But Fielding's proposed system does not limit personal and affective relations to the "private" realm of parochial benevolence, while mandating systems of disinterested judicial superintendence whose "ideology is that they embody no ideology" (Bender 176). The qualities that make a good vicar are personal qualities, but so are those that make a good justice of the peace. For Fielding, justice "is to be found in the untutored responses of good-hearted country gentlemen, and in the heterocosm of the novelist's art" (Potkay 111).

The parish has attributes—national coverage, affinal bonds, mutual interest, heterogeneity—that will later belong to the private home. It is a hybrid political entity, constituted by no particular act of government, sustaining an ancient lineage, and providing an arena in which the mechanisms of state authority can operate under the guise of private and affectively guided "care." Unlike the private home, however, the parish's pastoral functions do not depend upon a putatively thorough separation from external and statutory oversight that is in fact a reproduction of the national interest.[67] The parochial system is explicitly governmental at the same time as it nurtures kindred bonds and virtues. The parish's capacity to bound the knowledge, needs, and desires of the lower orders makes it an ideal disciplinary mechanism for Fielding. Even as it administers discipline, the supervisory class should gather from its parochial duties an impetus to discipline itself, to limit its own luxuries and waste.

Fielding's fiction demonstrates the epistemic basis of this managerial system, and his pamphlets follow the same logic: "What can be more shocking than to see an industrious poor creature who is able and willing to labor, forced by mere want into dishonesty[?]" (*Enquiry* 95–96). The comic author strives to frame a just imitation of nature, and the magistrate strives to foster a social order whose nature is worthy of a just imitation.

The parish is the primary topos of poverty management, but it might also be called the first topos (and topography) of the English novel. By the end of the eighteenth century, the home has become the major topos—not to say telos—of the novel (as it does, for a time, in poverty management). That is, both parish and home subsist in fiction as conceptual frames and localizing principles that help to organize representation of place, space, and social affiliation. Each, at times, borrows the attributes of other topoi, such as the *locus amoenus*, retirement, even the equivocal comfort of utopia (εὖ τόπος, "good place," or οὐ τόπος, "no place"). At other times, each topos exerts its influence by its absence, as a destination or object of desire, a mourned or alienated loss. I do not mean that novels after 1790 set their action only within homes, but that the topographic logics of novels tend to rely on domesticity and privacy: scenes are determined by their location either within or outside private space. Domesticity is carried into public spaces by characters, especially women, whose actions and motivations are expressly private, personal, and not engaged in any manifest way with mechanisms of law, politics, commerce, or civil administration.[68]

In the middle years of the eighteenth century, however, the spatial organization of fiction, and the mediation of its relation to external concerns like politics and nationality, are the domain of the parish and analogous small sociogeographic units whose relations to statute and governance are mixed, particularly the manor. Such is clearly the case in *Joseph Andrews* and *Tom Jones*, and it seems also true of *Pamela*, where Squire B abuses his patronal power and Pamela atones for his tyrannies by devoting herself to charity "to supply the deserving poor the loss they have sustained in the death of my honoured lady" (389). *Tristram Shandy*'s "world" is marked out by the Shandy estate, Toby's bowling-green theater of warfare, Yorick's "sallies about his parish" (17), and by the midwife's "small circle described upon the circle of the great world, of four *English* miles diameter, or thereabouts" (12). *Humphry Clinker* begins with Matthew Bramble's instructions to Dr. Lewis, to "tell Barns to thresh out the two old ricks, and send the corn to market, and sell it off to the poor at a shilling a bushel under the market price," and to settle a lawsuit with a "bad

neighbour" ("let him give five pounds to the poor of the parish and I will withdraw my action" [33]), and it ends with Winifred Jenkins-Loyd declaring, "All
the parish allowed that young 'squire Dallison and his bride was a comely pear
for to see" (395).[69]

Sentimental fiction in general looks, from this perspective, like nothing
so much as an incorporation of the clerical function and paternalistic oversight into representations of personal relations. Clerics frequently appear in
early novels as major, though seldom main, characters who take the roles of
commentator, advisor, guardian, and/or fool. By the early nineteenth century,
on the other hand, the parish is a residual and sometimes nostalgic discursive territory. Jane Austen's Tory leanings show in her devotion to circumscribed manorial realms: "3 or 4 families in a country village is the very thing
to work on" (*Letters* 275, September 9, 1814).[70] But her narratives concede the
incompatibility of tyrannical parochial authority with the self-determination
of competent young women: Elizabeth Bennett, for instance, reflects sourly
"that though this great lady [Catherine De Bourgh] was not in the commission of the peace for the county, she was a most active magistrate in her own
parish . . . [W]henever any of the cottagers were disposed to be quarrelsome,
discontented or too poor, she sallied forth into the village to settle their differences, silence their complaints, and scold them into harmony and plenty"
(*Pride and Prejudice* 141). Lady Catherine's surname suggests "borough," yet
another kind of social administrative unit, one that originates as the medieval
version of town government, and that can be numbered among the residual
paternalisms that Elizabeth must face down to establish her social/conjugal
aspirations. "I am only resolved to act," she tells Lady Catherine, "in that manner, which will, in my own opinion, constitute my happiness, without reference
to *you*, or to any person so wholly unconnected with me" (288). In *Emma*, Mr.
Knightley's manorial authority gives way at last to the imperative "that so long
as [Emma's] father's happiness—in other words his life—required Hartfield
to continue her home, it should be his likewise" (407). The system Fielding
sought to reform and bolster is, by Austen's time, in its final decline.

Fielding's attempt to save the parochial system is a scheme for poverty
management modeled by analogy on the epistemology he develops in his fiction and tied to it in practice: "There appear to me to be four sorts of political
power; that of bodily strength, that of the mind, the power of the purse, and
the power of the sword. Under the second of these divisions may be ranged all
the art of the legislator and politician, all the power of laws and government.
These do constitute the civil power; and a state may then be said to be in good

order, when all the other powers are subservient to this" (*Enquiry* xii). The power of the mind operates both from the top down and from the bottom up. It coordinates private and collective objectives: "no man can have this general philanthropy who hath not private affection" ("Characters of Men" 223). The partnership of judicial oversight and clerical care must harmonize unmediated intimacy with comprehensive disciplinarity. Fielding's epistemology is intuitive, but at the same time morally systematic. His poverty regime is homogeneous and national, but also the work of personal charitable impulses and kindred affections.[71] Leo Braudy writes, "Fielding's judge works in the courts of equity, upholding the importance of the specific situation and the individual nature of the case before him" (92), and the novels are a special means of access to both orders of vision at once—the comprehensive and the intimate. Fielding's various proposals, in sum, seek to reconcile universal improvement with uncoerced personal reciprocity: "If any society ever hath been or ever can be so regulated, that no talent in any of its members, which is capable of contributing to the general good, should lie idle and unemployed, nor any of the wants of its members which are capable of relief should remain unrelieved, that society might be said to have attained its utmost perfection" (Fielding, *Covent Garden Journal* 3).

This last observation comes from *A Plan of the Universal Register Office,* one of Fielding's final projects. The Office, a private business in central London, offered "the combined services of an employment agency, a financial institution, a real estate agency, a curiosity shop, and a travel bureau" (Goldgar xvi) and operated throughout the 1750s, closing at the behest of Fielding's brother John. It represents an attempt to "bring the world as it were together into one place" (Fielding, *Plan* 6) so as to provide "a method of communicating the various wants and talents of the members to each other; by which means they might be mutually supplied" (5). Here we find an urban variation on Fielding's parochial system. It seeks to supply a private nexus of provision that will overcome the inadequacy of all other attempts, which "are so far defective, as they fail to be universal" (5). Private wants meet their relief in a comprehensive system of cooperation that is at once charitable and mercantile, a homology later made monolithic by Adam Smith's theory of the simultaneity of self-interest and the common weal.[72] Its orchestration of need and provision also takes place under the eyes of qualified overseers: "the proprietors of this office are gentlemen, and men experienced in business; so it will be executed with the utmost care, regularity, and fidelity, and as much secrecy always as shall be desired by the parties themselves" (Fielding, *Plan* 9). An urban counterpart to the manorial interest watchfully coordinates the desires and expenditure of the great ("We shall plainly perceive his wants increasing with his riches" [4]) with the needs and capacities of the poor: "Virtue equals happiness, if at all, for and through the disinterested gentleman of considerable resources" (Potkay 118). The Universal Register Office, though not as successful as his Bow Street work, was as close as Fielding came to seeing his parochial vision realized in bricks and mortar.

Fielding's parish is a circle described on a circle. It has the same basic conceptual-rhetorical structure as other cherished but fading Tory ideals such as the body natural and body politic or Filmer's God-king-father system. That fundamental structure in these examples is the two-bodies trope: an instrumental metaphoric whose tenor and vehicle are the same term: "body" and "father," respectively.[73] "Church" is the governing signifier in the case of the parish system, and "home" anchors the privacy/nationality partnership that this study will pursue. The parish's two bodies, during the eighteenth century, suffer growing encroachment by agents of the body politic, so by Fielding's time the parish's relation to nationality is one of subordination and differentiation, not microcosm and equivalence. Parish authority descends from outside its borders; the parish itself is not in a rigorous sense a figure for the nation; and the relation of parish to parish is as much heterology as homology, and always was. It partakes of synecdoche insofar as it is always understood as an objective sector of the national space, but its very objectivity blocks its capacity to stand for the nation. Though it may have been the best means available for constructing a conceptual national totality, it also excludes most of its inhabitants from that totality—barring the subject of parochial care from meaningful engagement with the nation as spatial and communal corporation.[74]

The parish system fails to accommodate itself to the abstracted authority of the modern nation-state. Other, often disaccordant, systems are responsible for binding parishes into a national network. Eighteenth-century reforms to the parish system withdraw administrative operations, especially the law, to external loci.[75] The parish and the paternalism it entails in the cultural/political imaginary pass from a sphere of personal, minimally regulated relations in fraught negotiation with external governmental, administrative, and commercial forces to a derelict remainder of landed authority that is largely beneath the notice of statute law. We might conclude, finally, that Fielding's reforms did as much to facilitate the dismantling of the parish system as to stave off its decline. He vests administrative instrumentality in sentiments, habits of judgment, and rules of conduct that encourage mutually constitutive relations between the personal and the institutional, the local and the universal, the somatic and the abstract—modes of social affiliation that sustain modern domesticity. Consider the modern sense of the term *vagrant,* which no longer designates lack of a parish settlement, but rather lack of a home. The private home, we will see, has a much more robust capacity to translate and accommodate the political structures of modernity.

# 2

# An Englishwoman's Workhouse Is Her Castle

## Poverty Management and the Radcliffean Gothic

> Oh! Madam, were every young woman who voluntarily abandons the
> protection of her real friends to encounter the difficulties, and anxiety,
> to which I have been exposed; and were those to be publicly known,
> would it not have the happy effect, of rendering the tranquil home, dear
> to the daughters of innocence?
>
> —Anna Maria Bennett, *Agnes De-Courci*

The young unmarried woman in eighteenth- and nineteenth-century British fiction may be the most overdetermined character in all of English
literature. We always find congregating about her a throng of themes, contests,
anxieties, polemics, and proprieties. Our heroine has been seen dallying with
the formation of modern subjectivity, with public literacy and mass education,
and with the literary marketplace. She has been asked, and often coerced, to
represent domestic harmony, the aspiring middle class, patriotic sentiment,
reproductive sexuality, and the community of taste and decency. She stands
accused of sexual license, filial disobedience, material greed, seductive manipulation, laziness, inattention, miscegenation, and interfering with productive
labor, as well as graphomania, subversion of patriarchal authority, and consuming to excess the very novels in which she appears. She is endangered and
dangerous, innocent and guilty, prudent and wasteful, modest and brazen.
Among her responsibilities are paternity, legitimacy, property, social relations,
and the maintenance or overthrow of aristocratic privilege. Everywhere she
goes she is followed by a train of ghosts, papists, seducers, banditti, kidnap-
pers, Jacobins, and Jacobites. Her admirers call her protofeminist, exogamous,
and duplicitous, and her detractors charge her with the same. The young single woman is in fact double, or indeed multiple.

She is, as recent scholarship has thoroughly established, a privileged locus for the identification and examination of social anxieties.[1] My purpose here is to add yet another determinant to the list that already encumbers our heroine. She is also very frequently the focus of anxiety about the poor. She embodies their vulnerabilities and the dangers they pose, and in her fate we may generally discern ideological content relating to the handling of poverty. In *Joseph Andrews,* we have seen direct and explicit examination of rural poverty management, but here I will assert that debates over poverty acquire sufficient cultural prominence by the end of the eighteenth century to inflect most, if not all, narrative descriptions of the single woman and her fortunes, and that representations of and responses to poverty are pivotal to the formation of the modern middle-class home. Gothic fiction of the 1790s, I will argue, is especially dense with rhetorical and thematic echoes of the poverty debates, and the reverse is certainly also true. My exemplary text is Ann Radcliffe's 1791 *The Romance of the Forest,* which I will discuss in detail in the latter part of this chapter.

Pamphlet wars over poverty raged throughout the century, and the major themes of the 1790s were rising by the beginning of the 1780s. With the additional provocation of the French Revolution, there was ample incitement for a high pitch of public anxiety about poverty by the time Radcliffe wrote *The Romance of the Forest.* Her narratives have a great deal in common with writings about poverty from the 1790s and the early years of the nineteenth century. Her novels, and gothic fiction of her era generally, are deeply involved not only with digesting fears about what was happening in France, but also with sustaining a much longer cultural conversation about the poor in England. If sentimental fiction codified individual affective responses to particular examples of poverty and suffering, the first major wave of gothic fiction deals in conflicts between the self-governing subject and modes of collective determination—figuring contests over regulation and discipline of the poor as struggles between private subjects and mysterious, implacable mechanisms of coercion. The solitary pauper and the assembled poor in early gothic fiction have the same perfectly equivocal role that I ascribe to the young single woman: at one moment they are defenseless and dependent, but admirable and dignified; the next moment they are elusive, debauched, and treacherous. Following Radcliffe's lead, both novelists and poor-law advocates turn ever more toward the private home as the best means of containing dangerous social energies and of mediating the regulatory functions of authorized sexuality and ultimately of the nation-state.

The vogue for sentiment and its gothic mutations provided vocabulary and mise-en-scène for talking about the poor. Indeed, sentimentalism arguably began as a mode of talking about (and sometimes to) the poor.[2] The bleeding of sentimental language into political discourse is especially notable around the turn of the century, when philanthropic benevolence becomes more and more institutional and national, and advocates for the poor form alliances with evangelical activists such as Hannah More and the abolitionist William Wilberforce. Sir Egerton Brydges, M.P. for Maidstone, writes on the topic of poverty: "Never before did I meet with a subject in which the driest details of business were associated with all the best furniture of a poetic mind; where the blaze of fancy, and the best emotions of the heart could throw the truest, the most philosophical, and most virtuous light on a complicated subject of artificial legislation" (17–18). At the same time, radical and antisentimental writers like Jeremy Bentham, William Godwin, and Anna Laetitia Barbauld contested the terminology but affirmed the urgency of the poverty debates. The French Revolution, the final decay of parish governance, and the wage/food-price crises of the 1790s and 1800s forced most if not all representations of British nationality to reckon with the underclasses. As prominent traffickers in sentimental language, novelists could hardly avoid comparing the attributes and experiences of unmarried women with those of the poor. When we juxtapose representations of single women and paupers, we will find striking similarities in the kinds of condemnation or sympathy, bitter or happy ending they receive. In the following two sections of this chapter, I will trace key topics and developments in the various discourses on poverty in the second half of the century and their convergence around developing conceptions of the private home. In the remainder of the chapter, I will outline the coincident efforts of writers on poverty and writers of gothic fiction, particularly Ann Radcliffe, to install women as the superintendents of the poor and of the middle-class home.

## THE POORHOUSE IN RUINS

After 1782, by most accounts, discussion about and legislation for the poor took an ameliorating turn. Sidney and Beatrice Webb maintain that "the statute law as to the relief of the poor became . . . more exclusively generous and humane in character and intention" (*English Poor Law* 422).[3] According to Raymond Cowherd, "humanitarian reform of the poor law was begun by [retired merchant] Jonas Hanway" as early as the 1760s ("Humanitarian Reform" 329), but sweeping reform starts with Sir Thomas Gilbert's Act of 1782 (22

George III.c.83), which sought to expand and regulate the administrative divisions responsible for the impotent poor—a major blow to parish autonomy—and which also required the guardians of the able-bodied unemployed to find employment for them or else provide maintenance in lieu of wages (Webb and Webb, *English Poor Law* 274–75). Two more important acts were passed in the following decade, both introduced by Sir William Young. The Act of 1795 (35 George III.c.101) ended the removal of persons not actually in need of parish relief—facilitating William Pitt's goal of improving "the circulation of labour" (qtd. in Cowherd, "Humanitarian Reform" 334).[4] The second Young Act, passed in 1796 (36 George III.c.23), authorized justices to "order Outdoor Relief, 'notwithstanding any contract shall have been made for maintaining the poor' in a workhouse" (Webb and Webb, *English Poor Law* 282), allowing the magistracy, where they saw fit, to dispense with incarceration.[5]

Outside Parliament, Thomas Bernard's Society for Bettering the Condition and Improving the Comforts of the Poor (SBC), formed to promote Pitt's legislative goals, published its first annual report in 1797.[6] Hannah More's *Village Politics* (1792) and *Cheap Repository Tracts* (1795–99) were distributed in the millions with the assistance of more than 750 subscribers, sympathetic clergy, and societies set up by middle-class well-wishers (Stott 176–77). Some participants in the poverty debates had significant links to other reformers, such as the abolitionist William Wilberforce, the prison reformers John Howard and Elizabeth Fry, the factory reformer Sir Robert Peel the elder, and the educators Hannah More and Joseph Lancaster (Cowherd, *Political Economists* 2). Wilberforce and Pitt were also members of the SBC's inaugural committee.

Despite the humanitarian tone of the debates, however, historians generally agree that practical improvements to the systems of welfare and relief were no better than intermittent, particularly after 1793, when crops began to fail regularly.[7] Binding out children as apprentices and farming the labor of paupers occurred regularly and without effective checks or oversight. Land enclosures were also reaching a crescendo at this time, ravaging rural smallholdings: "The cottager without legal proof of rights was rarely compensated. The cottager who was able to establish his claim was left with a parcel of land inadequate for subsistence and a disproportionate share of the very high enclosure costs" (E. P. Thompson 217). The rural poor were more and more subject to the disciplinary mechanisms of privatization, commodity markets, and what would be called the "iron law of wages."[8] Even in the countryside, the factory/prison system that dominated the nineteenth century was taking shape.

In some regions, nonetheless, the generous impulses of reformers like

Hanway, Gilbert, and Young were echoed by intensification of outdoor relief (provision of money, rent, or goods in lieu of wages) in preference to indoor relief (confinement to workhouses). Many rural justices, as Young's 1796 law anticipated, refused to condemn paupers, especially children, to what they saw as intolerable workhouse conditions: "A considerable number of magistrates . . . frequently made orders to relieve the supplicant, in stark contradiction to the opinion of overseers and vestrymen" (Hitchcock, King, and Sharpe 11). In a session at Maidstone, Kent, in 1797, for instance, the justices observed that "where the labourer in husbandry . . . give [*sic*] their children an opportunity at the little village schools, of learning reading and writing . . . boarding them at their own cottages . . . they feel the enjoyment of domestic comfort and such young persons will generally prove the most healthy, the most virtuous, and the most useful members of society" (qtd. in Melling 156). Even before Young's law, the Speenhamland system "adopted by Berkshire magistrates in the spring of 1795 . . . provided subsidies according to a scale dependent on [the price of bread], and assured the poor a minimum income sufficient to prevent starvation" (Sherman 136). During this relatively brief period, when, in Frederick Morton Eden's view, the reformers' "humanity exceeded their good sense" (qtd. in Cowherd, *Political Economists* xiv), the universalizing concept of home blossomed, and, according to Geoffrey Taylor, indoor relief suffered a "complete breakdown" (17).

By 1800, the (increasingly nostalgic) paternalism of benevolent manorial overseers and the heterogeneous parochial curacy was "as [E. P.] Thompson points out . . . losing steam, becoming more ritual than real: 'paternalism was as much theatre and gesture as effective responsibility'" (Sherman 8). The merchant political economist Patrick Colquhoun denounces the Law of Settlements as "a legal warfare between parish and parish" (187–88) and laments that "the national principle established for the maintenance or relief of paupers, was originally lost sight of, in local or parochial provision . . . limiting the burden to a mere parochial fund laid the foundation of all the evils which have followed" (240). Although "the traditional parochial organization of England had by the end of the eighteenth century run its course" (Pounds 498), what remained consistent was the inconsistent kinds and quantities of relief from one parish and one county to the next during the last decades of the old poor law. Even so, Frederick Morton Eden claimed that "the greatest improvement, of modern times, respecting the care of the poor, or that, at least, which seems to have been most generally aimed at, has been taking the parochial poor out of the hands of overseers and church wardens" (1: v). Into the place of parish officials stepped the superintending middle class, including women.[9] The pauper's dwelling becomes, during this period, a more and more important administrative unit at the expense of the parish. It is the favored location for distribution of, and in a sense it is the actual substance of, relief. It also tends to be the place of contact between classes, especially when middle-class women are providers; Jane Austen is famously partial to scenes of well-to-do women visiting their condescension upon grateful paupers.

It is important, however, not to imagine that the conflicts over poverty management simply involved a battalion of teary-eyed evangelical benevolists lining up against another of coldhearted, quantifying natural-law economists. Sandra Sherman makes an error of that kind when she argues that the essential shift of the period is from old-order paternalism to quantification, which "*imagined* the poor by reconstituting their reality through quantifying protocols that submerged individual narrative—subjectivity—in statistics, input/output ratios, and institutional accounts that flattened personal distinctions" (3).[10] The appropriate distinction, according to Boyd Hilton, is between material and moral forms of intervention (87). Notably, the Clapham Sect, with William Wilberforce at its center and abolition among its chief doctrines, advocated no more than spiritual guidance for the poor.[11] They follow the evangelical "emphasis on life as a moral trial" (Hilton 90) and a natural-law understanding of providence, where the divine hand rarely if ever intervenes and economic intervention should be likewise avoided. Among the opponents of these "moderates," Hilton counts "extreme" evangelicals who are far more likely to suggest material aid for the poor, at least in part because they understand providence as much less mechanistic and more shaped by an active divine hand (13–17).

Neither moderate nor extreme economists show any interest in eliminating poverty altogether: "Without a large proportion of poverty," Patrick Colquhoun writes, "surplus labour could never be rendered productive in procuring either the conveniencies [*sic*] or luxuries of life" (8).[12] The agricultural economist Arthur Young is more blunt: "Everyone but an idiot knows that the lower classes must be kept poor, or they will never be industrious" (*Farmer's Tour* 4: 361). At issue is how the laboring poor can be valued in national ledgers of prosperity, and growth. Frederick Morton Eden argues from strict rationalism: "The only point of view, in which a nation can regard [plans for poor law reform], is to consider how far they actually do or do not promote the general weal, by raising the largest quantity of provisions, or materials for manufacture, at the least cost, their inconvenience to individuals will be softened and mitigated, indeed, as far as it is practicable, but by no means be suffered to counteract any new plans of improvement, of great and real national utility" (1: xiv). Writers who pursued these lines of thought further still, including Thomas Malthus, proposed the abandonment of all relief measures. At the other, interventionist, end of the spectrum, writers like William Young reject exclusive economism: "The eye of the philosopher and statesman looking over the people of a great country, cannot narrow its regard, to a consideration of them as mere instruments of manufacture, or tools of husbandry. It will look for another sort of wealth, than that accruing from returns to the chest of the exchequer. It will require that the wide face of the country should be a treasury of pure morals and unadulterated happiness: surely at least not adulterated by institution" (*Considerations* 16). Precise distinctions between schools of thought are hard or impossible to draw. Patrick Colquhoun, for instance, begins his treatise arguing that "poverty is a most necessary and indispensable ingredient in society" (7) and ends it claiming that "the strength and resources of a state can only be estimated by the quantum of moral virtue which prevails, since its offspring is sobriety and industry, producing, with an increase of wealth, an augmentation of comfort and happiness" (141). Poverty management is founded on a kind of brinksmanship wherein (depending upon one's position concerning intervention) the poor must be kept, or must keep themselves in a state that verges on insubsistence, but that can be celebrated as healthy, virtuous, happy, and the very soul of a prosperous nation.[13]

Complicating matters further in the later decades of the eighteenth century is the repudiation of *populationniste* theory, which had maintained a direct correlation between population and national wealth: "The *populationniste* believed that the only true wealth of a nation was the number of its inhabitants; people made a country opulent and rich" (Vaggi 38).[14] In Britain, *populationnisme* continued to find supporters until Malthus's *Essay on the Principle of Population* (1797), which forcefully, and successfully, repudiated any notion that the laboring poor were simply an undifferentiated national stock.[15] Indeed, Malthus foresaw exactly the opposite path of development from that predicted by *populationnisme*. The destiny of healthy and freely reproducing populations is, paradoxically, starvation: "The rosy flush of health gives place to the pallid cheek and hollow eye of misery" (Malthus, *Essay* 70). In the aftermath of *populationniste* theory, political economy and the preservation of the poor are complicated by the dangers of surplus labor and the possibility of overproduction and underemployment.[16]

Malthus himself advises the poor to shepherd their surplus labor: "We must . . . shew [the poor] that the withholding of the supplies of labour is the only possible way of raising its price; and that they themselves being the possessors of this commodity, have alone the power to do this" (*Essay* 133–34). Poverty-management policy consequently starts to encourage the laboring poor to restrain and manage their own productive energies and in doing so to distinguish their own interests from those of anyone else and of the nation: as Catherine Gallagher points out, Malthus's argument that population growth will lead to misery, vice, and starvation "ruptures the healthy body/healthy population homology" (39). The pauper's self-interest, like that of Adam Smith's merchant, serves the interests of all by neglecting or even opposing them.[17] In place of a reciprocal partnership between the body natural and the body politic, a new opposition raises a new conundrum: the suffering body in need of sympathy and sustenance fights for political and cultural influence against the idle body that needs to be made productive.

Elizabeth Hamilton, in her dedicatory preface to *The Cottagers of Glenburnie* (1808), applauds those who "do not fancy the whole duties of charity to be comprised in some efforts towards prolonging the sensitive existence of those who, without such relief, must perish; nor do they consider . . . the physical wants of the lower orders as the only wants that ought to be supplied . . . [P]recious in their eyes are the gleams of joy that illumine the poor man's cottage; sacred the peace that reigns in it; doubly sacred the virtues by which alone that peace can be established or secured" (xi). The suffering body and the idle body are, in other words, inseparable, though each asserts its truth to the exclusion of the other. Each embodies a fundamental premise about the drive to economic life that works to regulate the other under the rule of its own first principles. Each position insists that the other must be subordinate: either pleasure and sufficiency must follow from the effective harnessing of labor forces, or a population will ensure its productivity and prosperity if its fundamental comfort and contentment are guaranteed.[18] Catherine Gallagher proposes a pair of terms that equate roughly to the economic models I am identifying. The suffering body implies a "somaeconomics," which is "deeply rooted in British empiricism," but comes to full expression in the utilitarian theory of Jeremy Bentham: it seeks "to describe the theorization of economic behavior in terms of the emotional and sensual feelings that are both causes and consequences of economic exertions . . . 'happiness' or 'enjoyment' are the ultimate values, and wealth itself is defined as 'the means of enjoyment'" (3–4). The idle body, on the other hand, belongs to "bioeconomics": the Malthusian "concentration on the interconnections among populations, the food supply, modes of production and exchange, and their impact on life forms generally" (3). And "the two sorts of explanation overlap, for telling biological stories about the economy required attention to the sensations of economic actors, whose accumulated feelings, in turn, were used to explain both the quality and the quantity of economic life" (35).[19] The "problem" of poverty management, then, becomes the problem of relieving the immediate needs of paupers in a way that fosters, rather than obviates, their affective investment in contributing to the public weal by convincing them that the national interest is really the interest of each alone.

Metonymic relations between private subject and nation take the place of the old metaphoric ones: "National happiness," Elizabeth Hamilton declares, is "the aggregate of the sum of individual happiness and individual virtue. The fraternal tie . . . binds . . . not exclusively to the poor or to the affluent, it embraces the interests of all" (x). No longer is the body of a pauper, along with all other bodies, forfeit to "the corporal integrity of the monarch" (Foucault, *Power/Knowledge* 55), but rather "the body of society . . . needs to be protected, in a quasi-medical sense" (55). Poverty management passes from superintending a national stock to husbanding the moral sentiments and rational investments of the poor themselves, working to ensure that they feel they have a stake in the nation, both sentimentally and economically. Perhaps the most important practical consequence of this transition is the turn against workhouses: in 1787, the MP Thomas Gilbert, who had begun his reforming efforts two decades earlier with a plan for larger, more centralized workhouses (*A Scheme for the Better Relief and Employment of the Poor*), threw his weight in another direction, asking "whether it is not as unwise, as it is cruel, to break through all the connections of life, and shut up part of a family in the workhouse, without trying whether they may not be equally useful to themselves, and society, at their own homes" (*Considerations* 41). If the workhouse cannot ensure that the surplus energies of the poor are made productive, perhaps home can.

One of the most persistent themes of early and mid-eighteenth-century treatises on poverty had been proposals for workhouses that pay for themselves out of the proceeds of their inmates' production. The goal of setting paupers to productive work "seemed to offer not only the relief of the destitute without cost to the ratepayers, but even an increase in national wealth" (Webb and Webb, *English Poor Law* 408), but by the 1780s and 1790s, that aspiration was dead. No workhouse ever succeeded in breaking even, let alone yielding a return.[20] When the new poor law of 1834 instituted universal workhouse detention for those requiring welfare, it "had deterrence, not profit, as its *raison d'être*" (G. Taylor 18). At the end of the eighteenth century, however, carceral solutions were generally out of favor: John Howlett, vicar of Great Dunmow in Essex and defender of the Whig minimum-wage scheme, believed that "the utmost the district-houses of industry have affected . . . is, they have continued to maintain their paupers at double the sum per head they could have maintained themselves for in their own cottages" (*Examination* 39–40). Home seemed to offer what the workhouse could not, self-sufficiency: "It is a fact, that the poor are maintained much more comfortably, and at much less expense, at their own homes, than in workhouses . . . [I]f the poor were thus profitably and constantly employed, they would be almost always able to maintain themselves and their families, their honest exertions seldom failing to supply their expenses" (Cowe 50–51). The suffering body and the idle body might be persuaded to collaborate in relieving their mutual insufficiencies, paradoxically, if the two bodies were left to fight it out between themselves in a space of private self-determination.[21]

## A Stake in the Country: Cottages

"It is commonly observed," William Pitt wrote in 1797, "that the labourers who possess [their own cottages] are the most industrious, sober, and frugal, that they seldom apply to their parishes for relief, and that their houses have an appearance of neatness and comfort, not often met with elsewhere. If these were more attainable by the poor, frugality would revive among them, and young people would strive to lay up a sum of money for this purpose" (6). In the same year, the Board of Agriculture, a statutory body created by Parliament in 1793, published "the results of its national inquiry concerning the best form of cottage" (Crowley 183). If we believe the evidence of the presses, cottages were a new national calling, blooming over all the countryside where the dank, shadowy hulks of workhouses had been pulled down to make way.[22] The poet, novelist, and playwright Samuel Jackson Pratt (who also published under the name Courtney Melmoth) reports in his dedicatory epistle to the 1803 edition of *Cottage Pictures; or, the Poor* (published in 1801 as *Bread; or, The Poor*), "I shall be called upon, by Truth, to conduct my reader to the repositories of comfort which I have myself seen; to impress his mind with an idea of the well planed [*sic*] and appointed cottages I have myself entered; to describe the smiles of content and of health where I have seen them revel" (vi). However exaggerated the reports were, the ideological deep structures of home were taking shape in the cultural figure of the poor family's cottage.

"Every labourer, possessing such property of his own," Pitt continues in his *Address to the Landed Interest on the Deficiency of Habitations and Fuel for the Use of the Poor*, "would consider himself as having a permanent interest and stake in the country" (6–7). The cottage, embodying home and its universalizing principle, offered a means of bonding the poor to their nation. Five years after Pitt published his proposal, Thomas Bernard borrowed Pitt's phrase: "Cottagers possessing property . . . will acquire a degree of consolidated and defensive strength . . . Every individual will then have a stake in the country" (5: 51). Not long after that, Patrick Colquhoun suggested a system of friendly societies, enabling the poor to relieve themselves, which "will also excite a disposition to loyalty and subordination, by and interest, a stake in preserving, maintaining and defending the laws and constitution of the country" (137). Pitt, Bernard, and Colquhoun all adopt a metaphor of investment, a stake in the common wealth, that will encourage the investor to take care of the corporate property in which he holds a share.

"The poor man," Colquhoun adds, "would then feel that he had a home to fight for (from which he could not be removed), and a country to defend" (242). Colquhoun and his fellow cottagists imagine the poor, and wish the poor to imagine themselves, as economic actors participating in Adam Smith's national system, where self-interest contributes to the general prosperity but is also freely determined by each actor for himself: "The poor man, poor as he is, loves to cherish the idea of property. To talk of *my* house, *my* garden, *my* furniture, is always a theme of delight and pleasure" (Bernard 2:326). The rhetoric of economic investment seems almost invariably to borrow the registers of sentimental investment. Bernard cites William Paley's *Natural Theology* (1802) on the magical powers of private property: "'Property,' says Dr. Paley, 'communicates a charm to whatever is the object of it. It is the first of our abstract ideas; it cleaves to us the closest and the longest. It endears to the child its plaything, to the peasant his cottage, and to the landlord his estate'" (5: 27). Cottages make their inhabitants into economic actors even as they institute a sanctuary from the arena and conditions of economic striving.

Visions of contented cottagers were offered in service of poor-law reform as early as 1767: "The condition of the industrious, sober and virtuous labourer . . . perhaps ought rather to excite our envy than pity. Health and peace of mind, the choicest blessings reserved for mankind, are to be looked for in his humble cottage. His cares seldom exceed the limits of the day; the industry, frugality, and virtue of the parents being all the fortune his children will stand in need of" (*Inquiry into the Management of the Poor* 91). There is a clear continuity between this political grandiloquence and the traditional topoi of pastoral verse, but by the 1790s, provision, and preservation, of cottages is a refrain that belongs unmistakably to poor-law reformers. Thomas Bernard's SBC is particularly vocal: contributor Edward Parry Esq. laments in the society's first *Report* that the poor are "of necessity driven from their cottages to a society, which must disgust and distress them" (Bernard 1: 26). With an attached smallholding, the cottage makes an oasis of self-sufficiency: "Every cottage should have land enough about it to supply the family with vegetables at least, if not afford sustenance for a pig or a cow" (E. Wilson 11). Children, too, may participate by taking care of the garden and so "contribute largely to their own support, if not wholly maintain themselves" (Pitt 12–13). Indeed, the participation of women and children in subsistence labor that sustains the home helps to free up the labor time that adult males need to perform work whose productivity benefits the nation beyond the cottage doorstep.

It seems to me plausible that the new valuation of rural home-making was also informed by the annual Harvest-Home tradition, a "piece of natural religion, an ebullition of jocund gratitude to the divine source of all earthly blessings" (Chambers 2: 377), celebrated in most or all English districts with a variety of rituals and fêtes.[23] Robert Chambers's 1832 miscellany *The Book of Days* describes one version:

> The grain last cut was brought home in its wagon—called the *Hock Cart*—surmounted by a figure formed of a sheaf with gay dressings— a presumable representation of the goddess Ceres—while a pipe and tabor went merrily sounding in front, and the reapers tripped around in a hand-in-hand ring, singing appropriate songs . . .
>
> > "Harvest-home, harvest-home,
> > We have ploughed, we have sowed,
> > We have reaped, we have mowed,
> > We have brought home every load,
> > Hip, hip, hip, harvest-home!" (2: 377)

A 1787 play takes the title *Harvest Home; A Comic Opera* and concludes with an application of the Harvest-Home trope to something resembling the universalized home:

> Cleora: Who social pleasures love to share,
> Where rise, nor hall, nor costly dome;
> Far from the meager train of care,
> Come, smiling, to Love's Harvest-Home!
>
> (Dibdin 27)

Along with the celebration of plenty, the Harvest-Home also gathers all degrees together under a common dispensation, a holiday from strict social distinction that the middle-class home adopts as its permanent condition.[24]

Social indistinction within homes begins with social indistinction between homes: "considering the regular gradation between the plan of the most simple hut and that of the most superb palace," John Wood the Younger writes in 1781, "a palace is nothing more than a cottage IMPROVED" (1).[25] In 1798, the architect James Malton published fourteen designs for rural habitations in a "regular gradation, from a peasant's simple hut, to habitation worthy of a gentleman of fortune" (3).[26] The cottage industry nurtures the principle that lowly cot and stately country seat no longer differ from one another in kind, only in scale; they, and every degree of domicile between them, are all homes. Cottages, Malton writes, can "as well be the habitation of a substantial farmer or affluent gentleman, as the dwelling of the hedger or ditcher" (4). Wood implies further that home can be a space of sympathetic identification between classes: "In order to make myself master of the subject, it was necessary for me to feel as the cottager himself" (1), though his sentimental paternalism and the restriction of his designs to laborers suggest that the rehabilitation of the cottage did not really take place until the 1790s. The principle of homogeneity, nonetheless, is clearly one of the modern home's attributes from its earliest stages.

The vogue for cottage designs received impetus also from the Vitruvian primitivism of midcentury architectural theorists like Robert Morris, who explains that "the science I am treating on is made universal through necessity . . . [I]n every structure in every climate, Nature had dictated the architect to the disposal of it" (qtd. in Crowley 177). That principle of universal domestic refuge is sanctified by Felicia Hemans in her 1808 *Poems*, which features two short lyrics that encapsulate the idea:

> INSCRIPTION FOR A COTTAGE
> OH! give me, Heaven, whate'er my lot,
> Or in the palace, or the cot,
> A noble generous mind;

Exalted in a lowly state,
At fortune's favours not elate,
To all her frowns resign'd.

Song
SAY, does calm Contentment dwell,
In palace rich, or lowly cell?
Fix'd to no peculiar spot,
Gilded rooms, or simple cot,
She will grace the courtly scene,
Or love to haunt the village green:
Where Virtue dwells, Content must be.
And with her Felicity. (53–54)

The cottage exemplifies home's magical combination of a precise and sanctified personal topography that is simultaneously "no peculiar spot." The hierarchy of homes, from lowly cell to palace, is preserved and naturalized by its
very arbitrariness.[27]

This newfound cultural prestige, while legitimated by the pastoral tradition, inverts the predominant eighteenth-century connotations of the terms
*cottage* and *cottager*. John E. Crowley reports that before their meanings shifted,
they had been etymologically and legally linked to vagrancy: "Cottagers were
by definition tenants, usually with inadequate holdings in land to support a
family" (170). John Wood laments that "the greatest part of the cottages that
fell within my observation, I found to be shattered, dirty, inconvenient, miserable hovels, scarcely affording a shelter for beasts" (2). More than simply earning its redemption, the cottage improves its social pedigree from vagabond
lodging to middle-class ideal: "The inherent anti-urbanism of middle-class
culture was reflected in the quintessential image of early nineteenth-century
desirable housing, the *white cottage* with thatched roof and porch embowered
with honeysuckle and roses" (Davidoff and Hall 361). In 1794, Ann Radcliffe's
*The Mysteries of Udolpho* gives its heroine her start in a "summer cottage"
whose owner, our heroine's father, had made additions, but "would not suffer a stone of it to be removed, so that the new building, adapted to the style
of the old one, formed with it only a simple and elegant residence" (2). Jane
Austen makes fun of the cottage vogue in *Sense and Sensibility* when some of
the Dashwoods find Barton Cottage "defective, for the building was regular,
the roof was tiled, the window shutters were not painted green, nor were the
walls covered with honeysuckles" (30), and Willoughby declares, "were I rich

enough, I would instantly pull Combe [Magna] down and build it up again in the exact plan of this cottage" (73).

In fact, as early as 1801 the bourgeoisification of cottages was sufficiently established that Samuel Jackson Pratt could disparage middle-class appropriations of the agrarian ideal, linking them metonymically to what he sees as the causes of rural poverty—enclosure and large-scale accumulation of private wealth:

> Farm-house, and farm too, are in deep disgrace,
> 'Tis now the LODGE, the COTTAGE or the PLACE!
> Or if a farm, *ferme ornee* is the phrase![28]
> And if a Cottage, of these modern days,
> Expect no more to see the straw-built shed,
> But a fantastic villa in its stead! (42, lines 413–18)

The "Pride, thinly veil'd in mock humility" (43, line 419) that misappropriates and aestheticizes the cottage is the tyranny of the "village despot," "Possessing, yet encumbering the ground, / In deep carousal, high above his lord," (40, lines 366–67). For Pratt, bourgeois acquisitive aspiration (what he calls, in the poem's advertisement, "the system of diversified monopoly . . . with all that forms the hideous chain of rapacity and fraud") has undone the paternalistic bonds that formerly governed rural prosperity and domestic harmony. Indeed, Pratt borrows the antipaternalistic rhetoric of Wordsworth and radical writers and turns it on the very class that is benefiting from the decline of aristocratic paternalism.[29] The weight of evidence suggests that the middle classes, much more than the laboring classes, were the beneficiaries of the cottage "boom."

Among the benefits that the cottage vogue provided for the rising middle class was assistance in naturalizing the forms of property relations and contractual social relations that the middle class asserted over against what Robert Southey called the bonds of "grateful and honest dependence" between landholders and peasants (qtd. in Tobin 13). Common to most versions of the self-sufficiency argument for cottage provision is the appeal to familial affections, such as this early (1775) encomium from William Greaves to honest laborers, "whose wishes never aspired to more than a bare competence": "They live happy and contented, whilst they can cheerfully earn their bread, though with care and hard labour, surrounded by their families, their friends and old acquaintance" (22). To the bonds of family Greaves adds also a "powerful natal attachment" to one's place of birth and livelihood (21), and Thomas Bernard expands the same sentiment: "The cottager . . . centers all his desires to the spot where he was born, and the family to which he has given birth . . . The heart will always be *tremblingly alive* to the call, which summons him back to his home, and his family; and renews the sweetest sensations, which we ever enjoy in the sublunary world" (5: 49). The cottage home is, as I noted earlier, both a place of absolute personal specificity and "no peculiar spot"; there is no place like home.

Native affection's counterpart, the protocosmopolitan anxiety of nostalgia for one's distant native place/land, appears notably in Goldsmith's *The Deserted Village*, which laments the misery of poor emigrants forced to fly the village

> To distant climes, a dreary scene
> Where half the convex world intrudes between,
> Through torrid tracts, with fainting steps they go,
> Where wild Altama murmurs to their woe.
>
> ·  ·  ·  ·  ·  ·  ·  ·  ·  ·  ·  ·  ·
>
> Far different these from every former scene,
> The cooling brook, the grassy-vested green
>
> (19, lines 341–60)

There is, especially in the era of the French Revolution, a not-so-cosmopolitan resistance to the foreign: "If foreign commerce be considered with regard to its supposed influence on the moral character of a people, its tendency will be found to contract, and not to enlarge, to vitiate and not to refine the moral sentiment" (Archard 62). Self-sufficiency at the level of private domesticity had its national equivalent in strident promotion of the "home trade." "The History of Tom White, the Postilion," one of More's *Cheap Repository Tracts*, for instance, relates how Tom gives up his wandering life to turn farmer in his native village and finds there are "many temptations to send his corn at an extravagant price to a certain sea-port town," but Tom "would not be tempted to encourage unlawful gain; so he threshed out a small mow at a time, and sold it to the neighbouring poor far below the market price" (291). The rule of strict self-interest and the autonomy of private homes can, where hegemonic interests find an expedient, be explicitly suspended in favor of a superordinate and collective self-interest at the level of home nation.

From this survey of the poverty-management debates around the turn of the century, we can derive several crucial attributes of the private-home/home-nation coalition. These attributes are, let us note, conceptual and ideal, foundational elements eventually absorbed into the naturalized hegemonic figure of home. They include: *self-sufficiency*—a sustainable match between needs and resources nurtured by an immanent and uncoerced will to maintain and improve; *simultaneous personal specificity and homogeneous generality*—home is one's own personal sanctuary and no peculiar spot; *affective bonds naturalized under the sign of nativity, family, and nationality*—the site of a "powerful natal attachment" and the companionship of family and friends; *a metonymic relationship between private dwelling and nation*—derived from the "stake" in the national wealth offered to the cottager; and *universality*—as in the etymological extension of the word *home* to designate all from the humblest cottage to the grandest manor house and the common status of stake holder. All of these attributes can be found in a crucial passage written in 1796 by one of home's major synthesists, Sir William Young, M.P. for St. Mawes, Cornwall, and author of the poor-law acts of 1795 and 1796:

> The elements of national character are to be traced in the relations of the individual to the state . . . The industrious father of a cottage family leading forth his industrious sons to their morning work, forms a picture as gratifying to the statesman as to the moralist. Such a father of such a family is the most valuable of citizens: his labours, his morals, his affections, all interwoven and implicated, form a character on which the British Constitution may securely rest, and its statesmen well depend, for returns of profitable labour, and for happy and zealous defense of the country, he who hath *no home* to defend, hath *no country!* From the habits of domestic affections springs the sense of moral duties . . . Let the word HOME be appropriated to as many as the lot of life can admit to it, under human institution. (*Considerations* 17–18)[30]

From a marginal resort of vagrancy and destitution, the cottage home has been transformed into the essential principle of Englishness.

Young's vision of home is profoundly influential. Writers on poverty adopt its sentiments and logic for both pro- and antipaternalistic purposes as do poets. Samuel Jackson Pratt recapitulates Young wholesale:

> O give the heirs of poverty their cots,
> Attach them fondly to their native spots;
> Amidst their thorny paths entwine a flower—
> Theirs soft submission, thine attemper'd power;
> Force them no more like banish'd men to roam,

But give to each that balm of life—a *Home*! . . .
Content and Neatness, cottage gods! shall grace,
And Hope with Heav'ns own bloom shall mark the place;
And with them fair Frugality shall come,
And sage Oeconomy resume her home;

. . . . . . . . . . . .

O days devoutly wish'd, when hinds shall feel
A generous passion for the public weal;

. . . . . . . . . . .

A brave, intrepid, voluntary band,
Patient to till, and bold to guard the land. (83–84)

As part of the 1806 manuscript of *Home at Grasmere*, William Wordsworth composes a panegyric to home that comprises much the same set of values:

This small abiding-place of many men,
A termination and a last retreat,
A centre, come from wheresoe'er you will,
A whole without dependence or defect,
Made for itself, happy in itself,
Perfect contentment, unity entire.

. . . . . . . . . .

In this majestic, self-sufficing world (48)

He calls Dove cottage "a home / within a home" (52), evoking the private-home/home-nation correlation.

The first generation of British Romantic poets contributed a great deal to the hymnody of home. One of Samuel Taylor Coleridge's volumes published prior to *Lyrical Ballads* features a poem titled "Domestic Peace":

Tell me, on what holy ground
May Domestic Peace be found?
Halcyon daughter of the skies,
Far on fearful wings she flies,
From the pomp of scepter'd State,
From the Rebel's noisy hate.
In a cottaged vale She dwells
List'ning to the Sabbath bells! (60)

His vision of domestic peace is undoubtedly informed by his Pantisocracy project, with its self-sufficient, domestic retreat and its "cottag'd dell."[31] Coleridge's sometime collaborator in Pantisocracy, Robert Southey, was perhaps the most enthusiastic of all the early poets of home. His verse from the 1790s is crowded with homes, cottages, and paupers who yearn for them. In "Botany Bay Eclogues: Humphrey and William," William grieves for "A home so snug, so chearful too as mine," which he has lost after shooting partridges that ate his corn, but belonged to his "testy Squire": "I went to prison and my farm to ruin, / Poor Mary! for her grave the parish paid" (*Poetical Works* 5: 75). "I had a home once—I had once a husband— / Pity me Strangers!" cries "The Widow" to a passing carriage, which leaves her to die in the snow (*Poetical Works* 5: 106).

Southey's most elaborate celebration of home is his 1797 "Hymn to the Penates," a rambling, and self-pitying, expression of quite literal agoraphobia. The speaker wants only a spot

> Where my tir'd mind might rest and call it *home.*
> There is a magic in that little word;
> It is a mystic circle that surrounds
> Comforts and Virtues never known beyond
> The hallowed limit. Often has my heart
> Ached for that quiet haven; haven'd now
> I think of those in this world's wilderness
> Who wander on and find no home of rest
> Till to the grave they go! them POVERTY
> Hollow-eyed fiend, the child of WEALTH and POWER,
> Bad offspring of worse parents, aye afflicts.
>
> (*Poetical Works* 5: 136)

"HOUSEHOLD DEITIES!" he cries,

> Then only shall be Happiness on earth
> When Man shall feel your sacred power, and love
> Your tranquil joys. (5: 136)

Should such a time come, "then shall the city stand / A huge void sepulchre" (5: 136) while "shunning the polished mob," "by the evening hearth CONTENTMENT sits" (5: 129 and 132).

That poem provides an epigraph for John Wilson's "My Cottage," a naked (and dreadful) imitation of Wordsworth composed when Wilson was living at Elleray, on Windermere, and published in 1812. "Here," sings the writer who would later appropriate and mock James Hogg's Ettrick Shepherd persona,

> have I found at last a home of peace
> To hide me from the world; far from its noise,
> To feed that spirit, which, though sprung from earth,
> And link'd to human beings by the bond
> Of earthly love, hath yet a loftier aim
> Than perishable joy, and through the calm
> That sleeps amid the mountain-solitude,
> Can hear the billows of eternity,
> And hear delighted. (290)

Not one of these poems (*Home at Grasmere* included) has a great deal to recommend it, but the rise of home and the first emergence of English Romanticism clearly share some important cultural territory—most prominently, I would suggest, the constitutive opposition between originary, structureless autonomy and organic, determinate system. I will discuss home's role in more revered Romantic verse in my third chapter. Home is, for my present purposes, also a disciplinary mechanism just as much as is the iron law of wages.[32] It functions to maintain and extend class structures. An important difference between home and many other institutions of class organization, however, is that the primary objects upon which its management and enforcement are exercised are women.

## "Stock the Country with Beggars"

Once the poor are understood as a massive productive resource, the contest over poverty management can be understood as "battle between the landed classes and middle classes for the right to superintend the poor and, by analogy, the nation" (Tobin 3).[33] In fact, control over poverty management by the end of the eighteenth century seems to have been largely an object of struggle among middle-class theorists. The most audible voices for the old landed interest seem to have come from a few conservative clergy, such as Thomas Bere, curate of Blagdon, who accused Hannah More of seditious radicalism and her agents of Methodism (Stott 234–36). In its poor, during the period of the French Revolution, England foresees the imminent arrival of either prosperity (derived from effectively harnessed military and labor power) or anarchy (wrought by mobs of sturdy beggars). Responsibility for managerial discipline and consequently for whether prosperity or anarchy will prevail tends to fall on poor women. In fiction and in poor-law polemics, the double binds that divide women between innocence and depravity hinge upon their figuration (and therefore endangerment) of the nation *in potential:* "Never let it be forgotten," cautions Thomas Gisborne, a member of the Clapham Sect, "that female example, if it be thus capable of befriending the cause of religion and the interests of moral rectitude, is equally capable of proving itself one of the most dangerous of their foes" (249). The poor woman symbolically and literally brings with her consequences that *will* ensue.

In the previous chapter's discussion of *Joseph Andrews,* we heard Lady Booby's complaint about Fanny: "And so this wench *is to* stock the parish with beauties ...—but sir, our poor is numerous enough already; I *will have* no more vagabonds settled here" (246, emphasis added) and Mrs. Tow-wouse's: "We *shall have* thirty or forty poor wretches in red coats shortly" (49, emphasis added). The future tense is ubiquitous in eighteenth-century writings about poverty: we might also recall Fielding's warning in his *Enquiry into the Causes of the Late Increase of Robbers,* "that the streets of this town, and the roads leading to it, *will* shortly be impassable without the utmost hazard" (19, emphasis added). As is the case with Lady Booby's attack on Fanny, this future-tense register frequently makes use, both literally and figuratively, of the futurity conventionally implicit in pregnancy and the capacity to become pregnant. William Young, for instance, laments that removals often happen on "speculation ... of encrease of family ... by which, if not hastily removed, [new arrivals] might rent premises, pay rates, and acquire a settlement. Thus the principles of national population and wealth receive at once a check!" (*Observations* 34).

The vagrancy laws do express the speculative propositions that Young maligns: "And whereas women wandring and begging are often delivered of children in parishes and places to which they do not belong, whereby they become chargeable to the same; it is enacted, that where any such woman shall be so delivered ... the Churchwardens or Overseers may detain her till they can safely convey her to a Justice ... who may ... order her to be publickly whipt, and detained in the House of Correction" (*Statutes at Large* 101). Young's *populationniste* assumptions run up against other anxieties about a mobile and wantonly reproductive population. Indeed, his own act of 1795 left only three categories liable to removal before they became chargeable to the parish rates: "rogues and vagabonds," "idle and disorderly persons," and "every unmarried woman with child" (Webb and Webb, *English Poor Law* 343).[34] The clergyman John Trusler conjures up some of the abuses that were perceived to make the settlement and vagrancy laws necessary (but also inadequate) in a 1785 fictional criminal autobiography, whose narrator is head of a gang of thieves: "We took in three young women among us . . . They all proved pregnant before I quitted the company; and though I did not continue long enough to see how they got over the difficulty, I understood they meant either to drop their bastards in some distant parish, lay them at the doors of some gentlemen's houses, or swear them to persons that had been their common disturbers" (1: 83). At least in part because poor women were widely associated with the kind of abuses detailed here (defiance of settlement, bastardy, and false claims of paternity), removals were exercised against women—regardless of whether they were with child—much more often than against men.[35]

Although, as Wolfram Schmidgen has shown, bastardy lost much of its opprobrium in literary representations (and in fact acquired considerable value as a kind of exceptionalizing category for literary characters in eighteenth-century fiction), bastardy as a transgression against the poor laws was if anything subject to increasing censure and suppression.[36] (The same double principle applies to vagrancy, as I have shown in chapter 1.) Bastardy begets beggary, complains Josiah Childe: "They grow up with habits of idleness; become vicious, and stock the country at last with beggars" (qtd. in Rose 5).[37] It may contribute to the growth of a population that "would consist of a larger proportion of persons not capable of adding by their exertions to the resources of the state" (Malthus, *Letter to Samuel Whitbread* 30). Current methods of dealing with bastardy, according to the Reverend John Acland, a justice in Devon, allow a parish to "take advantage of another . . . [by] sending women to lie in of bastard children" (Acland 20). Acland's solution (proposed in 1786) is the repeal of virtually all settlement laws, as a result of which, he predicts, "honourable marriage, in which children will be provided for, as well as begot, will be hereby greatly encouraged and increased; and in consequence thereof, a much more numerous population (the greatest and the truest riches of a state) will most undoubtedly take place" (59). But Acland's assumptions are *populationniste* and lose traction in the 1790s under the pressures of wage-price upheaval and food shortages.

Malthus and other writers introduce to the economics of poverty management a greater attention to the private lives and sensations of the laboring classes: "I had certainly much rather that the poor were deterred from very early and improvident marriages by the fear of dependent poverty" (Malthus,

*Letter to Samuel Whitbread* 28).[38] Thomas Bernard agrees: "The Poor Laws of England have held out a false and deceitful encouragement to population. They promise that unqualified support, that unrestricted maintenance, to the cottager's family, which it is not *possible* for them to supply; thereby inducing the young labourer to marry, before he has made any provision for the married state; and in consequence, extinguishing all prospective prudence and all consideration for the future" (3.10–11). These socioeconomic disquisitions, along with Hannah More's *Cheap Repository Tracts* and any number of other works, formulate the principle that the poor must be taught to exercise restraint and prudence with an eye always to the future development of their own interests.

To a considerable extent, the future tense of poor-management debates follows from its proximity to political economy and the speculative, predictive phrasings typical of that discipline. The poor embody, for example, the available supply of surplus labor—labor whose yield is surplus value—so essential to increased wealth. The abstraction of labor required for such a model enables a conception of the poor as a reservoir of labor in potential—labor that is deferred and not yet used up. Over this supply the poor woman has several kinds of influence: She is its source—literally its mother (besides futurity, pregnancy is of course also a master trope for increase); she is a manager— "when a labourer is thus blessed with a frugal, industrious, and intelligent wife, he shews his attachment and good sense by leaving all domestic concerns to her prudent and superior management" (Cowe 86); she is an educator—"as teachers . . . British women had established a newly prominent social role by the beginning of the nineteenth century" (A. Richardson 167); and she provides the laborer with the object for which he strives and aspires—"he who does not make his family comfortable, will himself never be happy at home; and he who is not happy at home, will never be happy anywhere" (Bernard 2: 284).

As King and Tomkins note, "poor women were regarded as a pressing social and economic problem at the same time as some contemporary commentators were identifying their ability in bringing together and managing the different strands of the economy of makeshifts" (24).[39] From more than one part of the political spectrum, the solution proposed to problems of poverty management is effectively to teach—or force—the poor to manage themselves, with women as the primary managers. It is not hard to see how the middle-class home adopted this scheme for its universalizing purposes; in Nancy Armstrong's words: "If the marketplace driven by male labor came to be imagined as a centrifugal force that broke up the vertical chains organizing an earlier notion of society and that scattered individuals willy-nilly across the English landscape, then the household's dynamic was conceived as a centripetal one. The household simultaneously recentered the scattered community at myriad points to form the nuclear family, a social organization with a mother rather than a father at its center" (95). By the mid-Victorian period, if not well before, the middle-class wife/manager was an English commonplace: "Every wife is a steward of her husband's wealth, and should consider herself in that light. Every little act of carefulness, every piece of forethought, every prevention of accident, illness, or waste, becomes a sacred duty" ("Our Households" 76).[40]

The burden of futurity placed on the poor and particularly on poor women is supplementary to the charges placed on middle-class women, who are frequently made to signify the sociopolitical relations of developing capitalism. The supplementarity of this burden is a token of its residual persistence from aristocratic social relations, where women are unequivocally responsible for the stability of patriarchal landholding—better known as posterity than as futurity.[41] Middle-class women were, as Beth Fowkes Tobin puts it, "engaged in a radical reconstitution of public virtue that involved replacing the old aristocratic notions of public virtue, honor, and benevolence with new bourgeois notions of self-regulation and surveillance" (89), and their function was to offer, in Kate Ferguson Ellis's words, "stability . . . to a society whose aristocrats . . . had lost the capacity for moral leadership" (11). The middle-class woman's virtue is an essential underpinning for the credit (in every sense) and fidelity required by the transactional and contractual nature of all social relations under capital. The "very existence" of the middle class "depended on the establishment of creditworthiness" (Davidoff and Hall 21). The values embodied by middle-class women, however, are not commensurable with the speculative, to-be-realized component of social relations. The competent and reliable domestic woman cannot also signify in a manifest sense that which is deferred, not yet present, and likely to be lost altogether.[42] That honor falls to women of the laboring classes. They must bear responsibility for what will be and what will be lost.

Hence, even as the poor woman is ushered into her post as manager of the laboring classes, the weight of her responsibilities keeps her advocates and her doubters fretful and jittery. Jeremy Bentham, for instance, prefers to have the workhouse available as a carceral substitute when private domesticity breaks down: "The industry-house, like a well-regulated convent, but free from the objections that attach on convents, would restore the fugitive ['bad wife'], without spot or suspicion, to the marital arms" (*Pauper Management Improved* 219).[43] William Young envisions the opposite outcome: "Put the wife in the woman's ward of a workhouse, the children in another; wean the husband and father from the relative affections; he will fly from the roof, and a robber is set loose on the world, and an enemy created to the state" (*Considerations* 18). The tracts in general tend to agree that if the laboring classes cannot be kept productive and contented, they are likely to become an insurgent body bent on the destruction of England.

Many writers wax imaginative on the topic of disaffected paupers. Eden warns that where the poor go "without a home, or any asylum to shelter them from the inclemency of the weather . . . through the medium of these miserable outcasts of society, crimes are increased and become a regular trade" (1: 402), and John Hill seconds him: "When the labourers perceive they are not likely to receive their due recompense, not only will their affections be alienated from their superiors, but they will think themselves justified in opposing their own interest to that of the public" (62). The poor may form a corporate body directly opposed to the nation—an antination. The self-evident connection of such paranoia to the French Revolution is rehearsed by Arthur Young in two histrionic works, *The Example of France, A Warning to Britain* (1793) and *National Danger, and the Means of Safety* (1797). In the earlier work, Young counsels, "we see exactly in France, what is the case of an indigent poor possessed of power" (22), and, the French threat "is a moment that ought to bring political agitation to every bosom.—The question concerns not empires, kings, and ministers alone—it comes borne to our fortunes, our houses, our families" (120). William Young, in the same pamphlet that sketches the benefits of home, sums up anxieties about the homeless:

> In filling workhouses, we are manning, as it were, so many disaffected garrisons, the inmates of which in the first violence of popular commotion . . . will be let loose on the country, from a regard to which they have been so cruelly and forcibly weaned. They have been left no place of endearment, no point of home where to fix, and whence to stretch the compass of regard to the circle of family, to that of neighbourhood, to parish, to county, and till it reaches the periphery of the commonwealth, and becomes a national affection and patriotic support. (*Considerations* 18–19)

Note that Young here, and above, twice imagines the poor man being "weaned" from a figural breast. The nursing breast, which doubles as the "point of home where to fix," keeps the underclass circulating in a warm current of affection and contentment. Without it, other—undesirable—points "where to fix" are liable to crop up. It may also be worth recalling that it was poor women who provided wet-nursing to the affluent classes.[44] Economic analyses that define the poor as the source of national prosperity complete the picture: the breast at which the nation suckles, that which has a surplus of nourishment and whose owner has a strong motivation to share that nourishment, is that of the poor woman.

### HAMLET'S DAUGHTER

William Beckford published, in 1797, a gothic parody entitled *Azemia: A Descriptive and Sentimental Novel,* under the nom de plume Jacquetta Agneta Mariana Jewks, a narrator who often waxes digressive:

> If you shut me out from these realities [political topics], may I not be allowed a few extraordinaries . . . a castle or two, or an abbey—a few ghosts, provided I make out afterwards that they were not ghosts, but waxwork and pasteboard; and a little sprinkling of banditti, just to excite a small emotion of terror!—and then I may be able to fill up my little book without a word of politics, revolutions, or counter-revolutions, and prattle through my volumes as prettily and beat up my literary *pap* with as innoxious ingredients as the most straight-laced matrons, or rigid elders, can recommend for their babes and sucklings. (1: 64–65)

In spite of this disclaimer, a few pages later Mrs. Jewks introduces Mr. Wild-codger, who discourses on the poor at length:

> It is proposed, in order to accommodate the houseless, if any such there are (which however is their own fault), to have . . . various views painted of houses and seats, after the manner of Mr. Repton, and in the most picturesque point of view—such as Mr. Pitt's seat at Holmwood, Mr. Dundas' at Wimbledon, Mr. Rose's at Cuffnells, &c. &c. &c. and in contemplating these representations, the great affluence and flourishing state of their country, the wretched animals . . . may surely . . . forget all *their* trifling inconveniences in the great and patriotic sentiment of rejoicing in the prosperity of their country. (1: 90)[45]

Beckford's parody suggests that the popular Radcliffean and Minerva Press gothic of the 1790s was perceived to relate obliquely, and perhaps accidentally or haphazardly, to political matters. Mrs. Jewks's introduction of politics by means of disavowals implies that the distancing effects characteristic of the "feminine" gothic (foreign and historical settings, supernatural incidents) may not have distanced these novels from the sociocultural contexts of their production at all. Radcliffean romances may in fact have been understood as possessing the capacity to reflect in figural or cryptic ways on the political realities from which they ostensibly sequester themselves. As Harriet Guest speculates, the gothic "may constitute a region of extrapolitical activity that can reflect upon and inform, perhaps reform, the nature of what it is excluded from" (121). Certainly the provocative, agitating possibilities inherent in gothic romance were widely attested.[46]

Ann Radcliffe's particular political sentiments and affiliations are disputed.[47] In a recent biography, Rictor Norton marshals substantial evidence to balance a fair amount of speculation in making his case that Radcliffe "was fully aware of the radical politics of her time and sympathized with them" (x). He cites, for example, a diary observation by the engraver Joseph Farington that Radcliffe's husband, William, was "democratically inclined" (136). Certainly there were prominent and outspoken dissenters in Radcliffe's family and social circles, most notably Joseph Priestly. Norton seems to establish that Radcliffe was intimately familiar with religious-political factions that participated in the foments of the 1790s. Although Norton distinguishes rationalist dissent from the evangelical tradition, it seems no stretch to imagine Radcliffe as familiar with the terms and tactics of the poverty-management disputes. In any case, gothic fiction of the 1790s resonates with the poor-law debates not only in direct evocations of the topic, but also in its elastic and perverse strains of figuration that trace out all kinds of rhetorical and thematic equivalence to the discourses of poverty management. *Caleb Williams,* for instance, features explicit treatment of the topic: the forced removal of poor ailing Miss Melville leads to her death, and Caleb protests that the law is "better adapted for a weapon of tyranny in the hands of the rich than for a shield to protect the humbler part of the community" (76). In *The Monk,* more oblique/figural instances occur, such as the pregnancy of the novice Agnes, who finds herself shut away from the world where she fears, "it would be my fate to expire of hunger" (404). The abduction, pursuit, and confinement of young women, which is so rife in gothic fiction from this period, surely reflects the sheer cultural prominence of the plight suffered by—and threat posed by—women without means of support.

Radcliffe's *The Romance of the Forest* (1791) is an ideal example upon which to test my thesis that the poor debates resonate in fiction of the 1790s. It tells the story of Adeline, who enters the narrative unaware of her own surname, her parentage, or her place of origin. She is an apparent orphan and pauper, perhaps even illegitimate, cast upon the care of the La Motte family by an anonymous ruffian whom she believes to be her father. The La Mottes are themselves on the verge of indigence, fleeing creditors and officers of the law, and forced to seek asylum in a huge, moldering building filled with darkened recesses and menacing portent. Cast about from guardian to seducer to lover to surrogate parent until the mystery of her origins is settled and her pauper status finally erased, Adeline is a very strong example of the ways in which late-century fiction projects anxieties about poverty onto young single women.[48] She is both the problem and the solution.[49] She has the uncomfortable dis-tinction of being the embodying or determining feature of home—its primary agent—as well as the biggest threat to home—the unstable figure that may bring structures of family and property crashing down. She is at one moment the romance hero in quest for home.[50] At the next she is, as Michel de Certeau says, the other who authorizes discourse (68)—an object whose provoca-tive effects on desiring subjects legitimate authorial and readerly conclusions about propriety and truth.[51]

Besides an abundance of dangerous and endangered women, gothic fic-tion also shares a *locus classicus* with the poverty debates: the gothic castle is uncannily similar to the workhouse. William Pitt says, "This is no exagger-ated account of parish poor-houses in many parts of this Kingdom; they strike horror into the breast of every stranger who approaches them" (4). William Young agrees: "One principle is common to all these establishments . . . that principle is terror" (*Considerations* 22).[52] In *The Romance,* by comparison, Adeline describes the "desolate and mean" house where La Motte found her: "[My father] had ordered me confined in my chamber . . . I was assured that I had nothing to fear, and that I should live as well as if I was at liberty . . . The latter part of this speech seemed to contain an odd kind of comfort; I made little reply, but submitted to necessity . . . But why abandon me to the power of strangers, to men, whose countenances bore the stamp of villainy so strongly as to impress even my inexperienced mind with terror!" (41–42).[53] A man-uscript, written by her actual father, that Adeline finds in the novel's most prominent castle, Fontangville Abbey, reads: "O sound of despair! . . . Shut out from day, from friends, from life . . . in the prime of my years . . . I sink be-neath the—" (131). The lacuna in the manuscript at this moment invites us to imagine any number of awful tortures, including—in the gothic-figural sense offered by Harriet Guest—those of the workhouse.

The East Anglian poet and minister George Crabbe's depiction of the "pauper palace" in *The Borough* might as well be Fontangville Abbey or Udolpho Castle:

> That giant building, that high-bounding wall,
> Those bare-worn walks, that lofty thund'ring hall!
> That large loud clock, which tolls each dreaded hour,
> Those gates and locks and all those signs of power (204)

On first approaching Fontangville, La Motte "felt a sensation of sublimity rising into terror" (*RF* 15), and on entering, Adeline's feelings are much the same: "The partial gleams thrown across the fabric seemed to make its desolation more solemn, while the obscurity of the greater part of the pile heightened its sublimity, and led fancy on to scenes of horror" (17–18). The gothic castle, in a less concrete sense, embodies the fearsome institutions of arbitrary paternalism, and its customary state of decay implies, as William Hazlitt suggested in 1819, the decay of those institutions: "Mrs. Radcliffe's . . . mouldering castles, derived part of their interest, no doubt, from the supposed tottering state of all old structures at the time" (*Lectures on the English Comic Writers* 123).[54] "The sanctuary is prophaned," Radcliffe's Ellena protests in *The Italian;* "it is become a prison" (84).

The gothic castle in Radcliffe is the very antithesis of home, and exactly the same relationship subsists between the workhouse and home for the dominant voices of poverty management at the end of the eighteenth century. The Tory M.P. George Rose's assertion that inmates of the workhouse are "removed from the dwelling in which perhaps they were born, and separated from every one dear to them . . . by which misery and wretchedness is entailed on the individuals" (34) is equally applicable to any of Radcliffe's abducted heroines. Adeline stands out because she presents so many of the problems associated with poverty: she has no settlement; she cannot afford a tenancy; she may be a bastard; she cannot fend for herself. Adeline is a vagrant, but the agents who harass her are not representatives of institutional authority enforcing statutory management. Rather, the "officers" and "guardians" who pursue her and minister to her do so with strictly personal motivations that literalize the abstract institutional mandates of superintendence. Instead of paternalistic overseers she encounters actual fathers, suitors, and other representatives of literal/familial masculine authority. Those who hinder her or aid her do so from private affective intentions, not in service of regulations or policy.

The removals, relief, and efforts at settlement to which she is subjected are likewise governed by affective and extra-institutional impulses. At no point is she ever "on the parish." At every stage of her adventure, however, her pauper career has ready analogies to official forms of management: her castle confinement resembles a workhouse incarceration; La Luc's gentle supervision is a surrogate for the more benevolent forms of relief imagined by poor-management polemicists of the 1790s. Ambiguous, then malevolent, then sentimental manifestations of family entangle her at every stage, and stand in place of the equivalent mechanisms of state intervention. A romance set in contemporary England would confront the legal and institutional offices of poverty superintendence, but Radcliffe's geographical and historical displacement enables her to construct the fantasy of a poor-management system that depends not on the parochial and juridical systems of *Joseph Andrews* but on home. Adeline is not a vagrant in the statutory sense; she is homeless.

She is also, as women detached from prosperity and legitimacy must be, corruptible and potentially corrupting. Madame La Motte looks fearfully upon her son Louis's interest in Adeline: "She perceived that the beauty of Adeline had already fascinated his imagination, and she feared that her amiable manners would soon impress his heart. Had her first fondness for Adeline continued, she would still have looked with displeasure upon their attachment, as an obstacle to the promotion and the fortune she hoped to see one day enjoyed by her son. On these she rested all her future hopes of prosperity" (72). We see here again the future tension that poor women provoke so readily in onlookers. Often during the course of her adventures Adeline reflects woefully upon what is to come: "She . . . looked forward to the future with the most mournful apprehension. 'Should La Motte be seized, what was to become of her? She would then be a wanderer in the wide world; without friends to protect, or money to support her; the prospect was gloomy—was terrible!'" (58); and later: "The prospect of her future days was involved in darkness and uncertainty. Again she was going to claim the bounty of strangers—again going to encounter the uncertainty of their kindness; exposed to the hardships of dependence, or to the difficulty of earning a precarious livelihood" (173). This apprehensive, and suspenseful, attitude to futurity pervades Radcliffe's fiction, afflicting Adeline throughout and conditioning the reader's experience of the narrative.

More than simply narrative suspense, however, the phrase "mournful apprehension" (cited immediately above) generates a paradox. Adeline mourns that which has not yet come and therefore not yet been lost. This proleptic mourning seems to highlight the position of the poor woman in narrative, and in political economy. She is that which will have been lost. She will have been erased, by elevation to another status, as is the case with Adeline, or by absorption into productivity and the national wealth as the surplus whose use yields increase. Otherwise she will have failed to provide a "point of home where to fix" that can restrain crime and rebellion.[55] Analogous rhetoric appears often in tracts on poverty management. Thomas Bernard laments the "spiritless continuation of daily labour" that has "gradually deprived [the poor] of forecast, and of every effort that looks to futurity" (2: 4), and later he makes use of architectural metaphor: "If man had no hope of elevation . . . the foundations of society would be undermined, and the whole fabric moulder in a shapeless ruin" (3: 6). The poor, by this logic, need the sense of a happy ending to sustain their labors.

Proleptic mourning also alludes softly to one of Radcliffe's favorite sources, *Hamlet*. In her posthumously published preface, "On the Supernatural in Poetry," she defines the play's appeal: "The dark watch upon the remote platform, the dreary aspect of the night, the very expression of the officers on guard, 'The air bites shrewdly; it is very cold'; . . . are all circumstances which excite forlorn, melancholy, and solemn feelings, and dispose us to welcome, with trembling curiosity, the awful being that draws near; and to indulge that strange mixture of horror, pity, and indignation, produced by the tale it reveals" (147–48). Radcliffe rereads *Hamlet* as a kind of detective narrative, the uncertain future unfolded out of that scene by Hamlet's investigation: "Every circumstance of the scene contributes to excite some feeling of . . . expectation, in unison with, and leading on toward that high curiosity and thrilling awe with which we witness the conclusion of the scene" (148). Her whole narrative technique owes something to the ghost's words, "lend thy serious hearing / To what I *shall* unfold" (1197, I.v.5–6, emphasis added).[56] Like Hamlet's ghost, the manuscript that Adeline discovers and reads, unaware that her father was its author, offers to harrow up the soul: "To ye I speak—to ye reveal the story of my wrongs, and ask ye to avenge them . . . it imparts some comfort to believe it possible that what I now write may one day meet the eye of a fellow creature" (128). But Radcliffe's paternal ghost, not his heir, is the procrastinator; he does not know to whom he speaks, nor who his captors are, and he is unable to explain what has become of him.[57] His only specific request is that his reader mourn for him, the very act that Jacques Lacan identifies as uncompleted in *Hamlet*.[58] But here too Radcliffe's ghost procrastinates, countermanding his own request: "Yet stay your tears—your pity is now useless" (128).

Typically for Radcliffe, the heroine's father is both an object of sympathy and an authority who counsels restraint of sentimental excess. In *The Mysteries of Udolpho*, M. St. Aubert—a great weeper himself—warns his daughter: "Beware of priding yourself on the gracefulness of sensibility; if you yield to this vanity, your happiness is lost for ever. Always remember how much more valuable is the strength of fortitude, than the grace of sensibility" (80). The ghostly father's ambivalent advice to his daughter (St. Aubert is in his grave by the beginning of the following chapter) encapsulates the evangelical attitude toward the poor—at once tearful and hortatory. Emily and Adeline must carefully control their surplus sentimental energies, of which they have impressive supplies, and dispense them appropriately. Of course, the same rule applies to their economic bounties, when the young women have passed from paupers to middle-class paragons: "Not to [Adeline and Theodore] themselves was their happiness contracted, but diffused to all who came within the sphere of their influence. The indigent and unhappy rejoiced in their benevolence, the virtuous and enlightened in their friendship, and their children in parents whose example impressed upon their hearts the precepts offered to their understandings" (363). This superintendence of economic and affective abundance is an assertion of discipline over the formal, thematic, and readerly components of romance that seems readily comparable to the reform of romance attempted by Henry Fielding fifty years earlier.[59] It makes up, as I will explain in the final section of this chapter, part of a broadly reiterated self-regulatory schematic that is the most significant point of connection, in Radcliffe's fiction, between her representations of poverty and of home.

Before Adeline achieves her triumphant bourgeoisification in *The Romance of the Forest*, the process of installing her father as a kind of personal ghost imposes heavy psychic strain, on both father and daughter.[60] Her father, in his anonymous manuscript, reports that "this deathlike and perpetual silence—this dismal chamber—the dread of *farther sufferings* have disturbed my fancy" (133, emphasis added). Adeline's dread of what turn out to be *father* sufferings begins to get to her too: "Her fancy, which now wandered in the regions of terror, gradually subdued reason. There was a glass before her upon the table, and she feared to raise her looks towards it, lest some other face than her own should meet her eyes" (134). At a moment like this, I would argue, the overdetermination of Adeline's literary lineage presses close to the surface of the text. Part of the appeal of gothic fiction is its capacity to incorporate such traumatic literalization.[61] A number of times in this book the word *farther* appears to signal the frightful and mournful, yet ambiguous, futurity that hangs over the narrative and, homonymically, its disembodied embodiment in the figure of Adeline's already-lost but yet-to-be-discovered father. When La Motte first encounters Adeline, for instance, "every moment of farther observation heightened [his] surprise" (7); describing her captivity before La Motte took charge of her, Adeline says she "thanked God that he had preserved me this time, and implored his farther protection" (43); and while investigating the abbey, just moments before she discovers the manuscript, we find her "desirous . . . of examining farther" (116). In the final section of this chapter, I will analyze another persistent strain of suggestive phrasing that runs through this novel, intensifying its connections to the poverty debates.

## REMOVAL, RELIEF, SETTLEMENT

Adeline's moment of unwillingness to look in a mirror, "lest some other face than her own should meet her eyes," is another example of Radcliffe's favored technique of playing out sociopolitical problems in the registers of affect; we are not strongly encouraged to imagine that Adeline is actually the bastard of paupers, but at moments like this her uncertainty lets the possibility occur, as it were, in her own imagination. What a Radcliffe heroine feels and how her feelings generate bodily symptoms are often points of engagement with the political that evade the disavowal barring politics from the text's manifest content. For Adeline, the political is personal. In this section, I will argue that her connection to the poor-law debates is developed through Radcliffe's prominent use of words that are also key terms for the poor-law pamphleteers: *remove, relieve,* and, to a lesser extent, *settle.*

The opening chapter of the novel features both removals and relief. The La Mottes are fleeing Paris, "and such had been the precipitancy of this removal" that they have no time to inform their son (2). Soon after, Monsieur La Motte seeks shelter at a lonely cottage, but finds banditti there who demand that he depart and take Adeline with him; Adeline embraces the idea: "'Ah, Sir,' said she, 'Heaven has sent you to my relief'" (7). Within three chapters, the narrator is asking us to recollect "when [Adeline and the La Mottes] had settled at the abbey" (53). The only significant difference between Radcliffe's usage of the terms and their usage in the discourse of poverty management is that here they appear in the guise of private rather than institutional action.

Indeed, they are pointedly extralegal versions of statutory processes, which would seem to reflect the (more conceptual than actual) trend in poverty management away from direct bureaucratic and judicial enforcement and toward private care and domestic self-management. When we reach the conclusion of this novel by means of a pair of interlinked court cases that reassert authoritative property, lineage, and rule of law, we see an imaginative enshrining of home and private relief within what sounds a lot like Edmund Burke's beloved British constitution.[62]

Forms of the word *remove* occur, by my count, fifty times in *The Romance of the Forest.* The various forms of *relieve* appear a little over fifty times. By comparison, *Joseph Andrews,* a novel of similar length and with unambiguous interest in the terminology of poverty management, features *remove* in one form or another ten times, and *relieve* or *relief* just over twenty times.[63] Around half of Radcliffe's uses of *remove* refer to an involuntary relocation. On a number of occasions, we hear protests that either Adeline or Theodore is too ill to be moved: "A physician . . . pronounced her to be in a high fever, and said, a removal in her present state must be fatal" (12); "this gentleman [Theodore] cannot be removed in his present condition, without endangering his life" (177). Like Lady Booby, the Marquis invokes his authority in arbitrary fashion against the person who interferes with his desires, by sending Theodore to his regiment: "It was in consequence of having formerly observed the growing partiality between him and Adeline . . . that the Marquis had resolved to remove a rival so dangerous to his love" (200). After Adeline escapes the clutches of the Marquis, we find benevolent forms of removal: "'By all means have her [Adeline] removed hither,' said La Luc, whose eyes bore testimony to the tenderness of his heart. 'She can be better attended here than in Susan's cottage'" (257).

The good La Luc, who turns out to be Theodore's father, and by marital extension Adeline's, takes over the superintendence of Adeline after she has fled from the Marquis (with La Motte's guilt-stricken collusion). La Luc is a kindly clergyman in Savoy, modeled on the *vicaire savoyard* of Rousseau's *Emile.* Adeline becomes his charge in a revision of the novel's opening scene, where La Motte takes responsibility for her (La Luc's family finds her, "in a very small, close room, on a miserable bed . . . pale, emaciated, and unconscious of all around her" [256]). Having rescued Adeline after she escapes the poorhouse-like asylum in which La Motte had installed her, La Luc provides a regime of outdoor relief under which she recovers rapidly and flourishes. As chief officer of his parish, he does his best even though he cannot call on the assistance of the British constitution: the village is "an exception to the general character of the country, and to the usual effects of an arbitrary government . . . and these advantages it chiefly owed to the activity and attention of the benevolent clergyman whose cure it was" (240). He is apparently also a combination of squire and overseer: "His income from the parish was small, and what remained from the divided and reduced estates of his ancestors did not much increase it; but though he could not always relieve the necessities of the indigent, his tender pity and holy conversation seldom failed in administering consolation to the mental sufferer" (246). Radcliffe participates here in the nostalgic, but simultaneously transitional, view of the parish expressed elsewhere by Robert Southey: "A parish where the minister and the parochial officers did their duties with activity and zeal, might be almost as well ordered as a private family" (qtd. in Pounds 499). Both Radcliffe and Southey reflect, and promote, the absorption of social and affective bonds previously associated with the parish into those of family and home.[64]

A series of paternal figures struggle over Adeline's supervision, removing her either into their clutches, or out of their way. The Marquis and La Motte even collude in inventing a bogeyman version of her father who will steal her away if she is not obedient. The negotiations of those two men, which are frequently termed transactions, have the aspect of overseers contracting to farm out their charges to private manufacturers. Adeline's history of her upbringing (35ff.) and the subsequent *eclaircissement* of her childhood (332ff.) sound like a story of fostering or forced apprenticeship. In general, Radcliffe's consistent focus on the unjust and exploitive treatment that Adeline endures accords with laments offered on behalf of the poor in the period. Adeline's removal into the care of La Luc abolishes and makes amends for the corrupted forms of management that she has endured up to that point.

While Adeline is under La Luc's care, and at a few other points in the novel, *relieve* is used in a sense directly equivalent to that of poverty management—although like *remove*, it lacks an institutional or legal imprimatur. The majority of its more than fifty usages in the novel, however, make a metaphor of the term. It refers, as most modern usage of the word does, to the release of an uncomfortable blockage of affect: "Her mind being relieved . . . she became tolerably cheerful" (58). Within this metaphorical meaning, there is a further division: at some points the word has a kind of narratological sense; at other points it refers to bodily affective symptoms. The first of these two senses occurs when suspense is relieved: when an unknown visitor to the abbey turns out to be Louis La Motte, his father exclaims, "Your presence revived me, and

I was relieved at the same time from a load of apprehensions" (81); in order to justify a bout of eavesdropping, "Adeline remembered the hints of Theodore, and determined, if possible, to be relieved from the terrible suspense she now suffered" (117); and when Louis brings news concerning Theodore's death sentence, "Theodore and Clara with one voice called on Louis to relieve them from the tortures of suspense" (329). The second sense in which *relieve* is used refers to a bodily symptom alleviating (invariably a woman's, almost invariably Adeline's) emotional suffering: "She retired to her chamber, where . . . her oppressed heart found relief from tears" (112); "At length a deep sigh somewhat relieved her oppressed spirits, and her senses seemed to return" (134); "Her tears had somewhat relieved the anguish of her mind, and she again reposed in placid melancholy" (295).[65]

The narratological sense of *relieve* evokes Radcliffe's interpretation of *Hamlet*. The characters' repeated feelings of suspense followed by relief enact the experience that Radcliffe ascribes to her readers, and which also models the self-discipline required to contain surplus and unruly energies. The other feminine-affective usage of *relieve* seems characteristic of gothic fiction in its literalization of language that is usually metaphorical. Radcliffe's diction is that of hydraulics; she operates Adeline, and the narrative, like a construction of bladders, conduits, and valves that rise and fall, close and open.[66] Radcliffe's system allows blocked affect to be mitigated by transformation into bodily symptom and literal expulsion. Its effect is the dissipation of chaotic energies and unslaked passions so that no dangerous or unpredictable consequences follow. Adeline's affective blocking and unblocking implies that she has a capacity for self-relief. As a poor woman, her means of sustaining herself is to hoard her energies, unleashing their excesses in carefully controlled outbursts—most often out of sight of witnesses, unless the outburst is offered in exchange for benevolence: "La Luc rejoiced to see her weep, encouraged her tears, which, after some time, relieved her" (304). She exemplifies something very like the shepherding of energies that Malthus encourages in the poor. Stifled affect, like surplus labor, is a valuable excess, an unused resource that may be diverted to improper purposes; La Luc's daughter Clara, for instance, receives the gift of a lute from her father, "with more gratitude than she could express," and she "played it again and again till she forgot every thing besides. Her little domestic duties, her books, her drawing, even the hour which her father dedicated to her improvement . . . passed unheeded by" (249). What cures Clara of her folly is the realization that she has forgotten her accustomed duty of providing relief to a local pauper family: "'No food to-day!' said she to herself, 'and I have been playing all day on my lute, under the acacias by the lake!'" (250). With an instinctive capacity to control her eruptions, Adeline provides the model of a poor woman whose self-command, maintenance of energy, and safe disposal of uncontainable excess might be a guide to the laboring classes (and their patrons) in general.

*Settle* is a less common term in this novel. It occurs seventeen times and only three times to mean taking up residence: the first I have mentioned above and the succeeding two come in the denouement, when La Motte leaves "for England, where it was his design to settle" (354) and when his son "resigning his commission . . . settled on the borders of the lake" where Adeline and Theodore have made their home (363). Nonetheless, the progress of this narrative can be glossed as a series of removals, interspersed with provisions of relief that are never quite adequate until the conclusion when affairs are finally settled (354 and 356) and the virtuous settle down. The narrative business that enables these settlements substantially concerns the legal confirmation of Adeline's parentage and estate—the same basic question considered by justices hearing a settlement case at any parish quarter session in England. The fundamental lacunae of the novel have been the identity of Adeline's father and whether he left her mother with child, unmarried, in unfamiliar surroundings—who is *responsible* for her?

That Adeline is passed from father figure to father figure (in the conclusion, some "farther settlement" of her affairs delays her departure from Paris [356]) without encountering anyone who might be her actual mother suggests the avoidance of the one person who, in English law, could fix the identity of a child's father by force of her word alone: "No further evidence of fatherhood than the woman's oath was required for the issue of a warrant against the putative father" (Webb and Webb, *English Poor Law* 309).[67] A single-sheet engraving published in 1790 decries this law. It depicts a woman appearing before "Justice Juggle" to accuse "Toney" of impregnating her. Toney stands behind her, twisted and palsied, pigeon-toed, his arms and shoulders hunched, and his left eye closed. To her accusation he replies:

> And please ye Sir, I never knew
> This woman, any more than you!
> There's Tom, & Bob, & many more,
> Our parson too, knows she's a WHORE,
> Nor could I, was I paid to try,
> Deprive her of her Chastity

Half form'd by nature here I stand
Bereft the use of foot and hand.
Deficient I can't fill the station
That is design'd for propagation.

But the justice rules,

All you can say Toney is merely a farce
The law is as clear as your nose in my ——
Her Oath, not your word ipso facto must pass.
You must marry her Sir! or do this at least
Be confin'd in a Joal [*sic*], or pay well for a feast.[68]

This law would seem to help account for the preponderance of dead and missing mothers in Radcliffe's fiction and in that of many of her contemporaries.[69]

Because the mother can, by force of declaration, clear up the mystery that drives Radcliffe's master plot, she must be excluded from the narrative. Her absence is necessary to the novel's central mystery.[70] Yet what she could declare would establish not her own identity, but the father's. The very enunciation whose nonenunciation makes the mother central would erase her.[71] In an important sense, the heroine's mother cannot be fully present. In Radcliffean romance, the trace of the mother comes usually in the form of a resemblance between the heroine and a miniature portrait or some other character's lost beloved. The mother's only identity is her face, and our heroine has that written all over her face.

Even without her mother's help, Adeline discovers her father's identity and so finds a settlement. In an instant, "from an orphan, subsisting on the bounty of others, without family, with few friends, and pursued by a cruel and powerful enemy, she saw herself suddenly transformed to the daughter of an illustrious house, and the heiress of immense wealth" (346). She then undertakes a further transformation, making herself into something like a middle-class wife "to whom the splendid gaieties that courted [Theodore and Adeline] at Paris were very inferior temptations to the sweet domestic pleasures and refined society which Leloncourt would afford" (358).[72] And if "middle-class wife" is an anachronism in 1791 (not to mention in seventeenth-century Savoy), we can certainly say that Adeline becomes the "point of home where to fix": "not to [Adeline and Theodore] themselves was their happiness contracted, but diffused to all who came within the sphere of their influence"

(363). Her uncertain future—the risk to which she exposed herself—has been redeemed for the certain and stable value of the bourgeois marriage contract. The wasteful expenditure of aristocratic paternalism has been disciplined, and the surplus energies of the poor have been capitalized: as the celebration of the return home winds down, La Luc surveys "the scene—his children and people thus assembled around him in one grand compact of harmony and joy," after which "every cottager returned to his home" (362) without the least hint of trouble, treasuring up Adeline's lesson on resourceful self-management.

Radcliffe's convergent endings typify a growing imperative in English fiction where the conclusion of a marriage plot, which is to say the marriage, seems less momentous than the establishment of a home. The rhetoric of closure in late eighteenth- and early nineteenth-century fiction tends to dwell more on the glory of domesticity than on the pleasure of the connubial moment. Radcliffe's two major novels after *The Romance of the Forest* share with it conclusions that celebrate joyous homecoming and homemaking. The homes are particularly notable for their contracts, offering social security in exchange for self-discipline, forged with the local laboring poor. In *Udolpho*, "their present felicity . . . [Emily and Valancourt] solemnly vowed to deserve . . . by endeavouring to imitate [St. Aubert's] benevolence,—by remembering, that superior attainments of every sort bring with them duties of superior exertion,—and by affording to their fellow-beings, together with that portion of ordinary comforts, which prosperity always owes to misfortune, the example of lives passed in happy thankfulness to God" (671). In *The Italian,* the concluding party "was not given to persons of distinction only, for both Vivaldi and Ellena had wished that all the tenants of the domain should partake of it, and share the abundant happiness which themselves possessed" (412). Thomas Gisborne's *Duties of the Female Sex* codifies the Radcliffean resolution: "Home is the center round which the influence of every married woman is principally accumulated . . . the place where she will possess peculiar means of doing good among the humbler classes of society . . . Her habitual insight in to local events and local necessities, her acquaintance with the characters and the situations of individuals, enable her to adapt the relief which she affords to the merit and to the distress of the person assisted" (289–90). The vision of traditionary, obligatory paternalism that we found in Fielding has transformed into one of contractual, locally contingent maternalism.[73]

After the popular success of *The Romance of the Forest*, Radcliffe's growing embrace of home and assurance of its cultural significance is exemplified by her choice of epigraph for the first chapter of *The Mysteries of Udolpho* from Thomson's *The Seasons:*

> home is the resort
> Of love, of joy, of peace and plenty, where,
> Supporting and supported, polish'd friends
> And dear relations mingle into bliss. (1)

Unlike Adeline's, Emily's end is in her beginning, though for most of the interval between beginning and end, Emily's home is as lost to her as was Adeline's. Home becomes a marker of closure and partakes of the paradoxes attendant upon endings. Both home and narrative closure are destinations, points of completion, cessation, and renunciation: in her *Journey Made in the Summer of 1794,* Radcliffe praises home's "coveted stillness, in which the active find an occasional reward, and the idle a perpetual misery" (101).[74] But home and the closure of a marriage plot are also both sites at which renewal, growth, and continuity begin—only, however, in the aftermath of narrative (the ever after). In the founding of a home an economy of loss and stasis merges with an economy of circulation and expansion. Home is both stationary and dynamic. It is the reward of labor and the ledger of prosperity, but at the same time definitively separate from the marketplace and never overtly subject to the mediations of commodity value. It is the embodiment of good civil order and social discipline, but untouched by any instruments of the state or the public sphere.

Home is, finally, unrepresentable; it lies beyond the reach of narrative. Mary Brunton's 1811 novel *Self-Control,* a Scottish rewriting of both *Pamela* and *Clarissa* redacted through Radcliffean romance and North American captivity narrative, concludes that "the tranquil current of domestic happiness affords no materials for narrative. The joys that spring from chastened affection, tempered desires, useful employment, and devout meditation, must be felt—they cannot be described" (2: 467). The home life actually depicted in domestic fiction is provisional, an uneasy and turbulent arena that requires the normative force of the marital resolution to restore its proper sanctity. Narrative itself is always disruptive of the post-desiring Elysium of the ideal and ideologically replete home.[75] The mysteries of Udolpho may yield to narratorial elucidation, but those of home do not. Of course, domestic novels do conduct us into home lives, but those domestic scenes do not sustain the perfect compact of harmonious community, consummated aspiration, and radiant stillness that defines the home figure in its conceptual plenitude; they tend toward it, but its restoration comes after narration. The platitude "there's no place like home" captures this paradox in its equivocation: no figuration, representation, or comparison is adequate to home. As I noted in my introduction, home has the conceptual structure of the repressive hypothesis; it is both the cabinet that conceals a secret truth, and the secret itself.

In the cultural imaginary, every home is homologous to every other home, but also entirely singular and personal. It is a place of return and the reward of social duty but simultaneously fulfills nothing more than personal desire; depends on no statutory authority; and, like romance (according to eighteenth-century estimates), lacks authorized formal structure. As with Radcliffe's suspense narratology, we are encouraged to ignore the regular and formulaic conditions that have shaped our home and respond as though we could not have anticipated such a miracle, have never seen anything like it before. Every home is founded as though it were the first of its kind. The architectural theorist Robert Morris, for instance, relates his sense that cottages are constructed "as if the inhabitants had newly started into being, and were led by Nature and Necessity, to form a fabric" (qtd. in Crowley 177). Home offers a compelling and coercive fantasy of radical contingency combined with perfect naturalness. The inventors of the middle-class private home create a social figuration that is able to devour its own and other histories with astonishing rapacity. Not many comparable cultural objects or norms have been anything like as successful and as obstinate.

For a final token that Radcliffe's decade is decisive in the history of home, I will cite Margaret Cullen's little-known but emphatically titled *Home—A Novel*. A five-decker published in 1802, it tells an unremarkable tale of domestic virtue triumphant and love rewarded. It is noteworthy, I think, only for its title, and for the character of Mrs. Almorne, a magisterial champion of private domesticity who delivers a eulogy to home in the final pages: "The precedent of a few upright characters acting on such principles, will soon be followed by others, who are at present deterred from it merely through fear,— and thus the improper influence of consanguinity may gradually diminish, till it shall at length be destroyed . . . and Home, instead of being a prison in which the Virtuous are condemned to associate with the Vicious, will become a secure refuge from the wicked, and the most delightful asylum of Man" (5: 363). Home is, in this speech, extending its reach to incorporate and transform the unbounded domesticities and the undomestic subsistent lives of the eighteenth century into a self-sustaining, autotelic sanctum. Oppressive systems of patriarchal kinship give way to companionate and consensual kindred bonds. And the home expands from its conception in the principles of an upright few to realization as a universal haven. As soon as this all-nurturing asylum achieves hegemonic sway over the English cultural imagination, however, it vanishes. The most delightful asylum of Man is the "elfin grot" of "La Belle Dame sans Merci": its discovery is its loss and the nation that has triumphantly claimed it is doomed to wander forever after in a quest to rediscover and reclaim it.

# 3

# Home and Away

## Hegemony and Naturalization

If the heads of the Durbeyfield household chose to sail into difficulty, disaster, starvation, disease, degradation, death, thither were these half-dozen little captives under hatches compelled to sail with them—six helpless creatures, who had never been asked if they wished for life on any terms, much less if they wished for it on such hard conditions as were involved in being of the shiftless house of Durbeyfield. Some people would like to know whence the poet whose philosophy is in these days deemed as profound and trustworthy as his song is breezy and pure, gets his authority for speaking of "Nature's holy plan."

—Thomas Hardy, *Tess of the d'Urbervilles*

Something curious begins to happen in early nineteenth-century depictions of private domesticity. In the last decade of the eighteenth century, novelists, and others, had celebrated home as an enclosed, self-sustaining refuge, unchanging and impervious to the foreign. But homes in early nineteenth-century fiction take on a less idyllic aspect. Writers start to condemn them as enclosed, self-sustaining refuges, unchanging and impervious to the foreign. Home becomes boring and suffocating. At both the private and national levels, its profound inwardness feels more and more claustrophobic and solipsistic rather than safe and nurturing. In the 1790s, Robert Southey chose an epigraph from Hesiod's *Works and Days* for his "Hymn to the Penates": "That which is in the HOUSE is better since what is outside is damaging" (*Poetical Works* 5: 485 n. 3). Ann Radcliffe offers this reflection in her *Journey Made in the Summer of 1794*: "An Englishman . . . cannot help considering the natural security of his country, and rejoicing, that, even if the strong and plain policy of neglecting all foreign consequences, and avoiding all foreign interests . . . except the commercial ones, which may be maintained by a navy, should for ever be rejected, still his home cannot be invaded; and, though the expence of wars should make poverty general, the immediate horrors of them cannot enter the cities, or the cottages of an island" (187).[1] The Englishwoman's home prior to the turn of the century is a bulwark of self-fortification and her homeland provides sturdier ramparts still, though the whole retains the appearance of a warm, embowered cottage.[2]

The priest, poet, and Clapham Sect abolitionist Thomas Gisborne, in his 1797 *Enquiry into the Duties of the Female Sex,* warns that

> facility of access and intercourse expose women ... to the danger of acquiring a habit of continual visiting, and the other habits which St. Paul justly ascribes to those who have contracted the former. "They learn to be idle, wandering about from house to house ..." Domestic business is interrupted; vigilance as to family concerns is suspended; industry, reflection, mental and religious improvement are deserted and forgotten. The mind grows listless; home becomes dull; the carriage is ordered afresh; and a remedy for the evil is sought from the very cause which produced it. (285–86)

Gisborne exhorts women to follow St. Paul's admonition to be "keepers at home" (283), where domestic employments will guard against idleness and the temptation to become "tatlers also and busy-bodies, speaking things which they ought not" (286). His admonitions sound very like the kind of rhetoric that had been applied to paupers wandering between parishes earlier in the century. But a year earlier, Edmund Burke had already begun to chafe against the turn inward: "If we look to nothing but our domestick condition, the state of the nation is full even to plethory; but if we imagine that this country can long maintain it's blood and it's food, as disjoined from the community of mankind, such an opinion does not deserve refutation as absurd, but pity as insane" ("Regicide Peace" 195). Passages like that one appear to renounce a mood for which Burke had advocated in the *Reflections:* "Whenever our neighbour's house is on fire, it cannot be amiss for the engines to play a little on our own. Better to be despised for too anxious apprehensions than ruined by too confident a security" (92). Homeland security has, for Burke, shaded into paranoid excess.[3]

The turn against hermetic domestic regimes does not occur in a wholesale historical shift or a discrete historical moment. Indeed, what I am characterizing as a change of cultural attitude toward inwardly focused conceptions of home is not necessarily historically subsequent to what I described in the previous chapter as the emergence of the middle-class home. The two developments occur in parallel and without stably distinguishable beginning or end points or causal patterns. Both begin with a fundamental revision of relationships between private and public, and while the turn inward is a more evident drive in the early emergence of middle-class domesticity, the turn outward is crucial to the cultural shape and dimensions of home in its hegemonic form. I will argue in chapter 4 that Walter Scott's *Old Mortality* retells a tale of the emergence of modern domesticity that suggests a similar double development. That novel traces a domestic revolution produced by two opposing historical forces, which assault older forms of domesticity from antithetical positions: a statist perspective that mistrusts the insurgent secrecy of private households, and a rebel perspective that associates households with laws restricting the freedom of personal conscience.

Maria Edgeworth's 1809 *Ennui* concerns the stagnating effects of an unvarying domestic life. Her overleisured Earl of Glenthorn is literally sick of domesticity: "My home was disagreeable to me" (167), and, "unless roused by external stimulus, I sank into that kind of apathy, and vacancy of ideas, vulgarly known by the name of *a brown study*" (144). Where Thomas Gisborne a decade before had argued that "occupations which may prevent the languour and the snares of idleness, render home attractive, refresh the wearied faculties, and contribute to preserve the mind in a state of placid cheerfulness" (80), Edgeworth suggests the very opposite. The Earl's surfeit of introspection poisons the whole nation for him: "I was tired of England, and wanted to see something new, even if it were to be worse than what I had seen before" (169).[4] The solution to his problem involves leaving home (both private and nation), giving up his estate and fortune, going to law and to Ireland where he atones for his absenteeist landlording: "When I saw . . . the neat cottages, the well-cultivated farms, the air of comfort, industry, and prosperity, diffused through the lower class of people, I was convinced that much may be done by the judicious care and assistance of landlords" (307). Diligent labor sets him free from his boredom: "Occupation and hope, and the constant sense of approaching nearer to my object, rendered this mode of existence, dull as it may seem, infinitely more agreeable than many of my more prosperous days" (305). A consistent turning outward, venturing beyond the limits of his own home restores the Earl and his appetite for the pleasures of home: "Fortunately my marriage has obliged me to continue my exertions, and the labours of my profession have made the pleasures of domestic life most delightful" (321). I think it is hardly surprising that the growing prominence of cultural productions from and about the British peripheries should complicate literary representation of the home-nation complex and that national tales should be preoccupied by the relationship of private domesticity to nationality.[5]

More than one of Jane Austen's characters becomes acquainted with the oppressiveness and predictability of a confined home life. Catherine Morland's visit to Bath reveals to her that "I, who live in a small retired village in the country, can never find greater sameness in such a place as this, than in my own home" (*Northanger Abbey* 76). "Here," Henry Tilney scolds her, "you are in pursuit only of amusement all day long"; "and so I am at home," she replies, "only I do not find so much of it" (76). When she does return home, her dejection is such that her mother's homespun wisdom, "Wherever you are you should always be contented, but especially at home, because there you must spend the most of your time," provokes a blunt dismissal: "It is all the same to me" (225). Catherine is a victim of the corrupting effects of exposure to society and refinements beyond her native circle, and in that respect her restlessness resonates with the idea that the laborer's cottage, and the little parochial world surrounding it, provides a sphere in which social aspirations are limited by epistemic boundaries. What the poor don't know about, they will not covet.[6] But here and elsewhere Austen shows little patience for the ideal of home as epistemic limit, especially as it limits young, leisured women.[7]

Her endings, which famously treat declarations of love and celebrations of marriage with disdain, suggest that her narrators are bored with the business of closure and home-making and see it as hardly more than a fee levied against all the pleasures of the marriage plot.[8] This studied disinterest, or even disavowal, forms a part of what Mary Poovey calls "Austen's gestural aesthetic," where her narrator "gestures towards extratextual events but so carefully manages these allusions that the reader is invited back into the text instead of encouraged to go outside its pages" (*Genres* 363). Domestic fiction can bring us to the threshold of the private home, but it cannot provide actual entry. Such a reading accords with my argument that the enclosed realm of domesticity has acquired a sense of solipsism in the early nineteenth century. Indeed, the gesture of disavowal becomes something of a ritual in novel narrative through the nineteenth century: "The hand that traces these words, falters, as it approaches the conclusion of its task" (Dickens 453). Austen's narratorial disinterest in the business of endings generates an ironic solipsism analogous to, but distinct from, the solipsism she, along with many other writers, appears to associate with home.

A comparable reaction against closed and introverted systems was taking place in political economy too, led by theories envisioning the danger of stagnation, particularly those of Thomas Malthus.[9] Malthus believed that his theory of population proved "that a period of stagnation must finally arrive in every country from the difficulty of procuring subsistence" (*Principles* 1: 448). But he argued further that "an indisposition to consume in large quantities the goods produced at home, and a want of the means of barter may occasion . . . a similar stagnation at a very early period of a nation's progress" (1: 448).[10] His insistence on the need for continual provocation and refreshment of consumer desire—a prototypical demand theory of value—leads to a call for opening of markets: "No country with a very confined market, internal as well as external, has ever been able to accumulate a large capital, because such a market prevents the formation of those wants and tastes, and that desire to consume, which are absolutely necessary to keep up the market prices of commodities, and to occasion an increasing demand for them, and for the capital which is to produce them" (1: 448). Life in general, and economic circuits as the collective expression of life in modernity, must always be stimulated by external forces (scarcity or novelty) or they threaten to become decayed and depraved. Malthus also finds fault with the self-sufficiency model of the private home, where, aside from indolence, the other great threat to vigorous demand is consumers' disposition not to consume but "to save with a view of bettering their condition, and providing for their families in future" (1: 363). As a consequence, the consumer will "be satisfied with more simple clothing, but by this economy he would disable the manufacturer from purchasing the same amount of his produce" (1: 363).

Malthusian theory, along with the reinvigoration of laissez faire doctrine after the protectionist era of the French Revolution, revived Adam Smith's dictum that external trade may compensate for an imbalance of "produce and consumption" that would lead to the "annual decay" of the capital of "a nation which had no foreign trade, but which was entirely separated from all the world" (Smith, *Wealth of Nations* 439). Political economists saw a need to open the home nation again to the salutary currents of foreign trade, reanimating a home-trade that seemed in danger of stagnation and morbidity: "Unless consumption increases exogenously (either through stimulated desires for luxurious expenditure or increased foreign trade), then general gluts are not only possible but inevitable" (Kreisel, *Economic Woman* 34).[11] Along with letting the world back in, some writers proposed anticipating Malthusian population patterns and sending the poor out; among them was the economist, M.P., and retired Colonel Robert Torrens: "We should avail ourselves of the resources placed in our hands by the vast extent of unappropriated colonial territory ... The hive contains more than it can support; and if it be not permitted to swarm, the excess must either perish of famine, or be destroyed by internal contests for food" (qtd. in Snell 112). Malthus himself would later support that plan before a parliamentary committee (Snell 112).

This chapter will defend the argument that, by the end of the Napoleonic era, if not before, the middle-class private home, and the national domesticity that it helps to organize, are sufficiently established in British cultural life to be already objects of nostalgia. As soon as the figure of home starts to acquire the vestments of naturalness and universality that settle over fully developed ideological formations, its actual manifestations begin to seem inadequate or corrupted. Less and less an uncomplicated solution for social problems, home becomes a problem itself—a site at which the social order has fractured. Because it has presented itself as the means of restoring social cohesion, home comes to need repairs itself. The "attempt to construct ideological closure" that Jacob Torfing identifies in disciplinary cultural figures like home necessarily fails "to constitute a fully sutured space of representation" (118). Home has become a hegemonic object, "a discursive formation that provides a surface of inscription for a wide range of demands, views and attitudes" (Torfing 101), rather than something that is itself inscribed upon existing social surfaces. Percy Bysshe Shelley, for instance, scrawls a figural graffito on the figural wall of the national home: "All things have a home but one— / Thou, Oh, Englishman, hast none" ("Mask of Anarchy," *Major Works* 406, lines 203–4). His demand is not simply, and literally, for provision of sustenance and shelter; he conflates the absence of home with betrayals of social justice and liberty, the loss of hope and prosperity, and the fragmentation of English social bonds. His lament that there is no home confirms that home has a hegemonic hold on the cultural imagination. No longer a topic, home has become a topos—not an object of representation any more, but a mediating surface for representation. And because home vanishes from the field of representation, it becomes an object only recognizable in forms structured by absence, fragmentation, or distortion. The national tale straddles this same representational horizon. Its relationship to nationality is necessarily nostalgic, or at least backward-looking: the nations celebrated and mourned in national tales are not nations in the full sense anymore. They are lost origins, swallowed up by the home-figure that valorizes Englishness precisely by disappearing it, making it immanent.[12] From this point forward, evocations of home in British culture tend to focus on the need to rescue or restore its perpetually betrayed or threatened ideal.

As the logic of this transition predicts, evangelical zeal for home-providing solutions to indigent poverty faded rapidly after the 1790s. As early as 1800, the *Commercial and Agricultural Magazine* was reacting forcefully against the popular figure of the self-sufficient cottager: "A wicked, cross-grained, petty farmer is like the sow in his yard, almost an insulated individual, who has no communication with, and therefore, no reverence for the opinion of the world" (qtd. in E. P. Thompson 219). An 1818 polemic by the Earl of Sheffield disparaged out-relief and called for a reinvigorated workhouse system: "In general it would be better to receive the children which the parents say they cannot maintain, into a well-regulated workhouse; but if the habits and character of the parents are dissolute and immoral, it is particularly advisable to receive all their children, when they apply for relief, to separate them from depravity and bad habits" (126). In the 1820s, Charles Lamb attacked the "popular fallacy" that "home is home though it is never so homely": "the home of the very poor is no home!" (74). The poor cannot, after all, be trusted to shepherd their own resources and manage their own interests.

Home is no longer a policy instrument sponsored by limited political interests aiming to accomplish discrete political goals. It is now a privileged term evoked from virtually every political perspective. Anna Clark, from extensive analysis, finds that British radical politics in the early nineteenth century move "to unite the working class, by adopting a notion of domesticity, demanding access to the public sphere for working men and protection in the private realm for their women" (177). Anti-Jacobins like Edmund Burke and Arthur Young had, of course, been defending the home from the depredations of radicals and republicans since the beginning of the 1790s. Meanwhile, opposing sides in the slavery/abolition debate both adopt "the rhetoric of the interdependence of domestic and colonial interests" for their opposing purposes (Trumpener, *Bardic Nationalism* 164). No political interest can afford to leave home out of its doctrinal toolbox any more than it can neglect the appeal to Nature.

Home's early advocates have had their hegemonic moment.[13] I do not mean to imply that the triumph of home also marks the achievement of middle-class ascendancy. I am arguing that this particular cultural development is an example of what Antonio Gramsci calls "hegemonic activity even before the rise to power" (59). This is the period in which home (considered in light of the Foucauldian *dispositif*) enters into "strategic elaboration" and "a re-adjustment or re-working of the heterogeneous elements that surface at various points" (*Power/Knowledge* 195). The partnership between private home and national home is now a full-fledged figure for the body politic, a new Leviathan. The home's two bodies (private and national) displace the king's two bodies (natural and politic).[14] In this chapter, I will marshal a range of literary evidence for these ongoing transformations in the concept of home and their ongoing transformation of the nation. I will examine John Galt's story "The Buried Alive" as an effort to revivify gothic fiction after the Radcliffean gothic had fallen victim to the turn against solipsism. Then I will turn to William Wordsworth's protean figurations of home, especially in his Salisbury Plain poems, where home and the gothic castle of Stonehenge animate and confound one another. The homely and *unheimlich* ruin of Stonehenge recurs in Frances Burney's *The Wanderer*, and I will complete this chapter by returning there and observing her construction of a conceptual network from this oracular navel outward to all the homes of England.

## A Fine and Private Place

At pretty much the same time that we see a literary turn against the kind of home imagined in Ann Radcliffe's novels, we also see a literary-critical reaction against the Radcliffean gothic. The common terminology and rhetoric of these two reactions suggests that they are actually parts of a single reaction. Figures of solipsism and boredom litter critical dialogues on Radcliffe and the gothic, as they do expressions of disaffection with domesticity: "[Readers] admire one novel because it puts them in mind of another," complains an anonymous critic in *The Artist* in 1807; "By them it is required that a novel should be like a novel" (qtd. in J. T. Taylor 48). Reviewers grow more and more inclined to see in the labyrinthine Radcliffean plot what John Dunlop calls "passages that lead to nothing" (3: 387). Ghosts, banditti, and blood-stained scrolls lose their capacity to surprise: "The public soon, like Macbeth, becomes satiated with horrors, and indifferent to the strongest *stimuli* of that kind" (W. Scott, "Prefatory Memoir to Mrs. Ann Radcliffe" 120). Imagining Radcliffe's narratives as mechanisms, Scott pictures them with "springs which lie open indeed to the first touch, but which are peculiarly liable to be worn out by repeated pressure" (ibid.). Henry Tilney teases Catherine Morland with the prospect of a midnight adventure in the recesses of Northanger where she may discover "a dagger . . . a few drops of blood, and . . . the remains of some instrument of torture," but nothing "very remarkable" or "out of the common way" (Austen, *Northanger* 151). Sheer repetition makes even the most exciting (or comfortable) experience wearisome.

The narrowly circumscribed territory of novel narrative can enervate and deanimate its reading subject just as his home does to Edgeworth's Glenthorn. Edgeworth herself, in *Letters for Literary Ladies*, ventriloquizes this kind of lament: "I have heard that if these sublime geniusses [novel readers] are wakened from their reveries by the *appulse* of external circumstances, they start and exhibit all the perturbation and amazement of *cataleptic* patients" (37–38). Edgeworth would later receive credit, from Matthew Lewis's first biographer, Margaret Baron-Wilson, for helping Walter Scott to kill off tales of horror: "The novels of the 'wizard of the north,' following, as they did, the . . . productions of Miss Edgworth [*sic*], happily annihilated the class of works among which that of Lewis was so prominent . . . the monstrous and supernatural in fiction—having done their worst—were quietly consigned to the graves from which they might be said to have originally sprung" (qtd. in Robertson 32–33). Gothic novels can turn even skeptical readers into subjects fit only for the dissection table: "Attention flags," wails an anonymous reviewer of Eliza Parsons's *The Mysterious Warning*, "the mind experiences a kind of disappointment, loses the connections, proceeds languidly, and is not easily reanimated" (474); "We cannot think the wit of a brother critic far fetched," agrees a likewise anonymous reviewer of Matthew Lewis's *Bravo of Venice*, "when he compared that shelf in his library, on which the Tales of Wonder, The Venetian Bravo, and other similar productions were piled, to a galvanic battery" (255).[15] These novels reduce their readers to nothing more than organism, mechanism, or even undead matter sustained only by the novels themselves.

Confronted by these funeral orations and postmortem examinations, practitioners of gothic fiction in the early part of the nineteenth century take up the trope of reanimation and use it to resurrect the moribund genre. *Frankenstein* is the most famous example, but not Mary Shelley's only one; she also wrote a story titled "Roger Dodsworth, the Reanimated Englishman," whose narrator exclaims wistfully, "A novel idea is worth much in the commonplace routine of life, but a new fact, an astonishment, a miracle, a palpable wandering from the course of things into apparent impossibilities, is a circumstance to which the imagination must cling with delight" (43–44). Another galvanic narrative was published by the innovative Scottish novelist John Galt in *Blackwood's Magazine* for October 1821. Titled "The Buried Alive," it sheds light on rhetorical and cultural parallels in the historical developments of gothic narrative and middle-class domesticity.

Galt's tale is a very short piece, hardly three pages long, which relates in the first person an episode of catatonia that is mistaken for the death of the nameless narrator. "I had been for some time ill of a low and lingering fever," he tells us; "towards the evening, the crisis took place . . . and when it passed off, all my recollection returned with the most perfect distinctness, but the power of motion had departed" (35). He is declared dead, and though "I exerted my utmost power of volition to stir myself . . . I could not move even an eyelid" (35). After irreverent treatment by his undertakers, he is buried and begins to think himself genuinely dead: "This is death, thought I, and I am doomed to remain in the earth till the resurrection. Presently the body will fall into corruption" (37). Pure introspection becomes indistinguishable from death. In the midst of that thought, however, he hears the sound of shovels heralding grave robbers ("resurrection men"), who bring him very quickly to a medical school dissection table. Still conscious but immobile, he hears his quality as a subject approved; feels his nerves "rung and jangled like the strings of a harp" by a galvanic experiment; and finally, at the hands of the same doctor who attended his death, is "pierced . . . on the bosom" (38). The incision has its effect: "the ice of death was broken up—my trance ended. The utmost exertions were made to restore me, and in the course of an hour I was in full possession of all my faculties" (38).

Galt's tale adheres to conventional gothic themes of anxious confinement: the fever is a typical corollary to unrelieved passions.[16] But the vaguely defined domestic setting of "The Buried Alive" and the indistinct protagonist/narrator turn the Radcliffean resolution on its head. There is no revealed familial history and no decisive *eclaircissement* to bring us to a home-founding resolution. The "low and lingering fever" the narrator of "The Buried Alive" experiences is described only against a blurred domestic backdrop, glimpsed through the claustrophobic solipsism of his inactivity, not at all like the densely detailed surroundings of Radcliffe's sufferers. (There is also, we should note, no sense of the virtues that cluster around, or vices that sunder, the Radcliffean home.)

The obvious familiarity of Galt's scene to its occupant and the constant attendance of friends make clear enough the homeliness of the setting. The story bears some resemblance to an anecdote that Galt offers in his *Literary Life* of the decline and death of his friend Park, who "remained in the sobriety of home" (1: 215) while Galt sought his fortune in the world:

> I was struck with the alteration which his malady had caused; for its insidious malice made the symptoms of mortality not obvious, and I never suspected that the apparent contraction of his whole nature was but the visible effect of a consciousness that his part and purpose in

the world was done . . . I was present at his death. I have often since endeavoured to discover in what way the event affected me, sensible it did so to a great degree . . . I think . . . it was because I had no other alive to whom I could unbosom myself. (1: 216–17)

In this context, "The Buried Alive" seems vibrant with a yearning to resurrect a lost object of affection, and at the same time to escape from a subjectivity imprisoned by the inscrutability of other subjectivities—to achieve affective communion. At an earlier moment in the *Literary Life,* Galt worries that as "a man who has spent so many of his most active years in comparative solitude and sequestration," he "cannot fail to have acquired modes of reflection, as well as topics of thought, somewhat dissimilar to those which are commonly entertained" (1: 210). The subject that is genuinely sealed off from all others may cease to resemble other members of its species. The same must also be true of the hermetic home.

The almost pure interiority of the narrative voice in "The Buried Alive" is commensurate with the captivity Galt seems to associate with home life, and the puncturing of that interiority is definitively extradomestic. The narrator would seem to be suffering from an extreme incidence of the "brown study" of which Edgeworth's Earl of Glenthorn complains. Galt's story exemplifies the literary eminence of domesticity; it is not *about* home, but its semantics and its effects are dependent on the backdrop domesticity has provided for literary discourse. Home is the "surface of inscription" (Torfing 101) for this narrative of illness—the unnamed site of a nameless disease. As I have suggested, a paradoxical but predictable effect of home's rise to dominance is its relative disappearance from the foreground of representation. In the same manner, the paucity of direct attention to the form and function of the parish unit in earlier eighteenth-century writings bespeaks not its marginality, but its dominance. Fielding's thematizing of the parish implies cracks in its foundations, or rather in its status as one of the foundations of the social.

The "coveted stillness, in which the active find an occasional reward, and the idle a perpetual misery" (*Journey* 101) that Radcliffe lists among the virtues of home is literalized by Galt as a very unrewarding paralysis. The narrator's stasis conceals the investment of tremendous, indeed total, volition to no effect whatsoever. Domesticated to death, he becomes a subject-as-object. The more he is perceived to be no longer a subject, the more keenly he feels himself one. This speaking object witnesses his death, his mourning, his preparation and interment, his exhumation, and his subjection to medical experimentation. He is undead, one who haunts his own body. What brings him back to life and speech is a penetrative examination whose completion would reveal that there is no trace of the domestic subject in the scientific object. The incision opens an epistemic gap, a literalized space of inquiry where the incommensurable contents of the affective self and of the physiological object of investigation momentarily coincide, prompting a shocking but restorative epiphany. What the medical knife opens up is not so much the material body as the feeling subject. A wound occasioned by contact with a radical alterity— a scientific investigation whose object is, in multiple, conflicting senses, the subject—proves to have a kind of homeopathic effect. The forced confrontation of figural and literal interiors in a breach of their shared outer surface restores the porosity of that surface so the subject within can again communicate with its exterior.[17]

In "The Buried Alive," failure of the systems that sustain affective communion ("I heard the sound of weeping . . . I cannot describe what I felt") gets mistaken for a failure of the systems that sustain organic life ("the sense of life seemed to become more and more acute as my corporeal powers became weaker" [35]). The goal of materialist science—identifying mechanisms that sustain both organic life and affective selfhood—is obstructed by its dissective method: the self must be extinguished (or rather have been extinguished) before the organism can be galvanically reanimated and/or cut open. The implicit quest to make these two systems commensurable manifests, in a parallel form, Catherine Gallagher's distinction between bioeconomic and somaeconomic modes of analysis—between investigations into biological processes and interpretations of the affective self.[18] Just as participants in Romantic-era poverty debates seek to negotiate disjunctions between relieving the suffering body and making the idle body productive, the anatomists in "The Buried Alive" pursue what Adam Smith called "the unknown principle of animal life" (qtd. in Packham 468) that invigorates both affective sensation and organic animation.[19] They exemplify the incapacity of bioeconomic inquiry, which works exclusively on the idle body problem, to account for somaeconomic processes, the problem of the suffering body. Galt's anatomists do trigger a reconciliation of affective and organic life in their object of inquiry, but only because they unwittingly provoke the organic body to preserve itself by restoring to the affective self its capacity for bodily expression. The vital principle itself is not revealed; it preserves its mystery by revealing its efficacy (electricity is not the secret; the catatonic body is "rung and jangled like the strings of a harp" under its application but remains "as dead" [38]). As a narrative resolution, then, this one turns out to have something very much in common with those of Radcliffean and domestic novels: they too can be said to fall silent at the threshold of the very life principle toward which their narratives have striven, asserting the plenitude of home, but implying at the same time that the nature or essence of that plenitude cannot be plainly articulated, cannot be an object of instrumental knowledge.

"The Buried Alive" refigures the clash between the body affective and the body economic as an aporia within materialist life-science—and obliquely as the conflict between mourning the body—"my friend placed my head on what was deemed its last pillow, and I felt his tears drop on my face" (36)—and utilizing the cadaver—"I discovered that I was in the hands of two of those robbers who live by plundering the grave, and selling the bodies of parents, and children, and friends" (37).[20] Instrumental figurations of interiority (self and home) cannot dissolve this aporia; the home and its metaphorics must be opened up to exteriority and the literal. Radcliffe's heroines shore themselves up against all forms of penetration, figural or literal, finally expelling all that is alien and incommensurable, but Galt's nameless protagonist can only be released from his self-enclosure by an act of penetration.[21]

"The Buried Alive" offers to revivify the gothic by perforating boundaries between the home and the external or foreign that Radcliffe's narratives (along with great swathes of cultural production in the British 1790s) strove to seal. And writing in the Scottish realm of letters, Galt participates in a larger literary movement that brought to fiction the potent exteriority of history: Francis Jeffrey, reviewing *Waverley* in the *Edinburgh Review,* rejoices that "the reader . . . who . . . speedily comes to perceive that he is engaged with scenes and characters that are copied from existing originals . . . regards with a keener interest what he no longer considers as a bewildering series of dreams and exaggerations" (208). The Edinburgh reviewers clearly recognized that they were building their new metropolis of fiction on burial grounds that had been revered by gothic novelists before them: as William Gifford writes jauntily in a review of *Tales of My Landlord* (whose coauthor was Scott himself), "the persons of his drama . . . are evoked from their graves in all their original freshness" (469). And Scott makes facetious reference to this conceit in his preface to *Peveril of the Peak:* "Here you have a countess of Derby fetched out of her cold grave, and saddled with a set of adventures dated twenty years after her death" (28: lxxxv). The living dead are liberated from the vapored imaginations of gothic novelists and come to dwell among us as ghostly emblems of shared history and common national heritage. The essential hauntedness of home, both national and private, is a symptom of its incorporation of prior social and political orders. Terry Castle, speaking of *The Mysteries of Udolpho,* argues that "to be 'at home' is to be possessed by memory, to dwell with spirits of the dead" (234). Indeed, it is only during and after the rise of domesticity that revenants in narrative begin to take particular locations as the governing principle of their hauntings. Earlier literary ghosts such as Dante's Virgil, the elder Hamlet, and Banquo seem to have no particular concern for *where* they haunt. The era of the haunted house is also that of home. Scott's fiction exemplifies the function of mourning in the constitution of the domesticated nation, expanding to a national scope what we find in the familial plots of Radcliffe's romances.[22]

In the literary reaction against Radcliffean gothic, and in critical estimations of Radcliffe for a long time afterwards, her active part in the transition of home from limited corporate interest to hegemonic object was largely erased. Wylie Sypher, for instance, found Radcliffe preceded by and wholly in thrall to "bourgeois standards": "Her awareness . . . is so imperfect that she cannot be said to compromise [between economic and moral values]. Her fiction is meaningful because it so inadequately conceals the naked contradictions intrinsic in bourgeois Romanticism, a revolt so radically inhibited that it failed to be in a deep social sense creative" (qtd. in D. Rogers 27–29). For Sypher, Radcliffe is a product of already established bourgeois hegemony, a middle-class paragon whose subject matter is really only herself. I think it is telling that her first memoirist, Thomas Noon Talfourd, saw no such paragon, but a gentlewoman of an older caste, who "felt a distaste to the increasing familiarity of modern manners, to which she had been unaccustomed in her youth; . . . she preferred the more formal politeness of the old school among strangers" (13). The bourgeois-domesticated Ann Radcliffe has, nonetheless, been a biographical commonplace: "Waiting for William's return in these long evening hours, with all her household duties done and complete freedom from interruption assured, Ann began beguiling the time with putting down on paper some of the romantic scenes on which her imagination loved to dwell" (Grant 46). Bonamy Dobrée's introduction to the Oxford World's Classics edition of *The Mysteries of Udolpho* says simply, "She never entered the literary life, preferring to live quietly at home, writing by the fireside, not enjoying very good health" (ix).

Even Rictor Norton, whose biography rejects the sequestered and apolitical figure other biographers have constructed, begins his work declaring: "Her life resembles one of those manuscripts discovered in a gothic novel:

its leaves faded and almost indecipherable, pages torn in half, whole chapters missing . . . all adumbrating a secret hidden at the centre" (1). This domesticating impulse, along with the early nineteenth-century critical turn against gothic, participates in the naturalizing of home, the endlessly reproduced erasure of its historicity and cultural specificity. Reiterating and reproducing the naturalness of home has, since the early nineteenth century, been a fiercely durable and persistent tradition in English-language discourse of all varieties, as for example in Witold Rybczynski's assertion that "domestic well-being is a fundamental human need that is deeply rooted in us, and that must be satisfied" (217).[23] This chapter's purpose is not simply to reassert that the modern middle-class home is the legacy of such a naturalization, but that the naturalizing process drove many production lines in the British literary industry for the two decades between the end of Radcliffe's ascendancy and Galt's macabre story.

Margaret Cullen's 1802 novel *Home* seems to stand astride the transition between emergence and naturalization; the tone is equal parts polemical advertisement and triumphant paean: "The improper influence of consanguinity may gradually diminish, till it shall at length be destroyed . . . and Home, instead of being a prison in which the Virtuous are condemned to associate with the Vicious, will become a secure refuge from the wicked, and the most delightful asylum of Man" (5: 363). Cullen's imaginative conversion of the home from prison of consanguinity to citadel of consensual companionship evinces home's growing function as a disciplinary apparatus. That function is apparent in Jeremy Bentham's plan for his panoptic workhouse/prison, which will make carceral institutions as orderly as private homes: "It is in truth but through want of wisdom, not by any law of nature, that the disparity has remained so wide between penal justice and domestic discipline. *Good order* is a condition not less necessary to the delicacies of domestic comfort, than to the utmost severities of public justice" (*Pauper Management Improved* 221). Home has become the "natural" institution to which the workhouse is auxiliary. Where home had been a supplement to the major instruments of poverty management, they are now subordinate to it and appropriate their attributes from it. By the mid-nineteenth century, the name *home* can be applied to institutions for the care and incarceration of the indigent, elderly, diseased, and disabled; the poorhouse has become a category of home.

The discursive tactics evident in discussions of home at the end of the eighteenth century shift from what we might as well call a predominantly evangelical tone—proselytizing the home, debating and advertising its attributes—to a nostalgic one, emphasizing home's contiguity and continuity with historical forms of domesticity rather than its newness or its radical difference from earlier systems. A reviewer of Cullen's novel in the *Monthly Review* confirms that shift, exclaiming that "the very title itself would awaken our benevolence" (103). Mrs. Almorne, the novel's main polemicist for home, however, is "somewhat too romantic in her system": "her censure of affection shewn to unworthy relations is too unlimited. Attachments of this sort, being fixed in the mind by early impressions and associations, become a part of our nature, and answer many important purposes. The same process endears to us our native habitation, and our native country; and we cannot consent to break asunder this bond of 'natural affection'" (103).[24] The bonds of natural affection are now evidence of the naturalness of home. Another example, almost exactly contemporary with Cullen's, appears in Samuel Jackson Pratt's *Bread, or the Poor* (1801). In chapter 2, I cited his concluding exhortation, "Give to each that balm of life—a HOME!" (83, line 530), in parallel with William Young's 1796 call to arms: "Let the word HOME be appropriated to as many as the lot of life can admit to it" (*Considerations* 18). Unlike Young, however, Pratt spends the earlier part of his discourse establishing the sense that comfortable and independent domestic lives for the rural poor would amount to a restoration of an older, precapitalist vernacular order:

> Time was, when twice ten husbandmen were fed,
> And all their wholesome progeny found bread,
> And a soft home, each in his modest farm,
> By tillage of those lands—and raiment warm;
>
> .  .  .  .  .  .  .  .  .  .  .  .  .  .
>
> Past are these scenes, the bloomy substance fled,
> Lo! the thin shadows offer'd in their stead.
>
> (37–40, lines 299–302 and 357–58)

Pratt's nostalgia is strikingly similar to Oliver Goldsmith's in *The Deserted Village,* but the lost topos for which Pratt pines is not so much the golden-age *comitatus* that Goldsmith imagines as a world of rustic economists shepherding the health and prosperity of their private homes.

## "Sublime Retirement"

Among the processes of hegemonic transformation that take place over the eighteenth century, other important tropes and topoi precede home in acquiring naturalization. Prominent among them are some of the denizens and relics of ancient Britain, fixtures of what Katie Trumpener names "bardic nationalism." Anne Janowitz offers two useful examples. The first is the word *country:* "The sense of 'country' as rural terrain and 'country' as nation . . . began to melt one into the other . . . [T]he myth of rural England as well as the myth of the homogeneous coherence of the nation" was born (4). The second is the cluster of concepts and symbols embodied by ruins: "The hegemonic English group which imagines the community of 'Britain' calls upon the figure of ruin to secure its past, but by the ancillary naturalizing of the image precipitates a retrogressive ideology of ruralness which industrialization itself can neither exhaust nor even catch up with" (4). *Country* and ruins possess rhetorical and conceptual characteristics comparable to those of the modern home: *country* generates a postpatriarchal two-bodies metaphor (natural and politic) akin to that of home (private and national); ruins figure a merging of human endeavor with nature that obscures historical, political, and economic conditions.[25]

Frances Burney's *The Wanderer* and William Wordsworth's *Salisbury Plain* situate a paradigmatic ruin, Stonehenge, at the center of their meditations on home, its fissures, and its exclusions.[26] Stonehenge functions for both writers as a centerless center, able to figure both violent dispossession and the mystification of that dispossession by naturalized domestic institutions that are at once fortress-like and nurturing. In this section and the following one, I will examine Wordsworth's polemical themes of home and homelessness, beginning with poems from the first years of the nineteenth century in which Wordsworth deploys a highly intricate poetics of home. Then I will return to the earlier *Salisbury Plain* and its contestation of the models of home taking shape in English cultural and political life during the 1790s. I will argue that, in fact, Wordsworth articulates a detailed concept of homelessness in *Salisbury Plain* before the middle-class home has reached a comparable level of elaboration.

Wordsworth alludes to home and its attendant conceptual systems in a remarkable number of the poems he composed before 1810. *Home at Grasmere,* which was designed as a beginning for *The Recluse* and concludes with a version of the passage known as the "Prospectus," is the most fulsome. The immediate impetus of *Home at Grasmere* is Wordsworth's taking possession of Dove Cottage in 1799, where he resided with his sister Dorothy for something over eight years. The first complete manuscript of the poem, according to the Cornell edition, was composed between 1800 and 1806. I noted in chapter 2 this poem's endorsement of home's self-sufficiency—"Perfect contentment, unity entire . . . / In this majestic, self-sufficing world" (48, lines 170–204)—

and home's double signification—the "home / within a home" (52, lines 261–62).[27] The "dear valley" (46, line 135) where the speaker and his "Emma" make their abode is replete:

> What want we? Have we not perpetual streams,
> Warm woods and sunny hills, and fresh green fields,
> And mountains not less green, and flocks and herds[?]
> (46, lines 145–47)

Such repletion is sufficient not just to the wants and needs of these bourgeoisified returnees, but also to the vale's natural system of poverty management: "they who want are not too great a weight / For those who can relieve" (66, lines 447–48). Nature itself colludes in the domestic idyll:

> 'tis the sense
> Of majesty and beauty and repose,
> A blended holiness of earth and sky
> (46, lines 161–63)

The 1831–32 draft of the poem adds, "On Nature's invitation do I come" (43, line 71). And the idyll is portable:

> Our home was sweet;
> Could it be less? If we were forced to change,
> Our home again was sweet. (48, lines 179–81)

The abiding subject naturalizes his home, and it naturalizes him, grants him residency.

The sweeping optimism and personal contentment of this work make an intriguing contrast with the *Recluse* as a (conjectured) whole, whose projected scale and majesty, according to Wordsworth's plans for it, are hard to overstate.[28] The triumphal tone of this poem also celebrates Wordsworth's victory in his long struggle to establish his father's claims for salary from Lord Lonsdale, the landlord who loomed over Wordsworth's Lakes District childhood and familial dispossession.[29] In a 1793 letter, Dorothy Wordsworth had written, "We in the same moment lost a father, a mother, a home, we have been equally deprived of our patrimony by the cruel hand of lordly tyranny" (84). *Home at Grasmere*, and, for Tim Fulford, Wordsworth's poetics as a whole, "sought to master the masters of the land by articulating it in a way they could not" ("Fields" 61). This wresting of authority amounts to a kind of usurpation: "[Wordsworth] conceived poetry as an usurpation-through-language of the power of the landowner (of his claim upon the land and of his claim to possess a language which legitimately empowered him to decide)" (ibid.). The "usurpation" of Dove Cottage, then, transfigures a property transaction into an ostentatious wresting of patrimony from the grip of merciless patronal fingers.

Just as crucial as the usurpation itself is the overwriting of its transgressiveness by an originary right fixed in Nature, which is given voice by Wordsworth's organic language and a *locus* for this *genius* by the private home. Wordsworth's personal triumph over Lonsdale recapitulates synecdochally the historical naturalizing and universalizing of private property and bourgeois domesticity: "The unappropriated bliss hath found / An owner and that owner I am he" (*Home at Grasmere* 42, lines 85–86).[30] When Wordsworth figures his establishment of private property rights as a usurpation, he also demonstrates the eighteenth-century devolution of absolutism, identified by Michael McKeon, "whereby the absolute authority of the sovereign is internalized . . . as a sovereign attribute of the individual citizen" (*Secret History* 30): "The Lord of this enjoyment is on Earth / And in my breast" (Wordsworth, *Home at Grasmere* 42, lines 87–88). The expression of natural right and legitimate proprietorship proceeds from an inward place rather than an external or superordinate authority.

Before he completed *Home at Grasmere,* as many critics have noted, Wordsworth had chosen and refined, in *The Prelude,* the theme of uncertain and anguished wanderings rewarded by accession to a mastering poetic vision that orders, legitimates, and naturalizes, and that tends to coincide with a return home; *The Prelude* begins with a guiding question: "What dwelling shall receive me? . . . Underneath what grove / Shall I take up my home[?]" (1: 107, lines 11–13). Mary Jacobus calls this accession "the emergence of the prophetic poet-visionary" (84), and Paul de Man describes it as "the passage from a certain type of nature, earthly and material, to another nature which could be called mental and celestial" (*Rhetoric of Romanticism* 13). In the same book, de Man explains that the "transition" into the other nature is, for Wordsworth, "the essential moment above all other poetic moments"; the poet's consciousness enters "a reflective and silent world that stands nearer to an authentic understanding of our situation" (55). That last phrase could pass for a description of the Wordsworthian home, which also has the complex status of a transcendence that is not necessarily distinct from immanence.[31]

Two of *The Prelude*'s most-cited moments of visionary perception privilege home and "making abode" as signs of unnamable experience—or rather as signs of a recognition that can be named, but whose essence lies beyond representation. The later of these two moments occurs immediately after the passage through Simplon Pass in book 6, where the climbers fail to recognize the point at which they "had crossed the Alps" (1: 189, line 524) (the earlier moment I will discuss below). The poet redeems his disappointed epiphany in a flare of imagination:

> I was lost as in a cloud,
> Halted, without a struggle to break through.
> And now recovering, to my Soul I say
> "I recognise thy glory." In such strength
> Of usurpation, in such visitings
> Of awful promise, when the light of sense
> Goes out in flashes that have shewn to us
> The invisible world, doth greatness make abode,
>
> . . . . . . . . . . . . . .
>
> Our destiny, our nature, and our home,
> Is with infinitude and only there;
> With hope it is, hope that can never die
>
> (1: 190, lines 529–40)

As de Man notes, "the imagination appears there as the faculty . . . that projects us out of the everyday present into the future" (*Rhetoric of Romanticism* 57), but the better nature and destiny that open to the responsive intellect have a recognizable echo in the vernacular—home, where the abstract objective takes form in the function of dwelling, making abode. The unnamable thing (*thing* is a term that recurs strikingly often in *The Prelude*) can be communicated, not as itself but as immanence or possibility, in act or process:

> the soul,
> Remembering how she felt, but what she felt
> Remembering not, retains an obscure sense
> Of possible sublimity, to which,
> With growing faculties she doth aspire
>
> (1: 132, lines 334–38)

Verbs supplement uninscribable or unspecifiable nouns; *how* stands in for, and points the way to, *what.*

These ephemeral and inchoate glimpses acquire what little stability they can in the dwelling-function: what is beyond the representational power of language can nonetheless mediate itself, enunciate its hidden presence or catch "the light of sense," through the process of inhabitation, living within. In book 1, the poet recollects his early ambition, "with a frame of outward life," to "fix in a visible home / Some portion of those phantoms of conceit"—poetic subjects, new or old (1: 110, lines 129–31). What has no name may still at least be intimated, spoken *of* without being spoken, through our shared participation in home. In *Home at Grasmere,* Wordsworth repeats the principle, suggesting that home is not just the best, but the only pattern that can guide us to this place beyond names:

> no where else is found—
> No where (or is it fancy?) can be found—
> The one sensation that is here . . .
>
> .   .   .   .   .   .   .   .   .   .
>
> 'Tis (but I cannot name it), 'tis the sense
> Of majesty and beauty and repose,
> A blended holiness of earth and sky,
> Something that makes this individual spot,
> This small abiding-place of many men,
> A termination and a last retreat,
> A centre, come from wheresoe'er you will,
> A whole without dependence or defect,
> Made for itself and happy in itself,
> Perfect contentment, unity entire.
>
> (47–48, lines 135–70)

*Abiding* is the best term Wordsworth can find to name, without naming, the ideal relation between Nature and the private subject (the latter abides in the former) and something like the same relationship subsists between the demotic face of Nature and its transcendent self.[32] Home's suitability to such mediation may have to do with its tendency (which I define in chapter 2) to slip beyond the bounds of narration and representation. Its intuitive knowability paired with its inaccessibility to representation makes it an effective vehicle for other instances of unrepresentability.

The special status of abode-making also engages, and works to dissolve, the distinction, identified by Pierre Bourdieu, between *being* and *doing* (23–24). The former is the estate of "cultural nobility": "Like the titular members of an aristocracy, whose 'being' . . . is irreducible to any 'doing' . . . all their practices derive their value from their authors, being the affirmation and perpetuation of the essence by virtue of which they are performed" (23–24).

*Doing,* by contrast, is the inessential essence of "the holders of . . . uncertified cultural capital": "they *are* only what they *do,* merely a by-product of their own cultural production" (23). In *The Prelude,* "greatness" is reconceived in the essential "doing" of making abode. Wordsworth's project, then, includes a bourgeois appropriation and re-naturing—his "strength / Of usurpation"—of patriarchal/paternalistic essence and its legitimating figures. In *Home at Grasmere,* self-justifying private property rights displace, and incorporate, aristocratic title. Absolutism devolves: the sanctum of the invisible world is no palace or great house, but home, a "sublime retirement" (*Home at Grasmere* 191, line 723). Here is a counterpart to home as narrative closure, the finally unrepresentable end of aspiration. We recognize home, but it can only be present to us through inhabitation, dwelling with (or within), however momentary. Making abode is a privileged and expansive compound of being and becoming.

The earlier moment of visionary insight to which I refer above is the "mystery of words" sequence from book 5:

> Visionary power
> Attends upon the motion of the winds
> Embodied in the mystery of words;
> There darkness makes abode, and all the host
> Of shadowy things do work their changes there,
> As in a mansion like their proper home;
> Even forms and substances are circumfused
> By that transparent veil with light divine;
> And through the turnings intricate of verse,
> Present themselves as objects recognised,
> In flashes, and with a glory scarce their own.
>                       (1: 177, lines 619–29)

The Simplon Pass imagination episode essentially recapitulates this earlier one, where the elusive, invisible, and privative come to form and substance through the process of making abode, a process (working changes and turning intricately) that constitutes the recognizable object and endows it with a surplus of glory. The mystery of words, like the mystery that divides Galt's paralyzed subject from his would-be anatomists, consists of a signifying lacuna that is analogous to home—recognizable without being representable, at once a plenitude and a vacancy, and not susceptible to capture by positivizing inquiry.

The mansion as "proper home" also hints at a certain *entente* with classicist poetics, their proprieties and their figurations of greatness.[33] Wordsworth's phrasing might be compared with Ben Jonson's epigram on Sir Kenelm Digby:

> In him all vertue is beheld in State:
> And he is built like some imperial room
> For that to dwell in, and be still at home.
>
> (qtd. in Wayne 168)

Jonson likens the whole man to a grand interior that is really not interior at all. The great house confers its sublime properties upon its proprietor, according to the traditions of aristocratic sumptuary display. Wordsworth's revision depends on the action of dwelling, rather than the dwelling place. Where Jonson mediates the majesty of state through domestic habitation, Wordsworth proposes that a sublime privation dwells at the heart of privacy and allows flashes of contact with the visionary soul of Nature. A negation hidden in the Wordsworthian home, a kind of pure interiority inverts the classical order of substance and form and achieves brief but dazzling presence, which, in Miltonic terms, "substance might be called that shadow seemed, / For each seemed either" (51, lines 669–70). The limiting effect of the double simile ("*as* in a mansion *like* their proper home") implies not so much that house and home are secondary or supplementary, but that the explicit denotative power of language bows before the greater force of what it cannot say, what already inhabits, dwells within and between words.

The conception of home that informs these passages from *The Prelude* and *Home at Grasmere*, then, is thoroughly appropriated to de Man's "mental and celestial" nature. It is naturalized in the same paradoxical maneuver wherein Wordsworth unsettles the very objectivity of Nature by constituting its organic unity in a moment of return. In M. H. Abrams's classic formulation, "the terminus of all the poet's journeyings is not only home and paradise, but also a recovered unity and wholeness which he had experienced nowhere else except, 'As it found its way into my heart / In childhood'" (221). Only in the return of the mature poet to that essentially irretrievable experience can the "great Nature that exists in works / Of mighty poets" (*Prelude* 1: 177, lines 618–19) be realized. Wordsworth's use of home demonstrates, in metaphysical grandeur, the consequences of its naturalization in general; the transient flashes of presence and the necessary loss that precedes them assert that home is accessible only through exceptional endeavor, that it reveals itself only momentarily and as something to which we return. The inhabiting subject's relation to his own home is primarily an alienated one.[34] The very cultural shift that makes home the link between subject and soil, origin, and life-telos, simultaneously separates the subject irrevocably from her origin, just as the adult imagination can only grasp organic unity with Nature after losing that very unity.

Home is always founded on a rightful usurpation, a reclaiming. In one sense, it is the historical deposing of aristocratic-patriarchal derivative title and tenant obligation by private ownership; in another sense, it is the personal assertion of affective attachment to a lost childhood pastoral. Thus home's naturalization is also its removal to a place of inaccessibility that stands in place of an originary wholeness.[35] In a related sense, the inhabiting subject is alienated from her home *because* it is hers to the exclusion of others. The proprietorial imperative—every home must be *mine* to someone—means that all other homes are *not* home to me because they are *not mine*. Hence my own home is negated by the proprietary subjects who dwell in all the homes that surround mine. However joyfully I celebrate it, a thousand other homes deny that I am home at all. This compromising metaphysic is perfectly analogous to Jacques Lacan's formulation of the signifier: "A signifier is what represents the subject to another signifier. This latter signifier is therefore the signifier to which all the other signifiers represent the subject—which means that if this signifier is missing, all the other signifiers represent nothing. For something is only represented to" (*Ecrits* 694). As glossed by Slavoj Žižek, the "differentiality" between two opposing signifiers (here understood as *my home* and *another home* or *all other homes*) takes this form:

> The opposite of one term, of its *presence,* is not immediately the other term but the *absence* of the first term, the *void* at the place of its inscription (the void which *coincides* with its place of inscription) and the presence of the other, opposite, term *fills out* this void of the first term's absence ... Within a signifier's dyad, a signifier thus always appears against the background of its possible absence which is materialized— which assumes positive existence—in the presence of its opposite. (*For They Know Not What They Do* 22)

Home is everywhere and nowhere, just as nation is everywhere and nowhere. And home's mobility, along with its nationalization, means that even national borders do not mark a stable limit to home. It can be carried abroad, and has been by imperial delegations.

The visionary transition thematized so vigorously in *The Prelude* and *Home at Grasmere* also echoes and mystifies both Wordsworth's growing conservatism and the historical transition of the home figure from strategic object to "natural" unity. The question of where exactly Wordsworth's political allegiances lay from one year to the next, and how they developed has sustained long critical debate. His shifting attitudes to the poor and to poverty management are crucial territory in this campaign, which has engaged James Chandler, Marjorie Levinson, Alan Liu, David Simpson, Gary Harrison, and others.[36] Indeed, this ongoing discussion amounts to the only significant scholarly conversation on the topic of poverty in English literature of the (long) eighteenth century. My goal is not to offer any new evidence or insight concerning Wordsworth's political positions, but to trace his contributions to and borrowing from the conception of home, especially as it relates to poverty. After around 1800, in any case, reference to home in all English cultural production becomes less and less an indicator of political position and ever more a ground or precondition of political discourse itself. In general, I will accept Gary Harrison's assertion that the poems Wordsworth began in the 1790s and later revised "reveal the degree to which he later muted his radical critique as he became more reserved in his political opinions" (93).

Mary Jacobus's analysis of the way Wordsworth revises and incorporates *Salisbury Plain* into *The Prelude* persuasively explains Wordsworth's political transformation.[37] The later poem, she argues, suppresses the explicit oppositional politics of the earlier versions: where images of Druidic sacrifice had "functioned as Wordsworth's own allegory for the consuming violence of Britain's war-mongering imperialism" (83), in *The Prelude*, "his recently acquired ability 'to have sight / Of a new world' . . . demands his oversight of the most striking contemporary instance of the barbarism which he had originally associated with Stonehenge and which now takes its place in what Althusser calls 'the inner darkness of exclusion'" (86). Harrison believes that Wordsworth felt *Salisbury Plain* was "too politically volatile to risk publishing" (97) and blunted its critique over successive reworkings. Clifton Spargo argues that "the Wordsworth of 1802 is already becoming the late Wordsworth, a poet who withdraws from the specter of his more liberal, even revolutionary politics of the 1790s" (56). In Jacobus's dexterous phrasing, "traces of the *Salisbury Plain* poems which underlie [the Salisbury Plain] episode of *The Prelude* disrupt the surface of 'a work . . . like one of Nature's'" (88). I will turn my discussion now to the dissonant textual archaeology of those earlier works.

## "Homeless Near a Thousand Homes"

In verse written before the turn of the century, Wordsworth does not celebrate home with the same kind of abandon as he does in those later works I have discussed so far, but the term and concept has almost equal prominence. The works he composed in the 1790s, as Fred Randel demonstrates, often feature journeys that terminate in compromised and bitter homecomings (an important attribute of the home at Grasmere is its status as journey's end and site of return, but bitterness has no place there): "Nothing good has come of journeying for the characters in [*The Borderers*] or for those in the poems that eventually became 'Guilt and Sorrow.' Why, then, don't they go home? The possibility is repeatedly raised and shown to be a goal that is snatched away as soon as it is approached" (581).[38] Where the later poems tend to find means of overcoming subjective alienation, the earlier ones often focus on intractable cases of alienation and tend to represent them in the form of discordant relations between subjects and their homes.

The narrator of *Salisbury Plain* (composed 1793–94) relates, in the third person, a storm-lashed nighttime journey across the titular region in quest of "some cottage whither his tired feet might turn . . . / Or hovel from the storm to shield his head" (22, lines 56–60). He comes upon Stonehenge, which "seems an antique castle spreading wide" (23, line 78), but flees it when a subterranean voice warns him off—"Fly ere the fiends their prey unwares devour" (23, line 88). At length he finds respite in a hovel, which the narrator calls a *spital*—a wayside shelter for the indigent (abbreviated from *hospital*). Already hidden in this lonely shelter is a female vagrant, whose story of destitution makes up the remainder of the poem's narrative. The last 132 lines are prognostications on the tyranny and injustice that follows when nations "for empire strain" (36, line 448). *Salisbury Plain* "[m]easure[s] each painful step" (22, line 39) up through an increasingly figural hierarchy of asylums and homes. It begins bleak and literal: "Hard is the life when naked and unhouzed." The immediate troubles of the lonely traveler and his new friend are simple lack of adequate shelter—a "lonely cot" (32, line 349)—and of food—"hungry meal too scant for dog that meal to share" (26, line 171). Under the rudimentary eaves of the spital, the vagrant recalls her father's comfortable cottage "on the sweet brink / Of Derwent's stream" (27, lines 208–9), which was lost to "cruel chance and wilful wrong" (29, line 255). Debt leads to dispossession: "His all was seized; and weeping side by side / Turned out on the cold winds alone we wandered wide" (29, lines 259–61).

The vagrant-to-be procures four years of survival by marrying a youth of "tender voice and eye" (30, line 271), and keeping up a "constant toil" (30, line 290), but all domestic industry fails when "[f]or War the nations to the field defied" (30, line 295). Private troubles are linked by degrees to a national disorder: "How changed at once! for Labour's cheerful hum / Silence and Fear, and Misery's sweeping train" (31, lines 298–99). Military recruiters drag the family abroad, where "Want's most lonely cave" (31, line 309) would seem a better fate than "dog-like wading at the heels of War" (31, line 313), and

> All perished, all in one remorseless year,
> Husband and children one by one, by sword
> And scourge of fiery fever (31, lines 320–22)

She returns alone to England and vagrancy:

> And homeless near a thousand homes I stood,
> And near a thousand tables pined and wanted food.
> Three years a wanderer round my native coast
> My eyes have watched yon sun declining tend
> Down to the land where hope to me was lost;
> And now across this waste my steps I bend:
> Oh! tell me whither, for no earthly friend
> Have I, no house in prospect but the tomb.
>
> (33–34, lines 386–93)

The concluding warning against imperial ambition and war with France decries the hypocrisy of pursuing external military ventures, while "at home in bonds they drink / The dregs of wretchedness" (36, lines 447–48). This hierarchy is the basis for my claim that Wordsworth is one of the first writers to give full expression to the modern concept of homelessness—as a state not simply "unhoused," but constitutive of the very notion of home. *Salisbury Plain* dramatizes the equivocal relationship of homelessness to home; the latter arises ostensibly to eliminate the former, but tends to obscure homelessness instead of alleviating it—"homeless near a thousand homes I stood" (line 386). It is possible to argue that home has a supplementary relationship to homelessness, rather than, as we might expect, the other way around.

It seems to me that Wordsworth's Stonehenge/castle and his wandering supplicants are amply informed by the cultural-political resonances I connect to Radcliffe's poorhouse/castle and endangered heroines in the previous chapter. If Radcliffe appropriates rhetoric and concepts from the polemics of poverty management, Wordsworth here out-polemicizes the polemicists. His critique of national policy focuses precisely on the urgent need to fill the empty spaces where domesticity does not exert its magic power, fails to make land productive and buildings sheltering. At this moment, he appears to have allied himself with the evangelical reformers.[39] Home is strategically positioned as the means of fixing a system that exploits and excludes. It is sufficient and universalizable, though at the moment of *Salisbury Plain,* it remains an atypical feature of the English countryside, "Where all the happiest find is but a shed / And a green spot 'mid wastes interminably spread" (35, lines 422–23). The poem's demands include the conversion of waste grounds into home/ homes, a figural echo of the cottages-for-paupers movement that was coming to prominence as Wordsworth composed *Salisbury Plain.*

In "The Old Cumberland Beggar" (composed between 1796 and 1798), indigence dwells in a kind of private interminable waste:

> On the ground
> His eyes are turn'd, and, as he moves along,
> *They* move along the ground; and evermore,
> Instead of common and habitual sight
> Of fields with rural works, of hill and dale,
> And the blue sky, one little span of earth
> Is all his prospect. (*Lyrical Ballads* 230, lines 45–51)

The beggar's confined field of vision is the basis for what David Bromwich sees as a meditation "about what it means to be alienated from one's purposes, or dispossessed of one's full human faculties" (23). The narrow prospect, the lack in the beggar's vision, reminds others of a lack in their own:

> The prosperous and unthinking, they who live
> Shelter'd, and flourish . . .
> 
>        . . . behold in him
> A silent monitor, which on their minds
> Must needs impress a transitory thought
> Of self-congratulations (232, lines 111–16)

And each is reminded thereby of his "peculiar boons, / His charters and exemptions" (232, lines 117–18). The beggar's little span generates a comprehensive view that incorporates the blessings of domesticity, communal bonds, and sympathetic charity for the beggar who is himself the central, though excluded, figure in this visual economy. Henry Fielding's distinction between a broad manorial perspective and a confined parochial one has here been distilled to a distinction between the blindness of the homeless and the vision of the en-homed.

*Salisbury Plain* dramatizes a failure of that comprehensive domesticating vision, entering into and enlarging the empty prospect of the vagrant. James Chandler observes that "in 'The Old Cumberland Beggar,' the private charity of lowly cottage dwellers can both sustain the needy and redeem the rest. But in *Salisbury Plain,* such charity constitutes a tiny oasis that serves to damn rather than to save the barbarous region around it" (136). The plain itself is a null space at the heart of England. Like the "very ocean" with which it is explicitly paralleled, its emptiness is a stage for human despair. It is barren because it is unresponsive to the needs of the subject; "vacant the huge plain around him spread" (Wordsworth, *Salisbury Plain* 22, line 62). The plain also visits the sufferings of Tantalus on its protagonists in another way (apart from the "thousand homes" that give no shelter): it is sown all over with grain, but fields of grain are no better than "wastes of corn" (22, line 45) to our travelers. While it may be fertile and productive from a national perspective, it has no sustenance to offer the languishing wanderer. At the heart of the poem's critique is precisely this distance between the national logics of prosperity and sufficiency (effectively the discourse of political economy) and the material needs of the private subject—the female vagrant describes her return to England thus: "Some mighty gulf of separation passed / I seemed transported to another world" (33, lines 370–71). The "little span of earth . . . all his prospect" to which the Cumberland beggar's vision is confined here expands to a totalizing blankness. Where the Cumberland beggar cannot see the fertility and plenty around him, for the vagrants of *Salisbury Plain* fertility and plenty is the very substance of their deprivation; in the "wastes of corn" they see not prosperity and sufficiency, but the denial of such bounty to such as themselves.

Salisbury Plain and the "antique castle" at its center exert a centripetal pull that figures Wordsworth's logic of destitution; the vagrant's restless motion carries her toward a destination that is no destination. Stonehenge marks the vortex of an adductive void that negates all comfort, prosperity, and attachment. The unhomely presence (or rather constitutive absence) at the very center of the home nation generates what Janowitz calls a political uncanny: "This 'other region,' this terrain most unlike the fruitful country of nature's benevolence, is also England most *like* itself, since the monument Stonehenge is the marker of England's antiquity. The birth of the nation is here mapped onto the same 'spot' as the blasting of the nation" (96). This vision of Stonehenge marks a definitive merging of the gothic castle (and its double, the poorhouse) with the home; their constitutive opposition in the British cultural unconscious, proposed by Ann Radcliffe, is confirmed by Wordsworth. In *Salisbury Plain,* however, Wordsworth makes explicit the contradictions that this opposition encapsulates, while his later verse tends to neglect them.

Wordsworth's Stonehenge gives form to a number of instrumental figures that we find also, often as negations, in the conceptual matrix of the middle-class home. Aside from its ready evocation of the association between gothic castle and poorhouse, it is also a "powerful circle" within a circle, a radiant hub that draws the fascinated subject in—though in *Salisbury Plain* it then sends him fleeing, a token of that poem's insistence that the home nation continues to exclude those it has exploited and discarded. Stonehenge is also a point of origin, a place of nativity set beyond the bounds of memory and finally inseparable from nature itself. Seventeenth- and eighteenth-century treatises on Stonehenge become more and more eager to align it with heroic and romantic national origins. The architect John Wood of Bath even proposed it as the prototype of Greek columnar architecture: the "Delphick Temple in *Greece*" was, he argues, "a temple . . . of *British* institution [designed by King Bladud] as I shall hereafter make appear to you by the most irrefragable circumstances" (76).[40] Wood's conjectures underscore the oracular function attributed to Stonehenge and its builders, and revived by Wordsworth in the polemic of *Salisbury Plain.* The temple at Delphi, along with its oracle, was the site of the *Omphalos* (or one of them)—the navel of the world—and its British counterpart seems very much to be a kind of navel of the nation, at once a constitutive absence and a centering presence; it tells an oracular tale of the sturdiness and immemorial endurance of Britishness, its bloody origins, and the possibility that those origins may be incorporated and supplanted by a civilized home, which Stonehenge itself will monumentalize.

Stonehenge is, in other words, a ruin, which, having displayed its dreadful spectacle of collective bloodshed, can hopefully become the final resting place of such slaughter:

> Heroes of Truth pursue your march, uptear
> Th' Oppressor's dungeon from its deepest base;
>
> . . . . . . . . . . . . . . . . .
>
> pursue your toils, till not a trace

> Be left on earth of Superstition's reign,
> Save that eternal pile which frowns on Sarum's plain.
>
> (38, lines 541–49)

It is a site of mystery, a lacuna that cannot be brought finally to speech (the poem barely describes the structure itself). It is haunted, which is to say it is both the locus to which sentiment attaches (opposed to the "steeple-tower . . . / Where at my birth my mother's bones were laid" [30, lines 264–66]), and it is a theater of past transgressions that prefigure present ones ("Reveal with still-born glimpse the terrors of our ways" [35, line 432]). And it is a center that has no center, just as home is the center of a centerless system of power. The modernity of home depends on its uncentralized distribution of social relations: Thomas Madge, in an 1810 sermon on educating the poor, cites "the everlasting principle of conduct—let your benevolence circulate every where and centre no where" (4). One's own home is a center and origin point, but only through the dispensation of the overarching home figuration that disperses all private homes in a larger, centerless home. The personal centeredness of every home is overwhelmed by the decentering, centrifugal pull of the countless other homes that surround it. Stonehenge is a fitting emblem for home for exactly this reason. It is always only home from another perspective than one's own.

In the meantime, the "friendless hope-forsaken pair" who have shared shelter and story in this navel of the nation depart the next morning to find "that lowly cot," where they "shall share / Comforts by prouder mansions unbestowed" (34, lines 415–18). A cottage home, upon which they stumble, at long last provides sustenance. It has enough, indeed it has surplus, and its hospitality compensates directly for the exclusion our wanderers have endured: "For you yon milkmaid bears her brimming load, / For you the board is piled with homely bread" (35, lines 419–20). Again Wordsworth seems to endorse the predominant strains of evangelical poverty management of the period. The cottage home can provide both sustenance and affective connection. The authoritative "for you" that the narrator addresses to the friendless pair suggests, and encourages, the incorporation of the cottage home into the national order of vision, lets them see at last the possibility of plenty. But again, their cottage sanctuary is just "a shed / And a green spot 'mid wastes interminably spread" (35, lines 422–23) that "serves to damn rather than to save the barbarous region around it" (Chandler 136). General dissemination of cottage homes throughout the nation promises to resolve—but has not yet resolved—

the crises of poverty and imperialist excess. The triumph of the cottage over its menacing opposite, Stonehenge, would confine the latter to a memorial function. It might then become a vanishing origin point, a marker of the violent inception of culture, but also the spectacle that visibly forbids perpetuation of that constitutive violence in the form of exploitation and indigence.

Paradoxically, Stonehenge signifies and safeguards the domestication of this newly visible national interior. The ruined temple/castle becomes itself a version of the numinous, haunted, vanishing center that is the English home. A brief passage in book 2 of *The Prelude* recapitulates this figure on a modest scale with, "A grey stone / Of native rock, left midway in the square" of the poet's childhood village, which "was the home / And centre" of his "infantine" joys (1: 125, lines 33–36). It may be worth noting that Ann Radcliffe's last published work, *Gaston de Blondeville* appends a poem on Stonehenge that purports to explain why, on Salisbury Plain,

> corn will not spring,
> Nor a bird of summer will rest his wing,
> Nor will the cottager here build his home,
> Nor hospitable mansion spread its dome. (4: 154)

Radcliffe's Salisbury Plain is also a waste surrounded by plenty. I will not detail the lurid myth-romance that accounts for the desolation, but I will note that its unhomely influence is held in check by the spire of Salisbury cathedral, which "thus high they made, / All the land to watch and ward" (4: 156); "It could see on the wide horizon's bound / Each shade, good or bad, as it walked its round" (4: 156). The spire's guardianship is a modality of vision and is extended by its own visibility, so the "nighted traveller on the plain" may "perceive it faintly shine" (4: 157). Radcliffe's Stonehenge, like Wordsworth's, is a haunted monument to past oppression that establishes a collective order of benevolent and protective visibility.

In the first two versions of Wordsworth's Stonehenge poem (*Salisbury Plain* and "Adventures on Salisbury Plain," 1795–99), redemptive or even utopian cottage homes are only partial and isolated refuges. The radical strains of the early *Salisbury Plain* poems play out, as James Chandler notes, in Wordsworth's hostile treatment of paternalism: "The oppression is clearly that of one class over another, as emblematized [in 'Adventures on Salisbury Plain'] by the synecdoche of the manor's hegemony over the cottage: 'Then rose a mansion proud our woods among, / And cottage after cottage owned its sway' . . .

In *The Ruined Cottage,* by contrast, oppression is not mentioned as a cause, and *all* classes in the happy land suffer . . . [S]uffering occurs not at the hands of other human beings, but at the hands of heaven" (134). The revision of *Salisbury Plain* that Wordsworth finally deemed publishable, "The Female Vagrant," which appears in the 1798 *Lyrical Ballads,* has dropped the Stonehenge episode and focuses only on the vagrant's tale of woe. The description of her decaying fortune is largely intact, but the concluding stanzas introduce culpability and self-recrimination: "I have my inner self abused, / Foregone the home delight of constant truth" (58, lines 259–60). The vagrant now bears some blame for her condition, and the poem's thematic emphasis has shifted away from the open critique of exploitation that we see in *Salisbury Plain* toward a view that, at least partly, ascribes indigent suffering to punishment by a just providence. The introduction of providence seems to signal Wordsworth's growing reconciliation with the order of home and home nation that is taking a hegemonic hold over English private and public life. The later versions of the Salisbury Plain episode appear to presume that the "comforts," which were "by prouder mansions unbestowed" (*Salisbury Plain* 34, line 418), now emanate from all homes and that there are homes enough to ensure the circulation of general sufficiency to everyone who inhabits the greater home of England.

For the later Wordsworth, in other words, home's universalization would seem to have been accomplished. What was, in the "imperfect verse" (*Prelude* 1: 313, line 358) of *Salisbury Plain,* an instrument of political provocation has become, in *The Prelude,* "a sanctity, a safeguard, and a love" eternal and natural (1: 121, line 528). The function of home and abode-making has shifted in his poetics too. Home was a slogan for Wordsworth in 1793, signifying the possibility of a new organicism, but five years later, instead of defining the new home model that can revivify poetry and the poor, he is alluding to home's naturalness, permanence, and transcendence:

> whatever else there be
> Of power or pleasure, sown or fostered thus,
> Peculiar to myself, let that remain
> Where it lies hidden in its endless home
> Among the depths of time.
> (*Prelude* 1: 167, lines 194–98)

Home has become the place where visible Nature meets and "circumfuses" with invisible Nature. Wordsworth's struggle with antiquated poetic and political orders, and his break with the past to which they belong, has allowed him access to a much fuller and more abiding past whose immanence and permanence could not be brought to expression until the arrival of (or at) home.

## THE ORACLE AT THE POST OFFICE

In this final section, I will revisit Stonehenge with another literary vagrant, Frances Burney's Wanderer. Published in 1814, but more than a decade in composition, *The Wanderer* is unequivocally a narrative of return. It revisits the decade of the French Revolution and reviews its social effects on England through a protagonist whose identity and experience is consistently inflected by the motif of return, even as she obeys the Radcliffean narratology of first encounter and suspense. Helen Thompson notes the "disproportion between the novel's manifest content and its apparently endless recursivity" (965). In a telling moment of resistance to the readerly epistemology that entraps her, Burney's protagonist seeks respite in "the second volume of the Guardian," finding, "in the lively instruction, the chaste morality, and the exquisite humour of Addison, an enjoyment which no repetition can cloy" (508).[41] Burney's last novel also combines the thematics of vagrancy and poverty that its title implies with the conception of home as site of return that I locate in Wordsworth. Its relation to the hegemonic process at the heart of my discussion is complicated by its historical setting—the years of "the dire reign of the Terrific Robespierre" (11). I will argue that this work is strongly marked by its bifurcated investments in, on the one hand, the antipaternalistic domesticating rhetorics of the 1790s and, on the other, in the turn against solipsism and excessively paranoid domestic regimes of the postrevolutionary period. *The Wanderer* trembles with nostalgia for the moment at which the private home and nation home constitute one another. Insofar as it is a historical novel, its history is that of the triumph of the middle-class home and the domestication of England.

The Wanderer herself is a descendant of Radcliffe's Adeline (who claims some kinship in turn to Burney's Evelina)—penniless, homeless, unparented, and unsettled. But her ties to the rebellious French multitude are not so figural as Adeline's. The national scope of the danger that both Adeline and the Incognita may embody is explicit in the person of Burney's heroine and in every dimension of the narrative discourse. Radcliffe keeps Adeline always at a safe distance from national and contemporary politics; her Englishness (or her potential Jacobinism) and her modernity are not named as such. Burney's

acknowledgment of the bogeymen and bogeywomen that haunt her protagonist is set at a historical remove of twenty years or so, but its frankness about
"Female Difficulties" (the novel's subtitle) and about anxiety over feminine
agents of revolutionary insurrection is striking. That frankness is illuminated
by Burney's preface to *The Wanderer.* Referring to her dedication of *Evelina* to
her father, more than thirty years earlier, Burney declares that her "timid offering, unobtrusive and anonymous . . . reached its destination through a zeal as
secret as it was kind" (3). Now, though, "He, whom I dreaded to see blush at
my production," is "the first to tell me not to blush at it myself!" (4). Burney
extols the father who does not jealously confine his daughter.

The Wanderer's love interest, Harleigh, also exemplifies this unsuspicious
paternalism: he finds her "not, at least, without probity, since she prefers any
risk and any suspicion, to falsehood. How easily, otherwise, might she assume
any appellation that she pleased!" (33). Burney's acclaim for relaxed paternalism passes then to bolder claims for her work: it too may venture unsuper-
vised beyond the strict bounds of private domesticity. The domestic novel, in
other words, may be permitted to deal in national, historical, and philosophical themes: "I am aware that all which, incidentally, is treated in these volumes
upon the most momentous of subjects, may HERE, in this favoured island, be
deemed not merely superfluous, but, if indulgence be not shown to its intention, impertinent" (9). This novel is predicated upon the willingness of its
audience to construe itself as both a domestic body and a public one and to
allow intercourse between the private and public, the native and foreign in the
same discursive/generic arena.

*The Wanderer* is the story of a woman's wanderings through the depredations of paternalistic tyranny and domestic paranoia, as well as much of the geography of southern England. She first appears claiming to be a fugitive from
the French Terror, begging passage to England with a boatload of English es-
capees. It is night and she can barely be seen, only identified as a woman by her
voice. At first the characters surrounding her refer to her as "the Incognita,"
later they rename her Ellis, and finally she is revealed as Juliet Granville. The
narrative casts her as a lost, and sealed, letter in search of a destination, and
the prominence of correspondence in the novel underwrites this role. On first
arrival in England, she asks to be delivered to an address of a kind: Brighton
(Brighthelmstone) Post Office, where she hopes to collect a letter *poste res-
tante.* She refuses to reveal anything about herself: "Her birth, her name, her
connexions, her actual situation, and her object in making the voyage, resisted
enquiry, eluded insinuation, and baffled conjecture" (41). The jibe she en-

dures for seeking transport to Brighton—"an hundred or two miles is a good way to go for a letter!" (32)—emphasizes her category confusion over which (or who) is the letter and which the addressee.

A letter does await her in Brighton, but it is a foreign one, not the "inland letter" the Incognita seeks, which was supposed to "contain directions for the meeting" with an unnamed friend (32). "I have," she laments, "no direction from the person whom I had hoped to meet; and whose abode, whose address, I know not how to discover!" (66). In other words, she is a sealed package, delivered to a post office, seeking thence redirection to a private destination—she is, apparently, a letter personified. She also acquires a name from the missing letter: "L. S.," the only form of address it was supposed to carry. Nominalizing her new initials, the Incognita's friends and enemies begin referring to her as "Ellis," and the narrator does so too without comment or demur. The narrator's refusal to provide privileged readerly access into the Wanderer's history and subjectivity is widely remarked; Helen Thompson suggests that Ellis is effectively without interiority (971). Or we might read Ellis as an inscribed surface, folded in upon itself, repeatedly subject to scratching out and reinscription of new addresses, and only made legible by gradual unfolding. For the majority of the narrative L. S./Ellis does not have the figural spatiality, or fullness, that could make her a destination for communication, an addressee. She is much more like an article of correspondence than a corresponding subject. She is a lost letter in danger of being declared a dead letter or of having her seal violated.

In a sequence that recalls the Viola, Orsino, Olivia love plot from *Twelfth Night,* Ellis is coerced to act as a letter declaring the love of Elinor Joddrel (Burney's caricature of radical feminism) for Harleigh. Ellis is very unwilling to do so, and is mortified further when Harleigh misreads her intention as a declaration of *her* love for him. "Shall I be guilty," he pants, "of indiscretion, if I seize this hurried . . . moment, to express my impatience for a communication of which I have thought almost exclusively, from the moment I have had it in view?" (162–63). His declaration of love, quite conventional by Burney's standards, has the tone of written correspondence. Although Ellis does end by marrying Harleigh, at this moment he upsets the decorum of private correspondence and the progress of unspoken courtship.[42] Ellis responds to Harleigh by curtailing his efforts to read her message: "My commission admits as little of extension as of procrastination. It must be as brief as it will be abrupt" (163). Where she allows herself to become legible, Ellis tends to be misread and to incite mistaken or inappropriate responses. Elinor is apparently shrewd enough to have anticipated this effect: "My design," she tells Ellis, "in making you speak instead of myself, is a stroke of Machiavellian policy," whose purpose is, "to fathom what his feelings are for you!" (161). In Romantic-era fiction, the misinterpreted, intercepted, or misaddressed letter, as readers of *Emma* will affirm, generates replies that often reveal much more than an orthodox correspondence.

Not only does the Wanderer have no legible message and no destination, she has no imprint from a sender—neither address nor return address. She becomes the target of a question that marshals the tone of the narrative through most of the book, "without a name, without a home, without a friend?" (133), provoking endless speculative talk about where and to whom she belongs as well as disputes over whether or not she merits trust and asylum, whether she is fit to be received. Sealed correspondence almost automatically implies foreignness, ambiguity, and provocation, and the same is true of Burney's heroine.[43] One of her companions in the boat that brings her to England suspects that she is "our native enemy, that, I make no doubt, is sent amongst us as a spy for our destruction" (25). She captivates and unnerves those who encounter her like Helen Maria Williams's *Letters from France,* which were written and published in eight volumes from 1790 to 1796 and "widely excerpted, quoted, applauded and attacked in the British press" (Favret 53).[44] The intensive surveillance, and often suppression, of written correspondence in Britain during the period of the French Revolution, is a symptom in *The Wanderer* of the paranoid domestic regimes that this novel works to critique and imaginatively dissolve.

The initial boat ride establishes most of the Incognita's enmities and alliances—it is women particularly who object to her: Mrs. Maple, Mrs. Howel, Mrs. Ireton, and Elinor Joddrel. Ellis's exclusively male, and mostly chivalric advocates ensure that she gains asylum in their homes or those of relatives, though not a great deal of comfort. The suspicious women force her repeatedly to leave one home and beg admittance to another. And even her allies never abandon their efforts to break open the seals of her anonymity: "Accomplished creature!" Harleigh exclaims, "who and what are you?" (88). She threatens both domestic manners and national prosperity in the same way: by concealing messages that may carry the incendiary articles of an invasive exterior power—the laboring classes or the French, or both. The suspicious women treat foreign insurgency and improper personal aspiration as homologous threats to their established domestic orders: Mrs. Howel warns Ellis, "the inexperienced youth [Lord Melbury] whom you would seduce, is the only person that can fail to discover your ultimate design, in taking the moment of meeting with him, for quitting the honourable protection that snatches you from want, if not from disgrace: at the same time that it offers security to a noble family, justly alarmed for the morals, if not for the honour of its youthful and credulous chief" (564). Ellis has no designs upon the young lord, but her protests cannot persuade her opponents. Her silence has been extorted by a threat against the life of her guardian back in France—hardly an insurgency against the people of England, but perhaps a kind of dream inversion of that persistent anxiety. The surveillance and suspicion deployed against Ellis makes a ready analogy to what Mary Favret calls the "spy fictions" produced by 1790s treason investigations (41). "The sentimental and the feminine" in these cases "clearly served as a vehicle for the subversive": letters relating to personal and domestic matters were interpreted as insurrectionist codes.[45]

What I find particularly striking about this novel's fetishizing of correspondence is not just the prominence of letters per se (hardly a novel from the period fails to make one or more letters pivotal) but Burney's attention to the disseminatory systems of correspondence, the developing English mail service as it emerged from the deep restrictions of the 1790s and reinforced the expanding hegemony of private homes.[46] The postal service was an important instrument of the transformation of homes from simple spheres of refuge to stations in a social network, and the very substance of that network.[47] I am not speaking simply of letters, which have circulated in prose fiction since Richardson and before. By postal service I mean the transmission of correspondences within a self-aggregated, comprehensive, and national network, which begins to seem systematically operative in the Britain imagined by novels and other cultural productions well before the declaration of uniform postage in 1840.

John Palmer, who had organized the mail-coach system during the 1780s and 1790s, claimed in a 1797 pamphlet that "the arrival and departure of the mails all over the country, will now be regular, expeditious, and safe; on plain, simple, and certain principles" (43). An 1808 pamphlet, compiling parliamentary discussions of Palmer's case (he fought regularly and vociferously with the office of the Postmaster General), cites supporters claiming that "the services of Mr. Palmer are daily and hourly experienced by all ranks and descriptions of people" (*Debates* 61) and that "this stupendous engine is at this moment actually in motion, and will be so long as the kingdom shall exist" (73–74). Even if, as Christopher Browne insists, until 1840 the postal service remained "a slightly eccentric network served by a motley collection of postboys and robber-proof carts" (52–53), a pervasive, systematic, and above all *symbolic* postal network had sprung to conceptual life in England before Burney completed her novel. I think it is a measure of the wishful energy that Burney invests in her corresponding theme that there was no actual post office in Brighton in 1793 or even in 1814. According to the British Postal Museum and Archive, records indicate that the first full-fledged post office in the Brighton area was the Kemp Town office, founded in 1832.[48] Burney is not really mistaken, however: mail would have been collected at and distributed from Brighton at a letter receiving house or inn prior to 1832, and the term *post office* could as well be applied to such an establishment.[49]

In the early years of the nineteenth century, the British mail network was rapidly extending itself. In 1801, Post Office Secretary Francis Freeling set up courier teams to deliver mail to London homes (Browne 41–42). Cities such as Dublin, Edinburgh, Manchester, Bristol, and Birmingham also established their own penny posts. Just as important was the proliferation of cross posts under Palmer's mail-coach system.[50] Cross posts, also known as byposts, were mail routes that passed directly from one location outside of London to another without having to pass through the General Letter Office in London.[51] Although Robinson insists that, at this time, London was still "the great radiating center" of postal correspondence (234), the postal service was clearly organizing itself into the kind of decentralized network of nodal points and multiple connective arteries that I have identified with the private home, which also "recentered the scattered community at myriad points" (N. Armstrong 95).

As I have noted, the objective of free, comprehensive, and institutionalized intercourse between private homes was delayed for years by recurring crises over the passage of correspondence across national borders and fears of seditious conspiracies conducted by mail within Britain.[52] Those crises themselves generated popular political figurations (Favret's "fictions of self-defense") that cast England as an enclosed and nurturing domestic sphere in need of vigilant protection. Arthur Young, for instance, asked in 1797, "You, whose farms are spectacles of industry, and your houses the residence of ease and comfort; what steps have you personally taken to add to the defence of the country, and to enable you with effect to say, this house is my castle, I will defend it; this woman is my wife, or my daughter, and I will die, ere a ruffian invader shall deprive me of her?" (*National Danger* 9). Though the domesticating rhetoric that Young here exemplifies contributed to the formation of the home-nation figuration that this study is pursuing, its fortified and hostile defensiveness is precisely the target of the mitigating critiques that this chapter seeks to highlight. During the years of invasion anxiety, the mobility of the mail, like mobility among the poor, had as many opponents as advocates. The postal network that facilitated commerce and communication might also facilitate other networks of invasive or insurrectionist conspiracy. The postal service had to recover from its association with the seditious and vagrant agency of the letter before it could consummate the hegemonic cultural value that *The Wanderer* seems to design for it.

The network of public dissemination in which Ellis gets lost is charged with the same kinds of hostile and paranoid energies. At most places where she seeks asylum, she meets invasive inquiry and inhospitality. The sublime women maintain domestic tyrannies: "With a brow of almost petrifying severity, sternly fixing her eyes upon [Ellis], Mrs. Howel, for a dreadful moment, seemed internally suspended, not between hardness and mercy, but between accusation and punishment" (564). Margaret Ann Doody argues that the novel as a whole presents an England where people are "complacent, politically obtuse, and xenophobic . . . an affluent society turned in on itself and withering away" (326–28). Defense of home and hearth has bred solipsism and divisive passions. Behind the tyrant women lurks Lord Denmeath, head of the family that controls Ellis's patrimony, who has ordered that Ellis will "never be received nor owned in England" (645). Denmeath has offered a six-thousand-pound portion to the Frenchman who marries the unwanted heiress, a kind of *lettre de cachet* designed to eliminate her from the lineage. Most mysterious of all is an unidentified pursuer who forces Ellis to fly to increasingly desperate hideouts. In more humble homes, she finds hospitality and care, but remains imperiled by her pursuer and the oppressive need to labor for her subsistence.[53]

The laborers who shelter her also suffer the ill effects of a bare subsistence; Burney echoes the language of the evangelical poor-law reformers when she describes a laborer's expectations: "No view of amelioration to his destiny enlivened his prospect; no opening to better days spurred his industry; and, as all action is debased, or exalted, by its motive; and all labour, by its object; those who struggle but to eat and sleep, may be saved from solicitude, but cannot be elevated to prosperity" (699). The self-sufficient private home may be sufficient for subsistence, but it is not sufficient for happiness and prosperity after all. Thomas Bernard, by comparison, writes in the SBC reports that the "spiritless continuation of daily labour" has "gradually deprived [the poor] of forecast, and of every effort that looks to futurity" (2: 4). A "rigorous and inexorable breaking down of the distinctions between accomplishments and labor" is, as Judith Frank points out, the means by which Burney converts her fallen gentlewoman into a middle-class exemplar (173). Ellis's descent into labor prepares the way for her to demonstrate a shift from public (aristocratic/sumptuary) self-expression to modest and private intimate communication. The postal service, then, provides a network of communication and exchange for that kind of private and intimate, yet generalized, intercourse, which leads both to flourishing social relations between one home and the next and to the condensation of the network of private homes into a national collective home.

Ellis's escape from the interstices to which she has been repeatedly banished transforms those spaces of exclusion into the network of homes. The female Robespierres are overthrown, the *lettres de cachet* exposed and their authority destroyed, and closed private spheres are opened to enlightening intercourse with the world beyond their doorsteps. These reforms are accomplished after Ellis reaches at last a kind of destination at Stonehenge, when she has been, as Claudia L. Johnson observes of Burney's Camilla, "almost entirely emptied before she is accepted and loved" (146): "I have no heart!—I must have none!" Ellis protests at a moment of high duress (341). Hence, Ellis comes to Stonehenge as Wordsworth's female vagrant did, homeless near a thousand homes. Her emptiness and the blank hostility of the nation that surrounds her echo the void of Wordsworth's Salisbury Plain. After the eccentric Sir Jaspar Herrington abducts her to Wilton, the Earl of Pembroke's magnificent country seat, where she can think of nothing but hiding in "some empty apartment" (759), he takes her the following day to "a vast plain; nor house, nor human being, nor tree, nor cattle within view" (764). Left to herself and "excited by sympathy in what seemed lonely and undone . . . she now went on . . . till she arrived at a stupendous assemblage of enormous stones" (765). Here Ellis, renamed for the last time as Juliet Granville, finds herself in the midst of the immovable trace of Britain's elemental endurance.

Amid Stonehenge's desolate stones, paradoxically, she finds a perfect sympathetic engagement: "In a state of mind so utterly deplorable as that of Juliet, this grand, uncouth monument of ancient days had a certain sad, indefinable attraction, more congenial to her distress, than all the polish, taste, and delicacy of modern skill. The beauties of Wilton seemed appendages of luxury, as well as of refinement; and appeared to require not only sentiment, but happiness for their complete enjoyment" (765–66). Wilton and Stonehenge, two of England's recently consecrated national treasures (which is to say tourist destinations) counterpoint the Wanderer's deplorable but redeemable state.[54] "Exhausted by relating a history so deeply affecting to her" (754), unaware of any friendly intentions toward her in the world, and humiliated by complete exposure, she finds herself alone at a kind of origin point of her "loved, long lost, and fearfully recovered native land" (751). She falls into entranced communion with "this abandoned spot, far from the intercourse, or even view of mankind," which "blunted, for the moment, her sensibility, by removing her wide from all the objects with which it was in contact; and insensibly calmed her spirits; though not by dissipating her reverie" (766). National space finally crystallizes around Juliet.

She feels herself surrounded by overwhelming and empty literal space, but genuine national space must combine literal space with instrumental metaphorics of center and boundary, part and whole, interior and exterior. Touching, but not a homogeneous part of, the literal space of England, Salisbury Plain is arranged, by Juliet's meditation, into a provisional center where all the novel's oppositions intersect; present and past, English and foreign, address and destination, sympathy and antipathy, refinement and indigence, self-abasement and self-fulfillment, concealment and exposure. As the scene at which these antitheses terminate—can no longer be sustained—Stonehenge takes on their symbolic force and becomes a vehicle that generates the instrumental metaphor required to turn literal space into national space. It is an irreducibly authentic artifact, which "takes labor and imagines it in relation to all conceivable time" (Frank 181); it seems "to have been placed 'from the beginning of things'" without "any vestige of human art," yet "could only by manual art and labour have been elevated to such a height" (Burney, *Wanderer* 765). For Burney, Stonehenge incarnates, and inaugurates, English Romantic modernity. At her absolute extremity, Juliet is admitted at last to her native land, and at the same time she makes England actual and total. England, in a sense, comes into being when this exemplary subject finds herself at the primal signifier of its symbolic order. Her history exhausted, her enclosed and encrypted message finally parsed, the Wanderer acquires the spatial plenitude of subjective interiority in a Wordsworthian moment of sublime dwelling, effecting, as does Wordsworth, a revisionary usurpation of aristocratic title and authority: "[Juliet's] performance of dispossessed essence—a performance that can summon essence into being only as an effect—would, then, both prove the persistence of postrevolutionary rank and . . . irreducibly denature it" (H. Thompson 975). The null space of Stonehenge centers and gives concrete presence to the full, abstract, and figural space of the home nation—the governing interiority that authorizes Juliet's interiority. Stonehenge also, as in

Wordsworth, establishes the centerless dispersal of centers that characterizes the modern middle-class home.

Finally impervious to all examination because she has achieved a kind of emptiness, Juliet arrives at the edifice that stands guard over and stands for the edifices of home and of England. Communing with the symbolic, she becomes symbol. Sir Jaspar asks her, "Do you divine, my beauteous Wanderer . . . what part of the globe you now brighten?" (766), echoing Edmund Burke's rhapsody for Marie Antoinette: "Surely never lighted on this orb, which she hardly seemed to touch, a more delightful vision. I saw her just above the horizon, decorating and cheering the elevated sphere" (*Reflections* 75). The moment at which Juliet is most thoroughly evacuated and overwritten by politics, history, and the nation is the same moment at which her replete selfhood comes flooding back. She does not so much vanish into a figural representation of England as the reverse—her nation becomes a symbol of Juliet herself. Burney adds one more name to the Wanderer's nomenclature: "a female Robinson Crusoe," who has been "as unaided and unprotected, though in the midst of the world, as that imaginary hero in his uninhabited island, and reduced either to sink, through inanition, to nonentity, or to be rescued from famine and death by such resources as she could find, independently, in herself" (873). At the very last, Burney inverts the epistemological order that has governed the narrative: the Wanderer is no longer the flat enclosed surface that we took her for, scratched at, scribbled upon, and soiled by many curious examiners. She is revealed as not only a fulsome subject, but the only one, as the striving soul whose labors have made her island her own domain.[55]

Like Galt's "Buried Alive," Juliet has been isolated by a failure of affective communion and subjected to hostile investigations that threaten her life. The Wanderer has been not so much a dead letter as an undead letter, uncannily and unnaturally animated by unseen forces. Her revivification comes, as I have noted, where hostile and hospitable forces meet in multifarious negations. She reaches a destination that is also a point of origin. The logic of correspondence is satisfied, and she acquires a permanent address. Those who treated our heroine with suspicion or malice are locked out: "excluded from the happy hall, as persons of minds uncongenial to confidence; that basis of peace and cordiality in social intercourse" (872). Juliet's home establishes an open and harmonious network of sentiment and affiliation, an affective postal service. Some offenders are not just turned out of doors, but (at least figurally) cast out of the nation altogether: "The Admiral himself . . . insisted on being the messenger of positive exile to three ladies, whom he nominated the three furies; Mrs. Howel, Mrs. Ireton, and Mrs. Maple" (872).[56] Mrs. Maple's fear that the Incognita was "sent amongst us as a spy for our destruction" (*Wanderer* 25) turns out, ironically, to have been accurate. Home's exclusivity, nonetheless, is overwritten by a totalizing of its inclusivity. Those who are exiled have been convicted, so to speak, of transportable crimes and are consequently no longer inhabitants of Juliet's domesticated England. The homeless do not exist.

Besides expelling the overbearing patriarchalists and other uncongenials, Juliet also retraces the path of her flight through England: "No one to whom Juliet had ever owed any good office, was by her forgotten, or by Harleigh neglected. They visited, with gifts and praise, every cottage in which the Wanderer had been harboured" (872). In doing so, the pair mark out a network of homes joined by the intimate communication of gratitude and proven virtue.[57] She closes down the sumptuary excesses of the landholding classes and opens up the confined prospects of the laboring classes. Thus the centripetal effect of Juliet's Crusoe-fication is dissolved, and the momentary centering of England in her person and consciousness is dispersed across the land. The "happy hall" gathers England about it and links its radiant hub to the national home, whose many other radiant hubs combine with it to form the very model of an ideal postal economy.

Nicola Watson finds a similar programmatic in *Emma*, where Austen aims to "ensure a world of near-perfect, institutionalized intelligibility and legibility in which what Jane [Fairfax] says of the postal system would be true of social intercourse in general" (102).[58] I find this assertion hard to reconcile with Austen's gleeful interference with the passage of virtually any enunciation from addressor to addressee in *Emma*. Misdirected and intercepted correspondence makes a fine metaphor for both the narratorial application of irony and the devious plotting of *Emma*. And the value of eavesdropping is affirmed in the novel's conclusion, where Emma's reconciliation with Frank Churchill is enabled by her reading of a letter from Frank to Mrs. Weston (395–403), and even Mr. Knightley assents to Emma's entreaty that the letter "does [Frank] some service with you" (406). Jane Fairfax's faith in the postal service does not have a counterpart in *Pride and Prejudice,* where the portentous calm of Elizabeth's visit to Pemberley endures only while Jane Bennett's delayed letter, "on which it was marked that it had been missent elsewhere" (222), defers the news of Lydia's elopement.[59] Austen's narrators have a taste for the oracular, and interpretation of their "truths" is appropriately figured by the reading of intercepted and misdirected correspondence. In spite of my reservations, nonetheless, Watson's book provides substantial evidence of what we might call the postal-reform theme in postrevolutionary British fiction. *The Wanderer* is another text that accords with Watson's central theses.

*The Wanderer*'s ironies are not so misleading, or so dependent on messages winding up at the "wrong" destination, as Austen's. Burney's narrative drives toward the elimination of oracular tendencies in postal correspondence, imagining a postal network and a national sympathetic communion in which messages arrive at their proper destinations and express themselves without ambiguity or deviousness. As it is for Wordsworth in *Salisbury Plain,* Stonehenge is Burney's last resting place of oracular mystery. From her paradoxically restorative communing with the druidic oracle, the Wanderer emerges to decree that home will no longer hold its truths in exclusive and defensive secrecy, but enter into open and plainspoken intercourse. *The Wanderer* retells (or gives the form of a retelling to) the elimination of paranoia and solipsism from private home and home nation, their contracting of a partnership that is comprehensive, and their generation of institutions that look more like spontaneous and natural extensions of human kinship and sociability than instruments of governance. The emergent hegemonic figure of the postal service, which lends its naturalizing and universalizing force to a growing public monopoly, stabilizes itself in partnership with the growing hegemony of home. The topographic conundrum of Stonehenge mirrors and authorizes that of home. Both are haunted, unfathomable, and resolutely singular, yet simultaneously incorporative, effusive, and essentially British.

# 4

# There's No Home-Like Place

## Out of Doors in Scotland

"You are right, my friend—you are right," replied poor Dick, his eye
kindling with enthusiasm; "why should I shun the name of an—an"—
(he hesitated for a phrase)—"an out-of-doors artist?"

—Walter Scott, *The Bride of Lammermoor*

Just like their English counterparts, early nineteenth-century Scottish novelists tend to find home too hermetic or prison-like. In Elizabeth Hamilton's
1808 *The Cottagers of Glenburnie,* for example, the kindly but not indulgent Mrs.
Mason goes to live as housekeeper to the MacClarty family ("clarty" means
"dirty") in the remote Highland village of the title and finds their cottage intolerable because nothing gets in or out. The MacClartys cannot see "how small
a drain would carry [their dirty water] down to the river, instead of remaining
here to stagnate, and to suffocate [them]" (150–51); Mrs. Mason's bedchamber
is "without any circulation of air," and so "she immediately advanced to the
window, in the intention of opening it for relief. But, alas! it was not made to
open; and she heard for her comfort, that it was the same with all the other
windows in the house" (153); the windows are also opaque with grime; and
Mrs. MacClarty cannot conceive how moths could have gotten into the bed
linens, "for no ae breath o' wind ever blew here!" (154). Mrs. Mason succeeds
in correcting these faults, and many others, but the MacClartys are nonetheless struck ill later in the narrative by "infectious airs" that take the life of Mr.
MacClarty. Finally Mrs. Mason is forced to give up on her incorrigible hosts
and devote herself to running a school for boys, whose result is "improvements in the village of Glenburnie," which "had their origins in the spirit of
emulation excited among the elder school-boys, for the external appearance
of their respective homes. The girls exerted themselves with no less activity, to
effect a reformation within doors" (397).

Hamilton inaugurates what Ian Duncan terms the "Scottish school of domestic national fiction" (*Scott's Shadow* 79) with a novel whose "sketches were originally formed . . . as separate pieces, in form and size resembling the tracts in the Cheap Repository" (Hamilton v–vi). Another member of this not-so-extensive school, Mary Brunton's 1811 *Self-Control*, brings us Laura Montreville—an heir to the self-disciplined heroines of Ann Radcliffe—who exhibits the titular virtue despite her origins in "a household, bustling without usefulness, and parsimonious without frugality" (1: 6). Scots writers of the early nineteenth century often fault their national domesticity with cruel parsimony where there should be prudence and frugality, a flaw that is a subcategory of the larger problem of domestic hermeticism. We first encounter Brunton's Laura going for "a solitary ramble" from "her father's cottage . . . Her countenance was mournful, and her step languid; for her health had suffered from confinement, and her spirits were exhausted by long attendance on the deathbed of her mother" (1: 3). Her home is something that must, at first, be escaped.

Laura does escape her parental home and later follows Radcliffe's Adeline, Emily, and Ellena into a conventional romance-marital resolution, subsumed by an idyllic domestic settlement, but Brunton explicitly refuses to display the scene of contentment, or even to speak the name of home: "The tranquil current of domestic happiness," the narrator explains in the final paragraph, "affords no materials for narrative" (2: 467). Where Jane Austen is reticent about the happy homes that conclude her novels, Scottish writers regularly disavow the topic altogether, for reasons that I will elaborate in this chapter. Walter Scott's contribution to Scottish domestic national fiction, *Saint Ronan's Well*, also recognizes the limitations of home: "The invalid often finds relief from his complaints, less from the healing virtues of the Spa itself, than because his system of ordinary life undergoes an entire change, in his being removed from his ledger and account-books—from his legal folios and progresses of title-deeds—from his counters and shelves,—from whatever else forms the main source of his constant anxiety at home, destroys his appetite, mars the custom of his exercise, deranges the digestive powers, and clogs up the springs of life" (Author's Edition 33: iv–v). That caveat comes from Scott's 1832 magnum opus introduction to *Saint Ronan's Well*. The novel itself dwells very little on home as such, in either its private or national guises.

In early nineteenth-century English literary representations, the tensions and contradictions suspended in the dialectic between private home and home nation often threaten to break loose and upset that dialectical balance; "in the very reference to a 'home-country' lies the indication that the speaker is away from home" (George 2). But Scottish attempts to represent homes, I will argue, wrestle with contradictions a full degree more unruly. If the modern middle-class subject can be defined as the *aufhebung* of the dialectical opposition between private home and home nation, Scottish nationality destabilizes that opposition by interposing another opposition between the subject's nation of origin and her nation of residence: the nation a Scottish subject calls home is not England, which is persistently the nation that claims the title *home* for itself. Scottish subjects, as Ian Duncan remarks, "are obliged to reflect on their doubled relation to national identity as North Britons and Scots" (*Scott's Shadow* 116); "the subject belongs to a modern national culture by virtue of an original historical alienation within it" (59). It is for this reason that Scottish literature is more openly and avowedly a national literature than its English sibling.

England and Englishness construct themselves as an undifferentiated negative ethnicity against which all others register as positive difference.[1] In Sarah Green's 1824 (English) spoof *Scotch Novel Reading,* to be "national" is to allow positive difference to color one's thought and actions; the quixotic (English) heroine's judicious father (also English) tells her: "Without being national, I pronounce my fair countrywomen to be the most charming females in the whole world . . . and this is remarked of them by every liberal-minded and enlightened foreigner . . . Did you not see, my dear, that even the seemingly ignorant and truly national lady Macbane despised your folly, in your monkey-like imitation of Scotch dress and manners?" (1: 178–79). The "complete English guise" that our heroine reacquires after her father's admonishment, "neat, plain, and simple, with no other ornament than her own native beauty, health, innocence, and youth" (1: 179–80), completes a casual study of colonial asymmetry. The historical emergence of this English negative ethnicity, then, receives tremendous impetus from the homogenizing effect of the English private-home/home-nation partnership.

The ethnification of Scotland also exposes the modern home's propensity to undermine, rather than stabilize, bonds of mutuality and continuity. Deep-rooted, wide-spreading, and immutable social ties are presented, in *The Heart of Midlothian* for instance, as primitive:

> Perhaps one ought to be actually a Scotchman to conceive how ardently, under all distinctions of rank and situation, they feel their mutual connexion with each other as natives of the same country. There are, I believe, more associations common to the inhabitants of a rude

and wild, than of a well cultivated and fertile country; their ancestors
have more seldom changed their place of residence; their mutual recollection of remarkable objects is more accurate; the high and the low
are more interested in each other's welfare; the feelings of kindred and
relationship are more widely extended, and, in a word, the bonds of
patriotic affection, always honourable even when a little too exclusively
strained, have more influence on man's feelings and actions. (393)

Civic-minded disinterestedness is apparently little understood by the Scots,
and the obstinacy of their national affections here seems too exclusive to tolerate the homogeneous and itinerant affiliations of the middle-class home nation. Earlier in *The Heart of Midlothian,* Scott gently mocks the idea of unre-
flected attachment to one's native soil: Benjamin Butler is "a man of few words
and few ideas, but attached to [his hardscrabble smallholding] Beersheba with
a feeling like that which a vegetable may be supposed to entertain to the spot
in which it chances to be planted" (79). Despite the streak of native-attachment
rhetoric running through home's early promotions, the modern home is much
more characteristically mobile and adaptable than reverent to enduring soil
and society. Home's modern social network does indeed, as conservative writers feared, seem to corrode the bonds of "grateful and honest dependence"
(Southey qtd. in Tobin 13) that are nostalgically identified with prior orders.

Despite the antipathy to migration pervading the novels that Duncan calls
Scottish domestic national fiction, all of them (including *Saint Ronan's Well*)
feature characters moving their homes from England to Scotland and/or the
reverse. Scottish anxiety about migration invariably surfaces in novels as an
explicit problematic concerning the alienated relation the migrant domestic aspirant has to her new home in the other nation. Mrs. MacClarty in *The
Cottagers of Glenburnie* complains of Mrs. Mason's domestic reforming, "she
has been sae lang amang the Englishes that she maun hae a hantel o' outland-
ish notions" (151). Susan Ferrier's *Marriage* (1818) bounces north and south
several times. Its most disruptive character is the heroine's mother, Lady Ju-
liana, for whom leaving London might as well be moving to "what any one
unaccustomed to the hyperbole of fashionable language, would have deemed
Botany Bay" (184). She has to be exiled, finally, to France because she "found
foreign manners and principles too congenial to her taste ever to return to
Britain" (452). Our heroine, Mary, on the other hand, seems to agree with her
aunt Grizzy, who thinks "it will be a sad thing if you are obliged to stay in England" (452), and indeed, when Mary returns to the land of her birth, she finds

"the hills, the air, the waters, the people, even the *peat stacks,* had a charm that touched her heart, and brought tears to her eyes as they pictured home" (466). Ferrier negotiates her heroine's, and her own, approach to home through this peculiar specularization of gaze as Mary's eyes "picture" home, which seems to be something other than the scene in front of them. The oddly emphatic peat stacks suggest that a sense other than sight may be the immediate cause of Mary's tears. A parodically oversentimentalized distancing effect moderates what we might otherwise read as a fulsome and conventional homecoming and home-founding.

The concluding paragraphs of the novel do feature the soaring effusions we tend to expect, or did in the 1790s:

> Colonel and Mrs. Lennox agreed in making choice of Lochmarlie for their future residence; and, in a virtuous attachment, they found as much happiness as earth's pilgrims ever possess, whose greatest felicity must spring from a higher source. The extensive influence which generally attends upon virtue joined to prosperity, was used by them for its best purposes. It was not confined either to rich or poor, to cast or sect; but all shared in their benevolence whom that benevolence could benefit. And the poor, the sick, and the desolate, united in blessing what heaven had already blessed—this happy Marriage. (468)

Yet that paragraph sounds a little too familiar:

> Their present felicity . . . they solemnly vowed to deserve . . .—by remembering, that superior attainments of every sort bring with them duties of superior exertion,—and by affording to their fellow-beings, together with that portion of ordinary comforts, which prosperity always owes to misfortune, the example of lives passed in happy thankfulness to God. (Radcliffe, *Mysteries of Udolpho* 671)

> Not to themselves was their happiness contracted, but diffused to all who came within the sphere of their influence. The indigent and unhappy rejoiced in their benevolence, the virtuous and enlightened in their friendship, and their children in parents whose example impressed upon their hearts the precepts offered to their understandings. (Radcliffe, *Romance of the Forest* 363)

While I hesitate to claim unequivocally that Ferrier is satirizing the Radcliffean resolution, her conclusion is, first of all, unquestionably pastiche and therefore set in *some* kind of ironic frame. Second, Ferrier's borrowed ending indicates a kind of renunciation—of fiction's capacity to originate, a capacity analogous to, and enabled by, the originary power of home. For Ferrier, home's iterability seems to figure its loss rather than its immanence. The telos-as-origin is here no more than a signifier of literary convention. The home itself is already lost behind more than one historical horizon—the naturalization of home, the Act of Union, and now also the literary-historical ossification of domestic genre fiction.

In Scottish domestic fiction, Scots homes must contend with their English counterparts, which hold the patent on a natural and uncontradictory relation to their nation of affiliation. Hence, Duncan's phrase "Scottish domestic national fiction" is perfectly accurate. Unlike English domestic fiction, Scottish domestic novels cannot pretend that the national interior, which is the private home's immediate exterior, is simply and only a figural counterpart, a natural sameness-in-difference. It is always mediated by its relation to the paradigmatic English home nation: Hamilton, for instance, declares that "few of the children of Caledonia are deficient" in "warm attachment to the country of our ancestors," though differing from the English in their "partiality for national modes, manners, and customs" and their attitude to "national happiness" (viii–x).[2] The Scottish national literary project as a whole does not cease affirming that Scotland is the national heritage, history, and territory it produces.

But Scotland is not exactly a nation any longer. Nor, of course, is England, but sociopolitical representations of England are not framed by supplementarity, asymmetries of incorporation and subjugation, quite as obstructively as Scotland's are. The national tale labors under the imperative of presenting what Miranda Burgess calls an "organic, prepolitical body, bound together by customs and sentiments and by oral and written traditions that constitute a national culture" (35), a sameness without homogeneity. But for Scotland that imperative runs up against the constitutive difference and historical specificity of union. For even the fondest supporter of union, to think of Scotland as home in the full sense meant forgetting the 1707 act of renunciation that made it an incorporated territory within the extended British home nation, not to mention the English Alien Act of 1705, which offered Scots a choice between absorption and alien status.[3] Those two legislative thunderbolts make stubbornly particular and disruptive historical specificities in what is supposed to be an essentially ahistorical, aparticular stasis, the naturalness of home.[4]

In this last chapter, I will examine the reception of home in Scottish prose fiction, the complications produced by Scotland's positive difference from England, and particularly the efforts of Walter Scott to resolve some of those complications imaginatively and historiographically in *Old Mortality*. This final section of my argument concludes my account of the modern middle-class home's emergence and its consequent "disappearance" behind the horizon of its own unrepresentability. This chapter also gestures toward the colonial/imperial functions of home, its instrumentality for British overseas expansion and domination. As I noted in my introduction, postcolonial criticism has recently produced several excellent studies on these aspects of home's hegemonic value, and this book is indebted to them. Because Scotland is a kind of home front for empire, we probably should not be surprised that home is not, for the most part, treated with much effusiveness or explicit instrumentality in early nineteenth-century Scottish fiction.[5] I will argue, nonetheless, that Scots writers do strongly feel the influence of home's emergence in British politics and culture and pursue a variety of strategies to define its place in Scottish literature and life. As I showed in chapter 3, English writers of the early nineteenth century revise home to make it a scene of perpetual return, a place one has been before but where one never quite arrives. For Scots writers, it seems to me, home tends to take the form of a scene of departure, of farewell and backward glances. Rather than approaching, the Scottish subject is always receding from her home. The home where identity is undivided, where origin and aspiration, private autonomy and collective affiliation coincide, is already renounced, confiscated, or has vanished. The Scottish subject can only look forward to the hope of founding a new home-place, but that new home must be in some sense the habitation of exiles or émigrés, even when it is within the borders of Scotland.

## "Hame, Hame, Hame, to My Ain Country!"

The modern middle-class home's identification between private dwelling and nation—already a work of mystification—becomes even more tenuous when that identification cannot erase the constitutive difference it negates, when the subject of identification must recognize an irreducible otherness in herself. In a prefatory essay for the first issue of the first *Edinburgh Review* (1755), one of its founders, Alexander Wedderburn, writes: "The memory of our ancient state is not so much obliterated, but that, by comparing the past with the present, we may clearly see the superior advantages we now enjoy, and readily discern from what source they flow. The communication of trade has awakened industry; the equal administration of laws produced good manners; and the watchful care of the government, seconded by the public spirit of some individuals, has excited, promoted and encouraged a disposition to every species of improvement in the minds of a people naturally active and intelligent" (ii).[6] Scots nationality has not been annihilated, but it can no longer stand, autonomously, for itself. The comparative sense of collective advantage, the temporal displacement from origins, and the borrowed economies of order and improvement deny to Scots the kind of uncomplicated relation between private and collective affiliations that the English subject notionally enjoys. Scottishness is something more like a regional ethnicity (fortunately a "naturally active and intelligent" one).

Another enthusiastic unionist and cofounder of this short-lived journal, Adam Smith, contributed a letter to the second (and final) issue: "As, since the Union, we are apt to regard ourselves in some measure as the countrymen of those great men [Bacon, Boyle, and Newton], it flattered my vanity, as a Briton, to observe the superiority of the English philosophy" (66).[7] In 1755, the archaic foundations of the word *Briton* still showed pretty plainly through its postunion renovations.[8] The name's ancientness helps blur the time lag between the careers of Smith's adopted countrymen, Bacon, Boyle, and Newton, and the Act of Union; Britons, we should understand, have always had some natural collectivity, though the full flourishing of that communion has awaited modernity. The allusion to the great scientists suggests also that the first *Edinburgh Review* aimed to promote Scotland's incorporation into the Newtonian mechanical universe, taming the fragmentary temporalities, folkloric histories, uneven developments, antiquated property and family systems, and disorderly trade of Scots antiquity. Scottish history, commerce, law, and cultural geography are harmonized by a new, isotropic, British national space-time. That space-time is both a total quantifying and homogenizing system and an immaterial cloud of calculations that touches nothing and changes nothing, a comprehensive organizational matrix that disappears into the territory it captures.[9] Just as English ethnicity is a purely negative one, English space is a negative topographology.[10]

Almost seventy years after the first *Edinburgh Review* failed, William Hazlitt implied, in an essay on Walter Scott's fiction, that Scotland had still not been fully incorporated by Newtonian—and Smithian—quantification: "It has been asked, 'Have we no materials for romance in England? Must we look to Scotland for a supply of whatever is original and striking in this kind?' And we answer—'Yes!' Every foot of soil is with us worked up: nearly every movement of the social machine is calculable" (*Spirit of the Age* 127–28).[11] More striking, though, than the suggestion that cultivators of romance need territory undisturbed by science or civilization is the additional implication that romance writing may actually play a part in "working up" the fertile soil, perhaps converting it from primitive agrarian pasturage to the modern scientific farms of Arthur Young. This thesis has particular appeal for the historical romance of Walter Scott, whose tillage turns up the bones and relics of the Scottish past and arranges them in coherent, linear, autotelic narratives (multifarious paratexts notwithstanding). In Hogg's *The Queen's Wake,* "Walter the Abbott" takes up an ancient harp and

> The Border chiefs that long had been
> In sepulchres unhearsed and green,
> Passed from their mouldy vaults away,
> In armour red and stern array. (171)

The Waverley Novels bring the polyglot, recalcitrant, contradictory, and unlettered voices of Scottish history into coherent and closure-oriented story form.[12]

What I called, in chapter 2, Ann Radcliffe's suspense narratology is the principle that has ensured the exhaustion of England's romance resources. The fertility of fields that yield romance is quickly depleted, hence the critical complaints, which I detailed in chapter 3, that gothic romance was worn out by the early nineteenth century. Even an effective gothic narrative is only good for a first reading, and once the soil is thoroughly harrowed up, subsequent crops of the same species wither and die. Scott's historical romance turns that principle to advantage: if modern romance narratives can be told only once, then Scott's application of romance to Scottish history helps secure the primacy, singularity, and monumentality of his narratives: "Sir Walter may, indeed, surfeit us," Hazlitt says, "his imitators make us sick!" (*Spirit of the Age* 127). As the Great Unknown, the "Olympian storyteller," his bardic status and looming majesty are only reinforced, never diminished, by the satiric irony of epithets like Hogg's "Walter the Abbott."[13]

Rather than killing the text or at least destroying its fragile powers of fascination, as happens with the Radcliffean gothic, the first reading of a Waverley Novel already has the status of a kind of rereading, a return that grants the reader her affective encounter with the past but does not suffer for want of debased sensations like surprise, terror, and overwrought sympathy. Although

Scott is indeed using up Scotland's romance reserves, in doing so he is creating the authorized archive of a civilized sector of a civilizing empire.[14] The
Waverley Novels do render the figures that they exhume "from their graves in
all their original freshness" (Gifford, Review 469) dead a second time, but that
is exactly how the honored dead are made fit for nation- and home-forming
mourning. Scott had set out this scheme earlier in *The Lay of the Last Minstrel*,
celebrating both the bard whose "verse / Could call [ancient chiefs] from their
marble hearse" (68, lines 616–17) and

> . . . those, who, else forgotten long
> Liv'd in the poet's faithful song,
> And, with the poet's parting breath,
> Whose memory feels a second death.
>
> (69, lines 17–20)

The bard himself expires with the tale he tells; the Great Unknown is a voice
from the great unknown. Scott's fiction renders inert the disorderly and riot-
ous remainders of national history by subjecting them to the euthanizing processes of modern romance. His cavalier blending of fictionality and historical
factuality does not weaken his authority, but actually enforces it under the sign
of originality.[15]

The definition Scott constructs for romance in his "Essay on Romance"
carries us a step further: "The father of an isolated family, destined one day to
rise into a tribe, and in farther progress of time to expand into a nation, may,
indeed, narrate to his descendants the circumstances which detached him
from the society of his brethren, and drove him to form a solitary settlement
in the wilderness" (*Miscellaneous Prose Works* 6: 160–61). Scott emphasizes the
romance journey as exile, a departure from originary home (notably, a pre-
national one) and the eventual establishment of a new one in a new place.
For the purposes of my argument, what this tendency signifies is the impossibility of a genuine return home to an absolute origin.[16] Irreversible exile is
particularly characteristic of historical fiction. Scott's narratives consistently
recapitulate the figure of historical rupture that cuts off characters and nations
from prior social/political/domestic orders (both private and collective) and
forces them to establish new ones that embody dialectical resolutions of historical conflict. Even where characters do return to their ancestral dwellings
in the Waverley Novels, and often enough they do, they cannot simply rees-
tablish their homes in those places the way that Emily St. Aubert does in *The*

*Mysteries of Udolpho.* The site of resolution in a Waverley Novel, whether or not it is a home in any recognizably modern sense, is foremost a place at which a new order is established, a new "settlement in the wilderness."

Scottish literature is heavily inflected by topoi of exile and dispossession. In the Romantic era at least, Scotland appears as a geography whose outdoors overwhelms built interiors, and the chief activity going on among the hills and glens seems to be abduction, flight, and hiding. Certainly the Waverley Novels and the novels of James Hogg are heavily preoccupied with terrains that alternately frustrate and facilitate the movements and concealments of the characters in them. Dwellings, whether homes or otherwise, that are not sealed off tend to be literally or figuratively contiguous with the outdoors. Instead of in homes, characters often take "shelter" in caves, ravines, dense woods, battered hovels, or under the open stars. Houses that ought to be homes are frequently commandeered for nondomestic purposes, made scenes of action that mock any notion of separation between domestic spheres and public/political spheres. Whatever ought to be homely turns into something unhomely.

While there are plenty of cases of exile abroad in Scottish fiction, internal exile is more often the rule. Multitudes of characters find themselves foreigners at home, proscribed, dispossessed, and hunted on their own soil; their nativity, their patrimony, and what they tend to believe is their patriotism have been decreed treasonous or insurgent. The law, the military, and other mechanisms of state, instead of protecting and encouraging domestic order and social bonds, tear them (and themselves) apart. English novels do, often enough, present comparable narratives of flight, pursuit, confinement, and hiding, but the threatening forces are almost invariably private and insurgent themselves—Radcliffe's mercenary nobles and banditti, Lewis's perverted monastics, Godwin's chivalrous fanatic Falkland, Burney's and Austen's jealous matriarchs. While English heroines do get cut off from the safety of their homes and lose themselves in labyrinthine antihomes, they do not experience the entire apparatus of home—private and national—turning into a machine aimed at their destruction. In *Northanger Abbey,* for instance, the fundamental benevolence of English civil and political order premises Austen's satire: "In the central part of England there was surely some security for the existence even of a wife not beloved, in the laws of the land and the manners of the age. Murder was not tolerated, servants were not slaves, and neither poison nor sleeping potions to be procured, like rhubarb, from every druggist" (188). The more central, and hence further from peripheries and borders, the English home is, the less it suffers the depredations that stalk the outlying regions of the British Isles.

James Hogg's *Private Memoirs and Confessions of a Justified Sinner* offers a model case of internal exile. Set around the period of the Act of Union, the narrative (both narratives) actually visits Edinburgh during the unrest surrounding Scotland's last parliament, though neither narrator makes explicit mention of the business going forward in the halls of power. The *Confessions* is instead concerned with a jealous and deluded sibling's effort to wrest his patrimony—which includes the lavish family home of Dalcastle, the title of Laird, and legitimacy in the name of radical Calvinism—from his older, more Tory, and more convincingly legitimate brother. But, having claimed his perceived rights with the assistance of a malevolent shape-changer (Gil-Martin), the younger brother, Robert, is forced to flee the forces of law, personal vengeance, and his demonic accomplice. A caricature of extreme Scots Calvinism, Robert believes himself a crusader for his Kirk, but becomes instead a fugitive and vagrant, fleeing from asylum to asylum, each more pitiable than the last. At every potential home he seeks shelter, but is soon expelled when his infernal entourage spoils his welcome. There is no happy home and familial communion awaiting the protagonist to pacify his troubles and reconcile his alienated spirit. *The Confessions* spins out an extended play on possession and dispossession; Robert's repeated assertions in the latter part of his narrative that "I have two souls, which take possession of my bodily frame by turns, the one being all unconscious of what the other performs" (132) describe a psychic splitting that can readily symbolize his divided nationality.[17] Having contracted a partnership with what he takes to be a foreign power, Robert loses everything, including himself.[18] While two nations merge into one, one Scottish subject splits in two.

Most Romantic-era Scottish fiction is less bleak in its conclusions about whether Scottish subjects can reconcile themselves to the British home-nation system. Scott's *Old Mortality* will provide my main example. But exile and its less overtly coercive partner, emigration, feature so pervasively in Scots cultural production of the early nineteenth century that a few more examples are warranted, especially because they enable me to connect this portion of my study also to treatments of poverty. Probably the most significant actual historical processes that underlie the tropes of exile and emigration in Scots literature are the effects of the Highland clearances after the 1745 rebellion and the consolidation of immense landholdings across Scotland.[19] In an 1831 piece for the *Quarterly Journal of Agriculture*, James Hogg ascribes "the late decided change in the character of our peasantry" partially to "the gradual advancement of the *aristocracy* of farming, . . . district after district being thrown into large farms, which has placed such a distance between servants and masters, that in fact they have no communication whatever, and very little interest in common" ("On the Changes in the Habits" 50). There was, at the same time, a growing persuasion that Scots poverty generally could be eliminated by sending the poor to colonial territories with easily appropriable farmlands, particularly Canada, Australia, and, later, New Zealand.[20]

John Galt became a strong advocate of emigration (and was himself an emigrant to Canada and secretary of the Canada Company for five years, founding the city of Guelph in 1827 before returning to Scotland in 1829). His 1834 *Literary Life, and Miscellanies* features two disquisitions relating to the topic, in which he "attempted to show in what way the distresses of an old country might be alleviated by improving a new" (1: 216). The first of these disquisitions is titled "Colonization," and it lays out what Galt calls "my colonial system," which includes the proposition that Scotland's superfluity of laborers is likely to "engender dangerous discontents; people of property are averse to be taxed for the support of the able-bodied, and the able-bodied are naturally seditious against that frame of society which consigns them to poverty" (2: 40). The resemblance between Galt's cautionary tone and that of many 1790s English poverty writers is compounded by an almost equally familiar proposal that his solution will pay for itself: sale of colonial lands will fund "public works in the respective colonies, and defray the expense of removing to them the superabundant labourers from the mother country" (2: 43). "If we look at home," Galt warns, "all is in revolutionary fermentation, and it is only by casting our eyes to the colonies—those safety valves, to which the existing frame of society may owe its preservation—that the ebullition, the progress of knowledge may be continued with safety" (2: 46).[21] Unlike his English predecessors, Galt's proposals are emphatically centrifugal, directing idle and surplus energies outward rather than into closed, self-sustaining, and self-consuming economies.

The differences between English and Scottish poverty management are, according to Galt, significant and inveterate. Rejecting the "fallacy" that "an able-bodied labourer, who cannot find employment ought to be supported by his parish," Galt insists that the Scots have been wise enough to levy "no poor rates" (2: 44–45). R. A. Houston affirms Galt's claim in letter if not spirit: "The first noteworthy feature of Scottish relief is the enduring hostility of those who paid towards relief, mostly local landowners in the countryside,

to any form of rating to provide for the poor . . . Well-off rural Scots were prepared to pay towards the maintenance of the poor only provided their giving
was voluntary and their control over its destination was clear" (454). The distinction between Scottish and English procedures is by no means absolute:
"Scottish public poor relief was dispensed on a personal and *ad hoc* basis, or
it was administered piece-meal by parish 'Kirk Sessions'" (454). Despite a
general belief that Scotland had "a less generous system of poor relief than
in England . . . those who were unable to shift for themselves were certainly
cared for" (455). One striking difference obtains: "Out-relief was the norm.
Some of the larger towns experimented with poorhouses, workhouses, and
houses of correction . . . but there was none in the countryside and many
fewer than existed in England" (455). Houston speculates that "the contrasts
between Scotland and England have been overdrawn" (456), but he does indicate that the Scottish system tended to be more strongly manorial/patronal
and less parish-based than its English counterpart (456).[22]

Galt's emphasis on finding labor for the labor-less tallies with the way
most commentators, then and now, view the priorities of Scottish relief provision. His second essay on the topic in his *Literary Life, and Miscellanies,* "The
Timber Trade: As Respects the Poor Rates," adds to the benefits of exporting
laborers, those of importing the timber they cut. Should Scottish merchants
import Baltic timber instead of from North America, they "will lessen that
demand for labourers in the clearing of the [American] forest, which induces
so many thousands to emigrate yearly, and consequently cause an increase of
paupers at home, and indirectly nourish those mischievous sentiments which
endanger the very existence of the social compact itself" (2: 74). Galt advocates neither workhouses nor cottages, but sturdy ships and fond farewells for
"those unfortunate individuals, thousands on thousands, who have but the
workhouse and beggary before them, or the dreadful alternative of revolutionary crime" (2: 81). In early nineteenth-century Scottish thinking on poverty,
emigration plays a role that seems roughly analogous to that of home in England during the 1790s.

Felicia Hemans dramatizes sentimental ambivalence about emigration under
the rule of home in "Song of Emigration," published in *Blackwood's* in 1827:

> There was heard a song on the chiming sea,
> A mingled breathing of grief and glee;
> A man's voice, unbroken by sighs, was there,
> Filling with triumph the sunny air;

Of fresh green lands, and of pastures new,
It sang, while the bark through the surges flew.

But ever and anon
A murmur of farewell
Told, by its plaintive tone,
That from woman's lip it fell. (32)[23]

The masculine and feminine voices alternate throughout, expressing joy and desolation respectively:

"We will rear new homes, under trees that glow
As if gems were the fruitage of every bough;
O'er our white walls we will train the vine,
And sit in its shadow at day's decline,
And watch our herds, as they range at will
Through the green savannas, all bright and still"

· · · · · · · · · · · · · · · · ·

"But who will teach the flowers,
Which our children loved, to dwell
In a soil that is not ours?
—Home, home, and friends, farewell!" (32)

The voices also alternate stanza forms: the masculine using sestets of rhyming ten-syllable (though not iambic) couplets and the feminine following a loose ballad form. The implication seems straightforward enough: the masculine voice has a sterner and more modern, if faintly classicist (Georgic), progressivism, while the feminine stanzas evoke traditionary and homely yearning for natural bonds.

The Scots home tends to be riven in this way between forward-looking modernity and nostalgic organicism. The poet Allan Cunningham in the 1810 volume of (partly or wholly) forged traditional folk songs published by Robert Cromek, *The Remains of Nithsdale and Galloway Song,* includes verse that clearly aims to write home into Scots antiquity, particularly "Hame, Hame, Hame":

There's naught now frae ruin my country can save,
But the keys o' kind heaven to open the grave,
That a' the noble martyrs who died for loyaltie,
May rise again and fight for their ain countree.

It's hame, and it's hame, hame fain wad I be,
An' it's hame, hame, hame, to my ain country! (170)[24]

This song and many others affect Jacobite sentiment, thus inventing a Scots *hame* of immemorial provenance anchored to the Scots royal lineage.[25] "Hame, Hame, Hame" is featured in a section of the book titled "Jacobite Ballads, 1745" and comes with a headnote claiming, "This song is printed from a copy found in Burns's Common Place Book, in the Editor's possession" (169). The extensive details of origin and transmission attached to the songs suggest an extraordinarily inventive work of hoaxing, or at least imitation. I can find no evidence that any such commonplace book fell into Cunningham's possession. According to Cunningham's son, Peter, who printed a selected anthology of his father's poems in 1847, his father was an opportunist: "The idea of a volume of imitations passed upon Cromek as genuine remains flashed across the poet's mind in a moment" (xii).[26] Cunningham Junior also cites a note from *Jacobite Relics* by another capable hoaxster, James Hogg: "'Hame, Hame, Hame,' is taken from Cromek; and sore do I suspect that we are obliged to the same masterly hand for it with the two preceding ones" (26). The only evidence I can find of any earlier version of the song comes where Peter Cunningham includes in his introduction what purports to be a letter from Cromek to Allan Cunningham containing "Hame, Hame," which is an alternate version with a much sharper edge: "George, that vile usurper, / From Britain banished be" (xvii). "Is not this a heart-warming thing?" Cromek comments; "Don't give a copy of it under any pretence. Don't you think this song may be printed if the name of the King were omitted?" (xviii). The full extent of Cunningham's forgery and of Cromek's complicity seems uncertain, as indeed does the reliability of the account constructed by Cunningham *fils*.

Maurice Lindsay argues that "Many of [the *Remains*] were . . . Cunningham's own work, a fact of which Cromek has been accused of being perfectly well aware" (93). Lindsay also believes that one of "Cunningham's two best original songs" is "My Ain Countree" (93).[27] Walter Scott too has an opinion on the matter: "Luxuriance can only be the fault of genius, and many of your songs are, I think, unmatched. I would instance 'It's hame, and it's hame,' which my daughter Mrs. Lockhart sings with such uncommon effect" (qtd. in Lockhart 441 and in Cunningham, *Poems and Songs* 26). This disorienting maze of textual traces, whose effect is the obscuring of origins, mingles fictionality and historical factuality in ways similar to those I ascribed to Scott himself above, producing a "paradoxical logic of authentication" (Duncan, *Scott's*

*Shadow* 279) from the very traces of its forgery and plagiarism. Its application to the topos of home exemplifies what I am working to identify here: alienated voices speaking from exile, emigration, or proscription that lament their lost home and in doing so dissolve historical, or geographic, or political discontinuities that would otherwise sever the modern middle-class home from a naturalizing continuity with Scots antiquity.

One more example from Cunningham's "Jacobite Songs," "The Waes O' Scotland," borrows Wordsworth's *Girondin* incitement from *Salisbury Plain* and transfigures it for a nostalgic performance of internal exile. Where Wordsworth's lonely wanderer grieves, "homeless near a thousand homes I stood, / And near a thousand tables pined and wanted food" (lines 386–87), Cunningham's speaker encounters a "bonnie lass" who cries,

> O fatherless and motherless,
> > Without a ha' or hame,
> I maun wander through my ain Scotland,
> > And bide a traitor's blame.[28]

How our lass remains bonnie after the catalogue of injustice and deprivation she has endured is not explained, but more important is the sense that Jacobite rhetoric has lost its incendiary power and that it can therefore mediate the modern subject's nostalgic relation to her lost "countree." Instead of a sense of alienation produced by ruptured cultural and historical ties, the modern Scottish subject is offered the chance to find affiliation in the mourning and reenacting of her national provenance.[29]

The value of loss and dispossession as tropes of national origination is their tendency to obscure the origination itself. The constitutive violence of exclusion and coercion the modern home system continues to administer is erased by mourning for exclusions and coercions that precede modernity.[30] Nostalgia for the lost state of 'savagery' is simultaneously its renunciation. For English subjects, we have seen, home is the origin and end of aspiration, a place that is somehow lost because it is the destination of perpetual returns. For Scottish and other colonial subjects, and ultimately for English subjects too, home is not only suspended beyond the horizon defined by origin and end, but lost to an originary act of renunciation that cannot be called back. That renunciation may take a form as "natural" as maturation from youth to adulthood, or as historical as the Act of Union. Christian Johnstone's 1815 novel *Clan-Albin*, a narrative of the Highland Clearances, features a refrain often attributed to the MacLeod piper Donald Bàn MacCrimmon, *Cha till mi tuilleadh:* "this the glen whose every echo was ringing—*'We return, we return, we return no more!'"* (62). The Scottish home, if not every home, has a diasporic spirit.

## "Be It Ever Sae Hamely"

Having begun this study with a modification of romance in *Joseph Andrews,* we conclude with romance modified yet again in *Old Mortality.* As in Fielding's novel, there is no domestic space in *The Tale of Old Mortality* that looks much like the modern middle-class home. All of the domestic spaces in the narrative are archaic—attenuated by the feudal mode of production, kinship and clientage structures, regional "color," and political upheaval.[31] *Old Mortality* does indeed end with the establishment of a happy and presumptively bourgeois home, but the narrator, Peter Pattieson, "had determined to waive the task of a concluding chapter, leaving to the reader's imagination the arrangements which must necessarily take place" (349) and only changes his mind at the insistence of his acquaintance Miss Martha Buskbody, consumer of "the whole stock of three circulating libraries" (349). Even then, Pattieson does not actually specify *where* his principals, Henry Morton and Edith Bellenden, choose to live—the final domestic scene is Miss Buskbody's modest spinster lodgings, whence Pattieson flees, bidding her and us goodnight.

I will argue that the absence of the middle-class home in this novel is not contingent but determinate, signifying a historical watershed in the evolution of modern bourgeois domesticity as Walter Scott sees it. In the first place, *Old Mortality* is full to overflowing with other kinds of domesticity—literal, figurative, embattled, lost, destroyed, and recovered. From Morton's lurid vision of himself as villa-turned-fortress to the even more lurid image of Balfour standing in a cave brandishing the deed for Tillietudlem Castle, the novel's conflicts are insistently framed by modalities and distortions of home.[32] Harry Shaw insists, we should note, that Henry Morton's "spirit is clearly aristocratic" (192) and that the Covenanter uprising is a failed class rebellion (202), but he also admits that Morton embodies an awareness that, as a consequence of "bourgeois individuality," "members of postfeudal, postorganic societies" do not "belong" socially the way their ancestors did (203). Morton, like most of Scott's protagonists, is a protobourgeois subject, whose domestic inclinations and bland personality are descended most directly from the Radcliffean heroine. She too is a subject whose class has not yet coalesced around her and who moves through a decaying feudal environment. Scott's flirtation with anachronism in his protagonists is carefully constrained, and intermediated, by their positions at the edges of the central historical action, their status as internal exiles. They tend to remain peripheral to the historical machinations that overwhelm their personal travails. Only in the conclusions of Waverley Novels do the transformed milieus begin to reflect the bourgeois modernity that Scott's protagonists have been concealing in their own bosoms, uncertain whether it was good for anything more than to cause them suffering. Little wonder that Edward Waverley, Henry Morton, Frank Osbaldistone, and Darsie Latimer are adolescent or barely more; they feel the pangs of sentiments and affects that others do not feel so strongly, and they endure the alienation of sensitive souls.[33]

The omission of home from *Old Mortality* is also striking in the context of Walter Scott's fondness for marking narrative closure by allocating capitalized property. There are several important studies of the way Scott establishes that tactic in the conclusion of *Waverley,* particularly the transformation of the Baron Bradwardine's feudal estate into real estate.[34] A few important characters in *Old Mortality* aside from the central couple do get concluding property settlements, but those characters are not bourgeois exemplars, and they do not acquire anything resembling middle-class homes: Edith's mother, Lady Margaret Bellenden, regains proprietorship of Tillietudlem Castle and its domains; the faithful Cuddie Headrigg returns to his liege cottage on those domains; and Mrs. Wilson, housekeeper to Morton's uncle (and legator), continues to keep house. We can reasonably assume that Henry and Edith settle down at his ancestral home, Milnewood, under Mrs. Wilson's care, but Miss Buskbody's request for "a glimpse of their future felicity" (350) is not answered with any direct description of how or where they felicitate.[35] I do not suggest that Scott implies any future other than a happy and domesticated one for Henry and Edith. Rather, I want to take note of this ending's elaborate dance around the topic of home.

For a novelist working in 1818, home is the very topos of narrative closure. J. G. Lockhart reports a conversation from 1823, in which William Laidlaw advises Scott, "I have often thought that if you were to write a novel, and lay the scene here in the very year you were writing it, you would exceed yourself." "Hame's hame," Scott is said to have replied, "be it ever sae hamely" (505). Lockhart interpreted this exchange as the genesis of *Saint Ronan's Well,* which Scott described in his 1832 preface to the novel as "intended, in a word—*celebrare domestica facta*—to give an imitation of the shifting manners of our own time, and paint scenes, the originals of which are daily passing round us, so that a minute's observation may compare the copies with the originals" (Author's

Edition 33: iii).[36] The odd antiquarianism of the phrase *"celebrare domestica facta"* bespeaks Scott's disillusionment with a novel he considered less than successful, and perhaps also a terse irony concerning the role of home in Scottish life and letters: the phrase comes from Horace's *Ars poetica*, glossed by Basil Dufallo: "When praising the Roman genre of *fabula praetexta* . . . Horace remarks simply, 'nec minimum meruere decus vestigia Graeca / ausi deserere et celebrare domestica facta,' 'nor have those who dared to abandon the path of the Greeks and celebrate our homeland's deeds deserved the least honor'" (99). The private domestic lives of the Scots have not, as primary subject matter, made especially prestigious matter for the pen of the author of *Waverley*.

William Hazlitt calls Scott a "prophesier of things past" (*Spirit of the Age* 124), and one of *Old Mortality*'s key prophecies is the coming of the middle-class home. But an actual, unabstracted private home is, in the double historical perspective of this novel, both not yet established and already lost. The invention of the middle-class home is concealed by "the horizon at which—as for the individual subject, so for the nation—history comes to a stop" (Duncan, *Modern Romance* 53), and so in *Old Mortality* that horizon is invisibly demarcated by the absence of home. Historical propriety restrains Peter Pattieson from inserting an anachronistic middle-class home into his story of Scotland in the seventeenth century, and he is himself also shut out from conventional bourgeois domesticity. His visit to Miss Buskbody, "a young lady who has carried on the profession of mantua-making . . . for about forty years" (349), never quite achieves the status of courtship. He approaches her "with a palpitating heart," and they exchange compliments, but when he senses that she is "studying some farther cross-examination," he takes his hat and flees (349–52). Henry Morton and Edith Bellenden make their match too soon to enjoy genuine middle-class domestic bliss, while Pattieson and Miss Buskbody seem to have discovered the possibility a little too late. The etiology of the bourgeois home lies somewhere between the end of the Stuart succession and the end of this novel. There is a lacuna between the national union that the tale cannot relate and the personal union that the narrator cannot face, a story that cannot be told. It is the story of the modern home's conquest of national collectivity as well as private aspiration, its imposition of new laws and limits on both in the guise of total inclusion.

Scott has added to Austen's gestural aesthetic a kind of gestural historiography, alluding to a history and social reality beyond the text, but refusing to try to open the text up to it (extensive annotations notwithstanding): "I think," Peter Pattieson protests to Miss Buskbody, "a history, already growing vapid, is but dully crutched up by a detail of circumstances which every reader must have anticipated, even though the author exhaust on them every flowery epithet in the language" (350).[37] The modern home is set apart from the "historical planes of existence" (Kelly 144) because it is also set apart from the planes of fictional existence. *Old Mortality* thus manages both to historicize and to naturalize the modern home.[38] Scott outlines an etiology of bourgeois domesticity, but at the same time erases or disavows the historical grounds of its formation, especially the radical exclusions upon which it is founded and that it continues to enforce. The task of a historical novel, as Franco Moretti says, is to "represent internal unevenness . . . and then, to *abolish* it" (40). Accordingly, *Old Mortality*, like many of Scott's narratives, seeks to dissolve, or at least to palliate, the discomforting presence of English colonial hegemony in all spheres of Scottish life including the realm of intimacy and private refuge. Scott's "colonial subjection," as theorized by Caroline McCracken-Flesher, is revealed when, "in the moment of asserting national identity, the colonized subject pours his major effort into suppressing national difference" ("Thinking Nationally" 308). The middle-class home develops in this context as a mechanism of empire, a device capable of inserting one nationality into another, of anchoring identity categories and at the same time making them mobile. And Scotland, because of its political circumstances and its literary boom in the early nineteenth century, is a key proving ground for the new home in a new nation-state.

The historical antagonisms that drive the narrative of *Old Mortality* make domesticity (including its prebourgeois manifestations) a focus, even a topos, for their opposition. Both the state (which is to say the Stuart monarchy and its military representatives) and its primary opponent, the Covenanters, are fundamentally hostile to private households, and the shape of these hostilities helps to define their hostility to one another. Briefly: for the agents of the state, private households are hideouts and places of secrecy that conceal insurgency; for the Covenanters, the household sustains a law that competes with that of God, scripture, and the kirk (the Stuart monarchy, too, is a kind of household), and therefore they have renounced home—they are homeless, of the outdoors. The antithetical positions of the Stuart state and the covenanted nation allow Scott to play out the "historical" contest between open and closed forms of archaic domesticity, but just as importantly they enable him to figure a more modern dilemma between absolutes of state domination and personal autonomy: James II's unloved regime hardly needed Edmund Burke to revive its association with tyrannic absolutist power, and Scott works assiduously to define the Scottish "Whigs" as a radically individualist, contractual affiliation of private consciences united under the Covenants of 1638 and 1643.[39]

Scott's Covenanters present a limit case of the devolution of absolutism, "whereby the absolute authority of the sovereign is internalized . . . as a sovereign attribute of the individual citizen" (McKeon, *Secret History* 30).[40] The clash between Stuart (undevolved) absolutism and Covenanter conscience provides a surrogate for negotiations between monolithic, continuous state authority and private, voluntaristic political consent (or dissent), whose mediation and reconciliation the modern home-nation configuration is designed to effect. Henry Morton plays out some of those negotiations during his adventures. When he signs up with the Covenanters, he declares himself "willing to draw [his] sword for liberty and freedom of conscience" (170). "Desperate himself, he determined to support the rights of his country, insulted in his person" (114) and thus identifies with their extreme autonomism, which sets self in place of nation. His mentor-in-rebellion, Balfour, asks if his objective is "not that the church and state should be reformed by the free voice of a free parliament, with such laws as shall hereafter prevent the executive government from . . . trampling upon the consciences of men at their own wicked pleasure?" (170), to which Morton assents, but the perilous symmetry between the Covenanters' self-as-nation ethic and the Stuart monarchy's nation-as-self doctrine becomes clear to our hero, who is just the man to find a way between the two extreme alternatives.

The narrative of the troubles that perplex Henry Morton begins in a series of five scenes of hospitality—six if we count the narrator Peter Pattieson's "single glass of liquor" for Old Mortality in the prefatory chapter (11). The other five scenes are: Lady Margaret Bellenden's breakfast for King Charles II, years before—"the having given a breakfast to majesty, and received the royal salute in return were honours enough of themselves to unite her exclusively to the fortunes of the Stuarts" (19)—which she incessantly recounts; Morton's entertainment of those he has defeated in the popinjay shooting contest, during which the nemeses Bothwell and Balfour first clash; Morton's sheltering of Balfour in his uncle's stable, the crime for which the former is arrested; the dinner at Milnewood where Morton admits his crime to Bothwell and is arrested; and Lady Margaret's reception of Claverhouse and his dragoons, at which Morton's life is spared and his rebellion is spurred. No one is entertaining any angels unawares, except, perhaps, householders like Silas Morton who have "nae mark on their threshold for a signal that the destroying angel should pass by" (72).

But hospitality is, nonetheless, one of the laws of premodern Scots domesticity; after his arrest, Morton protests, "I am at least uncertain whether, even if I had known the crime, I could have brought my mind . . . to refuse a temporary refuge to the fugitive" (88). The domestic sphere, in this time and place, is not a sphere separated from the political because the law of hospitality makes it very difficult to consecrate any space as exclusively personal. The ancient "law" of hospitality is one of the antiquated domestic regulations that must be eliminated from Scottish households before the modern home can take up residence, as it were. In *Waverley*, the narrator repeatedly frowns at "the waste of [Fergus Mac-Ivor's] feudal hospitality" (158). Thresholds can be literally barred, as we will see, but the special figurations of private sanctuary are not protected and exalted by any traditionary or statute law. Domestic spaces in *Old Mortality* are riven by political forces so that they are hardly refuges and seldom even effective hiding places.

Compulsory hospitality defines the first of the interwoven contradictions that ensnare Morton. He is forbidden "to supply [Balfour or any rebel] with meat, drink, house, harbour, or victual, under the highest pains" (66), but he, and any other householder, cannot refuse the same to any red-coat that may request it: "the King's soldier cannot pass a house without getting a refreshment," Bothwell says; "In such houses as Tillie—what d'ye call it, you are served for love; in the houses of the avowed fanatics you help yourself by force; and among the moderate Presbyterians and other suspicious persons, you are well treated from fear" (75–76). At another moment he puts it more bluntly: "All's free where'er I come" (64); and the narratorial voice is more blunt still, referring to "the system of exaction and plunder carried on during these domiciliary visits" (62). The seventeenth-century Scottish private subject is required to maintain a home that is at once entirely open, and firmly closed. Scott represents coerced hospitality as the practical application of Stuart governance to the domestic realm.

Lady Margaret Bellenden keeps a loyalist household, welcoming the state's agents and expelling its enemies. Speaking of her locally famous breakfast for King Charles II, Lady Margaret explains that, "in whatever way his most sacred majesty ordered the position of the trenchers and flagons, that, as weel as his royal pleasure in greater matters, should be a law to his subjects, and shall ever be to those of the house of Tillietudlem" (95). As far as Lady Margaret is concerned, Tillietudlem is the state in miniature (or in metaphor), reproducing its ceremonies, ranks, and regulations, often with bathetic effect: she refuses to bring the "great Turkey-leather elbow-chair" out for Claverhouse to use as his "post in the attack upon the pasty" because "the throne," as she terms it, having "been once honoured by accommodating the person of our most sacred monarch . . . shall never . . . be pressed by any less dignified weight" (95–96).

The Stuart state is itself, as I have noted, also a kind of household, which is eager "to revive those feudal institutions which united the vassal to the liege-lord, and both to the crown" (14). But the prevailing indistinction between domestic space and other kinds of space (the halls of state or even just the outdoors) is approaching, we are encouraged to feel, a historical breakdown: "I'll hae nae whiggery in the barony of Tillietudlem," Lady Margaret informs Mause Headrigg, "the next thing wad be to set up a conventicle in my very withdrawing room" (55).[41] Lady Margaret's compliance with the procedures of state, including her expulsion of the estate's ploughman, Cuddie Headrigg, because of his mother's nonconformity, and her welcoming of the red-coats draws the wrath of rebels and leads to the collapse of her baronial idyll. The initial description of Tillietudlem's primitive domestic orders, however, is lavish and establishes a principle that the narrator sustains throughout *Old Mortality:* variant modes of domestic life are key measures of historical difference. "The breakfast of the Lady Margaret Bellenden," Peter Pattieson explains, "no more resembled a modern dejeuné, than the great stone hall of Tillietudlem could brook comparison with a modern drawing room. No tea, no coffee, no variety of rolls, but solid and substantial viands—the priestly ham, the knightly sirloin, the noble baron of beef, the princely venison pasty" (100). Even the provisions at Tillietudlem summon up the kind of political hierarchy that the modern private home proscribes.

Other households in the novel are not so open to the functions and functionaries of state power, but tend equally to frame comparisons between past and present. In these homes, exemplified by Milnewood, a less permeable boundary with the world outside prevails: "It was a universal custom in Scotland, that, when the family was at dinner, the outer-gate of the court-yard, if there was one, and, if not, the door of the house itself was always shut and locked" (62). This household is by no means a more modern one than Tillietudlem: the family consists of many servants and workers besides the proprietor's immediate kin; the house itself is decaying (37); and the domestics are "of a certain class . . . once common in Scotland, and perhaps still to be found in some old manor houses in its remote counties," who tend to be "ill-tempered, self-sufficient, and tyrannical" (40). But the inmates of Milnewood look out at the world without allowing the state's agents, or anyone else, to see in: Mrs. Wilson detects approaching red-coats through "some secret aperture with which most Scottish door-ways were furnished" (62).

Here is the crux of the Stuart state's antipathy toward private domesticity. Where a home is anything other than the kind of open, loyalist feudal demesne we see at Tillietudlem, its enclosure is potentially treasonous. The fact of concealment automatically implies insurgent machinations: the publican, Neil Blane, warns his daughter about Balfour: "let na him hae a room to himsel, they wad say we were hiding him" (27). Later, with Balfour stashed in his uncle's stable, Morton overhears a passing cavalry officer ask whose house Milnewood is; learn that the owner "frequents an indulged minister"; and respond: "Indulged? A mere mask for treason, very impolitically allowed to those who are too great cowards to wear their principles barefaced. Had we not better send up a party and search the house, in case some of the bloody villains concerned in this heathenish butchery [the murder of Archbishop Sharpe] may be concealed in it?" (41).[42] Indeed, one of the bloody villains *is* concealed in the house at the time. The suspicions of the state's agents tend to be accurate.

House-breaking in the name of the law seems to be, if not actually legitimate, at least discriminate. It is not simply the state's relation to domesticity that breaks down in *Old Mortality*. The home itself must also change. As Carolyn Austin observes of *The Heart of Midlothian*, "domestic isolation and the Waverley novels' ideology of a Great Britain founded on political inclusiveness distort each other when brought together" (622). *Old Mortality* shares in the business of working out a compromise between these positions. The antiquated Scottish national configuration of households within households is too centralized, centripetal, and hierarchical.[43] The new domesticity must be something between the too-open Tillietudlem and the too-closed Milnewood; the state itself must be excluded/withdraw itself from familial and household relations; and power must be distributed rhizomatically rather than in vertical orders of estate.

The cavalry officer's mistrust of the Indulgences also connects with an important thematic—masks and disguises—that runs throughout the novel in parallel with, and supplementary to, the theme of outmoded domesticity. The "mask of Indulgence" is, like archaic privacy, a necessarily equivocal sign that simultaneously legitimates status and enables its falsification.[44] Predictably, the Covenanters also despise the Indulgences, for reasons that are essentially identical to those of the state's agents. "That is but an equivocation—a poor equivocation," Balfour responds to Morton's profession of faith; "of all the baits with which the devil has fished for souls in these days of blood and darkness, that Black Indulgence has been the most destructive" (35). The same ambiguity appears in the disguise Morton dons to take part in the shooting contest and again when he is imprisoned at Tillietudlem. It also appears in Cuddie's "look of supreme indifference and stupidity which a Scottish peasant can at times assume as a masque for considerable shrewdness and craft" (63), and in Claverhouse's polished manners and grooming. Edith Bellenden appears in the Scots equivalent to the Restoration *beau monde*'s vizard mask when she visits the captive Henry Morton: "Jenny hastened, and soon returned with a plaid, in which Edith muffled herself so as completely to screen her face, and in part to disguise her person. This was a mode of arranging the plaid very common among the ladies of that century . . . so much so, indeed, that the venerable sages of the Kirk, conceiving that the mode gave tempting facilities for intrigue, directed more than one act of Assembly against this use of the mantle" (84). But Morton sees through her disguise intuitively: "for what other female in the house, excepting Edith herself, was like to take an interest in his misfortunes?" (87). Like the locked door of Milnewood, Edith's plaid is more effective as provocation than concealment.

Disguises in *Old Mortality* always fail, usually because the subject in disguise gives herself away unconsciously. When Bothwell administers the test oath, Mause Headrigg, whom Cuddie has tried to excuse as deaf, allows her divine zeal to flare out and in so doing upsets Bothwell's intention to overlook Morton's crime (68–69). Much later, having returned from a ten-year exile, Morton visits Milnewood, disguised by the passage of time, and gives himself away to Mrs. Wilson by speaking the name of his pet dog (316). Then, approaching the public house of Neil Blane, Morton wonders whether "his resumption of the dress which he had worn while a youth . . . might render it more difficult for him to remain *incognito*" (322). This last example implies not just that Morton is a poor student of dissimulation, but that his desire to conceal himself is by no means unalloyed.

The motif of disguise and its unsustainability in *Old Mortality* underscores the synonymy between privacy and secrecy that Scott associates with antiquated forms of domesticity and that will be broken by the Hanoverian social compact. (The "British Revolution" has taken place by the time Morton returns to Scotland in chapter 7 of the final volume, "and men, whose minds had been disturbed by the violent political concussion . . . had begun to recover their ordinary temper, and to give the usual attention to their own private affairs in lieu of discussing those of the public" [286]). Prior to the Revolution, open and sentimental intercourse is forestalled in Scott's seventeenth century because the social realm is fractured by stratification and contradiction. The forms of rule and compulsion that organize that older social order lack the naturalness toward which they are, nonetheless, approaching. Henry Morton leads us on a narrative and thematic trajectory toward a new open and sympathetic civility like that proposed by Adam Ferguson:

> The interests of society . . . and of its members, are easily reconciled. If the individual owe every degree of consideration to the public, he receives, in paying that very consideration, the greatest happiness of which his nature is capable; and the greatest blessing that the public can bestow on its members, is to keep them attached to itself. That is the most happy state, which is most beloved by its subjects; and they are the most happy men, whose hearts are engaged to a community, in which they find every object of generosity and zeal, and a scope to the exercise of every talent, and of every virtuous disposition. (59)

In Ferguson's and Scott's modern social realm, expression of attachment and civil engagement is no longer obligatory or coerced (or withheld in dissent) but pleasurable.[45]

The affective bonds of Fergusonian private selfhood function as mediators, constituting mutual interests (usually portrayed as impartial disinterest) and points of exchange between subjects. Social bonds are no longer barriers that make the personal or private unintelligible to others: "We love to chuse our object without any restraint, and we consider kindness itself a task, when the duties of friendship are exacted by rule" (Ferguson 87). Compulsory hospitality and its counterpart, reclusive secrecy, must make way for social exchange made free by its embodiment in voluntaristic and natural affective bonds. The state's relation to the private home should derive from the social relations natural to the latter, not engineered by the former. As Lisa Hill explains, Ferguson's model of historical development enables this kind of process: "Competition, conflict, belligerence and hostility indirectly preserve social cohesion and give rise to such beneficial institutions as an organised state, positive law and advances in defence technology and statecraft; social norms are shaped by and depend upon inter-subjective validation while moral judgements are reinforced by shared or mutual affective responses" (16). This gradual conversion of private passion into civil order seems to allow the development of a home (a relation between private home and home nation) that is at once natural and historically situated.

## THE DESTROYING ANGEL IN THE HOUSE

The complement to failed disguise in *Old Mortality* is misinterpretation, a process associated mainly with the Covenanters and their enthusiastic over-readings of scripture. But misinterpretation also governs a crucial plot development, Morton's decision to join the rebellion. The moment occurs in Til-lietudlem Castle when, shortly before his audience with Claverhouse, Morton overhears his beloved Edith in the act of begging his rival suitor, Lord Evan-dale, to exercise his influence with Claverhouse on Morton's behalf. What Morton overhears ("There is no friend I esteem more highly, or to whom I would more readily grant every mark of regard—providing—But—"), he interrupts with his own sigh, preventing Edith from pronouncing "the exception with which she meant to close the sentence" (108). Amid the confusion of interest and impartiality, rank and due deference, gallantry and rivalry, Morton decides that Edith's affection is lost to him, and the consequences are drastic indeed:

> That moment made a singular and instantaneous revolution in his character. The depth of despair to which his love and fortunes were reduced, the peril in which his life appeared to stand, the transference of Edith's affections, her intercession in his favour, which rendered her fickleness yet more galling, seemed to destroy every feeling for which he had hitherto lived, but at the same time, awakened those which had hitherto been smothered by passions more gentle though more selfish. Desperate himself, he determined to support the rights of his country, insulted in his person. His character was for the moment as effectually changed as the appearance of a villa, from being the abode of domestic quiet and happiness, is, by the sudden intrusion of an armed force, converted into a formidable post of defense. (114)

Disappointment in love, because it occurs in a social milieu where the personal and the political, the domestic and the national are dangerously fluid, is sufficient provocation for Morton to identify himself wholly with his nation. His private self is largely obliterated. Subsequently, and consequently, the figural annihilation of Scottish domesticity in the person of Morton also turns out to be quite literal throughout the West of Scotland; all homes are militarized or swallowed up by the theater of civil war.

As Harry Shaw argues, this "substantial equation of public and private spheres" is unusual for Walter Scott (193). At this moment, the collision of all the major components of personhood, domesticity, and nationhood produces a subject position that is unsustainable, but revolutionary. Morton experiences what Homi Bhabha calls an "unhomely moment," which "relates the traumatic ambivalences of a personal, psychic history to the wider disjunctions of political existence" (144). Morton embodies a merging of domestic and political aspirations that will lead to the shattering and reformation of both. In the morphological vocabulary of romance, Morton is the young hero departing from home, not to return until both he and his home are irrevocably changed. Scott ironizes the romance/allegorical implications of Morton's departure, by turning Morton over to the Covenanters, whose exaggerated, literalizing zeal for the allegorical becomes the register in which the short-lived, inside-out world of Morton's domestic revolution is represented.

Having escaped from his red-coat captors during the Battle of Drumclog, Morton joins the Covenanters and takes command of the rebels from his home parish. He finds himself in a state of radical homelessness. Domesticity is utterly removed from the haunts of the rebels. Where habitations are found, they are appropriated for warfare; Morton's first council of war takes place in "a shepherd's hut, a miserable cottage, which, as the only enclosed spot within a moderate distance, the leaders of the Presbyterian army had chosen for their temporary council-house" (176). The Covenanters' council hut is only barely an enclosure at all. It is part ruin and part figural outdoors: "the precincts of the gloomy and ruinous hut were enlightened partly by some furze which blazed on the hearth, the smoke whereof, having no legal vent, eddied around, and formed . . . a cloudy canopy . . . through which, like stars through mist, were dimly seen to twinkle a few blinking candles" (177). And in the council, loud voices call for the destruction of what domesticity remains elsewhere. The insane preacher Habbakuk Meiklewrath demands, "in a voice that made the very beams of the roof quiver," the despoliation of Tillietudlem: "Take the infants and dash them against the stones; take the daughters and the mothers of the house and hurl them from the battlements of their trust . . . Defile the house and fill the courts with the slain!" (181–82). Morton is horrified, and speaks up for moderation, but his words are not heeded.[46]

Again our hero is wracked by contradiction. To oppose the force that is ravishing the homes of Scotland, Morton has joined another force that also threatens to destroy any domesticity it finds. He holds to the cause, nonetheless, having renounced all ties that would give him reason not to rebel. Indeed, besides his antipathy for the state and his loss of Edith, Morton is also in rebellion against his own home and family, because of the "sordid parsimony which pervaded every part of his uncle's establishment" (38). He is unmoored: "I am sick of my country—of myself—of my dependent situation—of my repressed feelings—of these woods—of that river—of that house" (47). The domestic refuge that Morton wants for himself, his beloved, and his nation is nowhere actually extant, except insofar as his own virtues and aspirations are a kind of blueprint for it: "I am no slave . . . in one respect, surely. I can change my abode" (47). He is, in the early stages of the narrative, essentially an agent of negation: "A mild, romantic, gentle-tempered youth, bred up in dependence, and stooping patiently to the controul of a sordid and tyrannical relation, had suddenly, by the rod of oppression and the spur of injured feeling, been compelled to stand forth a leader of armed men" (215); "nothing remains for me now," he tells Cuddie, "but vengeance for my own wrongs, and for those that are hourly inflicted on my country" (124). So for a time he is content to side with the rebellion because the Covenanters' radical consciousness accords sufficiently with his own catachrestic identification with Scotland: "[He] felt his individual fate bound up in that of a national insurrection and revolution" (215).

That the metaphor of a villa-turned-fortress, and consequently of a self-turned-nation, is a catachresis would be evident to a character like Claverhouse, who cautions Evandale, "Should you wish . . . to rise to eminence in the service of your king and country, let it be your first task to subject to the public interest, and to the discharge of your duty, your private passions, affections, and feelings" (117). But, for a time at least, Morton is carried along by his identification, and the deranged scriptural terms in which the Covenanters speak provide a correlative to his state of mind. Ephraim MacBriar, for instance, exhorts the rebel army: "Your garments are dyed—but not with the juice of the wine-press; your swords are filled with blood . . . but not with the blood of goats or lambs; the dust of the desert on which ye stand is made fat with gore, but not with the blood of bullocks, for the Lord hath made a sacrifice in Borzah, and a great slaughter in the land of Idumea" (154). Morton does not embrace these garish, solipsistic allegories, but Scott implies that they are the consequence of a self-nation identification equivalent to Morton's.

At a crucial moment, Morton adopts a register of speech that comes close to that of the zealots: "The sword of liberty and patriotism is in my hand, and I will neither fall meanly nor unavenged. They may expose my body and gibbet my limbs, but other days will come when the sentence of infamy will recoil against those who may pronounce it" (215). He speaks these words to himself only. But, though his awareness of his own false consciousness takes some time to crystallize, he is able to recognize the catachreses in his fellow rebels' expressions: "I revere the Scriptures as deeply as you or any Christian can do," he tells Balfour; "I look into them with humble hope of extracting a rule of conduct and a law of salvation. But I expect to find this by an examination of their general tenor, and of the spirit which they uniformly breathe, and not by wresting particular passages from their context, or by the application of Scriptural phrases to circumstances and events with which they have often very slender relations" (170).[47] Morton's companions are intractable. They turn his nation into a kind of biblical wilderness around him, where home is not just lost, but renounced: "Well is he this day," cries MacBriar, "that shall barter his house for a helmet, and sell his garment for a sword, and cast in his lot with the children of the Covenant" (191)—ploughshares into swords.

Old Mortality himself preserves the Covenanter tradition of homelessness and exile within one's native land. Peter Pattieson refers to him as a "religious itinerant" and reports that "he is said to have held . . . a small moorland farm; but, whether from pecuniary losses, or domestic misfortune, he had long renounced that and every other gainful calling. In the language of Scripture, he left his house, his home, and his kindred, and wandered about until the day of his death" (9). Necessarily so, for the graves that he visits and restores "are often apart from all human habitation, in the remote moors and wilds to which the wanderers had fled for concealment" (9). The rebels that Old Mortality reveres conduct their conventicles under the open sky, and the battle at Drumclog is watched by "the women, and even the children, whom zeal, opposed to persecution had driven into the wilderness" (131). Their nation is the Kirk, and the expulsion of all "sectaries of various descriptions" would "re-edify in its integrity the beauty of the sanctuary" (152–53). It is, as that last phrase suggests, the Covenanters' ambition that no other edifice—state or home, literal or figurative—interpose itself between the subject and his church: "We have but one object on earth," says Balfour, "and that is, to build up the temple of the Lord" (188). The only sanctuary must be the nation-as-church.

The hostility of the Covenanters to private homes, and even more to baronial estates like Tillietudlem, is based in that figuration. Whereas for the state, all homes are havens for insurgency, for the rebels, all homes are limbs of the state and the established (English) church: they maintain a law that competes with the divine law. The firebrand MacBriar, for instance, decries the Erastianism of a church that would "place either King or parliament in [God's] place as the master and governor of his household" (171); Balfour congratulates Morton on his decision no longer to be "an indweller in the tents of Ham" (148); and later upbraids him for wishing to spare the defenders of Tillietudlem Castle: "There are those in yon dark Tower, over whom thou wouldst rather be watching like a mother over her little ones, than thou wouldst bear the banner of the Church of Scotland over the necks of her enemies" (208). The Covenanters' hostility to the private home is not the exact opposite of the state's—they do not see it as an agency of their oppression, so much as a kind of figuration that interrupts, and threatens to expose as catachreses, their scriptural visions of the nation of Scotland. For Scott's Covenanters, as for his loyalists, relationships between what we recognize as the private and the political are organized by metaphors, but to expose the metaphors as such is to imperil the integrity of those relationships.

Hogg and Galt also make renunciation of, or expulsion from, home a metonymic symbol for rebellion against dominant orders. In Hogg's poem *The Queen's Wake,* for instance, a contest between Scots bards ends with a shepherd from Ettrick placing second and rejecting his prize, proclaiming, "Your cottage keep, and minstrel lore,— / Grant me a harp, I ask no more" (168). The brownie in Hogg's Covenanter narrative *The Brownie of Bodsbeck,* who turns out to be one of the persecuted sect, tells the protagonist, "we were expelled from our homes, and at last hunted from our native mountains like wolves" (161). Galt's novel on the same topic, *Ringan Gilhaize,* begins with the protagonist recalling his grandfather's example: "After enduring for several years great affliction in his father's house . . . my grandfather entered into a paction with two other young lads to quit their homes for ever, and to enter the service of some of those pious noblemen who were then active in procuring adherents to the protestant cause, as set forth in the first covenant" (4). Ringan follows him into the legions of unhoused: "'You see, Ringan Gilhaize,' said the minister, '. . . we are mercifully dealt by—a rougher manner and a harder heart, in the agent of persecution that has driven us from house and home'" (170). Toward the end of the novel, he finds his home destroyed: "Then I rose again, and went towards the place where my home had been; but when I saw the ruins I ran back to the kirk-yard, and threw myself on the grave, and cried to the earth to open and receive me" (264). Both Hogg and Galt align grand, embracing conceptions of home more unequivocally and explicitly with coercive forms of domination than Scott does. Scott's narratives tend to drive toward a clear separation between spheres of private life and those where statecraft, warfare, trade, and the unsanctioned versions of those activities occur.[48] That tactic is key to his maintenance of the sense that an antediluvian naturalness survives in the home even as it transforms into the institution of origin and aspiration that is its distinctly modern guise.

*The Brownie of Bodsbeck* observes no such careful separation. Its tangle of private and public motivations, affects, and affiliations is not carefully unpicked, as happens in *Old Mortality* when Henry Morton's confusion of love rivalry with injured nationality is untangled and smoothed out. *The Brownie of Bodsbeck*'s political themes are densely intertwined with its domestic ones, not because politics and history invade and ravage private domesticity the way they do in Scott's novel, but because they are already immanent in the home and well up from within it.[49] The haunting of Chapelhope (the home in question) is a political uncanny, a merging of gothic *unheimlich* with Bhabha's unhomely.[50] "There were things about his house," the protagonist, Walter Laidlaw, discovers, "there were things seen, heard, and done there that he could nowise account for in a natural way, and though he resisted the general belief for a good while that the house was haunted, circumstances obliged him to yield to the torrent" (33). "I feared sair," he says to himself, "that a' wasna right about hame" (148) One member of the family, Walter's daughter Katherine, is not subject to these fears because she seems to be in league with the brownie (a creature that is understood as part revenant and part demon): "She's transplanted—she's no Keaty Laidlaw now, but an unearthly creature" (8). In Bhabha's terms, Walter feels a "shock of recognition of the world-in-the-home, the home-in-the-world" (141).

"There was," we learn about Chapelhope, "an outshot from the back of the house, called the Old Room, which had a door that entered from without, as well as one from the parlour within . . . anyone, with a little caution, might easily have gone out or come in . . . It contained a bed in which any casual vagrant or itinerary pedlar slept" (Hogg, *Brownie* 36), and the haunting emanates from there. This undiscerning provision of shelter to vagabonds implicates poor relief in the haunting of Chapelhope, as does the mysterious vanishing of dozens of the bannocks (oat or barley cakes) that the goodwife, Maron Linton, bakes in quantities that might seem supernatural in another context (6–7).[51] Of course, the Old Room, the zone of unmediated contact between domesticity and history, is providing shelter to the archetypes of Scottish homelessness, fugitive Covenanters, as well as a place for them to conspire with Katherine.

That Covenanters are hiding in the region is well known, yet the house-holders and their employees remain determined not to draw a connection between them and the haunting, a willed delusion that Katherine is happy to encourage: she warns her parents, "should you go with me into the Old Room just now, you might never be yourself again" (38). When he makes his appearance, Claverhouse spells out what the family cannot conceive: "Go and search every corner, chest, and closet in the house; for it is apparent that this is the nest and rendezvous of the murdering fanatics who infest this country" (58), but still no one draws the connection. The Covenanters keep their dependence on Walter and Maron's unwitting hospitality a secret from them because, as one eventually explains, "if you had taken pity on us, we knew it would cost you your life, and be the means of bereaving your family of all your well-earned wealth" (162). In secret recompense, they undertake some of the work of caring for the Chapelhope sheep unseen in the night, like helpful elves, which is pretty much what the beneficiaries of their assistance assume.

Claverhouse effectively colludes with the Covenanters in maintaining the mystery of the old room: Walter Laidlaw is arrested and later tried for his life not for sheltering rebels, but essentially because he fails to adapt his hospitality to suit the decorum required by representatives of the state: "I didna ken that he was a captain" is all he offers in defense of the blow he strikes one of Claverhouse's officer (139), minutes after grabbing Claverhouse himself by the neck. Unlike Scott's Henry Morton, Walter Laidlaw's honest, commonsensical, homegrown virtue does him no good at trial; "his own counsel were always trembling for him when he began to speak for himself" (139). Walter escapes punishment because he convinces the court that he is "nae whig, nor naething akin to them" (142), and the charge of sheltering and aiding the whigs is not pressed. Even after his release, as Katie leads Walter to the meeting at which his unwitting collusion with the Covenanters is revealed to him, he remains mystified: "Walter was busy all the way trying to form some conjecture . . . and began to suspect that his old friends, the Covenantmen, were some way or other connected with it; that it was they, perhaps, who had the power of raising those spirits by which his dwelling had been so grievously haunted" (157). They do, of course, have that power, though not as Walter understands it.

This ironic terror of, and refusal to contemplate, the possibility that political forces are immanent in the domestic sphere—Walter shows no fear of anything else, not even of Claverhouse himself—seems to me a marker of Hogg's satiric intervention in the history of home. Here, as in *The Confessions,* he intimates that the simultaneous conception of home—or any institution—as a transhistorical, apolitical essence *and* as a foundational figuration of civil, political, and national order requires willful forgetting or misrecognition. Indeed, an important piece of evidence that ghosts are at home in Chapelhope is Walter's wife Maron's misinterpretation of an overheard conversation in which Katherine addresses "Brownie." Rather than "the brownie," it turns out she was talking to John Brown, a Covenanter leader who has survived the execution that, according to historical record, ended his life in 1685. Hogg uses home's hauntedness to figure delusion or false consciousness. The householders at Chapelhope fail to understand that their private dwelling is a part of the political world. They can only comprehend the secret fact of immanent political and historical forces as ghosts, manifestations of subjects returning from the dead bringing punishment for old sins: in a characteristic piece of pastoral wise-foolery, Walter's shepherd Davie Tait complains, "the dead are as rife here now as the living—they gang amang us, work amang us, an' speak to us; an' them that we ken to be half-rotten i' their graves, come an' visit our firesides at the howe o' the night" (151).

The final chapter begins with an arch wink at the kind of concluding disavowal that Peter Pattieson offers in *Old Mortality* (and that Jane Austen's narrators also indulge), "I hate long explanations, therefore this chapter shall be very short," and it concludes without any implication of home's homeliness, but rather a selection of blessings from local luminaries:

> The old session-clerk and precentor at Ettrick said, "It was the luckiest thing that could have happened that [Walter] had come home again, for the poor's ladle had been found to be a pund short every Sunday" ... fat Sandy Cunningham, the conforming clergyman ... remarked, "that he was very glad to hear the news, for the goodman always gave the best dinners at the visitations" ... Even old John of the Muchrah remarked, "that it was just as weel that his master was come back, for he had an unco gude e'e amang the sheep when ought was gaun wrang on the hill." (167–68)

There is no domesticating settlement here, no compact of social harmony and mutual affection, only a resumption of quotidian self-interests. The very last paragraph deliberately interrupts the conventional literary benediction that passes the reader back to her domestic surrounds: "If there are any incidents in Tale that may still appear a little mysterious, they will all be rendered obvious by turning to a pamphlet, entitled, A CAMERONIAN'S TALE ... But any reader of common ingenuity may very easily solve them all" (168). The unclosure of this closing paragraph blurs the horizon at which fictional representation yields to extraliterary reality. Hogg refuses the gestural aesthetic of domestic fiction in favor of interpretive indeterminacy.

Morton's participation in Walter Scott's version of the Covenanter rebellion comes to an end in yet another scene of compromised hospitality. After the disastrous Battle of Bothwell Brigg, he and Cuddie cease their flight at "a large and solitary farmhouse, situated in the entrance of a wild and moorish glen, far remote from any other habitation" (259). When the inhabitants of the house refuse him admittance, Morton climbs in a window and finds himself surrounded by "several of those zealots who had most distinguished themselves by their intemperate opposition to all moderate measures" (260). The solitary house on the moor is a fitting place to stage the conclusion of Morton's civil war. In the most tenuous of domestic spaces, far from contact with any other homes, his captors conduct a summary trial that is in many respects the counterpart to the trial that Morton endured in Tillietudlem at the hands of Claverhouse. The two trials bookend his rebellion: the earlier one began at dawn; this one ends at midnight. Again he is condemned and again escapes at the last extremity, but this time his rescuer is Claverhouse. The first trial had turned Morton into a creature apart, a liminal being (neither person nor nation, but both at once): at Tillietudlem, Claverhouse had observed of him: "He is tottering on the verge between time and eternity, a situation more appalling than the most hideous certainty; yet his is the only cheek unblenched, the only eye that is calm, the only heart that keeps its usual time" (117). The second trial and condemnation returns him to himself: "It was with pain that he felt his mind wavering when on the brink between this and the future world" (264). From this precipice he returns, recovering his private selfhood.

Even though he renounces his personal war against the Stuart state and evades its sternest sanctions, Morton still cannot find a happy home in Scotland. His punishment is an exile that takes up the next ten years of his life—and none of the narrative. The Scotland from which he departs is barren of domestic refuge and comfort. Lady Margaret's precious "throne" has been destroyed in the sack of Tillietudlem (283), and the Bellendens have been forced to leave the castle by a claim of prior title from Sir Basil Oliphant, which Balfour facilitates by concealing the document that would establish Lady Margaret's legitimate title (284–85). Milnewood lies under threat of state forfeiture for Morton's treason (283), and Major Bellenden dies brokenhearted from the strain of his sister-in-law's dispossession and the ruinous lawsuit that follows it—"creditors came to [his mansion] Charnwood and cleaned out a' that was there" (294). Morton comes back in 1689, following the Prince of Orange, whom he has served for the duration of his exile and whose Glorious Revolution has fulfilled Meiklewrath's final prophecy to Claverhouse: "Behold the princes, for whom thou hast sold thy soul to the destroyer, shall be removed from their place, and banished to other lands" (268). The ellipsis of Morton's ten-year exile from a land where the forms of domesticity that he knew have been largely wiped out provides a lacuna capacious enough to encompass and effectively swallow up the vanished horizon of the modern home's historical emergence. He returns under a new civil authority as the agent of a new domestic order.

## FRUCTIFICATION

Returning as a stranger, disguised by passing time and rumor of his death, Morton finds Cuddie and Jenny maintaining a modestly blissful home at Fairy-knowe:

> The hut seemed comfortable, and more neatly arranged than is usual in Scotland; it had its little garden, where some fruit-trees and bushes were mingled with kitchen herbs . . . and the thin blue smoke which ascended from the straw-bound chimney . . . shewed that the evening meal was in the act of being made ready. To complete the little scene of rural peace and comfort, a girl of about five years old was fetching water in a pitcher from a beautiful fountain of the purest water, which bubbled up at the root of a decayed old oak tree, about twenty yards from the end of the cottage. (288)

We might imagine that Scotland's domestic idyll is already realized (and English dominion scaled back to, or naturalized as, an antique symbol guarding the wellspring), but Cuddie laments the loss of "the bonny barony, and the holms that I hae ploughed sae aften, and the Mains and my kale-yard, that I suld hae gotten back again, and a' for naething . . . but just the want o' some bits of sheep-skin" (292). Edith and her grandmother remain unjustly dispossessed, and Edith is on point of entering into a marriage with Lord Evandale based more on obligation—for "so many services, as hardly left her a title to refuse his addresses"(309)—and belief in Morton's decease than on affection. Conflict continues in the Highlands, where Claverhouse has joined the Highland clans and lost his life fighting against the new monarchy. His client loyalty to the house of Stuart, instead of to the state as such, marks precisely the style of civic duty and honor that is in rapid decay under the "prudent tolerance" of William and Mary (286).

Lord Evandale is also enthralled by the old forms of clientage and kinship: "You must be aware, my dear Edith," his sister says in vaguely Burkean phrases, "how often family connections, and early predilections, influence our actions more than abstract arguments" (299). Evandale possesses the chivalric features of Burkean civic masculinity, but he must make way for Morton, who comes as an agent of the new statute law of private property and personal responsibility.[52] Evandale announces that he means to exercise his early predilections by assuming the post at the head of the Jacobite army left vacant by Claverhouse. His last intended act before departing is to marry Edith so that his estate cannot be denied to her by his "heirs of entail" or "forfeiture as a traitor" (302). This, and other remaining feudal modes of conduct, still remain to be eliminated, or at least circumscribed by the emergent social contract of William and Mary. Domestic bliss must be achieved not by manipulation of entail and royal favor, but by mutual aspiration and endeavor, and after the explicit renunciation of the older forms.

In this postrevolutionary world, the rejection of feudal or chivalric imperatives need not involve wholesale national conflict. From the perspective of the Lowland setting of *Old Mortality*, the ongoing strife in the Highlands is very much at a remove: "the general state of the Highlands was so unruly, that their being more or less disturbed was not supposed greatly to affect the general tranquility of the country" (286). The new government is much less hostile to the private home than the previous one and hence privacy and intimacy begin to flourish: "men, whose minds had been disturbed by the violent political concussion, and the general change of government in church and state, had begun to recover their ordinary temper, and to give the usual attention to their own private affairs in lieu of discussing those of the public" (286). Indeed the secure and stable home is, according to the logic of bourgeois domesticity, a necessary condition for intimacy. The struggles and contradictions that had overwhelmed Morton and Edith are now either already dissolved, or resolvable at the level of personal action. The state refuses any longer to oppose those parties to the Covenanting cause that still consider themselves oppressed: "as the murmurers were allowed to hold their meetings uninterrupted, and to testify as much as they pleased against Socianism, Erastianism, and all the compliances and defections of the time, their zeal, unfanned by persecution, died gradually away" (287). Edith frees herself from fealty and obligation to embrace a rising ethic: "Forgive me—" she tells Evandale, "I must deal most untruly by you, and break a solemn engagement. You have my friendship, my highest regard, my most sincere gratitude . . . But, O, forgive me, for the fault is not mine—you have not my love, and I cannot marry you without a sin!" (305). The marital union, like the political union of Scotland and England, will be structured by a companionate ethos, not an overtly asymmetrical one of obligation and subjugation.

In *Waverley*, Scott had already done the work of concluding a novel with an English-Scottish marital union to sanctify the political union of England and Scotland. In *Old Mortality*, he is working on a more subtle and intricate pageant, arranging the awkward pairing of English rule with a Scottish conception of home. His key maneuver is substituting the Declaration of Right in place of the Act of Union as the founding document of the British home nation. By locating the resumption of "private affairs in lieu of" the all-consuming pressures of "those of the public" in "the year immediately subsequent to the British Revolution" (286), Scott installs the Glorious Revolution and its constitutional repercussions in place of union as the moment that a modern home nation begins to arise in Scotland.[53] Like the middle-class home, the Glorious Revolution is actually nowhere to be found in this novel; it falls into the unnarrated interval of Morton's exile. The narrator accounts for the ten-year lacuna with a brief meditation on the free discretion of "tale-tellers," who are "not tied down . . . to the unities of time and place" (286). The narrator would, nonetheless, appear to feel constrained ("years . . . glided away ere we find it possible to resume the thread of our narrative" [286]) by a unity of nation. Only when Morton is on Scottish soil can his tale be told. This special contingency is yet another example of Scott's negotiation between historicizing and naturalizing. Where the facts of historical development are unyielding, literary proprieties provide a means of sustaining authority.

Making the Glorious Revolution the constitutive political-historical absence in *Old Mortality* is another component of Scott's simultaneous historicizing and naturalizing strategy. By leaving out the middle-class home, he leaves equivocal its naturalness and/or historicity, and the same is true of the post-Williamite social contract. Just as Adam Smith adopts Bacon, Boyle, and Newton as his countrymen when he assumes the name of Briton, the Declaration of Right fudges the difference between adoptive and lineal kinds of patrimony. Morton returns to a nation that has already embraced a foundational social contract that is not revolutionary at all but consonant with nature and the perdurable constitution, just as Edmund Burke prescribed it: "An irregular, convulsive movement may be necessary to throw off an irregular, convulsive disease. But the course of succession is the healthy habit of the British constitution" (Burke, *Reflections* 109). The assimilative and domineering aspects of union are not so much disarmed or rebutted as displaced by a different negation: the end of feudal clientage and the emergence of personal proprietorship.[54] This shift is dramatized in another scene that revises an earlier one: Morton's second jilting. After his return he finds yet again that he has apparently lost Edith to Evandale. This time, instead of transforming himself into a grand catachrestic metaphor, Morton remains a humble metonymy: "There are periods of mental agitation when the firmest must be ranked with the weakest of his brethren; and when, in paying the general tax of humanity, his distresses are even aggravated by feeling that he transgresses, in indulgence of his grief, the rules of religion and philosophy, by which he endeavours in general to regulate his passions and his actions" (309). No longer a revolutionary outrage, disappointment in love is now nothing more than a private ordeal.

The reformation of property relations is completed when Morton confronts Balfour, ostensibly to recover the document that will restore Tillietudlem to Edith's family. But Morton's encounter with Balfour seems more akin to Edith's rejection of Evandale than to a climactic standoff. It takes place at the mouth of the cave in which Balfour has been hiding, amid a landscape whose symbolic gendering I will discuss below. The document Morton seeks ends up burned, and he fails in his mission (the castle is restored by the expedient of Sir Basil Oliphant dying without a will [350]). Instead we find that the residue of political force at the level of privacy is erotically charged male rivalry. "Thou has my secret," Balfour tells Morton; "Thou must be mine, or die!" (341). Of course, Morton chooses neither option. Although he has failed to recapture the document he wanted, the structural purpose of this scene is his renunciation of that kind of rivalry along with the feudal property system that nurtures it. He claims to have come with no hope of winning Edith's hand, that the happiness he seeks is "Lord Evandale's and that of his bride" (339), thus renouncing another rivalry at the same time. Rather than fight Balfour, Morton "sprung past him, and exerting that youthful agility of which he possessed an uncommon share, leaped clear across the fearful chasm which divided the mouth of the cave from the projecting rock on the opposite side" (341). Strikingly, the opposition between cave and projecting rock enables us to read Balfour as the feminized party in this relationship.

That figural gendering is consistent with the many other traces of eroticized male rivalry in this novel. Several of the most potently martial characters in *Old Mortality* are coded at times either as effeminate, or erotically invested in a male opponent, or both at once. Balfour's first meeting with Bothwell, for instance, is a wrestling match: "With that he dropped his coarse grey horseman's coat from his shoulders, and extending his strong brawny arms with a look of determined resolution, he offered himself to the contest. The soldier was nothing abashed by the muscular frame, broad chest, square shoulders, and hardy look of his antagonist, but, whistling with great composure, unbuckled his belt, and laid aside his military coat" (31). Their second, decisive, fight is similarly bravura. Later we encounter the Crown's ranking representative: "It was impossible to look at the Duke of Monmouth without being captivated by his personal graces and accomplishments . . . Yet, to a strict observer, the manly beauty of Monmouth's face was occasionally rendered less striking by an air of vacillation and uncertainty" (243). Morton himself has a similar quality—or had it before his exile—Cuddie says of him, "his face was made of a fiddle, as they say, for a' body that looked on him liked him" (291).[55] The most notable alloy of feminine and masculine in the novel, though, is Claverhouse: "His gesture, language, and manners, were those of one whose life had been spent among the noble and among the gay. His features exhibited even feminine regularity. An oval face, a straight and well-formed nose, dark hazel eyes, a complexion just sufficiently tinged with brown to save it from the charge of effeminacy . . . a profusion of long curled locks . . . which fell down on each side of his face, contributed to form such a countenance as limners love to paint and ladies to look upon" (100). Whatever the complexion, the description is certainly feminizing. The narrator repeatedly describes Claverhouse in these terms, while also admiring his skill as a warrior and officer.

With this theme of mingled masculinity and femininity, Scott stirs up the cultural mythology of seventeenth-century aristocratic homoeroticism that runs broadly through anti-aristocratic discourse of the eighteenth and nineteenth centuries: for example, "Sergeant Bothwell saluted the grave and reverend lady of the manor with an assurance which had something of the light and careless address of the dissipated men of fashion in Charles the Second's time" (77). This strain of bourgeois prudishness has much in common with contemporary attitudes to the officers of standing armies, who, being equally happy to "fight, or to do nothing," are generally "found to be made up . . . of effeminate coxcombs, or of bold profligates" (Dyer 42). Mary Wollstonecraft too complained that "officers are . . . particularly attentive to their persons, fond of dancing, crowded rooms, adventures, and ridicule. Like the *fair sex*, the business of their lives is gallantry.—They were taught to please, and they only live to please" (24). Although Scott shares somewhat less sympathy with Wollstonecraft than with Burke, he seems here in tune with her aversion to fops, who "may follow the example of other, hypersexualized men and begin to hanker for something 'more soft than woman' and . . . 'attend the levees of equivocal beings,' as Wollstonecraft termed homosexuals" (C. Johnson 11). It may be pertinent that the only virtue Morton displays in the course of the narrative that is in any sense exceptional or heroic is his skill at shooting popinjays.[56]

Soldierly effeminacy in *Old Mortality* is a symptom of the indivision between domestic and political realms that the novel emphasizes so persistently as central to its clash of historical forces. Claverhouse in particular is an unsettling combination of domestic and political personalities. He is just as at home on the battlefield as in the parlor. During the Battle of Drumclog, for instance, "Evandale could not forbear remarking the composure of his commanding officer. Not at Lady Margaret's breakfast-table that morning did his eye appear more lively, or his demeanour more composed" (143). His equal facility for domestic comfort and for martial ferocity makes Claverhouse a treacherous fellow: "The severity of his character . . . lay concealed under an exterior which seemed better adapted to the court or the saloon than to the field," but his manners conceal "that disregard for individual rights which [political] intrigues usually generate" (100–101). At least a provisional separation of spheres would seem to be the logical corrective to this refractory masculinity. The disorders resulting from gallantry in men of action may be eliminated by clear and secure boundaries between domestic and extradomestic space.

One more theme follows from the queering, and subsequent dequeering, of martial masculinity: fertility and nurturance. A number of times we hear Covenanters offering the invocation to "fructify." During their first meeting, Balfour asks Morton "whether the words he had spoken over-night had borne fruit in his mind?" (46); Peter Poundtext is described as "a fructifying preacher" (60); Poundtext himself says of Meiklewrath, "our violent brethren will have it, that he speaketh of the spirit, and that they fructify by his pouring forth" (181); and in a parley, an emissary gives letters to Evandale, advising him "to fructify by the contents, though it is muckle to be doubted" (200). In his preaching after Drumclog, Gabriel Kettledrummle attacks Charles II, "observing, that, instead of a nursing father to the Kirk, that monarch had been a nursing father to none but his own bastards" (153); Major Bellenden laments Morton's rebellion: "I ought to have been aware that I was nursing a wolf-cub, whose diabolical nature would make him tear and snatch at me"

(202); and I have already noted the passage where Balfour compares Morton to "a mother [watching] over her little ones" (208).[57] These figures of speech provide the Covenanting equivalent to the effeminacy of the Cavaliers. The figural masculine appropriation of childbearing and nurture also signifies failures of division between domestic and political spheres. Symbolically, these perverse mothers are either barren, or the bearers of monsters—all they produce are grotesque, distorted rhetoric and garish visions of a sanctified nation. As MacBriar puts it: "These are the latter days, when signs and wonders shall be multiplied" (181).

The scripture that underpins and unravels the fertility theme is Matthew 7:20, "by their fruits ye shall know them," a passage to which the (relative) moderate Poundtext refers: "We judge of the tree by the fruit" (180). Claverhouse seems subject to that judgment: "My marriage-bed," he laments, "is barren" (165). Civil strife and the obliteration of domesticity wipe out fertility. The first glimpse we see of Scotland after the Glorious Revolution features "boughs of flourishing orchards, now loaden with summer fruit"; "a sunny bank, which was covered by apple and pear trees"; and "fruit-trees and bushes . . . mingled with kitchen herbs" (288). Literal fruit remedy the desolation of the previous era. But all is not yet entirely well; as Morton advances to meet Balfour for the final time, he passes into a landscape "which had once been a wood, but was now divested of trees, unless where a few, from their inaccessible station on the edge of precipitous banks, or clinging among rocks and huge stones, defied the invasion of men and of cattle, like the scattered tribes of a conquered country, driven to take refuge in the barren strength of its mountains. These too, wasted and decayed, seemed rather to exist than to flourish, and only served to indicate what the landscape had once been" (325). Here we meet the last vestiges of the old orders, whose extinction now will clear the way for the new domesticity, both private and national. Balfour stands in his cave, a savage, empty, atavistic shelter, clutching a document that is a symbolic last link to feudal lineage landholding. The queering and proscription of aberrant masculinities follows from their termination in mutually lethal homoerotic rivalries and histrionic male pregnancies. The abjection of such masculinity as primitive or historically superseded is finally a symptom of the regulatory power that the modern home acquires over gender and sexuality.

Morton leaves Balfour in his cave and returns to Fairy-knowe just in time to receive Evandale's dying gift, the hand of Edith. This conclusive moment is

as ludicrous and functionary as any Scott ever wrote.[58] Its melodramatic liter-
alism is matched by its strident allegory of class triumph. Scott brings us to the
doorstep of the bourgeois home and the borders of the Hanoverian nation.
The home that we almost enter reorganizes the figural relations between itself
and the nation. No longer is the home either a metaphor for, or an antithesis
to, the nation. Instead it is a space that is simultaneously different from public/
political space, and the very substance of the nation. The private home is a
synecdoche for the nation and a metonymy for all other private homes. It is
a refuge from the turmoil of historical events, but also the measure by which
the nation's prosperity is reckoned. It dismantles the opposition between state
and subject so that rebellious sparks go "unfanned by persecution" (*Old Mortality* 287). Likewise, the subject, because home is the very embodiment of
his needs and desires, cannot fail to be contented. The simultaneous anchoring and dissolving of the self, the personal, the private accomplished by the
cultural hegemony of home is vertiginous. It may be that Peter Pattieson takes
flight from this very self-dissolution when he flees Miss Buskbody, and in
that impulse we may locate his affinity with Old Mortality's abandonment of
his home. The Scottish home is, to use a weathered modifier, always already
diasporic. So it should be no surprise after all that Scott does not conduct us
into the bourgeois home. We would find there, in the sanctum of the British
Empire's most sacred institution, a paradigmatic experience of postcolonial
alienation.

For all of its warmth, comfort, prosperity, and safety, one of the modern
home's most important attributes is inhospitality. Built on a renunciation of
ancient and feudal laws of hospitality, the middle-class home embodies the
right of refusal to any visitor or supplicant. At the national level, the home
nation counts among its primary functions the policing of entrants, immigrants, and applicants for state assistance. Such discriminations are the implicit
prerogatives of privacy and sovereignty, but home does more than arbitrate
admissions and expulsions; it treasures up alienation and dispossession as its
most fundamental values. The poorly concealed secret of home is that it has
no interior, no sanctuary or shelter, and no place of sufficiency. Home recedes
from every approach and every effort to articulate its presence. It cannot compensate, or make amends for histories of lack, exploitation, and displacement
because its plenitude is founded on obscuring those histories while maintaining their privations: home has incorporated the poorhouse and its descendant
institutions, and it polices boundaries that are not boundaries from a center

that is no center. For the modern, English-speaking subject, home constitutes her interiority by requiring her to exteriorize herself; it grants her autonomy by subjecting her to its nature; and it recognizes her singularity by codifying it in universal laws. Perhaps the best figure for the modern middle-class home, as it actually is, is the closet.

# Conclusion
## This Home Is Not a House

One of the attributes that has helped home maintain such a durable and tenacious influence in English-speaking territories is the difficulty of defining its essential attributes. Definitions of home tend to rely on negation (home begins where narratable action ends; it is untroubled by commerce, history, and politics) or on supplementarity (home is the outward expression of self; it is the scene of enjoyment, the fruit of one's labors). It has stationed itself beyond the threshold of the world as the definitive interior that orients all exteriority: "So far as the anxieties of the outer life penetrate into [the home], and the inconsistently-minded, unknown, unloved, or hostile society of the outer world is allowed by either husband or wife to cross the threshold, it ceases to be home; it is then only a part of that outer world which you have roofed over, and lighted fire in" (Ruskin 18: 122). Home has established resilient dialectical partnerships between itself and virtually all forms of social life.[1]

Or we might call home the dream navel of capital, an indecipherable jumble of all the purposes, interests, and values of social relations under the capitalist dispensation, which is the end of them all. End in both senses: home provides the boundary at which the iron laws of economic value cease to operate, beyond which other modes of value can be conceived, but it is also the telos of economic action:

> For this the hardy sons of labour toil;
> For this has learning pour'd the midnight oil;
> For this through trackless deeps the sailor roves;
> This arms the patriot for the land he loves;
> If lib'ral thought extend its gen'rous views,
> Or private aims to public good conduce,
> Their various aims in one—one object blend—
> Still to one point their fondest wishes tend:—
> Home—since the reign of guilt and death began,
> 'Tis all of Eden left to exil'd man! (A. Knight, *Home* 83)[2]

All of home's values are shaped by and germane to capital, but because it is the realization of industry, profit, and prosperity, the mechanisms of capital are prohibited from appearing as themselves within the domestic sanctum.[3] By the mid-nineteenth century in the United States, according to Kirk Jeffrey, home was definitively "an enclosure emphatically set apart from activities and priorities of the world . . . [U]ltimately the individual found meaning and satisfaction in his life at home and nowhere else" (24). Krishnan Kumar cites the popular sense that home is "perhaps the sole remaining site of satisfaction in late industrial society" (204) and "the principal source of identity and personal fulfillment" (206). This bourgeois orthodoxy has inverted the necessity-freedom opposition conventionally understood as central to Aristotelian political philosophy, which theorized "the antithesis between the political activities of the citizen and the economic activities of household management in terms of the philosophical antithesis of freedom and necessity" (McKeon, *Secret History* 7). Home has become the sphere in which humanity achieves liberation and self-actualization, while the sphere outside is defined by necessity, struggle, and animal subsistence.

Perhaps the most comprehensive negative definition of home is its opposition to the state. Home is where the state is not.[4] The Western liberal state marks its own limits as the protector and facilitator of home life: according to natural-rights theory, for instance, "the primary object of government is to secure to individuals a zone of negative freedom, consistent with the like rights of others, in which to care for themselves and to pursue their own chosen callings" (Malloy 36). In 1842, the Anglo-Irish free-market advocate William Cooke Taylor wrote: "The family is the unit upon which a constitutional government has been raised . . . Hitherto, whatever else the laws touched they have not dared invade this sacred precinct; and the husband and wife returning home from whatever occupations or harassing engagements, have there found *their* dominion, *their* repose, *their* compensation . . . There has been a sanctity about this . . . home life which even the vilest law acknowledged and the rashest law protected" (qtd. in Williams 178). The liberal state cannot define its own good in terms that are not effectively those that define the good of the home and its inhabitants: "The intimate space of the household is both end and origin of the liberal polity" (Johnston 4). This state of affairs is, in Hannah Arendt's view, cause for lament: "The contradiction between private and public, typical of the initial stages of the modern age, has been a temporary phenomenon which introduced the utter extinction of the very difference between the private and public realms . . . [T]he public . . . has become a function of the private and the private . . . has become the only common concern left" (69). In the social, economic, and political spheres beyond our private retreats, "everyday affairs have to be taken care of by a gigantic, nation-wide administration of housekeeping" (Arendt 28). For Arendt, any notions of the public, political, or collective are merely supplementary functions of the governing concepts of privacy and the personal.

Private institutions other than home (clubs, schools, corporations) also define themselves in part by the state's absence, but they too are in some sense servants of the private home or the home nation and most often both. Both the state and other private institutions find opportunities to negate the sovereignty of home where they can invoke the same systems of rights, property, and bodily integrity that home itself consolidates.[5] Home, in other words, articulates the conditions under which actually existing homes may be canceled. Indeed, as I have suggested, the hegemonic concept of home cancels all actual homes. Because boundaries that exclude economics, history, and politics from domestic life are never other than provisional or contingent structures of fantasy and effects of ideology, actually existing homes are fallen worlds, adrift in chains of signification. They cannot genuinely embody the immaculate, unrepresentable asylum that the full conditions of home's hegemony dictate. There really is no place like home.

So the domestic uncanny is not the symptom of an intrusion into the home by some external power or agency but rather a fissure, like the crack that sunders the House of Usher, through which home's hidden apparatus of coercion, historical determination, and power distribution casts its tenebrous glow.[6] Freud famously discovered that "among its different shades of meaning the word '*heimlich*' exhibits one which is identical with its opposite, '*unheimlich*.' What is *heimlich* thus comes to be *unheimlich*" (222). The English word *homely* has not developed such a conspicuous semantic doubling (*asylum* has, though it does not function adjectivally), but home as a representational object or topos in English-language literature is endlessly hospitable to the intrusion of the monstrous, unnatural, and incommensurable.[7] Where home is an explicit or even implicit object of representation, we expect its perversion or disruption. The unnatural is the very nature of home.

We might conclude, then, that home is impossible ⌐ more than negation, failure, or lack, but we should be caref discriminately a principle that poststructural language nd to be the plain condition of signification in general: us the seeds of its own deconstruction; ideology unrave cular contests the universal; the subject is always inscribed in the symbolic order. *Home,* like every other privileged signifier, masks its own lack by compensating for the lack in what it negates: the world outside where presence is perpetually forestalled by economics, politics, history, and other mediating social relations. But there is a particular (perhaps unique) complication in the signifying function of *home:* its unusual deployment of proprietorship. I observed in my introduction that the word *home* always carries with it an implied possessive: home cannot be home unless it is somebody's home. Commodities and labor, as Marx demonstrated, are susceptible of indeterminate ownership or nonownership— indeed, ownership under the rule of commodity is never without some indeterminacy.[8] A bed does not need an owner to be a bed, nor does a house, but only where there is a notional subject who claims "mine" can there be a home.

This special proprietorship, then, is at once the most thorough expression of the logic of private property, and the annihilation of that logic. On the one hand, home complies with consumer desire by assuaging lack but assuring continuity of desire and production; it follows the dictates of commodity fetishism: "a mere 'reflective determination' of an object or person is misperceived as its direct 'natural' property" (Žižek, *Plague of Fantasies* 100); and it is alienable: "If we were forced to change, / Our home again was sweet" (Wordsworth, *Home at Grasmere* 48). On the other hand, home transcends the constrictions of private property: it is an inalienable feature of self without reference to property rights, like my favorite flavor, my first kiss, or my best effort; a particular edifice, territory, or nation will always be my home, and may be so while overlapping with, yet exclusive of, claims from other subjects upon the same places and without regard to fee-simple ownership or tenure.

Home also has the social prestige of the anticommodity; under Western capitalism, home is a sanctuary where the inexorable logic of economic determination cannot penetrate:

> There is a magic in that little word;
> It is a mystic circle that surrounds
> Comforts and Virtues never known beyond
> The hallowed limit. (Southey, *Poetical Works* 5: 136)

Commodities flow into the middle-class home, where their value is nullified. Domestic labor adds nothing to the stock of available capital. And yet home is not understood as wasteful or destructive of value: "The household is no longer a unit of common production but of common consumption" (Weber, *Economy and Society* 375).[9] Home distills the metaphysic of commodity value into the quintessence of value itself. Freed from its measurement and mediation functions, value within the mystic circle can be imagined as transcendent realization, perfect sufficiency: "A whole without dependence or defect, / Made for itself, happy in itself" (Wordsworth, *Home at Grasmere* 48). Even aesthetic value is less uninhibited than the quintessential value of home. Aesthetic value, by most accounts, is *for* a subject, the property of an object or of a relation between subject and object. Home is *of* a subject. Its value is not transferable and has no kind of specie convertibility. It is "unity entire," a "self-sufficing world."

Nor does use value register within doors: "Home certainly cannot be defined by any of its functions. Try the idea that home provides the primary care of bodies: if that is what it does best, it is not very efficient; a health farm or hotel could do as well . . . We will dismiss the cynical saying that the function of the home in modern industrial society is to produce the input into the labor market. As to those who claim the home does something stabilizing or deepening or enriching for the personality, there are as many who will claim that it cripples and stifles" (Douglas 288). The same virtues that gild home's hegemonic figuration translate into the shortcomings of its private franchise operations. And yet the defectiveness of actually existing homes does not blemish home itself. Home is not disparaged by the faults of homes; its impermeability to everyday social relations—which never really shake off the grime of economics, law, and power—only reinforces its prestige. The reason why the "anxieties of the outer life" (Ruskin) and its "harassing engagements" (Cooke Taylor) never penetrate the sanctum of home is that nothing penetrates it. Home, "with its laughably complex, tyrannical rules, unpredictably waived and unpredictably honored, and never quite amenable to rational justification" (Douglas 298), recedes from us. It waits in the next room. It promises to arrive next year. It waves to us from photographs.

But this account might suggest too strongly that home is simply ideational, only an abstraction mistaken for material reality. The Romantic-era poetics of evanescence, which flourished at the same time as home's cultural reification, seem to help condition its elusiveness:

> In such strength
> Of usurpation, in such visitings
> Of awful promise, when the light of sense
> Goes out in flashes that have shewn to us
> The invisible world, doth greatness make abode

. . . . . . . . . . . . . . .

> Our destiny, our nature, and our home,
> Is with infinitude and only there.
>
> (Wordsworth, *Prelude* 1: 190)

The poetics of home, which is to say the representational strategies that developed as a means of presenting home's unrepresentable essence, have much in common with Romantic modes of figuration, whose purpose is to summon up but not actually articulate transcendence:

> Even forms and substances are circumfused
> By that transparent veil with light divine;
> And through the turnings intricate of verse,
> Present themselves as objects recognised,
> In flashes, and with a glory scarce their own.
>
> (Wordsworth, *Prelude* 1: 177)

Access to the Romantic sublime comes through mediating phenomena, made legible by the reader's competency in language that has not lost its links to nature, the divine, or the real: "The wisdom that actualizes nature, and compels her to be its interpreter, makes itself understood-and communes with the human mind" (Coleridge MS Notebook, qtd. in Fulford, "Coleridge" 38).

Which is to say poets resorted to accretions of sign and figuration whose cumulative effect was the expression of sublime experience:

> Thy light alone-like mist o'er the mountains driven,
> Or music by the night-wind sent
> Through strings of some still instrument,
> Or moonlight on a midnight stream,
> Gives grace and truth to life's unquiet dream.
>
> (Shelley, "Hymn to Intellectual Beauty," *Major Works* 115)

As Paul de Man puts it: "The subjectivity of experience is preserved when it is translated into language; the world is then no longer seen as a configuration of entities that designate a plurality of distinct and isolated meanings, but as a configuration of symbols ultimately leading to a total, single, and universal meaning . . . [T]he symbol is founded on an intimate unity between the image that rises up before the senses and the supersensory totality that the image suggests" ("Rhetoric of Temporality" 188–89). In his *Defence of Poetry*, Shelley codifies the figural process:

Poetry defeats the curse which binds us to be subjected to the accident of surrounding impressions. And whether it spreads its own figured curtain, or withdraws life's dark veil from before the scene of things, it equally creates for us a being within our being. It makes us the inhabitants of a world to which the familiar world is a chaos. It reproduces the common universe of which we are portions and percipients, and it purges from our inward sight the film of familiarity which obscures from us the wonder of our being. It compels us to feel that which we perceive, and to imagine that which we know. It creates anew the universe, after it has been annihilated in our minds by the recurrence of impressions blunted by reiteration. (*Major Works* 698)

This passage might read just as cogently if *home* were substituted for *poetry*. Home has that same indeterminacy: Is it a hieroglyph haunting the figures on a curtain or does it lie hidden behind the veil? It reveals itself to us as a pattern generated by the confluence of social signs and processes, whose synthesis has been composed by poets of another sort. It weaves, as if by magic, a totality and a world out of disorder and, regardless of its contingencies, we persist in apprehending it as natural.

Home is an effect of social practices. If it is a magical tapestry, it is woven from aspiration, striving, discipline, coercion, and other strands of sociopolitical life. Insofar as it is what Shelley calls the "scene of things," home is the reconciliation and reproduction of heterogeneous purposes in "common" vernacular. In the final portion of this conclusion, I will attempt to identify and define some of the important figures in (or behind) the curtain: social values, doctrines, and imperatives that have been stabilized and naturalized in the modern conceptual and practical orders of home, and therefore social forces that participated in the formation of home and that continue its development, modify its chattels and dimensions, and will eventually transform it into something else entirely or consign it to dereliction.

## PARTIAL SCHEMATIC OF THE MODERN MIDDLE-CLASS HOME

### *Inhospitality*

Riley, whose spirit of tormenting, springing from bilious ill humour, operated in producing pain and mischief . . . Ireton, whose unmeaning

pursuits, futile changes, and careless insolence, were everywhere productive of disorder . . . and Selina, who, in presence of a higher or richer
acquaintance, ventured not to bestow even a smile upon the person
whom, in her closet, she treated, trusted, and caressed as her bosom
friend; these, were excluded from the happy Hall.

—Frances Burney, *The Wanderer*

Home's aura of warmth, charm, and nurturance, is subordinate to its reification
of proprietary volition. Any visitor or supplicant must negotiate the householder's strict right of refusal. Ancient and feudal codes of indiscriminate hospitality have been repudiated in favor of privacy and prudent shepherding of
resources. One of the principal functions of the home nation is appraisal and
policing of all entrants, immigrants, asylum seekers, and applicants for any
part of its resources.

## Iterative Singularity

We see Huts and Cottages built in the same Manner, just as if the inhabitants had newly started into Being, and were led by Nature and Necessity, to form a Fabric for their own preservation.

—Robert Morris, *Rural Architecture*

Every private home is invented as though it were the first and only one of its
kind. The oedipal family ruptures, and sons and daughters reject patriarchal
determination so they may create themselves and their world anew. A nation
celebrates the overthrow of tyranny, the expulsion of invaders, or collective
acts of resolute sacrifice as the historical moment at which birth and majority
simultaneously arrived. Home is consecrated in self-assertion and gives form
to autonomy and self-determination. But every originary moment of this kind
is also the restoration of a natural order, a repetition, and a renunciation of
autonomy under the rule of the next attribute on this list: comprehensive
homogeneity.

## Comprehensive Homogeneity

A Palace is nothing more than a Cottage IMPROVED.

—John Wood the Younger, *A Series of Plans for Cottages*

Forms of collectivity and affiliation that may be partial, unstable, or contradictory—affinal and consanguineal bonds, nativity, nostalgia, heritage, adoption,

suffering or bereavement, proximity (geographic or other kinds), proprietorship, diaspora, oppression—can be accommodated within home's field of incorporative sameness that has no absolute qualitative content. The only attribute that two or more homes must have in common is homeness itself, and two or more inhabitants of the same home need not share anything more than their affiliation in that home. Home naturalizes a collectivity that effaces economic and other kinds of social inequity, asymmetries in social privilege and prestige, and varieties of difference that might otherwise obstruct the particular communal unity that any given home defines. The identity between one home and any other home is uncanny; their sameness cannot be expressed in precise conceptual or perceptual attributes. Which is not to argue that specific social attributes (family, language, ethnicity, historical solidarity) cannot be asserted as necessary qualifications for participation in a home. Indeed, all homes effectively do mandate such qualifications, but home itself legislates no fixed specificity as to those qualifications. Its conditions for belonging can be set and altered as domestic power relations dictate. Hence, home's comprehensive homogeneity can justify and enforce measures of inclusion and exclusion within the home or home nation and at its borders.

## Sufficiency

> The condition of the industrious, sober and virtuous labourer . . .
> perhaps ought rather to excite our envy than pity . . . His cares seldom
> exceed the limits of the day; the industry, frugality, and virtue of the
> parents being all the fortune his children will stand in need of.
>
> —Anonymous, *Inquiry into the Management of the Poor*

Bourgeois aspiration finds its realization in home. Prosperity, companionship, self-expression, identity, happiness, contentment, and effort rewarded are all deeply bound up in it. Indeed, the cultural imaginary of English-speaking nations can hardly conceive such satisfactions without home. While the bounties reaped from striving and affluence may include a great deal more than a happy home, the first proponents of home engraved on its foundation stone the principle that a happy home can, and even ought to, be enough. Thus domestic labor has gone unrewarded because the domestic laborer is required to understand herself as already rewarded. The home nation follows the same logic: patriotic sentiment commands adulation for this land and no other. The homeland is by definition the supreme adequacy of patriotism; one cannot feel patriotic affection for someone else's homeland. Home's degradations and injuries must be collectively resented, and it must be defended without mercenary concern for wage or recompense, just as domestic labor must be its own reward. Both private home and home nation are also governed by the principle of the commonwealth. They provide unified and bounded spheres of subsistence, hierarchies of responsibility, and means to adjudicate property sharing and apportionment.

## Fictionality

> The precedent of a few upright characters acting on such principles, will soon be followed by others . . . and Home, instead of being a prison in which the Virtuous are condemned to associate with the Vicious, will become a secure refuge from the wicked, and the most delightful asylum of Man.
>
> —Margaret Cullen, *Home—A Novel*

In my introduction, I suggested that domestic fiction is the discursive mode best able to represent home, but the analysis that followed showed that even domestic fiction finally defers home for the aftermath of narrative representation. Just as the nation is, in Benedict Anderson's famous formulation, an imagined community that cannot be experienced in total presence, the private home has the special privilege of being a falsehood that is nonetheless true. Home is an essence without essence, a dispersed center, a place without absolute location, and a perfect stasis that is ceaselessly mobile and circulatory.

## Transformativity

> If pity's boon the dreary hearth illumes,
> And fashion drops one feather from her plumes,
>
> .  .  .  .  .  .  .  .  .  .  .  .  .  .
>
> Labour, and Liberty, and radiant Health,
> Shall fill the country with a country's wealth.
>
> —Samuel Jackson Pratt, *Cottage Pictures*

Home turns abstractions like value, comfort, security, happiness, and affluence into chattels, fixtures, walls, and clothing, and back again. It does so by providing a space in which the material goods of home become a kind of stage set for the performance of home's intangibles, and where the tangible and intangible form an indissoluble identity and interdependence. The boundary between literal and metaphoric becomes highly permeable within a home. Home also transforms the self: "If you lived here, you'd be home."

## Relational Figurations

> We have given to our frame of polity the image of a relation in blood; binding up the constitution of our country with our dearest domestic ties; adopting our fundamental laws into the bosom of our family affections; keeping inseparable, and cherishing with the warmth of all their combined and mutually reflected charities, our state, our hearths, our sepulchres, and our altars.
>
> —Edmund Burke, *Reflections on the Revolution in France*

The private home is a synecdoche but also a metaphor for the home nation; every private home is a constituent part that goes to make up the whole, and every private home is also the vehicle for a figuration that expresses the essential qualities of the home nation. The home nation by the same token has a metonymic link to the private homes within (and often enough beyond) its borders, but is also evoked as a vehicle for metaphors that define the private and personal. The private home is a portion of the home nation, and the home nation is an assembly of private homes. Each can also function as the opposite of the other, as the constitutive lack that authorizes the other, and an abstraction or generalization of the other. Neither comprehends all that lies within national boundaries: the nation contains more institutions than the private home, and not all that happens in the private home is domestic per se. But the home-ness of either home is capable of passing beyond its own boundaries. Private transactions can occur in public spaces, and Englishness can be established outside of England. The home figuration comprehensively and elastically coordinates and reconciles the rhetorics of the personal with those of the national and back again, translating modes of valuation and participatory justice from one to the other.

# Notes

## Introduction

1. Patrick Spedding has outlined the shortcomings of full-text searches in the *ECCO* database in a recent *Eighteenth-Century Studies* article.

2. Private dwelling and nation have long shared more than one title: *domestic* has also had the capacity to signify both since at least the mid-sixteenth century (*OED* 4: 944).

3. Alison Blunt cites the 1935 Government of India Act, which states: "An Anglo-Indian is a person whose father or any of whose other male progenitors in the male line is or was of European descent but who is a native of India. A European is a person whose father or any of whose other male progenitors in the male line is or was of European descent and who is *not* a native of India" (3). "Although written out of this definition," Blunt goes on, "the maternal line of descent for Anglo-Indians usually included an Indian woman, often as far back as the eighteenth century" (3).

4. "It is in the heyday of British imperialism that England gets defined as 'Home' in opposition to 'The Empire' which belongs to the English but is not England" (George 4).

5. "The public realm, when conceived as the homeland, is explicitly modeled on an idealized version of the private realm of the household or family" (Kumar 208).

6. The song "Home! Sweet Home!" was composed in 1823 by Sir Henry Bishop (music) and the expatriate American John Howard Payne (lyrics) for the opera *Clari, Maid of Milan*. Its most famous couplet is, "Mid pleasures and palaces though we may roam, / Be it ever so humble, there's no place like home."

7. One of Charles Lamb's "Popular Fallacies," originally printed in the *New Monthly Magazine* in the mid-1820s, is titled "That Home Is Home Though It Is Never So Homely."

8. A medley of dramatic entertainments thematizing *home* begins to accumulate on the English stage from the mid-1780s on. They include Cobb, *Strangers at Home* (1786); Dibdin, *Harvest Home* (1787); Holman, *Abroad and at Home* (1796); and Dallas, *Not at Home* (1809).

9. The poem was first published in 1801 as *Bread; or, The Poor,* and still bears that title at the beginning of the text itself; only the frontispiece of the 1803 edition names it as *Cottage Pictures*.

10. Romantic-era English nationalism "aimed to homogenize the private and public meanings carried in the words 'home' and 'domestic' . . . and to make home-life underwrite the authority of administrative institutions like the Home Office, as well as notions of a home-country" (Lynch 45).

11. Gaston Bachelard shows that, while the linguistic specificity of home may be stubborn, its universalizing metaphysic has passed beyond the borders of English-speaking nations: the place of dwelling [*maison*], he declares, "is a privileged entity for a phenomenological study of the intimate values of inside space, provided, of course, that we take it in both its unity and its complexity and endeavor to integrate all the special values in one fundamental value" (3).

12. Mary Ellen Hombs, director of the Legal Services Homelessness Task Force, writes of the 1987 Stewart B. McKinney Homeless Assistance Act: "The bill never was and could never be enough. It contained primarily emergency assistance, plus a little help for preventive programmes and transitional measures . . . The preventive measures were in fact mere deterrents; true preventive measures would ensure that housing was decent and permanently affordable, and that wages and benefits were sufficient to keep a household from permanently living at risk of homelessness. The bill did not even contain a right to emergency shelter, much less a guarantee of housing, yet it was 'full funding' of the McKinney Act which presidential candidate George Bush advocated in the 1988 campaign" (116–17).

13. The constitutive supplement is a paradoxical logic that Jacques Derrida has famously scrutinized and explicated: "The supplement supplements. It adds only to replace. It intervenes or insinuates itself *in-the-place-of* . . . If it represents and makes an image, it is by the anterior default of a presence. Compensatory and vicarious, the supplement is an adjunct, a subaltern instance which *takes-(the)-place*" (145).

14. The eighteenth-century poor were an undifferentiated mass in the cultural and juridical imaginary, including both wage laborers and the unemployed, as well as orphans, the elderly, and the impotent (see Cowherd, *Political Economists* 2).

15. See John Broad, "Housing the Rural Poor in Southern England, 1650–1850," for a careful assessment of relations between polemical and practical applications of the workhouse system.

16. Sherman's *Imagining Poverty* "is not a book about late-eighteenth-century novels, though it began . . . when I asked how a genre concerned with subjectivity—the novel—could ignore ubiquitous depictions of pain" (1). To date, only two other monographs by literary scholars have confronted relationships between fiction and poverty in eighteenth- and early nineteenth-century England. Beth Fowkes Tobin's *Superintending the Poor* (1993) examines the "battle for the superintendency of the poor" as a conflict whose objectives are not simply control over poverty management, but outright cultural and political hegemony. The right to manage poor relief and discipline, Tobin argues, becomes a crucial field of contention between the emerging bourgeoisie and Britain's declining oligarchies. Judith Frank's *Common Ground* (1997) is less intimate with the pamphlet materials of the eighteenth-century poor debates and more interested in defining the aesthetics of poverty in fiction. She does, nonetheless, work to define some of "the ways the poor shape dominant culture" (3). Following the work of Peter Stallybrass and Allon White, Frank finds that the role played by poverty in eighteenth-century fiction has much to do with the way "the characters of gentlemen and gentlewomen are represented as formed through acts of imitation of and identification with the poor" (4). I will refer to all three of these books in the course of my study.

17. "Outdoor relief" was the provision of relief in the form of food, clothing, money, shelter. "Indoor relief" was confinement to a workhouse, poor house, or house of correction. K. D. M. Snell argues that the "generous, flexible, and humane" qualities of parish relief were actually declining by 1780, before the homes-for-paupers vogue had even begun (107).

18. See Sherman 136.

19. For an enumeration of these acts, see the beginning of chapter 2.

20. Young was author of two of the most prominent parliamentary acts that sought to promote outdoor relief.

21. For a detailed examination of the lead-up to, passage of, and implementation of the 1834 Poor Law, see M. A. Crowther, *The Workhouse System: 1834–1929.*

22. See Bentham, *Observations on the Poor Bill Introduced by the Right Honourable William Pitt* (1797).

23. *Populationniste* theory is based on the "law" that a nation's wealth could only be augmented by an increase in its population, generally indexed to the theory that all productive increase must originate in agriculture. The decline of populationism, initiated in France by François Quesnay, was completed in Britain by Thomas Malthus (see, for instance, Vaggi *The Economics of François Quesnay* 38).

24. Poovey renounces her own method in *Genres of the Credit Economy: Mediating Value in Eighteenth- and Nineteenth-Century Britain* (338–52). For a succinct repudiation, see Kreisel, *Economic Woman* 16–18.

25. Although, as I noted earlier, there have been few studies of the relationship between poverty and fiction in the period, William Wordsworth's poetic and political engagement with poverty has generated a very large body of scholarship, and analyses of writers in the radical tradition also touch regularly on the history and rhetoric of the poverty debates. Domesticity, I need hardly observe, is not by any means an underserved topic in critical examinations of eighteenth- and nineteenth-century literature.

26. See, for instance, Smart 162–64; Olssen 89–110; and Foucault, *Remarks* 150–57.

27. Marx's example of a simple abstraction is labor.

28. Michael McKeon has, famously, used the simple abstraction to locate the origins of the English novel: "My procedure in this study will be to work back from that point of origin [the stabilization of the conceptual category 'novel'] to disclose the immediate history of its 'pre-givenness'" (*Origins* 19).

29. The ruling corporate body implied by Gramscian theory is not necessarily reducible to social class defined according to classical Marxian economism: "Gramsci's opposition to economism was central to his concentration on the autonomy of the cultural sphere, and on elements of culture such as the nation and ethnic identity" (Olssen 96).

30. "The problem is at once to distinguish among events, to differentiate the networks and levels to which they belong, and to reconstitute the lines along which they are connected and engender one another. From this follows a refusal of analyses couched in terms of the symbolic field or the domain of signifying structures, and a recourse to analyses in terms of the genealogy of relations of force, strategic developments, and tactics" (Foucault, *Power/Knowledge* 114).

31. "The generality that I try to make apparent is not of the same type as others. And when I am blamed for localizing problems, confusion is created between the local character of my analyses and an idea of generality similar to the one usually discussed by historians, sociologists, economists, etc." (*Remarks* 154).

32. A number of scholars have made detailed and convincing attempts to reconcile significant features of the Gramscian and Foucauldian canons. Mark Olssen, for example, argues that "what Foucault adds to Gramsci, apart from a more open conception of social structure,

then, is an understanding of how various complex social techniques and methods central to the construction of identities, values, and political settlements are constituted and how they operate. Foucault offers a more developed set of concepts through which the microphysics of the constitution of hegemony is understood in terms of the exercise of multiple processes (techniques, strategies) of power and effects. That is precisely what Gramsci on his own account was unable to do" (104). Other efforts to find compatibility between Gramsci and Foucault include Chantal Mouffe's influential suggestion, at the end of her essay "Hegemony and Ideology in Gramsci," that the two might make common cause; Mouffe and Ernesto Laclau's *Hegemony and Socialist Strategy;* Barry Smart's "The Politics of Truth and the Problem of Hegemony"; Joan Cocks's *The Oppositional Imagination;* and Peter Ives's *Language and Hegemony in Gramsci.*

33. As soon as the "small-time operators" who were the progenitors of middle-class social orders "have set in motion the new social apparatus, it not only maintains and perpetuates itself, constantly justifying the expansion of its own scope and operations, but also renders increasingly invisible the human agency that put it in place . . . a whole set of laws, surveillance procedures, and self-regulating 'habits' follow quite naturally" (Trumpener 155).

34. The opposition between collective home and autonomous home also has a resemblance to the opposition between *langue* and *parole* of structuralist linguistics.

35. *Adam Bede*'s fourth chapter is titled "Home and Its Sorrows," and features Adam's recollection of running away when "he could bear the vexations of home no longer" (55). The book is set in the "dear times" of the 1790s, "when wheaten bread and fresh meat were delicacies to working people" (53–54). Eliot seems to refute the optimistic home of the 1790s in the terms it invented: "Nature, that great tragic dramatist, knits us together by bone and muscle and divides us by the subtler web of our brains; blends yearning and repulsion; and ties us by our heart strings to the beings that jar us at every moment" (46).

36. In *Households of the Soul,* Vincent Pecora finds that reactions such as Stevenson's and that of Tennyson's Ulysses against "the bourgeois household of modern Western capitalism" make up part of the genesis of a modern "imaginary vision," the noble household: "Whether it retains the aura of the princely estate, feudal service, or the tribal chief's clan . . . in the modern imagination, the sumptuary and liturgical impulses of these diverse households . . . amount to a unified conceptual (or ideological) field organized around patron-client relations rather than market forces" (x–xi). Its function is to maintain a "latent continuity . . . between (1) the masculine and often overtly communal adventure of empire, (2) a cultivated fantasy of patriarchal order and noble resistance to 'common,' utilitarian, and market-oriented duties at home, and (3) an aestheticized version of some 'work of noble note'" (12). Nostalgic attachment to this mythic realm of "noble expenditure," even though it is antithetical to the bourgeois sphere of "'natural' production and consumption," enables bourgeois culture to conceive of enterprise beyond the confines of home and to entertain the unruly aesthetics of modernist artistic production (xi).

37. Michael McKeon finds the process under way in the mid-eighteenth century: "It was on this model of the voluntaristic yet systematic interaction of private desires and interests that contemporaries imagined mysterious new public institutions as impersonal personalities, local and private motives somehow writ large and public" (*Secret History* 31), and largely complete by the end of the Napoleonic era: "The vexed relationship between the family and the state that structures much early modern thought on this subject has been decisively internalized and privatized" (692). Hannah Arendt sees the triumph of private life as the great catastrophe of

modernity: "The contradiction between private and public, typical of the initial stages of the modern age, has been a temporary phenomenon which introduced the utter extinction of the very difference between the private and public realms . . . the public . . . has become a function of the private and the private . . . has become the only common concern left" (69).

38. All citations of *The Prelude* will be taken from this version, designated the "AB-Stage Reading Text," from 1805–6.

39. "The rhetoric of 'Home' in most disciplines," Rosemary Marangoly George writes, "is an ahistoric, metaphoric, and often sentimental story line" (11).

40. "So far as the anxieties of the outer life penetrate into [the home], and the inconsistently-minded, unknown, unloved, or hostile society of the outer world is allowed by either husband or wife to cross the threshold, it ceases to be home; it is then only a part of that outer world which you have roofed over, and lighted fire in" (Ruskin 18: 122).

41. As it developed, the realm of private life became, according to Nancy Armstrong, "a strictly female field of knowledge" (14).

42. "Fictionality is an intrinsic attribute of home" (George 11).

43. Michael McKeon makes an analogous point, arguing that for studies governed by the quest for a truth somewhere behind representations, "domesticity becomes only partly legible, occluded by a modern myopia that bears some relation to the tendency to misread the technology of realism . . . as an ideology of transparent immediacy rather than a method of mediation" (*Secret History* 715).

44. Krishnan Kumar outlines these developments: "Starting sometime in the early seventeenth century, this promiscuous world was ordered and tidied up. Houses—upper-class houses to start with—began to reflect a marked degree of segregation of the status and functions of husband and wife, parents and children, masters and servants, friends and family. Boundaries were more strictly drawn—in paths and hedges, bricks and mortar, as well as in social customs—between the private and intimate world of the home and family, and the public world of acquaintances, business associates, and strangers" (209).

45. *At homeness* is a phrase developed in sociological studies to designate a variety of affective situations: personal, local, and national. See, for instance, Anne Buttimer, "Social Space and the Planning of Residential Areas" 47.

46. Elijah Anderson's *The Cosmopolitan Canopy: Race and Civility in Everyday Life* addresses similar questions about urban public spaces and has comparable homiletic motivations to Oldenburg, but shows a lot more political sophistication.

47. Important studies of home's functions in colonial and postcolonial contexts include hooks, *Yearning: Race, Gender, and Cultural Politics;* George, *The Politics of Home;* Grewal, *Home and Harem;* Hall and Rose, eds., *At Home with the Empire;* and Bhabha, "The World and the Home."

48. Mary Poovey's *The Proper Lady and the Woman Writer* (1984) and Nancy Armstrong's *Desire and Domestic Fiction* (1987), with its famous claim that "the modern individual was first and foremost a woman" (8–9), feature particularly important analyses of the ways in which eighteenth- and nineteenth-century British women writers designed and promoted bourgeois domesticity.

49. Other recent works that have investigated women writers' involvement with the formations of domestic ideologies in this period include: Butler, *Jane Austen and the War of Ideas;*

Todd, *The Sign of Angellica;* Ty, *Unsexed Revolutionaries;* Watson, *Revolution and the Form of the British Novel;* and Gonda, *Reading Daughters' Fictions.*

50. "If, in twentieth-century narratives, notably the psychoanalytic, the family has routinely been depicted as thwarting self-realization, the new Enlightenment domesticity liberated individuality" (Porter, *Creation of the Modern World* 281).

51. In *Dickens and the Concept of Home,* Frances Armstrong acknowledges that "it became conventional, in the late eighteenth century, to write about the home" (3). Nancy Armstrong argues that the "doubled social world" inaugurated by the triumph of middle-class private domesticity "was clearly a myth before it was put into practice . . . for almost a century" before the mid-Victorian period (95). That phrasing is unfortunate; it implies a certain teleology and, I think, mistakes the cultural place of myth: it is the Victorians for whom home is a myth.

52. Nor will I make broad claims about the functions of *home* in nations and territories outside of Britain, in periods outside the eighteenth and nineteenth centuries, or in languages other than English.

53. "The domestic novel is striated with the signs of its vigorous efforts to, not separate itself from the world, but absorb and incorporate the world within its virtual domain" (McKeon, *Secret History* 715).

54. "When is the word 'home' shrunk to denote the private, domestic sphere and when is the 'domestic' enlarged to denote 'the affairs of a nation'?" (George 13).

55. "Just as the family unit had been identified with a privately owned piece of the world, its property, society was identified with a tangible, albeit collectively owned, piece of property, the territory of the nation-state, which . . . offered all classes a substitute for the privately owned home of which the class of the poor had been deprived" (Arendt 256).

56. One body natural becoming an unlimited number of private bodies is one implication of what Michael McKeon calls the devolution of absolutism, "whereby the absolute authority of the sovereign is internalized . . . as a sovereign attribute of the individual citizen" (*Secret History* 30).

57. "It's the body of society which becomes the new principle in the nineteenth century. It is this social body which needs to be protected, in a quasi-medical sense. In place of the rituals that served to restore the corporal integrity of the monarch, remedies and therapeutic devices are employed, such as the segregation of the sick, the monitoring of contagions, the exclusion of delinquents" (Foucault, *Power/Knowledge* 55).

58. "In the old system, the body of the condemned man became the king's property, on which the sovereign left his mark and brought down the effects of his power. Now he will rather be the property of society, the object of a collective and useful appropriation" (Foucault, *Discipline and Punish* 109).

59. "The family organization, precisely to the extent that it was insular and heteromorphous with respect to the other power mechanisms, was used to support the great 'maneuver' employed for the Malthusian control of the birthrate" (Foucault, *History of Sexuality* 100).

60. "The liberal household continues to exist as the site of ends rather than nonmarket means, and that as such the intimate space of the household is both end and origin of the liberal polity" (Johnston 4).

61. "The separation out of domesticity transvalues it from a means to an end, from an instrumental signifier to a self-sufficient signified" (McKeon, *Secret History* 327).

62. This conception of power is the Foucauldian one. See, for instance, *The History of Sexuality*, 1: 93–97: "[Power] must not be sought in a unique source of sovereignty from which secondary and descendent forms would emanate; it is the moving substrate of force relations which, by virtue of their inequality, constantly engender states of power, but the latter are always local and unstable. The omnipresence of power: not because it has the privilege of consolidating everything under its invincible unity, but because it is produced from one moment to the next, at every point, or rather in every relation from one point to another" (93).

## 1. "Stock the Parish with Beauties"

1. English rural economies were "dominated by a three-class system. For a fixed annual rent, landowners leased their acres to tenant farmers, who relied on wage labour to carry out most of the work" (Offer 1). In a study based on the account book of the Thornborough estate in Yorkshire from 1749 to 1773, Elizabeth Waterman Gilboy estimates that a laborer might expect to earn around £9 per year, "with a pound or two extra through the work of his wife or child" (395), which "could compete successfully . . . with wages in the West and North of England" while lagging behind rates in districts closer to London (398). Of those wages, Gregory Clark estimates that agricultural laborers would need to expend an average 77 percent on food and beer, leaving an average of 6 percent for housing (493).

2. "Only those who could get a certificate of future support and good character from their parish of settlement could be absolutely sure that they could move outside their home parish and not face removal. Not until 1795 did people without a settlement gain the legal right to remain in a parish until they actually became chargeable on the poor laws" (Lees 29).

3. *Joseph Andrews* will be cited parenthetically hereafter as *JA*.

4. Michael McKeon notes the uneasy sense in Fielding that "social station is arbitrary" and that "relative placement" is what remains of the old orders (*Origins* 408).

5. Emulation itself, as the social form of imitation, was not presumed to be necessarily transgressive. It might just as readily promote virtue: "Examples work more forcibly on the mind than precepts: and if this be just in what is odious and blameable, it is more strongly so in what is amiable and praiseworthy. Here emulation most effectually operates upon us, and inspires our imitation" (*JA* 15). Carolyn Steedman writes: "Emulation theory was elaborated for the main part, out of eighteenth-century employers' routine condemnation of their servants' supposed habit of copying the manners, and behavior, and above all, the dress of their betters, revealing to their masters and mistresses their true desire to be like them . . . [B]ut there is very little evidence that it was a practice among servants, rather than an elaborate anxiety of employers, that expressed the hope that the servants might be doing just that: watching them, their betters; knowing them, copying them" (334).

6. In Pat Rogers's view, "issues related to crime and the law underlay [Fielding's] entire career as an author, even his earlier days as a dramatist and journalist" (137).

7. Fielding's close attention to the connections between geography and social relations would seem to account for his tendency to speak of hierarchies as topographies.

8. The transition from patriarchal obligation to contractual ties has been very widely studied. Recent examples include Davidoff and Hall, *Family Fortunes*; Tadmor, *Family and Friends in Eighteenth-Century England*; and Perry, *Novel Relations*.

9. Don Wayne writes of Penshurst House: "The purpose for which the great country houses

were built is now obsolete. Yet a house of this type, which was once the theater for the enactment of a certain concept of 'home,' may retain a vestige of that purpose even if, as in most cases, the home has been transformed into a museum" (11–12).

10. This aspect of *Joseph Andrews* recalls Fielding's ties to the Tory Satirists, whose quarry included French *romans héroiques* and similar English amatory fiction (especially that of Eliza Haywood), notably in chapter 14 of *Scriblerus*, "The Double Mistress" (65–78). Modern prose fictions, such as "the *Telemachus* of the Arch-bishop of Cambray" (*JA* 3), for which Fielding feels some esteem, are allowed the title of epic since it is "much fairer and more reasonable to give it a name common with that species from which it differs only in a single instance" (3).

11. Fielding's title page for *Joseph Andrews* stipulates that the novel is "written in imitation of the manner of Cervantes." His quixotic satire differs from that of Charlotte Lennox, whose Female Quixote gets her hands on a "great store of romances, and, what was still more unfortunate, not in the original French, but very bad translations" (7). Where Fielding locates quixotic delusion in modern forms of social aspiration, Lennox's Arabella imbibes a variety of antiquated notions from her French *romans*. Modern manners are also lampooned as antithetical to the substantial personal and social virtues that Arabella possesses in spite of her misconceived precepts.

12. See, for instance, Battestin, *The Moral Basis of Fielding's Art*; Paulson, *Satire and the Novel in Eighteenth-Century England*; and Bender, *Imagining the Penitentiary*.

13. "Fielding at once articulated a cultural system in his fiction and took a vital formative role in shaping a paradigmatic social system" (Bender 139).

14. Paul Slack notes that broad cooperative interventions had been attempted even before the full codification of the "old poor law": "They occurred chiefly in corporate towns, and—in the period from 1570 to the 1630s—in municipalities ruled by Puritans. In Norwich and other East Anglian towns in the 1620s, alliances of godly magistrates and ministers sought to remodel their little commonwealths, and they used the management of the poor as a tool for that purpose" (16). The locus classicus of almost all poor-management discussion in the eighteenth century is rural and parochial. Not many writers are willing to examine urban examples in detail, or to shape their proposals around any conceptual geography other than the country parish.

15. See Webb and Webb, *Parish* 36–37.

16. As the Webbs see it, the eighteenth century was the period during which local government was gradually and haphazardly reorganized around a "distinction between the administration of local affairs and the execution of national justice" (*Parish* 282) whose key point of intersection and distribution was the county. There were also divisions of governance between parish and county that Briggs et al. describe as intermediate levels: the hundred ("a sub-unit of the county, containing usually half a dozen or so parishes") and the borough (town jurisdictions) (54).

17. Richard Burn, whose multivolume *Justice of the Peace and Parish Officer* (1755) was the standard eighteenth-century work on the topic, writes: "It is not easy to fix any rule for distinguishing, in the abstract, between what things are the subject of orders of Justices, and what of convictions by them" (qtd. in Webb and Webb, *Parish* 281n).

18. An important part of the appeal of the parish to Fielding and other poor reformers is its essentially continuous descent from the earliest English Christian-era social administra-

tions. Even today, "the majority of parish churches in rural England . . . derive from the patronal churches of Saxon thegns or Norman lords" (Pounds 29).

19. Malcolm Kelsall states that in the previous century, the great manor houses that Jonson, Herrick, Carew, and other poets "celebrate had already been separated from the centres of power" (44).

20. Fielding's benevolent patriarch, "whose power rests on closely aligned territorial and judicial functions . . . exploits the feudal residues contained within the eighteenth century's more mediated relationship between government and property to project a communal pattern in which these two aspects seem to belong together naturally, even while they are no longer organically linked" (Schmidgen, *Eighteenth-Century Fiction* 79).

21. Although Fielding's narrator disdains romance, the novel is a parody and therefore retains the basic narrative structure of the form it deprecates.

22. The anonymous author of *An Essay on Civil Government* (1743) complains that soldiers in a standing army make "very pernicious members of society. They bully and abuse the country people about them; they disturb the villages and towns; they riot and commit excesses; they debauch and entice many young people of both sexes to their ruin and infamy. These evils they would not be capable of committing . . . did they earn their bread by hard labour" (338). Later in *Joseph Andrews*, Parson Adams encounters a gun-wielding gentleman who laments that there is no game in the area because "the soldiers, who are quartered in the neighbourhood, have killed it all" (114).

23. Deborah Valenze considers it "noteworthy" that after midcentury we find "the mobilization of an image of the poor as a social threat" (27).

24. In evoking "kindred bonds," I refer to a distinction now standard in social history between the propertied system of patrilineal descent and the more communal mingling of familial and affinal relations identified, for instance, by Randolph Trumbach, who distinguishes "two opposing systems of kinship—patrilineage for the great and kindred for the poor" (4).

25. Roger Lund points out that *Joseph Andrews* actually is burlesque, suggesting that "by denying that *Joseph Andrews* is burlesque, Fielding is merely anticipating the most immediate objections that might have been made to the ridiculous treatment of his characters" (113), but formally speaking, *Joseph Andrews* is also romance. What matters is the heuristic and epistemic means by which Fielding distinguishes his fiction from these disavowed genres.

26. For conceptual analysis of commercial humanism, see Pocock, *Virtue, Commerce, and History*, particularly chapter 2.

27. For extended discussion of eighteenth-century debates over the representation and embodiment of monetary value, see James Thompson, *Models of Value: Eighteenth-Century Political Economy and the Novel*. Thompson argues that Fielding is very much interested in anchoring represented value in "safe, stable, unchanging property, much like a landed estate, suspended within the patriarchal system of continuity" (154).

28. French critics, particularly Boileau and Dacier, had popularized and extensively annotated Aristotle's poetics in the later seventeenth century, devoting a good deal of attention to Aristotle's rule that "the Poet ought rather to chuse Impossibilities, provided they have a Resemblance to the Truth, than the Possible, which are Incredible with all their Possibility" (Dacier 407).

29. Pope, Swift, and Arbuthnot all made gleeful fun with untethered linguistic matter, particularly puns (see Alderson, "The Augustan Attack on the Pun"; and Attridge, *Peculiar Language* 188–95).

30. See, for example, the exchange between Sparkish and Horner in *The Country Wife:*
SPARKISH. "Did you never see Mr Horner? He Lodges in Russell Street, and he's a sign of a man, you know, since he came out of France." Heh, hah, he!
HORNER. But the devil take me, if thine be the sign of a jest. (243)

31. For discussions of Addison's conflicted feelings about autonomous form, see Sitter, "About Wit"; MacKenzie, "Breeches of Decorum"; and Mackie, *Market à la Mode.*

32. In this respect, Fielding's caricature of romance resembles the excremental negativity that Dryden and Pope call "Dulness." Indeed, Fielding's allusion to Milton goes by way of the *Dunciad,* in which the goddess Dulness is "the seed of Chaos, and of Night" (340.4.13), and book 4's invocation of the muse bids her, "Indulge, dread Chaos, and eternal Night! / Of darkness visible so much be lent" (339.4.2–3).

33. Dacier overreaches in offering a rationale for Aristotle's dictum that "the poet ought rather to chuse impossibilities, provided they have a resemblance to the truth, than the possible, which are incredible with all their possibility" (Dacier 407), which, for Fielding, would sanction chimerical forms of romance.

34. The *Enquiry* sets some of its informative passages on a similar footing: "This picture, which is taken from the life, will appear strange to many; for the evil here described, is, I am confident, very little known, especially to those of the better sort" (71).

35. In his early nineteenth-century "Essay on Romance," Walter Scott adheres to the formal principles of Fielding's definitions for romance and the modern novel, while dispensing with Fielding's ethical priority: romance is "a fictitious narrative in prose or verse; the interest of which turns upon marvellous and uncommon incidents," while the novel is "a fictitious narrative, differing from the Romance, because the events are accommodated to the ordinary train of human events, and the modern state of society" (6: 155–56). Notably, Scott also lists the vagrancy laws as one of the causes of the decline of romance: "The statute of the 39th of Queen Elizabeth . . . ranks those dishonoured sons of song [minstrels] among rogues and vagabonds" (6: 196).

36. Before he comes to his detailed discussion of ridicule in the preface to *Joseph Andrews,* Fielding connects his preliminary rejection of the burlesque to Shaftesbury: "I apprehend, my Lord Shaftesbury's opinion of mere burlesque agrees with mine, when he asserts, 'There is no such thing to be found in the writing of the Antients'" (5).

37. Participants in the debate over ridicule as a test of truth include Bishops Berkeley and Warburton, Mark Akenside, John Brown, and Henry Home, Lord Kames. Alfred Owen Aldridge insists that Shaftesbury did not propose the test of truth, but "merely began the debate over ridicule by discussing its social utility"; Berkeley was first "to refer to ridicule as a test of truth . . . and after his use of the phrase, nearly every eighteenth-century writer on ridicule took it up" (129).

38. Michael McKeon is not the only recent critic of Fielding to ignore the contest over ridicule. Judith Frank also makes no mention of the debate in her examination of poverty and the preface to *Joseph Andrews,* and nor do Ronald Paulson's numerous discussions of Fielding touch on it. Lund also misses the connection, even though he cites Shaftesbury's provoking observa-

tion (99). Simon Dickie has published a long and meticulously researched article titled "*Joseph Andrews* and the Great Laughter Debate" that, rather surprisingly, shows no awareness of the controversy. Richard Terry notes briefly that Mark Akenside seems to have been aware of "the discussion of ridicule contained in [*Joseph Andrews*]'s preface" (120). Thomas B. Gilmore also glances in a footnote at Fielding's involvement with the debate (5 n. 10). But we must go back as far as 1959 to find any sustained discussion of these questions, in William B. Coley's "The Background of Fielding's Laughter."

39. Fielding implies here not that a pauper may misapportion his income to give an affected appearance of finery (the commodities he lists are far beyond the means of any actual pauper), but that the possessor of flowers, plate, or china is most certainly not a pauper.

40. In Roger Lund's view, Fielding treats ridicule not as "a weapon that is consciously wielded by the satirist or the burlesque writer, but an inevitable condition arising from the object of ridicule itself" (97).

41. A brief, anonymous treatise on the restraint of appetites, titled *'Tis All a Cheat; or The Way of the World* and published in 1720, demonstrates that Fielding's moral economy of pauperism has its precedents: "My Poverty and these Rags . . . are enough to tell ye that I am an honest Man, a Friend to Truth, and one that will not be mealy mouth'd, when he may speak it to the purpose. *Some call me the* Plain Dealer, *others the* Undeceiver General" (3).

42. "Fielding's satire," as Charles Knight sees it, "uses the central characters as touchstones through whom others reveal their hypocrisy" (76).

43. In *Tom Jones*, Fielding's narrator asks, "What demonstrates the beauty and excellence of anything, but its reverse?" (183).

44. Jacques Derrida argues, for example, that writing supplements (and thereby authorizes the "presence" of) speech where it provides fixed signs and iterability: "If it represents and makes an image, it is by the anterior default of a presence" (145).

45. For extended discussion of Fielding's Latitudinarian tendencies, see Battestin, *The Moral Basis of Fielding's Art* 52–84.

46. Steedman cites James Beattie's "On Laughter, and Ludicrous Composition. Written in the Year 1764," which calls the English sociopolitical system "most favourable to *comic* writing . . . where persons of all ranks, and those ranks so very different, and the public welfare depends on their living on good terms . . . each within the sphere of his own prerogative" (qtd. in Steedman 330n).

47. *Satire and the Novel in Eighteenth-Century England* 96ff.

48. I think that the fictive or epistemic social transgression that this positioning of readers implies does not trouble Fielding because its purpose is to impose such strong restraints on affectation and improper mobility.

49. "The 'judge in every man's breast' . . . comes to be apprehended invisibly as authority in the liberal state" (Bender 179–80).

50. Numbers 47 (June 13, 1752) and 49 (June 20, 1752).

51. Opening book 12 of *Tom Jones*, Fielding's narrator dwells briefly on mob economics: "By the poor here I mean that large and venerable body which, in English, we call *the mob*. Now, whoever hath had the honour to be admitted to any degree of intimacy with this mob, must well know that it is one of their established maxims to plunder and pillage their rich neighbours without any reluctance; and that this is held to be neither sin nor shame among them. And so

constantly do they abide and act by this maxim that, in every parish almost in the kingdom, there is a kind of confederacy ever carrying on against a certain person of opulence called the squire, whose property is considered as free-booty by all his poor neighbours" (540).

52. In the social pamphlets, Christopher Parkes argues, Fielding "imagines a nation in which boundary lines all connect with each other to form a complete containment network" (19–20).

53. "Wandering is the cause of the mischief, and that alone to which the remedy should be applied" (Fielding, *Enquiry* 65).

54. Fielding's use of the term *home* in this passage clearly refers to the pauper's parish of settlement. In his urban magistracy, Fielding needed more elaborate strategies than the simple familiarity of fellow parishioners. He developed "registers to counter the criminals' control over time and space in a city with many dark places and unknown corners. It was a city where they could disappear. It was also a place where they could easily disguise themselves to take advantage of the multitude of transactions between strangers that took place every day" (Ogborn 220). The register system, nonetheless, has organizing structures analogous to Fielding's parochial system: local and personal encounters are recorded and collated for incorporation into a managerial superstructure that distributes its surveillance and its dispensation through the mediation of its local agents.

55. The all-intrusive surveillance that Richardson's Pamela ascribes to her master seems more like an omniscient authority than the kind of inquiry that Bender identifies with Fielding's narrators.

56. Advice manuals for servants and those who govern them reinforce the local and limited order of vision within which the laboring classes are confined, as Carolyn Steedman shows: "Servants were advised to look at, and look up to, their employers in order to both anticipate their wishes and also in order to learn how to be what was wanted," and "masters and mistresses were counseled to watch their servants' behavior and their apprenticeship in that pleasing watchfulness" (337).

57. Bender calls Fielding's planned system of national administration a "superficially backward-looking project" (185). I am arguing that old-order social relations play a more integral role than Bender grants them.

58. *Amelia* features a disquisition that speaks to the importance Fielding places on social station in the operations of the British constitution: "Good laws should execute themselves in a well regulated state; at least, if the same legislature which provides the laws doth not provide for the execution of them, they act as [watchmaker George] Graham would do, if he should form all the parts of a clock in the most exquisite manner, yet put them so together that the clock could not go . . . To say the truth, Graham would soon see the fault, and would easily remedy it. The fault, indeed, could be no other than that the parts were improperly disposed" (19–20).

59. Michael McKeon observes that "customary noblesse oblige and the hallowed system of the English law seem able to redeem themselves as the best scheme of social justice available" (*Origins* 403).

60. I mean only to suggest that his proposals for reform of poverty management at a national and comprehensive level were ineffectual. As Bender and others have documented, Fielding achieved a great deal in his renovation of judicial practice and criminal investigation, as well as the general administration of welfare measures within the London parishes that he oversaw as a magistrate.

61. Fielding's ally Charles Gray asks, "If men of rank and fortune will not be persuaded to give themselves a little trouble of this sort, in a bare inspection of their own parishes and near neighbourhoods, how can it be expected that there will be a more industrious application to the business of a whole county if the parish laws should be abrogated?" (v).

62. "Because there was no central policymaking authority, types and amounts of relief altered from parish to parish" (Sherman 7).

63. Richardson's Mr. B. also holds at least one advowson, which he exercises to provide a living for Mr. Williams (*Pamela* 376).

64. Christopher Parkes is mistaken in claiming that when Joseph returns to the Booby estate, "instead of proceeding to the habitation of his father and mother" (*JA* 42), he contravenes the law of settlement (Parkes 21). Joseph does not act in defiance of that law; the duration of his service to the Booby family entitles him to a settlement in their parish regardless of his dismissal. Parkes's claim relies, in any case, on a partial citation; he has elided an additional phrase: Joseph goes back to Lady Booby's parish "instead of proceeding to the habitation of his father and mother, *or to his beloved sister Pamela*" (emphasis added). While one may claim a settlement in the parish of one's parents, one may not do so in that of a sibling.

65. Lawyer Scout and his efforts to thwart the tenantry on behalf of Lady Booby would appear to have a precursor in a steward-lawyer about which one of Captain Hercules Vinegar's correspondents complains in the *Champion* of February 12, 1740. To a claim against a horse's cropped ears, the slippery lawyer responds, "with a sneer, that, since my horse's ears were cut off, it would be impractical for me to recover them, since they were now no longer horses in the eye of the law; for that Littleton (I think that was the man's name) says, that a horse is an entire thing, and not capable of being severed" (172). Thomas Littleton, a footnote tells us, was a fifteenth-century jurist who wrote a similar maxim in his *Treatise on Tenures* (Fielding, *Champion* 172 n. 6).

66. "Transparency is the convention that both author and beholder are absent from a representation, the objects of which are rendered as if their externals were entirely visible and their internality fully accessible" (Bender 201).

67. Not until the 1790s does the decisive transfer of parochial functions to domestic institutions (and their ideological representations) get under way—a transaction I will examine in my second chapter.

68. "The domestic novel is committed to the idea that collective norms can only be a function of individual experience within the realm of the private" (McKeon, *Secret History* 715).

69. Michael McKeon sees in Matthew Bramble, "a familial and 'feudal' care for his tenants that evokes an organic community hierarchically stratified by relations of personal dependence . . . Brambleton Hall presents the image of a Horatian 'country retreat'" (*Secret History* 680–81). McKeon insists that *Humphry Clinker* is, nonetheless, a "great domestic novel" (680), though I maintain my own distinction over and against McKeon's.

70. In a remarkable analysis, William Nelles demonstrates that the range of Austen's narratorial omniscience (for which he prefers the term "mind reading") has a strict limit: "An Austen narrator can only read minds within a radius of three miles of her protagonist; this is specified as being precisely the distance from Longbourn to Netherfield . . . and also from Kellynch Hall to Uppercross Cottage" (123).

71. In Roy Porter's view, the eighteenth-century poverty-management system worked as

Fielding intended: "The poor law served as a thorough-going system of support for and control over parishioners, complementing the family as the main regulator of life" (*English Society* 144).

72. Michael McKeon argues that the Register Office aims to orchestrate "the accommodation of 'private' particulars to a 'public' standard of the general" (*Secret History* 30).

73. Laurence Sterne parodies the decay of the two-body tropes with Toby's bowling green war that cannot continue once the actual continental war has ended and with Walter's disastrous efforts to form Tristram's destiny through anatomy.

74. "In this restraint I confine myself entirely to the lower order of people" (Fielding, *Enquiry* 8).

75. Church courts, N. J. G. Pounds reports, were losing jurisdiction throughout the century: "The secular courts kept nibbling away at the pretensions of the ecclesiastical, and succeeded in diverting an increasing volume of court business in their own direction" (324).

## 2. An Englishwoman's Workhouse Is Her Castle

1. The germinal moment of these analyses is historically much closer to the eighteenth century than to our own—Hegel's interpretation of *Antigone*: "The community . . . creates for itself in what it suppresses and what is at the same time essential to it an internal enemy—womankind in general. Womankind—the everlasting irony of the community—changes by intrigue the universal end of government into a private end, transforms its universal activity into a work of some particular individual, and perverts the universal property of the state into a possession and ornament of the family" (288).

2. The shared figurations and concurrent developments of sentimentalism, economics, and domesticity have been widely studied in literary scholarship and other disciplines. Prominent works include: Pocock, *Virtue Commerce and History*; Pateman, *The Sexual Contract*; J. Thompson, *Models of Value*; Motooka, *The Age of Reasons*; Skinner, *Sensibility and Economics in the Novel*; and Copeland, *Women Writing about Money*.

3. Raymond Cowherd stresses the ascendancy, in the 1790s and early 1800s, of evangelical Wesleyan and Whitfield revivalists in the poverty debates (*Political Economists* xiv–xvi).

4. *Removal*, *relief*, and *settlement* are key terms in the poor debates. Briefly, removal was the forced transportation of paupers to the parish at which they were legally settled (a status determined by complex conditions) and where they were entitled to relief, which was the provision of subsistence in a poorhouse or workhouse or by other means. For detailed historical and theoretical discussions of English and European approaches to poverty, at the level of the state, in political economy, and across the social classes, see Webb and Webb, *English Poor Law History*; Taylor, *The Problem of Poverty: 1660–1834*; Cowherd, *Political Economists and the English Poor Laws*; Henriques, *Before the Welfare State*; Porter, *English Society in the Eighteenth Century*; Slack, *The English Poor Law, 1531–1782*; Lees, *The Solidarities of Strangers*; and Snell, *Annals of the Labouring Poor*.

5. "Outdoor relief" is the provision of money and "relief in kind" that enables paupers to live in their own homes rather than in workhouses, which provide indoor relief.

6. Sir Thomas Bernard, 3rd Baronet, was the second son of Sir Francis Bernard, 1st Baronet. His father was governor of the Massachusetts Bay Colony from 1760 to 1770.

7. Recently "an optimistic interpretation of statutory poor relief" has emerged, "which stresses material generosity, in both the amounts of money redistributed and the types of assis-

tance countenanced by local authorities, and the humanity of a face-to-face, parochial system," but an opposing school of thought insists that "historians should in fact emphasize the *insufficiency* of welfare en masse" under the old poor law (King and Tomkins 4, 9). "'Welfare,' as it was practiced in the centuries between the first Tudor laws and the revision of 1834," according to Lynn Hollen Lees, "was neither uniformly harsh nor benign. Some of the poor benefited from relative largesse; others found it punitive and discriminatory" (19). K. D. M. Snell, by comparison, argues that "one can be surprised by the generous and encompassing nature of relief" (105), although the "generous, flexible, and humane" standards of provision decline after around 1780 (107).

8. See, for example, Henriques, *Before the Welfare State*, 24. The phrase "iron law of wages" was coined by Ferdinand Lasalle in the mid-nineteenth century. Subsistence theories of wages were, however, certainly emerging by the beginning of the nineteenth century. See, for instance, Antonella Stirati, *The Theory of Wages in Classical Economics: A Study of Adam Smith, David Ricardo and Their Contemporaries*.

9. "The middle ranks were to take a custodial role in steering society through the shoals of industrial capitalism . . . As paternalism receded from the economic arena, hierarchy and deference were reinscribed within relationships between classes" (Valenze 142).

10. Sherman's argument is founded on a false opposition between quantifying approaches that vest their authority in disavowal of imagination—"they could not imagine that they were imaginative. But they were" (3)—and "unscientific" approaches that embrace the imagination. She acknowledges that "a renovated paternalism followed Adam Smith and Thomas Malthus" (5), but her account ends up implicitly endorsing naïve literary verisimilitude, sympathetic obligation, and old-fashioned paternalism as the citadels of human self-realization. It is also not the case that quantification rose only in the later eighteenth century: "The golden age of political arithmetic is generally held to fall between the Restoration and the Hanoverian accession, it is often held that in eighteenth-century England, unlike the seventeenth and nineteenth centuries, there was little or no quantitative enquiry . . . In fact, far from such approaches being rare, they were fairly common, providing an important way whereby contemporaries saw, described, and, to a lesser extent, explained the world in which they lived" (Hoppit 516).

11. Named for the London suburb where William Wilberforce and fellow abolitionist Henry Thornton lived, the Clapham Sect included Thornton's brother Samuel, who was governor of the Bank of England; Hannah More; Thomas Gisborne; and John Shore, Baron Teignmouth, governor general of India from 1793–97 (see, for instance, Hilton 7ff.).

12. The term *poor* did not designate "destitution and dependence upon charity or public assistance" exclusively until the nineteenth century (Cowherd, *Political Economists* 2). During the eighteenth century, the indigent or unemployed poor were interchangeable with the laboring poor who survived on daily wages, as well as orphans, the elderly, and the impotent.

13. The English merchant-philanthropist Jonas Hanway writes in 1767: "The spring of health to the state, the ability of defence, the fountain of comfort, convenience and opulency, and a redundancy of the ornaments of life, all, confessedly, arise from the labour of the poor; therefore the preservation of the poor is the first lesson in political arithmetic" (1: 16).

14. Among the most prominent exponents of *populationnisme* was Victor de Riqueti, Marquis de Mirabeau, who claimed to have renounced it after meeting François Quesnay (Vaggi 22), founder of the Physiocratic school and author of the principle that "capital accumulation

[generated by agricultural industry] rather than population growth is the way to wealth, prosperity, and a strong nation" (Groenewegen 252).

15. *Populationnisme* was not without opponents prior to Malthus. In the 1780s, Joseph Townsend, for example, "defended the Workhouse test and the pulling down of cottages as necessary checks on an excessive population" (Cowherd, "Humanitarian Reform" 332).

16. This shift is also predicated on widespread rejection of Jean-Baptiste Say's Law, the "rule" that production could not exceed consumption. David Ricardo summarizes it in his *Principles of Political Economy and Taxation:* "A demand is only limited by production. No man produces but with a view to consume or sell, and he never sells but with an intention to purchase some other commodity ... By producing, then, he necessarily becomes either the consumer of his own goods, or the purchaser and consumer of the goods of some other person" (192–93).

17. "By pursuing his own interest he frequently promotes that of the society more effectually than when he really intends to promote it" (*Wealth of Nations* 399).

18. A persuasive analysis by Catherine Packham locates the etiology of this persistent opposition at least partly in the figurations that Adam Smith borrows from the vitalist life science of the Edinburgh Enlightenment to produce "a naturalized and cohesive image of the economy as a living organism, an image which both emphasizes the relation between worker and system (by seeing the former as a vital life-force internal to the body of the latter) and simultaneously effaces the worker (by reducing him to a figural life-force)" (469).

19. The complementary opposition between bioeconomics and somaeconomics has some resemblance to the distinction between Foucauldian and Gramscian analytics, which I discuss in the introduction to this book. For example: "The corollary of the expressed objective of Foucault's various analyses, namely to 'create a history of the different modes by which in our culture human beings are made subjects,' is a revelation of the forms of government and self-government to which human beings have been subject, where the concept of government refers to 'the way in which the conduct of individuals or groups might be directed,' that is an action or practice synonymous with the achievement or exercise of hegemony" (Smart 160).

20. The expenses of running workhouses and the ineffectiveness of their productive facilities doomed them to "utter failure" (Webb and Webb, *English Poor Law* 233).

21. The vitalist analogies that Catherine Packham finds operating in Smithian economics apply also to the disciplinary functions associated with home: "Actions, of adjustment and response to economic reality, operate like the self-regulatory efforts of the vitalists' animal economy, through which it preserves its health and maximizes its well-being ... [T]heir combined effort is beneficial to the larger system; and ... they are not controlled by an external, overseeing function, such as the sovereign or government" (476). Home is like a living body: "a self-directing organism following the 'wisest' course of action involuntarily, unconsciously, and independently of any external intervention" (476).

22. The vogue for cottages reversed a state of affairs that had prevailed generally since a 1589 statute "againste the erectinge and mayntayninge of Cotages" (31 Elizabeth I.c.7), which Theodore Barlow (a "Gentleman of the Middle Temple") explained in 1745:

> It being observed that the great increase of cottages abated the industry of the working people, many of whom preferred indigence with idleness, to plenty acquired by labour, and thereby naturally fell to pilfering; the legislature thought proper to restrain the increase of cottages as follows:

> No person shall build or erect . . . any manner of cottage for habitation or
> dwelling . . . except he lay to such cottage or building four acres of ground at
> least . . . There shall not be any inmate or more families than one dwelling in
> any one cottage. (153)

The 1589 law "remained in force until 1775 when it was repealed by a short act whose preamble cited the difficulties poor people had in finding 'habitation' and a fear of the lessening of population" (Broad 156).

23. Chapter 53 of *Adam Bede* describes a Harvest-Home supper.

24. "In the North," according to an 1826 "anecdote," Harvest-Home is celebrated "by a supper given on the last day of reaping, which is called the *mell-supper;* when the evening is spent in singing, dancing, and the utmost conviviality, in which the master and mistress of the house equally participate with the reaper and the plough-boy" (Percy and Percy 13: 156–57).

25. John Wood the Younger was the son of John Wood, the architect of Bath's eighteenth-century revitalization.

26. Other works that provided plans for rural cottages include Pitt, *Address to the Landed Interest;* and Elsam, *An Essay on Rural Architecture.*

27. Tricia Lootens observes that Hemans's later poem "The Homes of England" "links 'stately,' 'merry,' and 'cottage' dwellings within a harmonious national hierarchy whose unity of 'hut and hall' seems as much defensive as organic" (248).

28. *Ferme ornée* was introduced to the vocabulary of English landscape design by Stephen Switzer, author of *The Nobleman, Gentleman, and Gardener's Recreation* (1715) and later versions retitled *Ichnographia Rustica* (1718 and 1742) (see Turner 495). "Ornamental farm" is an accurate translation.

29. E. P. Thompson endorses the substance of, if not the doctrine behind, Pratt's complaint: "It became a matter of public-spirited policy for the gentleman to remove cottagers from the commons, reduce his labourers to dependence, pare away at supplementary earnings, drive out the smallholder" (219).

30. Young was an ally of William Pitt until 1801, but was also a slave owner and active opponent of William Wilberforce's abolitionism. In 1807, he became governor of Tobago, and remained so until he died in 1815 (see Matthew and Harrison, *Oxford Dictionary of National Biography* 60: 950).

31. "I seek the cottag'd dell, / Where Virtue calm with careless step may stray," from "Pantisocracy" (Coleridge 57). For further analysis of the domestic values key to Pantisocracy, see C. Smith, *A Quest for Home.*

32. Home "is extremely coercive, but the coercion is anonymous, the control is generalized. The pattern of rules continually reforms itself, becomes more comprehensive and restrictive, and continually suffers breaches, fission, loss at the fringes" (Douglas 306).

33. "What both sides shared," according to Sarah Lloyd, "was an extremely narrow concept of lower-class autonomy, or capacity for independent action, which they regarded as behaviour that had to be contained" (101).

34. The Webbs point out that, because the law of settlement applied only to those "coming to inhabit" a parish (*English Poor Law* 334), Young's law actually left unmarried pregnant women as the last part of the population wholly immobilized by the Law of Settlements; "rogues and vagabonds" and "idle and disorderly persons" were covered instead by the vagrancy laws.

35. Ursula Henriques asserts that "single women, widows with children, and deserted wives with families were most often removed," while single men were far more likely to be granted settlement or left alone (14). According to K. D. M. Snell, because illegitimate children were settled in the parish of their birth, it was not unusual to see "the removal of mothers before birth (at times by gangs of local men without the warrant of a removal order), sometimes during labour itself, to ensure that birth took place across parish boundaries" (107).

36. "The structural function of the bastard figure in the eighteenth-century novel has centrally to do with that figure's ability to mediate greater social diversity in a society that continues to articulate identity through a vertical sense of social place . . . [T]he bastard operates as a figure of observation and social description. While these figures are utilized and presented differently—from Johnson's and Chesterfield's discursive statements on bastardy and social observation to the implicit and explicit observational roles of Tom [Jones] and [Frances Burney's] Evelina—they are all closely linked to the problem of comprehending the increasingly complex social structure of eighteenth-century Britain through the modified conceptual tools of the old society" (Schmidgen, "Illegitimacy" 156–57).

37. A share of blame for illegitimate births often falls on workhouses. A committee investigating the "House of Industry" in Melton in 1791, for instance, reports that "it has . . . been long a practice to receive into your house at the approach of winter a number of lazy, notorious and abandoned prostitutes who, tainted with the foulest of diseases, resort thither for cure; and when the summer advances then quit their retreat . . . often leaving as a pledge an unaffiliated child" (quoted in Webb and Webb, *English Poor Law* 144).

38. George Eliot's Adam Bede, whose story is set in the last years of the eighteenth century, seems to be a doctrinaire Malthusian laborer: "He had long made up his mind that it would be wrong as well as foolish for him to marry a blooming young girl, so long as he had no other prospect than that of growing poverty with a growing family . . . He had not enough money beforehand to furnish even a small cottage, and keep something in reserve against a rainy day. He had good hope that he should be 'firmer on his legs' by-and-by; but he could not be satisfied with vague confidence in his arm and brain; he must have definite plans and set about them at once" (229). Eliot is not, at this moment, incorporating shades of historical detail with her finest brush.

39. The phrase "economy of makeshifts" is widely used in histories of poverty provision to encapsulate the widely various strategies and means made use of by the poor to survive. It "has become the organising concept for a number of historians of English welfare who wish to stress the disparate nature of income for poor households, in contrast to a concurrent research trend which would allow parish poor relief a predominant role" (King and Tomkins 1).

40. "You must either be house-Wives, or house-Moths," John Ruskin explains to the young women of England; "remember that. In the deep sense, you must either weave men's fortunes, and embroider them; or feed upon, and bring them to decay" (18: 337).

41. Vincent Pecora argues that what remains of aristocratic social order is overwritten by an "imaginary vision" of the noble household, which haunts the private home and whose function is to ensure "latent continuity . . . between (1) the masculine and often overtly communal adventure of empire, (2) a cultivated fantasy of patriarchal order and noble resistance to 'common,' utilitarian, and market-oriented duties at home, and (3) an aestheticized version of some 'work of noble note'" (12).

42. In a latent or repressed sense, of course, the middle-class woman does indeed signify the risks of investment, but I would argue that what is repressed along with those risks is the middle-class woman's doppelgänger (or one of them), the pauper that she will become if her creditworthiness fails her.

43. Bentham's reformed workhouse proposal includes plans for a structure essentially identical to his panopticon prison.

44. See, for instance, Fildes, *Breasts, Bottles, and Babies.*

45. Wildcodger seems to be a caricature of Arthur Young, whose *A Six Weeks Tour through the Southern Counties of England and Wales* features both a discourse on the state of the poor and extensive descriptions of grand country seats.

46. James Watt explains that Radcliffe's novels were "seen to provide what Scott described as 'a solace from the toils of ordinary existence,' a benign and comforting form of 'transport'"; Scott's commends Radcliffe, in other words, for steering clear of the kinds of provocation that he sees other gothic fictions indulging (110).

47. See Watt 110ff. for a survey of some important analyses of the political implications in Radcliffe's romances.

48. Adeline is also, despite her seventeenth-century French origins, "an incarnation of Englishness," as Cannon Schmitt observes of her fellow heroine, Ellena from *The Italian* (855).

49. Adeline embodies the ambiguity typical of gothic heroines, "who move between idealized exempla and cautionary protagonists" (Benedict 234).

50. In his "Essay on Romance," Walter Scott writes: "The father of an isolated family, destined one day to rise into a tribe, and in farther progress of time to expand into a nation, may, indeed, narrate to his descendants the circumstances which detached him from the society of his brethren, and drove him to form a solitary settlement in the wilderness" (*Miscellaneous Prose Works* 6: 160–61).

51. Consider, for example, La Motte's first encounter with Adeline: "Notwithstanding his present agitation, he found it impossible to contemplate the beauty and distress of the object before him with indifference. Her youth, her apparent innocence—the artless energy of her manner forcibly assailed his heart . . . He endeavoured to comfort her, and his sense of compassion was too sincere to be misunderstood. Her terror gradually subsided into gratitude and grief. 'Ah, Sir,' said she, 'Heaven has sent you to my relief, and will surely reward you for your protection: I have no friend in the world, if I do not find one in you'" (5–7).

52. As far back as 1769, the Reverend Richard Burn was lamenting that poor provision was designed "not with any intention of the poor being better provided for, but to hang over them *in terrorem*" (*Justice of the Peace* 3: 507).

53. *The Romance of the Forest* will be cited parenthetically hereafter as *RF.*

54. Two pamphlets from 1788 bear out Hazlitt's claim: "[The poor law] is a wise, humane, and magnificent code, and would, like many a venerable Gothic pile in the kingdom, fully, and for many years to come, answer well the charitable and pious purposes for which it was constructed by our forefathers . . . [but] it suffered like some of those venerable and more antient monuments" (*Defence of the Statute* 4); "Our general system of poor laws is a venerable pile, raised by skilful architects, and stands a distinguished monument to the wisdom and humanity of the British nation" (Howlett, *Insufficiency of the Causes* 105).

55. Radcliffe's ever-threatening banditti—who seldom actually show up—seem to echo por-

tents of pauper insurgency such as William Young's ("in filling workhouses, we are manning, as it were, so many disaffected garrisons"): "It had frequently occurred to La Motte, that this apparently forsaken edifice might be a place of refuge to banditti. Here was solitude to conceal them; and a wild and extensive forest to assist their schemes of rapine" (21).

56. Radcliffe's attachment to the narratorship of Hamlet's ghost is explicitly acknowledged in *A Sicilian Romance*, which takes "I could a tale unfold" for its title-page epigraph, and in *The Italian*, where the mysterious monk Zampari commands Vivaldi, "Listen to what I shall unfold!" (321).

57. Terry Castle's "The Spectralization of the Other in *The Mysteries of Udolpho*" is the classic study of Radcliffe's hauntings: "We feel at home in Radcliffe's spectralized landscape, for its ghosts are our own—the symptomatic projections of modern psychic life" (237).

58. See "Desire and the Interpretation of Desire in *Hamlet*."

59. "The narratorial commentary about the need to regulate passion and sensibility which runs alongside the presentation of Emily's enthusiasm in *Udolpho*, for example, in fact constitutes only one of a number of regulatory mechanisms internal to Radcliffean romance. Just as Radcliffe foregrounded the efforts of her central characters to maintain a rational sense of perspective throughout their various trials, so too did her works address the contemporary concern about the 'disciplining' of readers" (Watt 111).

60. The paternal hauntings literalize the spectralization of paternalism; the old systems of social order become ghostly as they are absorbed, transformed, and abstracted by the institutional relations of the modern social body. Because, as Foucault puts it, the family is "insular and heteromorphous with respect to [public institutional] power mechanisms" (*History of Sexuality* 100), the young woman's self-control sounds much more plausible to a novel-reading public (I imagine) when it takes the form of obedience to the desires of her dead father than if she were explicitly assuming the symbolic garb of the middle-class woman: both token and manager of property/value.

61. Margaret Homans, in *Bearing the Word*, gives a detailed account of the significance of literalization in writing by nineteenth-century women authors (26ff.).

62. "We have given to our frame of polity the image of a relation in blood; binding up the constitution of our country with our dearest domestic ties; adopting our fundamental laws into the bosom of our family affections" (Burke, *Reflections* 100).

63. In a survey of other eighteenth- and early nineteenth-century novels, I have found the following frequency of usage for variants of *remove* and *relieve*:

|  | Remove | Relieve |
|---|---|---|
| *Tristram Shandy* | 6 | 7 |
| *Humphrey Clinker* | 32 | 11 |
| *Caleb Williams* | 50 | 16 |
| *The Mysteries of Udolpho* | 72 | 52 |
| *The Monk* | 25 | 24 |
| *Northanger Abbey* | 9 | 12 |
| *Mansfield Park* | 35 | 27 |
| *Waverley* | 32 | 21 |

Only *Caleb Williams* makes use of the word *remove* with comparable frequency to Radcliffe, and no text features *relieve* with even half Radcliffe's frequency (bearing in mind that *Mansfield Park* is a much longer novel than *The Romance of the Forest*).

64. N. J. G. Pounds implies strongly that nostalgia for parochial community is, by the end of the eighteenth century, compensatory: "There had, in fact, long been a growing aloofness between parishioners and their parochial institutions" (499), and what remained of parish management consisted more and more of judicial and punitive functions generally doled out by county officials.

65. There is one incident of a male character relieving a blockage of affect in a comparable way: when the Marquis finds that La Motte has helped Adeline escape, he curses them both and "to invent and express these terms seemed to give him not only relief, but delight" (238). This relief differs in two respects: it is pleasurable, and it cannot be termed a bodily symptom. Notably, much is made of La Luc's grief over his dead wife and his frequent contemplative moods, but at no point does he ever relieve himself by sighs, tears, or any other discharge.

66. The "hydraulic principle," which, in Ronald Paulson's view, "Swift employed in *The Tale of a Tub*," dictates that "if your passion is blocked at one opening it will find a way out another— will be displaced to something else" ("Fielding, Hogarth, and Evil" 188).

67. This legal provision is represented in the example I cite above from John Trusler's *Modern Times* of women who "drop their bastards in some distant parish, lay them at the doors of some gentlemen's houses, or swear them to persons that had been their common disturbers" (1: 83), and Walter Scott evokes it in *The Heart of Midlothian*, when the beadle of an English parish asks Madge Wildfire, "Hast thou brought ony more bastards wi' thee to lay to honest men's doors?" (324).

68. Fores, "A Charge of Bastardy before Justice Juggle" (facsimile in collection of Yale University Lewis-Walpole Library).

69. Ruth Bienstock Anolik, in a wide-ranging essay, provides several explanations for the preponderance of maternal absences in gothic fiction. Among them she identifies "literalization of coverture and primogeniture" (26); "the necessity of the mother's absence to allow for the narratable deviance upon which the Gothic thrives" (28); and the "Gothic masterplot" of "the individuation of the young woman, denoted by her escape from the mother who is constructed as the spectral Other, threatening to dissolve the boundaries of the daughter's identity" (30). My goal here is not to dispute any of Anolik's postulates, but to add another.

70. *Tom Jones* is, of course, also framed by the absence of maternal testimony concerning the protagonist's paternity.

71. Margaret Homans gives an elegant analysis of erasures of the maternal in the first chapter of *Bearing the Word* (1–39).

72. In *The Mysteries of Udolpho*, Emily too prefers a modest residence: "Since both Valancourt and herself preferred the pleasant and long-loved shades of La Vallée to the magnificence of Epourville, they continued to reside there" (672).

73. Robert Miles argues that, at the end of Radcliffe's narratives, "what is installed is not glorified feudalism but an order based on the progressive promises of female sensibility. Here the bourgeois values of individualism and 'companionate marriage' triumph over the prejudices and vices of a passing aristocratic, patriarchal regime" (76–77).

74. My analysis of the economies of romance narrative, labor capitalization, and home implies an account of circulating energies that endorses Peter Brooks's amalgamation, in *Reading for the Plot*, of psychoanalytic models of psychic energy with narrative theory. Closure binds the unruly energies of sensational fiction in a manner that is analogous to the disciplinary organization of home: "We emerge from reading *Beyond the Pleasure Principle* with a dynamic model

that structures ends (death, quiescence, nonnarratability) against beginnings (Eros, stimulation into tension, the desire of narrative) . . . Crucial to the space of this play are the repetitions serving to bind the energy of the text so as to make its final discharge more effective. In fictional plots, these bindings are a system of repetitions which are returns to and returns of, confounding the movement forward to the end with a movement back to origins" (107–8).

75. "As a dynamic-energetic model of narrative plot, *Beyond the Pleasure Principle* gives an image of how the nonnarratable existence is stimulated into the condition of narratability, to enter a state of deviance and detour (ambition, quest, the pose of a mask) in which it is maintained for a certain time, through an at least minimally complex extravagance, before returning to the quiescence of the nonnarratable" (Brooks 108).

### 3. Home and Away

1. As Cannon Schmitt sees it, the "remainder of anxiety and paranoia" that the resolutions of Radcliffe's novels fail to gratify or assuage, is her "signal contribution to the formation of the Englishwoman": "Even more characteristic of . . . the Englishwoman than a given set of character traits is an attitude of paranoia and a habit of surveillance" (871).

2. Eileen Cleere sees a comparable orientation in conduct literature: "Conduct book writers like [Hannah] More, Maria Edgeworth, and Elizabeth Hamilton . . . were explicitly promoting a patriotic system of internal management for the purpose of homeland defense. Not only did conduct book writers like these provide upper- and middle-class women with a program of thrift and domestic economy that helped them participate in the war effort, they often placed female labor at the hidden center of patriarchal agricultural policy, rendering every wife and daughter not a soldier but a gardener of the British empire" (5). "Conduct books," Cleere continues, "instructed women to become participants in a form of economic isolationism that was both personal and political" (12).

3. "In the palpable night of their terrors, men under consternation suppose, not that it is the danger which, by a sure instinct, calls out the courage to resist it, but that it is the courage which produces the danger. They therefore seek for a refuge from their fears in the fears themselves, and consider a temporizing meanness as the only source of safety" (Burke, "Regicide Peace" 193).

4. It is true that Gisborne refers to women and Edgeworth's Earl is not a woman, but I will demonstrate that the shift in attitudes to domestic confinement in the first decades of the nineteenth century cannot be explained away by the doctrine of separate spheres.

5. Edgeworth is one of the progenitors of the national tale, which took shape around the moment of political union between England and Ireland. Her contribution to the genre's construction of national culture and national character has been carefully mapped. See, for instance, Kowaleski-Wallace, *Their Fathers' Daughters*; Corbett, *Allegories of Union*; Burgess, "Violent Translations"; and Trumpener, "National Character, Nationalist Plots."

6. Jeremy Bentham argues that workhouses, and poverty management in general, should confine the poor to an epistemic realm where they have "no unsatisfied longings, no repinings, nothing within knowledge that is not within reach" (quoted in Himmelfarb 83).

7. In *Pride and Prejudice*, Charlotte Lucas disappoints Elizabeth Bennett with her acceptance of Mr. Collins: "I am not romantic, you know. I never was. I ask only a comfortable home" (105). Elizabeth's "distressing conviction that it was impossible for that friend to be tolerably happy in

the lot she had chosen" (105) reads as disillusionment with the sexual institutions that her own class offers in place of aristocratic ones. *Mansfield Park,* on the other hand, defies this pattern: "With so much true merit and true love, and no want of fortune or friends, the happiness of the married cousins must appear as secure as earthly happiness can be.—Equally formed for domestic life, and attached to country pleasures, their home was the home of affection and comfort" (321), but Nina Auerbach finds this novel's fictive world "terrifyingly malleable" and its conclusions impossible to trust (220).

8. Deanna Kreisel examines the paradoxes of Austen's plotting in "Where Does the Pleasure Come From? The Marriage Plot and Its Discontents in Jane Austen's *Emma.*"

9. Eileen Cleere's analysis of the "home trade" movement implies that the majority of political economists continue to favor an enclosed market until the conclusion of the Napoleonic period. She cites "Napoleon's famous assessment of early nineteenth-century Britain as a nation of shopkeepers," interpreting it as "both a cultural insult and an economic warning; without trade routes and trading partners, without colonies or colonial exports, England's vast but undiversified wealth would practically evaporate" (4).

10. "The main human traits" that Christopher Herbert sees in Malthus's anthropology, "the permanent ones of the human biological constitution, are sluggishness, listlessness, amorphousness, inertia" (112).

11. The transition from closed and self-sufficient models of home to more open and permeable ones coincides roughly with the shift from physiocratic to classical political economy: "The eighteenth-century Physiocrats had emphasized the circularity of economic operations, their organic and self-contained nature; only with the classical economists do we see an economic model which describes the ballooning of the economy through surplus, accumulations of capital, and credit" (Kreisel, *Economic Woman* 46).

12. "There is no longer any original essence, only an ever pre-givenness, however far knowledge delves into its past" (Althusser qtd. in McKeon, *Origins* 19).

13. The hegemonic moment is the moment "in which one becomes aware that one's own corporate interests, in their present and future development, transcend the corporate limits of the purely economic class, and can and must become the interests of other subordinate groups too" (Gramsci 181).

14. Elizabeth Kowaleski-Wallace calls this historical transition "the implementation of a particular mode of domesticity necessary to the purposes of new-style patriarchy . . . [O]lder-style patriarchy, with its emphasis on paternal prerogative, hierarchy, and the exercise of force, had gradually yielded to new-style patriarchy with its appeal to reason, cooperation between the sexes, and noncoercive exercises of authority" (110).

15. Unsigned review of *The Mysterious Warning,* by Eliza Parsons, *Critical Review,* 2nd ser., 16 (1796): 474. Unsigned review of *The Bravo of Venice,* by Matthew Lewis, *Critical Review* 3rd ser., 5 (1805): 252–56. As Ian Duncan notes, "public experiments upon the cadavers of executed felons by Luigi Galvani's nephew Giovanni Aldini attracted popular attention and scientific debate in Great Britain in the first three decades of the nineteenth century" (*Scott's Shadow* 209).

16. Galt relates in his 1834 *Literary Life* that his own recollection of Radcliffe's fiction "at times . . . comes upon me like the lamp-light shadow of some phantasm in an 'eerie' fit . . . I can recollect no work by which I have been more affected" (1: 24–25).

17. One of Scotland's best-known inheritors of the gothic tradition, Robert Louis Stevenson published an odd poem, "The Celestial Surgeon," in 1886 that reiterates Galt's procedure:

If I have moved among my race
And shown no glorious morning face;
If beams from happy human eyes
Have moved me not; if morning skies,
Books, and my food, and summer rain
Knocked on my sullen heart in vain:—
Lord, thy most pointed pleasure take
And stab my spirit broad awake. (qtd. in Kreisel, "Wolf Children" 24)

The revivifying incision also has a provenance in eighteenth-century medical practice: in cases of epileptic stupor, Brandy Schillace reports, "stabbing inside the nose or under the fingernails" was a measure of last resort (279).

18. See chapter 2 for an outline of Gallagher's bioeconomic/somaeconomic distinction.

19. Galt affirms the adjacency of life science and affective engagement in his memoir *Literary Life* when, censuring George IV's spectacular 1824 visit to Edinburgh, he writes: "Had George the Fourth's performance of Crispianus in the Scottish metropolis been a truly royal avatar . . . he would at least have given one day to the inspection of the hospitals, of the receptacles of the houseless, and of the haunts and habitations of the miserable and forlorn . . . [Rulers] must visit the charnel-house—lift the lid, and learn what is man, as they shudder at the carcass; or, in other words, make themselves acquainted with the inevitable lot of humanity" (1: 241–42).

20. There is a third kind of disjunction pertinent to Galt's text: the compromised home-nation configuration of the Scottish subject, where a strong identification between private and national figures of domesticity is undermined by the foreignness that interposes itself between the English model and its Scottish subordinate. I will discuss this alienating complication in more depth in my final chapter.

21. Frances Burney's Juliet, heroine of *The Wanderer*, follows the Radcliffean prescription, confessing at the novel's close, "Many efforts, many conflicts . . . in my cruel trials, I have certainly found harder; but none, none so distasteful, as the unremitting necessity of seeming always impenetrable—where most I was sensitive!" (861).

22. I discuss this function in Scott's fiction and James Hogg's parody of it in "Confessions of a Gentrified Sinner: Secrets in Scott and Hogg."

23. My citation does not do full justice to Rybczynski's method; he does argue, on the same page, that "Domesticity . . . has existed for more than three hundred years" (217) rather than since time immemorial. His historicizing of home retains some transhistorical categories that he identifies most often as characteristically human, but which are mystifications of class, gender, and cultural specificity. As a work of popular history, however, his book does not deserve a wholesale scholarly dismissal.

24. Unsigned review of *Home—A Novel*, by Margaret Cullen, *Monthly Review* 41 (May-August 1803): 102–3.

25. Frances Burney, for instance, describes the monumental ruin of Stonehenge as seeming "like some rock, to have been placed 'from the beginning of things;' and though not even the

rudest sculpture denoted any vestige of human art, still the whole was clearly no phenomenon of nature" (*Wanderer* 765).

26. One of Ann Janowitz's key chapters in *England's Ruins* concerns *Salisbury Plain,* and her analysis offers useful insight, upon which I will draw, into the way Stonehenge becomes an uncanny double for England itself, at both private and national levels.

27. As in previous references to this poem, I am using the B manuscript assembled in Beth Darlington's Cornell edition of the poem unless otherwise noted.

28. Fred V. Randel observes that the "certitude of 'Home at Grasmere,'" bolstered by the concluding lines, "On Man on Nature and on human life," give "the exceptional grandiloquence and dogmatism of a great manifesto" (587).

29. Tim Fulford gives a lucid account of the significance of the Lonsdale dispute to *Home at Grasmere*: "The politics of landscape dwelt upon in *Home at Grasmere* can be brought into focus through an examination of Wordsworth's difficult negotiation of the social dispossession he himself suffered as a member of the rural economy. Wordsworth's father was the land agent and steward in Cumberland and Westmoreland of Lord Lowther, the Earl of Lonsdale. Lonsdale was the most powerful landowner in the Lake District . . . When Wordsworth senior died, in 1787, Lonsdale refused to pay a debt of nearly £5000 owed to him" ("Fields" 62). The legacy was finally paid in 1802, after James Lonsdale's death, by his heir, William Lowther.

30. Wordsworth seems in accord with William Paley on the topic of private property, which "communicates a charm to whatever is the object of it. It is the first of our abstract ideas; it cleaves to us the closest and the longest. It endears to the child its plaything, to the peasant his cottage, and to the landlord his estate" (Paley qtd. in Bernard et al. 5: 27).

31. William Hazlitt, discussing the relationship of nature to poetry, writes, "nature is a kind of universal home, and every object it presents to us an old acquaintance . . . they speak always the same well-known language . . . like the music of one's native tongue heard in some far-off country" (*Lectures on the English Poets* 103).

32. "'Home' may be the God-term without God," Andrew Bush proposes; "one may be agnostic as to historical and material existence, for what is of the essence is rather a form of relation. Where 'God' is the God-term, that relation is holiness; where it is 'home,' the matter would seem to be a question of belonging" (72).

33. Mary Jacobus identifies the mansion as a Wordsworthian idiom that "'Tintern Abbey' helps us to gloss as the mind ('thy mind / Shall be a mansion for all lovely forms')" (99).

34. Kate Rigby, discussing *Home at Grasmere,* observes that "dwelling . . . is always in some sense re-inhabitation, even if the place where you dwell also happens to be the place where you and possibly your forbears were born" (137).

35. "A certain kind of itinerancy is not necessarily incompatible with dwelling. Indeed, there is a sense in which not being at home, experiencing the place in which one lives, tarries or strays as unknown or strange, is of the very essence of dwelling" (Rigby 137).

36. Chandler, *Wordsworth's Second Nature;* Levinson, *Wordsworth's Great Period Poems;* Liu, *Wordsworth: The Sense of History;* Simpson, *Wordsworth's Historical Imagination;* Harrison, *Wordsworth's Vagrant Muse.* See also Bromwich, *Disowned by Memory;* and significant articles by Spargo, "Begging the Question of Responsibility"; and Dick, "Poverty, Charity, Poetry: The Unproductive Labors of 'The Old Cumberland Beggar.'"

37. Wordsworth did not publish *Salisbury Plain.* Its many revised versions include "Adventures on Salisbury Plain," "Guilt and Sorrow," and "The Female Vagrant."

38. Other poems that feature such failures include *The Ruined Cottage* and *Peter Bell* (the latter not published until 1819, but begun in 1798).

39. In Alex Dick's view, Wordsworth "opposed utilitarian attitudes toward poverty" and "favored 'local charity' . . . to encourage participation in the nexus of communal obligations which inspire work, independence, trade, self-sufficiency and growth" (370–71). "The Old Cumberland Beggar," which is Dick's primary example, at times adopts explicitly the registers of evangelical poverty management: "deem not this man useless—. Statesman!" (*Lyrical Ballads* 230, line 67), the speaker declares, and later, "May never house, misnamed of industry, / Make him captive" (233, lines 172–73).

40. Wood argues that the temple at Delphi was probably built by King Bladud (whom he also deems the founder of the Druidic religion) during an extended sojourn in Greece, where he "made himself famous . . . for his oracles" (10). Stonehenge itself, according to Wood, was built much later, but on principles established by Bladud.

41. More than a dozen times in *The Wanderer* the following basic sequence is played out: (1) Juliet arrives at a house where she will board, and almost immediately she attracts attention to herself. (2) A woman (usually one of the "three furies") takes a dislike to her. Children are entranced by her. A young man (or an old one) tries to declare his love. (3) Juliet is asked to perform in some way—music, acting, singing, needlework, conversation—and/or she is asked to reveal her identity. (4) She refuses any performance or revelation, precipitating a crisis. (5) She tries to hide, then decides to leave. (6) There are more attacks from women and defenses by men. (7) She makes her escape and is subsequently vindicated in some way.

42. In *Evelina,* a similar breach of etiquette, in written form, interrupts the developing attachment between Evelina and Lord Orville, though in that instance the indelicate letter is a forgery (286–90).

43. "Letters in the novels of the post-revolutionary years are always liable to go astray," Nicola Watson argues, "to engage in duplicity and deception, or to circulate out of control, relativizing competing discourses and thus putting social consensus in jeopardy" (16–17).

44. "In the 1790s," Mary Favret writes, "the public was asked to imagine the letter as the tool of division—of spies, Jacobinical conspiracies and seditious corresponding societies" (198). Nicola Watson concurs: "The letter as a double agent . . . is unmasked by its subjection to a process of recirculation, surveillance, edition, censorship and commentary" (70).

45. "In order to shore up the notion of a nation embattled, the letters of Jacobinical conspirators would have to have been invented even if they had not been intercepted . . . [T]he treasonous conspirator . . . would then occupy a role similar to the sentimental heroine's. Both served as the object of one invasion (rape or surveillance) and the symbol of another invasion (against 'domestic' terrain). The Home Office and the English home produced these fictions of self-defense" (Favret 40–41).

46. See Favret 30–33 and 39–41 for details of the acts against treasonous correspondence and the interception and suppression of private correspondence that they licensed.

47. Mary Favret cites Jacques Derrida's suggestion that "The movement of letters (the 'Post') is the system which produces and determines privacy" (14).

48. My thanks to Jamie Ellul, Records Officer, British Postal Museum and Archive. In his

e-mail, Ellul noted that it is very difficult to determine what offices the British Post maintained in the Brighton area prior to 1832.

49. I am grateful also to Susan Whyman for her advice and correction on this and other details in my description of postal history.

50. See Robinson, *The British Post Office* 238.

51. "A cross post could carry a by-letter from Bristol to Chester, but if the letter went from Bristol to Chester via London it was not a by-letter" (Robinson 65).

52. The manuscript of *The Wanderer* itself came close to confiscation when Burney returned to England in 1812: "The officer at the customhouse at Dunkirk was not prepared for the sight of all those papers fresh from Paris, and harboured the worst of suspicions . . . 'He sputtered at the mouth & stamped with his feet.' His tirade continued, the officer making accusations of 'traitorous designs' while the author of the manuscript . . . 'stood before him with calm taciturnity'" (Doody 316).

53. Judith Frank provides an analysis of Ellis's experience as a temporary member of the laboring poor in her conclusion to *Common Ground* (169–83).

54. John Towner describes what he calls the "discovery of Britain" in the later eighteenth century, typified by the growing popularity of "the Wye Valley, North Wales, Derbyshire, and parts of Scotland," and the gradual replacement of "classical tourism" by tourism in search of scenery (147–57). The Salisbury region, in which the Wanderer finds herself, gathered many of its tourists from nearby Bath Spa. Country houses, such as Wilton, "by the eighteenth century," were drawing more and more visitors "from the urban middle classes" as well as the "antiquarians" and "adventurous traveller[s]" who had been poking their noses in since the sixteenth century (Towner 33). Thomas Martyn's *The English Connoisseur* (1767) includes a thorough catalogue of the arts and antiquities at Wilton (1:84–129) for the "rising connoisseur" and the "yet uninformed observer of these valuable collections" (1: i).

55. The most famous of all literary visits to Stonehenge concludes *Tess of the d'Urbervilles* in a sequence that revises Burney's. Tess, having laid herself "upon an oblong slab," exclaims, "I don't want to go any farther . . . [N]ow I am at home" (393). "I think," Angel responds, "you are lying on an altar" (393).

56. As Jenny Bourne Taylor observes, home "has tended to be based on certain forms of prototypical experience, often extrapolated from particular life-stories . . . in particular a notion of native experience, of origin, of 'home' as both the producer, and the product of a certain experience of exile" (87).

57. Fiona Robertson points out that this pattern of returns is to be found also in *The Mysteries of Udolpho*: "All the scenes of early trial and suffering are ritually revisited and redeemed after the flight from Udolpho" (79).

58. Jane Fairfax says: "So seldom that any negligence or blunder appears! So seldom that a letter among the thousands that are constantly passing about the kingdom is even carried wrong—and not one in a million, I suppose, actually lost!" (qtd. in Watson 103).

59. The letter's misdirection, we should note, is blamed on Jane's having "written the direction remarkably ill" (222).

## 4. There's No Home-Like Place

1. I distinguish my usage of "negative ethnicity" from that of Koigi wa Wamwere in the book to which he gives the same title: "I use 'ethnicity' only to refer to positive ethnic pride and 'negative ethnicity' to indicate ethnic hate and bias" (22). Eric Hobsbawm's usage also differs from my own, is in a sense the opposite: "'Visible' ethnicity tends to be negative, inasmuch as it is much more usually applied to define 'the other' than one's own group" (66).

2. "The nationality that Scotland by itself cannot provide is supplied by English models" (Duncan, *Scott's Shadow* 59).

3. See McCracken-Flesher, "You Can't Go Home Again" 24.

4. David Deans, when reminded of "the oaths to government extracted from the established clergyman, in which they . . . homologate the incorporating Union between England and Scotland, through which the latter kingdom had become part and portion of the former," is apt to "cry out, 'My bowels!—my bowels!—I am pained at the very heart!'" (*Heart of Midlothian* 435).

5. James Kerr, in *Fiction Against History*, cites Michael Hechter's use of the term *internal colonialism* to define the relationship between the central and peripheral regions of Britain: "The relationship between Britain, the Highlands, Wales and Ireland was a 'colonial situation,' in which the dominated territories were condemned to an instrumental role with regard to the British 'metropolis'" (125 n. 7). Hechter borrows the term from Russian and Italian sources: "Initially coined by Russian populists to describe the exploitation of peasants by urban classes, it was later adopted by Gramsci, Lenin, Preobrashensky, and Bukharin to characterize the persisting economic underdevelopment of certain Russian and Italian regions" (xiii–xiv).

6. For attribution of this unsigned essay, see, for instance, Kidd, "The Ideological Importance of Robertson's *History of Scotland*" 130. This *Edinburgh Review* has no direct relation to the one founded by Francis Jeffrey in 1802; it only lasted two issues.

7. Also unsigned. Attribution: Lomonaco, "Adam Smith's 'Letter to the Authors of the Edinburgh Review.'"

8. "Briton. A native of Britain: a. In history and ethnology: one of the race who occupied the southern half of the island at the Roman invasion, the 'ancient Britons.' b. A Welshman. c. Since the Union of England and Scotland: a native of Great Britain, or of the British Empire; much used in the eighteenth century" (*OED* 2: 563).

9. According to Mary Poovey, "in the late seventeenth century Sir Isaac Newton recast the notion of isotropic space, which, in addition to its mathematical regularity, was held to be independent of all time, matter and motion" (*Making a Social Body* 28). Newton himself writes: "Absolute space, in its own nature, without relation to anything external, remains always similar and immovable. Relative space is some moveable dimension or measure of the absolute spaces; which our senses determine by its position to bodies; and which is commonly taken for immovable space" (qtd. in R. Schwartz 260).

10. In its assertion of totality and universality, what I am calling British national space-time is comparable to Fernand Braudel's conception (following Wolfram Eberhard) of "world-time": "a type of time experienced on a world scale . . . which is not however, and never can be the sum total of human history" (17–18).

11. Fernand Braudel refers to this kind of exception to world-time as "neutral zones" (42), which, predictably, are constitutive of world-time; as Saree Makdisi observes "homogeneous

time, like homogeneous space, is far from being smooth; the structuring principle of its homogeneity is unevenness" (*Romantic Imperialism* 63).

12. We should note that the fiction of James Hogg and John Galt frequently resists Scott's harmonizing and unifying imperative, but, even by their own acknowledgment, Hogg and Galt have little success in undermining the dominance of Scott's historiographic/narratological paradigm.

13. "The effect of [Scott's incognito] would seem to be the creation of a deeper and more implicit bond with his readers, an oblique way of insisting that they recognize the presence of the Olympian storyteller" (Waswo 308).

14. For Ian Duncan, "a romance revival may underwrite the extinction of the traditional form of life it salvages as an aesthetic trophy or talisman for the modern ideological assembly of a national culture" (*Scott's Shadow* 186).

15. "The act of invention that coins a resemblance *as* an original . . . The self-referencing rhetoric of fiction subsumes (but does not cancel) the burden of historical reference, perfecting a paradoxical logic of authentication" (Duncan, *Scott's Shadow* 279).

16. Consider the famous metaphor for progressive history coined by Scott in the "Postscript" to *Waverley:* "Like those who drift down the stream of a deep and smooth river, we are not aware of the progress we have made, until we fix our eye on the now distant point from which we have been drifted" (492).

17. Caroline McCracken-Flesher argues that "the narrator's sense of dislocation both from his community and from himself is a problem distinct to . . . Scotland's post-colonial figuration" ("You Can't Go Home Again" 24).

18. Robert is convinced for a while that Gil-Martin is Czar Peter of Russia and feels "disposed to yield to such a great prince's suggestions without hesitation" (130).

19. For discussions of Scott's relationship to the clearances and emigration, see Makdisi, "Colonial Space and the Colonization of Time in Scott's *Waverley*"; and Sussman, "The Emptiness at the Heart of Midlothian: Nation, Narration, and Population."

20. For the history of Scots emigration in the eighteenth and nineteenth centuries, see McCarthy, ed., *A Global Clan*; and Richards, *A History of the Highland Clearances.*

21. It seems likely that Galt was familiar with Robert Torrens's 1817 *Paper on the Means of Reducing the Poor Rates,* which advocates emigration for unemployable laborers and refers to colonization as a "safety valve" (qtd. in Snell 112).

22. Walter Scott details English poverty management carefully and accurately in *The Heart of Midlothian* and clearly implies its difference from the Scottish system. Jeanie Deans throws herself on the mercy of the parish of Willingham in Lincolnshire and is conducted "to his Reverence, in the first place, to gie an account o' thysell; and to see thou come na to be a burthen upon the parish" (325), under threat that should she not "answer the Rector all the better," she will receive "lodging at the parish charge" (325).

23. Hemans had published a comparable meditation—"The Emigrant"—fifteen years earlier in *The Domestic Affections.*

24. The poem has also been printed under the title "It's Hame and It's Hame" as well as "My Ain Countree."

25. Caroline McCracken-Flesher argues that Walter Scott chose Jacobitism as a cultural frame within which British union could be naturalized: "Scottish Jacobitism had been an

empty sign after the Scots' 1746 defeat at Culloden; indeed, after the Hanoverian succession, it lacked relevance, never mind power. Therefore Scott could inscribe within it both Scotland and England with no risk to the separate Scottish subjectivity he had carefully located within Calvinism" (308). So successful was this maneuver that Queen Victoria "sported the tartan at Balmoral, figured herself as a sentimental Jacobite, and lamented dearly beloved Scott alongside dearly beloved Albert" (309).

26. Peter Cunningham reports that Robert Cromek "was a man of considerable enthusiasm and ability, but he knew little about poetry and absolutely nothing about the poetry of Scotland. He was precisely that kind of person to believe everything he was told on that subject, and having a vague notion that the traditional songs of Scotland were pathetic and beautiful, he was ready to accept as such, all verses written in the Scottish dialect, that breathed the sentiments and passions of lowly rural life" (xxix–xxx).

27. Another of Cunningham's lyrics, "The Sun Rises Bright in France," makes use of the refrain "my ain countree," but I am confident that Lindsay is referring to "Hame, Hame, Hame."

28. Quoted from the version printed in Peter Cunningham's edition (30). Commentators cited on the same page concur in calling this poem "modern."

29. In *The Empire Writes Back,* Ashcroft, Griffiths, and Tiffin pose a set of questions that seem pertinent to the kind of diasporic consciousness I am proposing: "What does 'home' mean in the disrupted world of colonial space? How can 'home' become the transformative habitation of boundaries? For certainly that *unheimlichkeit,* that 'unhousedness' or 'uncanniness' which characterizes much colonial displacement, is a primary force of disruption in postcolonial life. Can it also be a source of liberation?" (218).

30. Modern nation-states "need historical novels," Franco Moretti claims, "to represent internal unevenness . . . and then, to *abolish* it. Historical novels are not just stories of the border, but of its erasure, and of the incorporation of the internal periphery into the larger unit of the state, a process that mixes consent and coercion—Love, and War . . . Love, between the man from England and the woman from the Lowlands estate: a miniature of a national union based on the agreement, the mutual desire of the more 'civilized' spaces. But war (and no prisoners), against the still 'savage' space, so that the state may finally achieve Weber's 'monopoly of legitimate violence'" (40).

31. The Waverley Novels do a great deal to help formulate what Vincent Pecora calls the "noble household," an invented history that identifies precapitalist domesticity with extended families, communities of obligation, and "the aura of the princely estate, feudal service, or the tribal chief's clan" (x).

32. Gary Kelly says of Scott's novels in general, "the romance journey often takes the form of a departure from home, and excursion into the public, social, and historical planes of existence, and a return to a home, often with a new wife or husband" (144).

33. These pangs of bourgeois maturation are some of "the typically human terms" through which Scott's novels help "great historical trends become tangible" (Lukács 35). Lukács's principle has close connections to Michael McKeon's proposal that "the domestic novel is committed to the idea that collective norms can only be a function of individual experience within the realm of the private" (*Secret History* 715).

34. See Duncan, *Modern Romance;* Makdisi, "Colonial Space and the Colonization of Time in Scott's *Waverley*"; and Schmidgen, *Eighteenth-Century Fiction and the Law of Property.*

35. As Edith is Lady Bellenden's "only hope" (351), we should expect Tillietudlem to pass on to her and her spouse at some point. Otherwise, all we know is that "once a year, and not oftener, Mr and Mrs Melville Morton dined in the great wainscotted-chamber [at Milnewood] in solemn state" (352). Like Radcliffe's concluding couples, I imagine, Henry and Edith would find any more sumptuary indulgence than that too rich for their modest tastes.

36. Mark Weinstein, editor of the Edinburgh Edition of *Saint Ronan's Well,* notes that the chronology of that novel's composition makes Lockhart's speculation "unlikely" (376).

37. See Poovey, *Genres of the Credit Economy* 363, for her delineation of the "gestural aesthetic," and chapter 3 of the present work for my assertion that it illuminates relations between narrative and home.

38. "Although the complicit subject's strategy may require constructing two narratives for the colonized nation, one that offers a locus for separate subjectivity, and one that inscribes the subject within the colonial narrative, the dualism is carefully distributed across singular narratives. So even in the act of claiming liberty, of claiming difference, the colonized subject remains subjected, remains primarily complicit" (McCracken-Flesher, "Thinking Nationally" 308).

39. The National Covenant of 1638 preceded the Solemn League and Covenant of 1643.

40. "The absolute rejection of all those demands made by the state which went 'against the conscience' and the demand for 'freedom of conscience'" were construed by Puritans, according to Max Weber, as "absolute right[s] of the individual *against* the state" (*Protestant Ethic* 212). One of Scott's clearest expressions of what he sees as Covenanter autonomism is the wistful obduracy of David Deans in *The Heart of Midlothian.* Deans recalls a post-1688 meeting of "the Anti-popish, Anti-prelatic, Anti-erastian, Anti-sectarian, true Presbyterian remnant," who have, ironically, "divided into many petty sects" and gather to dispute whether even a "faint shade of subjection to constituted authority" might be acceptable (201). "I am *not* a MacMillanite, or a Russellite, or a Hamiltonian, or a Harleyite, or a Howdenite," Deans tells Baillie Middleburgh, "I will be led by the nose by none . . . I have my own principles and practice to answer for"; "you are a *Deanite,*" Middleburgh replies (199).

41. The definition of a conventicle is a worship meeting held outdoors.

42. The Acts of Indulgence of 1669 and 1672 allowed dissenting Presbyterian ministers to return to the established church. Many did so, arousing, as Scott presents it, the fury of hard-line loyalists and radical Cameronians alike.

43. A passage from *Rob Roy* explains the "concentric bulwarks with which a Scotchman fortifies himself": "Surmount this mound [patriotism], you find an inner and still dearer barrier— the love of his province, his village, or, most probably, his clan; storm this second obstacle, you have a third—his attachment to his own family . . . It is within these limits that a Scotchman's social affection expands itself, never reaching those which are outermost, till all means of discharging itself in the inner circles have been exhausted. It is within these circles that his heart throbs, each pulsation being fainter and fainter, till, beyond the widest boundary, it is almost unfelt" (7: 157–58).

44. The equivocation of masks is a favorite theme of Restoration comedy: "I assure you," Mrs. Dainty announces in *The Country Wife,* "women are the least masked when they have the velvet vizard on" (137). The events of *Old Mortality* take place in the later Restoration period (aside from the novel's conclusion, after 1688), and Scott alludes explicitly to the vizard mask in a note added to the Author's Edition of *Old Mortality:* "Concealment of an individual, while

in public or promiscuous society, was then very common. In England . . . the ladies used vizard masks for the same purpose . . . This is repeatedly alluded to in Pepys's Diary" (*Old Mortality,* ed. Davidson 465 n. 15. I have consulted the Oxford World's Classics edition for this reference because the Edinburgh Edition follows the text of the 1816 *Tales of My Landlord.* All other references to *Old Mortality* are from the Edinburgh Edition.).

45. Scott's sympathy for Fergusonian models of civil order has not been widely discussed. P. H. Scott finds the pair very much in accord: "The extent to which Scott's views on the importance of the community echo those of Adam Ferguson is very striking. Of all the 'giants' (to use his own word) of the Enlightenment who influenced Scott, Ferguson was, I think, the most important. Scott had, of course, a close personal relationship with him through his friendship with his son" (209). "As far as I know," P. H. Scott continues, "Scott never specifically mentions Ferguson's *Essay* . . . Perhaps he had absorbed it so completely that he took it for granted" (209). Certainly I think Walter Scott is an advocate of Ferguson's law of unintended historical consequences: "Like the winds, that come we know not whence, and blow whithersoever they list, the forms of society are derived from an obscure and distant origin . . . and nations stumble upon establishments, which are indeed the result of human action, but not the execution of any human design" (Ferguson 119).

46. Scott's representation of civil war is almost certainly influenced by the example of the 1798 Irish rebellion, particularly in light of the rebellion's well-explored prominence in the genesis of the national tale. In her discussion of women's narratives of the Irish rebellion, Susan Egenolf discovers a breakdown of domestic separation comparable to that in *Old Mortality:* "Homes lost their conventional domestic functions and were absorbed into the rebellion, often employed as military headquarters or infirmaries or burned to the ground by either faction" (218).

47. This passage typifies what Caroline McCracken-Flesher calls Scott's effort to "suppress the doctrinal Calvinist voice, to write it out of its religious inheritance" ("Thinking Nationally" 305).

48. The "substantial equation of public and private spheres" that occurs in *Old Mortality* when Morton chooses "to support the rights of his country, insulted in his person," is "uncharacteristic of Scott in general," and "he introduces enough dissonance to make us question this blending" (Shaw 193–94).

49. Scott, in his introduction to *The Minstrelsy of the Scottish Border,* writes: "It seems no improbable conjecture, that the Brownie is a legitimate descendant of the Lar Familiaris [household god] of the ancients" (1: 150).

50. "In order to appear as material or empirical reality," Bhabha writes, "the historical or social process must pass through an 'aesthetic' alienation, or 'privatization' of its public visibility. The discourse of 'the social' then finds its representation in a kind of *unconsciousness* that obscures the immediacy of meaning, darkens the public event with an 'unhomely' glow" (143). The "unhomely" is clearly an adaptation of the *unheimlich,* but, instead of teasing subjectivity with an inorganic doubling of itself, the unhomely invests history and the objective world with a menacing sense of subjective determination, a narratedness: "It has less to do with forcible eviction and more to do with the uncanny literary and social effects of enforced social accommodation, or historical migrations and cultural relocations" (Bhabha 141). The unhomely, effectively, is the uncanny, reconceived from an extrasubjective or transsubjective perspective. Something

very like the unhomely is at play in *Old Mortality* in scenes like Morton imagining himself as a villa-turned-fortress, and Balfour at the cave mouth, which I will discuss in more detail below.

51. Maron has "baken in our house these eight days . . . sax dizen o' dizens" of bannocks, by her own count (6–7).

52. "In the old line it was a succession by the common law; in the new, by the statute law operating on the principles of the common law, not changing the substance, but regulating the mode and describing the persons" (Burke, *Reflections* 105).

53. "Scott stands, with Burke and Wordsworth . . . affirming the establishment of 1688, when domestic history was supposed to have culminated" (Duncan, *Modern Romance* 53).

54. Scott puts rhetorical and thematic emphasis on the Burkean analogy between collective liberty and private property: "By a constitutional policy, working after the pattern of nature, we receive, we hold, we transmit our government and our privileges in the same manner in which we enjoy and transmit our property and our lives" (Burke, *Reflections* 120).

55. Cuddie describes Morton to Morton himself, whom the ploughman has not yet recognized, implying that Morton is no longer tainted by the ensnaring masculine charms that had prevailed before the rebellion and the Revolution.

56. In *Ivanhoe,* the squire Damian is described thus: "The fond fool was decked in a painted coat, and jangling as pert and as proud as any popinjay" (17: 219)

57. "During his English reign King James [I] was frequently hailed as the 'nutritius' (nursing father) of the church, an image that he himself had used in *Basilikon Doron* and *The Trew Law of Free Monarchies* . . . which had its roots in Isaiah 49:23 ('kings shall be thy nursing fathers')" (Doelman 1–2).

58. "Lord Evandale, taking their hands in his, pressed them both affectionately, united them together, raised his face, as if to pray for a blessing on them, and sunk back and expired in the next moment" (349).

## Conclusion

1. "The home," Georg Simmel wrote at the beginning of the twentieth century, is (for women in the first instance) "an aspect of life and at the same time a special way of forming, reflecting, and interrelating the totality of life" (qtd. in Kumar 204).

2. From *Home: A Poem,* by Ann Cuthbert Knight (1788–1860), who emigrated from Scotland to Canada in 1815, the year of the poem's publication. She has no connection to the abolitionist Ann Knight (1786–1862).

3. Home "is not a monetary economy, though a household could be" (Douglas 297).

4. Homeland Security, the Surveillance Society (see, for instance, Wood, *A Report on the Surveillance Society*), and Facebook may be dissolving the last functional distinctions between home and state, but at this moment they retain some recognizable sociopolitical prestige.

5. "The natural-law principles that justify the individual right to property lay down corresponding duties to reflect the equal health, safety, moral, and property rights of neighbors. This interplay between duty and rights generates specific justifications for the regulation of property under the police power and the taking of property under the eminent domain power" (Malloy 36).

6. Anthony Vidler speaks of "the house, haunted or not, that pretends to afford the utmost security while opening itself to the secret intrusion of terror" (11).

7. As I note in chapter 4, Homi Bhabha has sought to develop *unhomely* as a complement to the uncanny, which imbues history with a frightening sense of subjective determination, a psychopathology perhaps of the all-engulfing social sphere described by Arendt—"a hypertrophied and distorted outgrowth of the private" (Kumar 214).

8. Commodities are "merely congealed quantities of homogeneous human labour, i.e. of human labour-power expended without regard to the form of its expenditure. All these things now tell us is that human labour-power has been expended to produce them, human labour is accumulated in them. As crystals of this social substance, which is common to them all, they are values" (Marx, *Capital* 128).

9. Parsimony, improvidence, and sumptuary excess, which are unquestionably domestic maladies, force economic reckonings that disrupt the rule of home: consider, for instance, the "sordid parsimony" of Milnewood in *Old Mortality,* which is counterposed to Tillietudlem's regal hospitality, marking neither house as comfortably home-like (see chapter 4 in this work).

# Works Cited

Abrams, M. H. "*The Prelude* and *The Recluse:* Wordsworth's Long Journey Home." *William Wordsworth's "The Prelude": A Casebook.* Ed. Stephen Gill. Oxford: Oxford UP, 2006: 209–24.

Acland, John. *A Plan for Rendering the Poor Independent on Public Contribution Founded on the Basis of the Friendly Societies Commonly Called Clubs.* Exeter: R. Thorn, 1786.

Addison, Joseph, and Richard Steele. *The Spectator.* Ed. Donald F. Bond. 5 vols. Oxford: Clarendon, 1965.

Adorno, Theodor. *Minima Moralia: Reflections on a Damaged Life.* Trans. E. F. N. Jephcott. New York: Verso, 2006.

Akenside, Mark. *The Pleasures of the Imagination: A Poem.* 3rd ed. London: R. Dodsley, 1744.

Alderson, Simon J. "The Augustan Attack on the Pun." *Eighteenth-Century Life* 20.3 (1996): 1–19.

Aldridge, Alfred Owen. "Shaftesbury and the Test of Truth." *PMLA* 60.1 (1945): 129–56.

Allan, Graham, and Graham Crow, eds. *Home and Family: Creating the Domestic Sphere.* London: Macmillan, 1989.

Anderson, Benedict. *Imagined Communities: Reflections on the Origins and Spread of Nationalism.* London: Verso, 1983.

Anderson, Elijah. *The Cosmopolitan Canopy: Race and Civility in Everyday Life.* New York: Norton, 2011.

Anolik, Ruth Bienstock. "The Missing Mother: Negotiations of Motherhood in the Gothic Mode." *Modern Language Studies* 33.1/2 (2003): 24–43.

Archard, T. *Suppression of the French Nobility Vindicated . . . To Which Is Added a Comparative View of Dr. Smith's System of the Wealth of Nations with Regard to France and England.* London: J. Debrett, 1792.

Arendt, Hannah. *The Human Condition.* 2nd ed. Chicago: U of Chicago P, 1958.

Armstrong, Frances. *Dickens and the Concept of Home.* Ann Arbor: UMI Research Press, 1990.

Armstrong, Nancy. *Desire and Domestic Fiction: A Political History of the Novel.* Oxford: Oxford UP, 1987.

Ashcroft, Bill, Gareth Griffiths, and Helen Tiffin. *The Empire Writes Back: Theory and Practice in Post-Colonial Literatures.* 2nd ed. London: Routledge, 2002.

Astell, Mary. *Some Reflections on Marriage. Political Writings.* Ed. Patricia Springborg. Cambridge Texts in the History of Political Thought. Cambridge: Cambridge UP, 1996. 1–80.

Attridge, Derek. *Peculiar Language: Literature as Difference from the Renaissance to James Joyce.* New York: Routledge, 2004.

Auerbach, Nina. "Jane Austen's Dangerous Charm: Feeling as One Ought about Fanny Price." *Jane Austen: New Perspectives.* Ed. Janet Todd. New York: Holmes and Meier, 1983. 208–23.

Austen, Jane. *Emma.* Ed. James Kinsley. Oxford World's Classics. Oxford: Oxford UP, 1980.

———. *Jane Austen's Letters.* Ed. Deirdre le Faye. Oxford: Oxford UP, 1995.

———. *Mansfield Park.* Ed. Claudia L. Johnson. Norton Critical Edition. New York: Norton, 1998.

———. *Northanger Abbey.* Ed. Marilyn Butler. Penguin Classics. London: Penguin, 2003.

———. *Pride and Prejudice.* Ed. Vivien Jones. Penguin Classics. London: Penguin, 1996.

———. *Sense and Sensibility.* Ed. Ros Ballaster. Penguin Classics. London: Penguin, 2003.

Austin, Carolyn. "Home and Nation in *The Heart of Midlothian.*" *SEL* 40 (2000): 621–34.

Bachelard, Gaston. *The Poetics of Space.* Trans. Maria Jolas. New York: Orion Press, 1964.

Bannet, Eve Tavor. *The Domestic Revolution: Enlightenment Feminisms and the Novel.* Baltimore: Johns Hopkins UP, 2000.

Barlow, Theodore. *The Justice of the Peace: A Treatise Containing the Power and Duty of that Magistrate.* London: Henry Lintot, 1745.

Baston, Thomas. *Thoughts on Trade, and a Publick Spirit.* London: 1728.

Battestin, Martin C. *The Moral Basis of Fielding's Art.* Middletown, CT: Wesleyan UP, 1959.

Beckford, William. *Azemia: A Descriptive and Sentimental Novel.* 2 vols. London: Sampson Low, 1797.

Bender, John. *Imagining the Penitentiary: Fiction and the Architecture of Mind in Eighteenth-Century England.* Chicago: U of Chicago P, 1987.

Benedict, Barbara. *Curiosity.* Chicago: U of Chicago P, 2001.

Benjamin, David N., ed. *The Home: Words, Interpretations, Meanings, and Environments.* Ethnoscapes series. Aldershot: Avebury, 1995. 1–14.

Bennett, Anna Maria. *Agnes De-Courci: A Domestic Tale.* 4 vols. Bath: S. Hazard, 1789.

Bentham, Jeremy. *Observations on the Poor Bill Introduced by the Right Honourable William Pitt.* Pamphlet. 1797.

———. *Pauper Management Improved.* London: R. Baldwin and J. Ridgway, 1812.

Bernard, Thomas, et al. *Annual Report of the Society for Bettering the Condition and Increasing the Comforts of the Poor* [SBC]. 9 vols. London: W. Bulmer, 1798–1817.

Bhabha, Homi. "The World and the Home." *Social Text* 10.2–3 (1992): 141–53.

Blunt, Alison. *Domicile and Diaspora: Anglo-Indian Women and the Spatial Politics of Home.* Oxford: Blackwell, 2005.

Blunt, Alison, and Robyn Dowling. *Home.* Key Ideas in Geography. London: Routledge, 2006.

Bourdieu, Pierre. *Distinction: A Social Critique of the Judgement of Taste.* Trans. Richard Nice. Cambridge: Harvard UP, 1984.

Braudel, Fernand. *Civilization and Capitalism, 15th–18th Century: The Perspective of the World.* Vol. 3. Trans. Siân Reynolds. Berkeley and Los Angeles: U of California P, 1992.

Braudy, Leo. *Narrative Form in History and Fiction: Hume, Fielding, and Gibbon.* Princeton: Princeton UP, 1970.

Briggs, John, Christopher Harrison, Angus McInnes, and David Vincent. *Crime and Punishment in England: An Introductory History.* London: UCL Press, 1996.

Broad, John. "Housing the Rural Poor in Southern England." *Agricultural History Review* 48.2 (2000): 151–70.

Bromwich, David. *Disowned by Memory: Wordsworth's Poetry of the 1790s.* Chicago: U of Chicago P, 1998.

Brooks, Peter. *Reading for the Plot: Design and Intention in Narrative.* Cambridge: Harvard UP, 1984.

Brown, John. *Essays on the Characteristics.* London: C. Davis, 1751.

Browne, Christopher. *Getting the Message: The Story of the British Post Office.* Stroud: Alan Sutton, 1993.

Brunton, Mary. *Self-Control.* 2 vols. Edinburgh: Manners and Miller, 1811.

Brydges, Egerton. *Letters on the Poor Laws.* London: Longman, Hurst, Rees, Orme, and Brown, 1813.

Burgess, Miranda. "Violent Translations: Allegory, Gender and Cultural Nationalism in Ireland, 1796–1806." *Modern Language Quarterly* 59.1 (1998): 33–70.

Burke, Edmund. "First Letter on a Regicide Peace." *The Revolutionary War 1794–97; Ireland.* Ed. R. B. McDowell. Oxford: Clarendon Press, 1991: 187–64. Vol. 9 of *The Writings and Speeches of Edmund Burke.* 9 vols. 1981–91.

———. *Reflections on the Revolution in France.* Edited by Conor Cruise O'Brien. London: Penguin, 1986.

Burn, Richard. *The History of the Poor Laws: With Observations.* London: A. Millar, 1764.

———. *The Justice of the Peace and Parish Officer.* 11th ed. 3 vols. W. Strahan and M. Woodfall, 1769.

Burney, Frances. *Evelina.* Ed. Margaret Anne Doody. Penguin Classics. London: Penguin, 1994.

———. *The Wanderer.* Ed. Margaret Ann Doody, Robert L. Mack, and Peter Sabor. Oxford World's Classics. Oxford: Oxford UP, 1991.

Bush, Andrew. "Overhearing Hollander's Hyphens: Poet-Critic, American-Jew." *Diacritics* 30.2 (2000): 70–87.

Butler, Marilyn. *Jane Austen and the War of Ideas.* Oxford: Clarendon, 1975.

Buttimer, Anne. "Social Space and the Planning of Residential Areas." *The Human Experience of Space and Place.* Ed. Buttimer and David Seamon. London: Croom Helm, 1980. 21–54.

Castle, Terry. "The Spectralization of the Other in *The Mysteries of Udolpho.*" *The New Eighteenth Century: Theory, Politics, English Literature.* Ed. Felicity Nussbaum and Laura Brown. New York: Routledge, 1987. 231–53.

Chadwick, Edwin. *Report from E. Chadwick Esq. on London and Berkshire.* London, 1833.

Chambers, Robert, ed. *The Book of Days: A Miscellany of Popular Antiquities.* 2 vols. London: W. and R. Chambers, 1832.

Chandler, James. *Wordsworth's Second Nature: A Study of the Poetry and Politics.* Chicago: U of Chicago P, 1984.

Clark, Anna. *The Struggle for the Breeches: Gender and the Making of the British Working Class.* Studies on the History of Society and Culture 23. Berkeley: U of California P, 1995.

Clark, Gregory. "Farm Wages and Living Standards in the Industrial Revolution: England, 1670–1869." *Economic History Review* n.s., 54.3 (2001): 477–505.

Cleere, Eileen. "Homeland Security: Political and Domestic Economy in Hannah More's *Coelebs in Search of a Wife.*" *ELH* 74.1 (2007): 1–25.

Cobb, James. *The Strangers at Home: A Comic Opera in Three Acts.* 2nd ed. London: Harrison & Co., 1786.

Cocks, Joan. *The Oppositional Imagination: Feminism, Critique, and Political Theory.* London: Routledge, 1989.

Coleridge, Samuel Taylor. *The Complete Poems.* Ed. William Keach. Penguin Classics. London: Penguin, 1997.

Coley, William B. "The Background of Fielding's Laughter." *ELH* 26 (1959): 229–52.

Colquhoun, Patrick. *A Treatise on Indigence.* London: J. Hatchard, 1806.

Copeland, Edward. *Women Writing about Money: Women's Fiction in England, 1790–1820.* Cambridge: Cambridge UP, 2004.

Corbett, Mary Jean. *Allegories of Union in Irish and English Writing, 1790–1870: History and the Family from Edgeworth to Arnold.* Cambridge: Cambridge UP, 2000.

Cowe, James. *Religious and Philanthropic Tracts.* London: J. Robson, 1797.

Cowherd, Raymond G. "Humanitarian Reform of the English Poor Laws from 1782 to 1815." *Proceedings of the American Philosophical Society* 104.3 (1960): 328–42.

———. *Political Economists and the English Poor Laws.* Athens: Ohio UP, 1977.

Crabbe, George. *The Borough: A Poem in Twenty-Four Letters.* 6th ed. London: J. Hatchard, 1816.

Crowley, John E. "'In Happier Mansions, Warm and Dry': The Invention of the Cottage as a Comfortable Anglo-American House." *Winterthur Portfolio* 32.2/3 (1997): 169–88.

Crowther, M. A. *The Workhouse System: 1834–1929: The History of an English Social Institution.* London: Routledge, 1983.

Csikszentmihalyi, Mihaly, and Eugene Rochberg-Halton. *The Meaning of Things: Domestic Symbols and the Self.* Cambridge: Cambridge UP, 1981.

Cullen, Margaret. *Home—A Novel.* 5 vols. London: J. Mawman, 1802.

Culler, Jonathan. "Omniscience." *Narrative* 12:1 (2004): 22–34.

Cunningham, Allan. *Poems and Songs.* Ed. Peter Cunningham. London: John Murray, 1847.

———. *The Remains of Nithsdale and Galloway Song: With Historical and Traditional Notices Relative to the Manners and Customs of the Peasantry.* Ed. Robert Cromek. London: Cadell and Davies, 1810.

Dacier, André. *Aristotle's Art of Poetry. Translated from the original Greek, according to Mr. Theodore Goulston's edition. Together, with Mr. D'Acier's notes translated from the French.* London: Browne and Turner, 1705.

Dallas, Robert Charles. *Not at Home.* London: B. Crosby and Co., 1809.

Davidoff, Leonore, and Catherine Hall. *Family Fortunes: Men and Women of the English Middle Class, 1780–1850.* Women in Culture and Society Series. Chicago: U of Chicago P, 1987.

de Certeau, Michel. *Heterologies Discourse on the Other.* Trans. Brian Massumi. Theory and History of Literature series. Minneapolis: U of Minnesota P, 1986.

de Man, Paul. *The Rhetoric of Romanticism.* New York: Columbia UP, 1984.

———. "The Rhetoric of Temporality." *Blindness and Insight: Essays in the Rhetoric of Contemporary Criticism.* 2nd ed. Minneapolis: U of Minnesota P, 1983. 187–228.

de Vries, Jan. "Between Purchasing Power and the World of Goods: Understanding the Household Economy in Early Modern Europe." *Consumption and the World of Goods.* Ed. John Brewer and Roy Porter. London: Routledge, 1993. 85–132.

*Debates in Both Houses of Parliament in the Months of May and June 1801: Relative to the Agreement Made by Government with Mr. Palmer, for the Reform and Improvement of the Post-Office and its Revenue.* London: Longman, Hurst, Rees, and Orme, 1809.

*Defence of the Statute Passed in the Forty-Third Year of Elizabeth, Concerning the Employment and Relief of the Poor.* Bury St. Edmund's: J. Rackham, 1788.

Derrida, Jacques. *Of Grammatology.* Trans. Gayatri Chakravorty-Spivak. Corrected ed. Baltimore: Johns Hopkins UP, 1998.

Dibdin, Charles. *Harvest Home; A Comic Opera in Two Acts.* London: Harrison & Co., 1787.

Dick, Alex. "Poverty, Charity, Poetry: The Unproductive Labors of 'The Old Cumberland Beggar.'" *Studies in Romanticism* 39 (Fall 2000): 365–96.

Dickens, Charles. *Oliver Twist.* Ed. Philip Horne. Penguin Classics. London: Penguin, 2002.

Dickie, Simon. "*Joseph Andrews* and the Great Laughter Debate." *Studies in Eighteenth-Century Culture* 34 (2005): 271–332.

Doelman, James. *King James I and the Religious Culture of England.* Studies in Renaissance Literature. Cambridge: D. S. Brewer, 2000.

Doody, Margaret Ann. *Frances Burney: The Life in the Works.* New Brunswick: Rutgers UP, 1988.

Douglas, Mary. "The Idea of Home: A Kind of Space." *Social Research* 58.1 (Spring 1991): 287–307.

Dryden, John. *Selected Poems.* Ed. Steven N. Zwicker and David Bywaters. Penguin Classics. London: Penguin, 2001.

Dufallo, Basil. "Words Born and Made: Horace's Defense of Neologisms and the Cultural Poetics of Latin." *Arethusa* 38 (2005): 89–101.

Duncan, Ian. *Modern Romance and Transformations of the Novel.* Cambridge: Cambridge UP, 1992.

———. *Scott's Shadow: The Novel in Romantic Edinburgh.* Princeton: Princeton UP, 2007.

Dunlop, John. *The History of Fiction.* 3 vols. London: Longman, Hurst, Rees, Orme, and Brown, 1814.

Dyer, George. *The Complaints of the Poor People of England.* London: J. Ridgway, 1793.

Dyson, Jeremiah. *An Epistle to the Rev. Mr. Warburton. Occasioned by His Treatment of the Author of "The Pleasures of the Imagination."* London: R. Dodsley, 1744.

Eden, Frederick Morton. *The State of the Poor.* 3 vols. London: J. Davis, 1797.

Edgeworth, Maria. *"Castle Rackrent" and "Ennui."* Ed. Marilyn Butler. Penguin Classics. London: Penguin, 1992.

———. *Letters for Literary Ladies.* London: J. Johnson, 1795.

Egenolf, Susan B. "'Our Fellow Creatures': Women Narrating Political Violence in the 1798 Irish Rebellion." *Eighteenth-Century Studies* 42 (2009): 217–34.

Eliot, George. *Adam Bede.* Ed. Margaret Reynolds. Penguin Classics. London: Penguin, 2008.

Ellis, Kate Ferguson. *The Contested Castle: Gothic Novels and the Subversion of Domestic Ideology.* Urbana: U of Illinois P, 1990.

Ellul, Jamie. "RE: Research Enquiry." E-mails to Scott R. MacKenzie. July 20 and 23, 2007.

Elsam, Richard. *An Essay on Rural Architecture Illustrated with Original and Oeconmical Designs.* London: E. Lawrence, 1803.

*An Essay on Civil Government.* London: R. Willock, 1743.

Favret, Mary. *Romantic Correspondence: Women, Politics and the Fiction of Letters.* Cambridge Studies in Romanticism. Cambridge: Cambridge UP, 1993.

Femia, Joseph V. *Gramsci's Political Thought: Hegemony, Consciousness, and the Revolutionary Process.* Oxford: Clarendon Press, 1981.

Ferguson, Adam. *An Essay on the History of Civil Society.* Ed. Fania Oz-Salzburger. Cambridge Texts in the History of Political Thought. Cambridge: Cambridge UP, 1995.

Ferrier, Susan. *Marriage.* Ed. Herbert Foltinek. Oxford World's Classics. Oxford: Oxford UP, 1986.

Fielding, Henry. *Contributions to the Champion and Related Writings.* Ed. W. B. Coley. The Wesleyan Edition of the Works of Henry Fielding. Middletown, CT: Wesleyan UP, 2003.

———. *"The Covent Garden Journal" and "A Plan of the Universal Register Office."* Ed. Betrand A. Goldgar. The Wesleyan Edition of the Works of Henry Fielding. Middletown, CT: Wesleyan UP, 1988.

———. *An Enquiry into the Causes of the Late Increase of Robbers.* Dublin: G. Faulkner et al., 1751. All citations of *Enquiry* refer to this edition.

———. *An Enquiry into the Causes of the Late Increase of Robbers and Related Writings.* Ed. Malvin R. Zirker. The Wesleyan Edition of the Works of Henry Fielding. Middletown, CT: Wesleyan UP, 1988.

———. "Essay on the Knowledge of the Characters of Men." *Miscellanies.* 2nd ed. 3 vols. London: A. Millar, 1743. 1: 181–227.

———. "A Fragment of a Comment on Lord Bolingbroke's Essays." *A Journal of a Voyage to Lisbon.* London: A. Millar, 1755. 221–45.

———. *"Joseph Andrews" and "Shamela."* Ed. Douglas Brooks-Davies and Martin C. Battestin. Oxford World's Classics. Oxford: Oxford UP, 1999.

———. *A Proposal for Making Effectual Provision for the Poor.* London: A. Millar, 1753.

———. *Tom Jones.* Ed. John Bender and Simon Stern. Oxford World's Classics. Oxford: Oxford UP, 1996.

Fildes, Valerie A. *Breasts, Bottles, and Babies: A History of Infant Feeding.* Edinburgh: Edinburgh UP, 1986.

Fores, S. W. "A Charge of Bastardy before Justice Juggle." Single-sheet engraving. November 20, 1790.

Foucault, Michel. *Discipline and Punish: The Birth of the Prison.* Trans. Alan Sheridan. New York: Vintage, 1979.

———. *The History of Sexuality: Volume 1, An Introduction.* Trans. Robert Hurley. New York: Vintage, 1990.

———. *Power/Knowledge: Selected Interviews and Other Writings, 1972–1977.* Ed. Colin Gordon. Trans. Colin Gordon et al. New York: Pantheon, 1980.

———. *Remarks on Marx: Conversations with Duccio Trombadori.* Trans. R. J. Goldstein and J. Cascaito. New York: Semiotext(e), 1991.

Fox, Lorna. *Conceptualising Home: Theories, Laws and Policies.* Portland, OR: Hart, 2007.

Frank, Judith. *Common Ground: Eighteenth-Century English Satiric Fiction and the Poor.* Stanford: Stanford UP, 1997.

Freud, Sigmund. "The Uncanny." *The Standard Edition of the Complete Psychological Works of Sigmund Freud.* Ed. and trans. James Strachey. 22 vols. Hogarth Press: London, 1953–75. 17: 217–56.

Fulford, Tim. "Coleridge, Böhme, and the Language of Nature." *Modern Language Quarterly* 52.1 (March 1991): 37–52.

———. "Fields of Liberty? The Politics of Wordsworth's Grasmere." *European Romantic Review* 9.1 (1998): 59–86.

Gale Cengage Learning. *Eighteenth-Century Collections Online.* gale.cengage.com. http://galenet.galegroup.com/servlet/ECCO?locID=ubcolumbia.

Gallagher, Catherine. *The Body Economic: Life, Death, and Sensation in Political Economy and the Victorian Novel.* Princeton: Princeton UP, 2006.

Galt, John. "The Buried Alive." *Tales of Terror from Blackwood's Magazine.* Ed. Robert Morrison and Chris Baldick. Oxford: Oxford UP, 1995. 35–38.

———. *The Literary Life, and Miscellanies.* 3 vols. Edinburgh: Blackwood, 1834.

———. *Ringan Gilhaize.* Ed. Patricia J. Wilson. Edinburgh: Association for Scottish Literary Studies/Scottish Academic Press, 1984.

George, Rosemary Marangoly. *The Politics of Home: Postcolonial Relocations and Twentieth-Century Fiction.* Glasgow: HarperCollins, 2000.

Gifford, William. Review of *Tales of My Landlord. Quarterly Review* 14 (January 1817): 430–80.

Gilbert, Thomas. *Considerations on the Bills for the Better Relief and Employment of the Poor.* London, 1787.

———. *A Scheme for the Better Relief and Employment of the Poor.* London, 1764.

Gilboy, Elizabeth Waterman. "Labour at Thornborough: An Eighteenth-Century Estate." *Economic History Review* 3.3 (1932): 388–98.

Gildon, Charles. *The Laws of Poetry.* London: J. Morley, 1721.

Gilman, Charlotte Perkins. *The Home: Its Work and Influence.* Reprint. Classics in Gender Studies series. Walnut Creek, Calif.: Altamira, 2002.

Gilmore, Thomas B. *The Eighteenth-Century Controversy over Ridicule as a Test of Truth: A Reconsideration.* School of Arts and Sciences Research Papers No. 25. Atlanta: Georgia State U, 1970.

Gisborne, Thomas. *An Enquiry into the Duties of the Female Sex.* London: Cadell and Davies, 1797.

Godwin, William. *Caleb Williams.* Ed. Maurice Hindle. London: Penguin, 1988.

Goldgar, Bertrand A. "Fielding, Politics, and 'Men of Genius.'" *Henry Fielding (1707–1754): Novelist, Playwright, Journalist, Magistrate: A Double Anniversary Tribute.* Ed. Claude Rawson. Newark: U of Delaware P, 2008. 257–70.

———. "General Introduction." *"The Covent Garden Journal" and "A Plan of the Universal Register Office,"* by Henry Fielding. Ed. Goldgar. The Wesleyan Edition of the Works of Henry Fielding. Middletown, CT: Wesleyan UP, 1988. xv–liv.

Goldsmith, Oliver. *The Deserted Village.* London: W. Griffin, 1770.

Gonda, Caroline. *Reading Daughters' Fictions, 1790–1834*. Cambridge: Cambridge UP, 1996.

Gramsci, Antonio. *Selections from the Prison Notebooks*. Trans. Quinton Hoare and G. N. Smith. New York: International, 1971.

Grant, Aline. *Ann Radcliffe*. Denver: Alan Swallow. 1951.

Grant, John. "Foucault and the Logic of Dialectics." *Contemporary Political Theory* 9.2 (2010): 220–38.

Gray, Charles. *Considerations on Several Proposals Lately Made for the Better Maintenance of the Poor*. London, 1751.

Greaves, William. *Reasons Humbly Submitted to the Honourable Members of Both Houses of Parliament for Introducing a Law to Prevent Unnecessary and Vexatious Removals of the Poor*. Cambridge: Francis Hodson, 1775.

Green, Sarah. *Scotch Novel Reading; or, Modern Quackery*. 3 vols. London: A. K. Newman and Co., 1824.

Grewal, Inderpal. *Home and Harem: Nation, Gender, Empire, and the Cultures of Travel*. Durham, NC: Duke UP, 1996.

Groenewegen, Peter. *Eighteenth-Century Economics: Turgot, Beccaria and Smith and Their Contemporaries*. Routledge Studies in the History of Economics. London: Routledge, 2002.

Guest, Harriet. "The Wanton Muse: Politics and Gender in Gothic Theory after 1760." *Beyond Romanticism: New Approaches to Texts and Contexts: 1780–1832*. Ed. Stephen Copley and John Whale. London: Routledge, 1992. 118–39.

Habermas, Jürgen. *The Structural Transformation of the Public Sphere: An Inquiry into a Category of Bourgeois Society*. Trans. Thomas Burger. Cambridge: MIT Press, 1991.

Hall, Catherine, and Sonya O. Rose, eds. *At Home with the Empire: Metropolitan Culture and the Imperial World*. Cambridge: Cambridge UP, 2006.

Hamilton, Elizabeth. *The Cottagers of Glenburnie: A Tale for the Farmer's Ingle-Nook*. Edinburgh: Ballantyne, 1808.

Hanway, Jonas. *Letters on the Importance of the Rising Generation of the Labouring Part of Our Fellow Subjects*. 2 vols. London: A. Millar and T. Cadell, 1767.

Hardy, Thomas. *Tess of the d'Urbervilles*. Ed. Tim Dolin. Penguin Classics. London: Penguin, 2003.

Harrison, Gary. *Wordsworth's Vagrant Muse: Poetry, Poverty and Power*. Detroit: Wayne State UP, 1994.

Harvey, Karen. "Men Making Home: Masculinity and Domesticity in Eighteenth-Century Britain." *Gender and History* 21.3 (November 2009): 520–40.

Hazlitt, William. *Collected Works*. Ed. P. P. Howe. 21 vols. London: J. M. Dent and Sons, 1930–34.

———. *Lectures on the English Comic Writers*. Vol. 6 of *Collected Works*. Ed. P. P. Howe. 21 vols. London: J. M. Dent and Sons, 1930–34.

———. *Lectures on the English Poets*. Vol. 5 of *Collected Works*. Ed. P. P. Howe. 21 vols. London: J. M. Dent and Sons, 1930–34.

———. *The Spirit of the Age*. In *The Selected Writings of William Hazlitt*. Ed. Duncan Wu. 9 vols. London: Pickering and Chatto, 1998. 7: 75–262.

Hechter, Michael. *Internal Colonialism: The Celtic Fringe in British National Development*. Berkeley and Los Angeles: U of California P, 1975.

Hegel, Georg Wilhelm Friedrich. *Phenomenology of Spirit.* Trans. A. V. Miller. Oxford: Oxford UP, 1977.

Hemans, Felicia. *The Domestic Affections.* London: Cadell and Davies, 1812.

———. "The Homes of England." *Blackwood's Edinburgh Magazine* 21.124 (April 1827): 392.

———. *Poems.* Liverpool: Cadell and Davies, 1808.

———. "Song of Emigration." *Blackwood's Edinburgh Magazine* 22.128 (July 1827): 32.

Henriques, Ursula R. Q. *Before the Welfare State: Social Administration in Early Industrial Britain.* London: Longman, 1979.

Herbert, Christopher. *Culture and Anomie: Ethnographic Imagination in the Nineteenth Century.* Chicago: U of Chicago P, 1991.

Hill, John. *The Means of Reforming the Morals of the Poor by the Prevention of Poverty.* London: John Hatchard, 1801.

Hill, Lisa. *The Passionate Society: The Social, Political and Moral Thought of Adam Ferguson.* International Archives of the History of Ideas 191. Dordrecht, Netherlands: Springer, 2006.

Hilton, Boyd. *The Age of Atonement: The Influence of Evangelicalism on Social and Economic Thought, 1785–1865.* Oxford: Clarendon Press, 1988.

Himmelfarb, Gertrude. *The Idea of Poverty.* New York: Knopf, 1984.

Hitchcock, Tim, Peter King, and Pamela Sharpe. Introduction to *Chronicling Poverty: The Voices and Strategies of the English Poor, 1640–1840.* Ed. Hitchcock, King, and Sharpe. New York: St. Martin's Press, 1997. 1–18.

Hobsbawm, Eric. *Nations and Nationalism Since 1780: Programme, Myth, Reality.* 2nd ed. Cambridge: Cambridge UP, 1992.

Hogg, James. *The Brownie of Bodsbeck.* Ed. Douglas S. Mack. Edinburgh: Scottish Academic Press, 1976.

———. "On the Changes in the Habits, Amusements and Condition of the Scottish Peasantry." *A Shepherds Delight.* Ed. Judy Steel. Edinburgh: Canongate, 1985. 40–51.

———. *The Private Memoirs and Confessions of a Justified Sinner.* Ed. P. D. Garside. The Sterling/South Carolina Research Edition of the Works of James Hogg. Vol. 9. Edinburgh: Edinburgh UP, 2001.

———. *The Queen's Wake: A Legendary Poem.* Ed. Douglas S. Mack. The Stirling/South Carolina Research Edition of the Collected Works of James Hogg. Vol. 14. Edinburgh: Edinburgh UP, 2004.

Holman, J. G. *Abroad and at Home: A Comic Opera in Three Acts.* London: George Cawthorn, 1796.

Homans, Margaret. *Bearing the Word: Language and Female Experience in Nineteenth-Century Women's Writing.* Chicago: U of Chicago P, 1986.

Hombs, Mary Ellen. "Reversals of Fortune: America's Homeless Poor and Their Advocates in the 1990s." *The Question of "Home."* Spec. issue of *New Formations* 17 (Summer 1992): 109–25.

Hope, Christopher. *Darkest England.* London: Macmillan, 1996.

Hoppit, Julian. "Political Arithmetic in Eighteenth-Century England." *Economic History Review* 49.3 (1996): 516–40.

hooks, bell. *Yearning: Race, Gender, and Cultural Politics.* Boston: South End Press, 1990.

Houston, R. A. "Poor Relief and the Dangerous and Criminal Insane in Scotland, c. 1740–1840." *Journal of Social History* 40.2 (2006): 453–76.

Howlett, John. *Examination of Mr. Pitt's Speech in the House of Commons on Friday, February 12, 1796, Relative to the Condition of the Poor*. London: W. Richardson, 1796.

———. *The Insufficiency of the Causes to Which the Increase of Our Poor and of the Poor's Rates Have Been Commonly Ascribed*. London: W. Richardson, 1788.

Hunt, Pauline. "Gender and the Construction of Home Life." *Home and Family: Creating the Domestic Sphere*. Ed. Graham Allan and Graham Crow. London: Macmillan, 1989. 66–81.

Hutcheson, Francis. *Reflections upon Laughter*. Glasgow: R. Urie, 1750.

*An Inquiry into the Management of the Poor*. London: Benjamin White, 1767.

Ives, Peter. *Language and Hegemony in Gramsci*. London: Pluto Press, 2004.

Jacobus, Mary. *Romanticism, Writing, and Sexual Difference: Essays on The Prelude*. Oxford: Clarendon Press, 1989.

Janowitz, Anne. *England's Ruins: Poetic Purpose and the National Landscape*. Oxford: Basil Blackwell, 1990.

Jeffrey, Francis. Review of *Waverley. Edinburgh Review* 24 (Nov. 1814–Feb. 1815): 208–43.

Jeffrey, Kirk. "The Family as a Utopian Retreat from the City: The Nineteenth-Century Contribution." *Soundings: An Interdisciplinary Journal* 55 (Spring 1972): 24–36.

Johnson, Claudia L. *Equivocal Beings: Politics, Gender, and Sentimentality in the 1790s: Wollstonecraft, Radcliffe, Burney, Austen*. Chicago: U of Chicago P, 1995.

Johnson, Samuel. *A Dictionary of the English Language*. 2 vols. 4th ed. Dublin: Thomas Ewing, 1775.

Johnston, Susan. *Women and Domestic Experience in Victorian Political Fiction*. Contributions in Women's Studies No. 186. Westport, CT: Greenwood Press, 2001.

Johnstone, Christian. *Clan-Albin: A National Tale*. Ed. Andrew Monnickendam. Glasgow: Association for Scottish Literary Studies, 2003.

Jones, Anthea. *One Thousand Years of the English Parish: Medieval Patterns and Modern Interpretations*. London: Windrush Press, 2000.

Kelly, Gary. *English Fiction of the Romantic Period, 1789–1830*. Longman Literature in English Series. London: Longman, 1989.

Kelsall, Malcolm. *The Great Good Place: The Country House and English Literature*. New York: Harvester Wheatsheaf, 1993.

Kerr, James. *Fiction Against History: Scott as Storyteller*. Cambridge: Cambridge UP, 1989.

Kidd, Colin. "The Ideological Importance of Robertson's *History of Scotland*." *William Robertson and the Expansion of Empire*. Ed. Stewart J. Brown. Ideas in Context series. Cambridge: Cambridge UP, 2008. 122–44.

King, Steven, and Alannah Tomkins, eds. *The Poor in England, 1700–1850: An Economy of Makeshifts*. Manchester: Manchester UP, 2003.

Knight, Ann Cuthbert. *Home: A Poem*. Edinburgh: J. & C. Muirhead, 1815.

Knight, Charles A. "*Joseph Andrews* and the Failure of Authority." *Critical Essays on Henry Fielding*. Ed. Albert J. Rivero. Critical Essays on British Literature Series. New York: G. K. Hall, 1998. 69–82.

Kowaleski-Wallace, Elizabeth. *Their Fathers' Daughters: Hannah More, Maria Edgeworth, and Patriarchal Complicity*. Oxford: Oxford UP, 1991.

Kreisel, Deanna K. *Economic Woman: Demand, Gender, and Narrative Closure in Eliot and Hardy.* Toronto: U of Toronto P, 2011.

———. "Where Does the Pleasure Come From? The Marriage Plot and Its Discontents in Jane Austen's *Emma.*" *Persuasions* 29 (2007): 217–26.

———. "Wolf Children and Automata: Bestiality and Boredom at Home and Abroad." *Representations* 96 (2006): 21–47.

Kumar, Krishnan. "Home: The Promise and Predicament of Private Life at the End of the Twentieth Century." *Public and Private in Thought and Practice: Perspectives on a Grand Dichotomy.* Ed. Jeff Alan Weintraub and Kumar. Chicago: U of Chicago P, 1997: 204–36.

Lacan, Jacques. "Desire and the Interpretation of Desire in *Hamlet*" Ed. Jacques-Alain Miller. Trans. James Hulbert. *Yale French Studies* 55.6 (1977): 11–52.

———. *Ecrits.* Trans. Bruce Fink, Héloïse Fink, and Russell Grigg. New York: Norton, 2006.

Laclau, Ernesto, and Chantal Mouffe. *Hegemony and Socialist Strategy: Towards a Radical Democratic Politics.* 2nd ed. New York: Verso, 2001.

Lamb, Charles. "That Home Is Home Though It Is Never so Homely." *The Essays of Elia.* 2nd ser. London: Edward Moxon, 1840. 72–74.

Lamb, Jonathan. "Exemplarity and Excess in Fielding's Fiction." *Critical Essays on Henry Fielding.* Ed. Albert J. Rivero. Critical Essays on British Literature Series. New York: G. K. Hall, 1998. 94–111.

Laslett, Peter, ed. *Household and Family in Past Time: Comparative Studies in the Size and Structure of the Domestic Group over the Last Three Centuries in England, France, Serbia, Japan and Colonial North America, with Further Materials from Western Europe.* Cambridge Group for the History of Population and Social Structure. Cambridge: Cambridge UP, 1974.

Lees, Lynn Hollen. *The Solidarities of Strangers: The English Poor Laws and the People, 1700–1948.* Cambridge: Cambridge UP, 1998.

Lennox, Charlotte. *The Female Quixote.* Ed. Margaret Dalziel. Oxford World's Classics. Oxford: Oxford UP, 1989.

Levinson, Marjorie. *Wordsworth's Great Period Poems.* Cambridge: Cambridge UP, 1986.

Lewis, Matthew. *The Monk.* Ed. Howard Anderson. Oxford World's Classics. Oxford: Oxford UP, 1980.

Lindsay, Maurice. *The Burns Encyclopedia.* 3rd ed. New York: St. Martin's Press, 1980.

Liu, Alan. *Wordsworth: The Sense of History.* Stanford: Stanford UP, 1989.

Lloyd, Sarah. "'Agents in Their Own Concerns'? Charity and the Economy of Makeshifts in Eighteenth-Century Britain." *The Poor in England, 1700–1850: An Economy of Makeshifts.* Ed. Steven King and Alannah Tomkins. Manchester: Manchester UP, 2003. 100–36.

Lockhart, John Gibson. *The Life of Sir Walter Scott, Bart.* London: Adam and Charles Black, 1893.

Lomonaco, Jeffrey. "Adam Smith's 'Letter to the Authors of the Edinburgh Review.'" *Journal of the History of Ideas* 63.4 (2002): 659–76.

Lootens, Tricia. "Hemans and Home: Victorianism, Feminine 'Internal Enemies,' and the Domestication of National Identity." *PMLA* 109.2 (1994): 238–53.

Lukács, Georg. *The Historical Novel.* Trans. Hannah Mitchell and Stanley Mitchell. New York: Humanities Press, 1965.

Lund, Roger. "Augustan Burlesque and the Genesis of Joseph Andrews." *Studies in Philology* 103.1 (2006): 88–119.

Lynch, Deidre. "Nationalizing Women and Domesticating Fiction: Edmund Burke and the Genres of Englishness." *Wordsworth Circle* 25.1 (1994): 45–49.

MacKenzie, Scott R. "Breeches of Decorum: Addison, Montaigne, and the Figure of a Barbarian." *South Central Review* 23:3 (2006): 99–127.

———. "Confessions of a Gentrified Sinner: Secrets in Scott and Hogg." *Studies in Romanticism* 41.1 (Spring 2002): 3–32.

Mackie, Erin. *Market à la Mode: Fashion, Commodity, and Gender in the "Tatler" and the "Spectator."* Baltimore: Johns Hopkins UP, 1997.

Madge, Thomas. *The Importance of Education to the Poor Stated.* Bury St. Edmund's: G. Ingram, 1810.

Makdisi, Saree. "Colonial Space and the Colonization of Time in Scott's *Waverley.*" *Studies in Romanticism* 34 (1995): 155–87.

———. *Romantic Imperialism: Universal Empire and the Culture of Modernity.* Cambridge Studies in Romanticism no. 27. Cambridge: Cambridge UP, 1998.

Malloy, Robin Paul. *Private Property, Community Development, and Eminent Domain.* Law, Property and Society series. Aldershot: Ashgate, 2008.

Malthus, Thomas. *An Essay on the Principle of Population.* Ed. Philip Appleman. New York: Norton, 1976.

———. *A Letter to Samuel Whitbread, Esq. M. P. on His Proposed Bill for the Amendment of the Poor Laws.* 2nd ed. London: J. Johnson, 1807.

———. *Principles of Political Economy.* Ed. John Pullen. Variorum ed. 2 vols. Cambridge: Cambridge UP, 1989.

Malton, James. *An Essay on British Cottage Architecture.* London: Hookham and Carpenter, 1798.

Martyn, Thomas. *The English Connoisseur: Containing an Account of Whatever Is Curious in Painting, Sculpture, etc. in the Palaces and Seats of the Nobility and Principal Gentry of England, Both Town and Country.* 2 vols. Dublin: T. and J. Whitehouse, 1767.

Marx, Karl. *Capital.* Vol. 1. Trans Ben Fowkes. Penguin Classics. London: Penguin, 1976.

———. *Grundrisse: Foundations of the Critique of Political Economy.* Trans. Martin Nicolaus. Pelican Marx Library. London: Allen Lane, 1973.

Matthew, H. C. G., and Brian Harrison, eds. *Oxford Dictionary of National Biography.* 60 vols. Oxford: Oxford UP, 2004.

McCarthy, Angela, ed. *A Global Clan: Scottish Migrant Networks and Identities since the Eighteenth Century.* International Library of Historical Studies 36. London: Tauris, 2006.

McCracken-Flesher, Caroline. "Thinking Nationally/Writing Colonially? Scott, Stevenson, and England." *Novel: A Forum on Fiction* 24 (1991): 296–318.

———. "You Can't Go Home Again: James Hogg and the Problem of Scottish 'Post-Colonial' Return." *Studies in Hogg and His World* 8 (1997): 24–41.

McKeon, Michael. *The Origins of the English Novel, 1600–1740.* Baltimore: Johns Hopkins UP, 1987.

———. *The Secret History of Domesticity: Public, Private, and the Division of Knowledge.* Baltimore: Johns Hopkins UP, 2005.

Melling, Elizabeth, ed. *The Poor*. Maidstone: Kent County Council, 1964. Vol. 4 of *Kentish Sources*. 6 vols. 1959–69.

Mellor, Anne K. *Romanticism and Gender*. New York: Routledge, 1993.

Miles, Robert. *Ann Radcliffe: The Great Enchantress*. Manchester: Manchester UP, 1995.

Mills, A. D. *A Dictionary of English Place Names*. New York: Oxford UP, 1991.

Milton, John. *Paradise Lost*. Norton Critical Edition. 2nd ed. New York: Norton, 1993.

Mirowski, Philip. *More Heat Than Light: Economics as Social Physics, Physics as Nature's Economics*. Cambridge: Cambridge UP, 1989.

Mohanty, Chandra Talpade. *Feminism without Borders: Decolonizing Theory, Practicing Solidarity*. Durham, NC: Duke UP, 2003.

Mohanty, Chandra Talpade, and Biddy Martin. "What's Home Got to Do with It?" *Feminism without Borders: Decolonizing Theory, Practicing Solidarity*. By Mohanty. Durham, NC: Duke UP, 2003. 85–105.

More, Hannah. "The History of Tom White, the Postilion." *Cheap Repository Tracts; Entertaining, Moral, and Religious*. London: F. and C. Rivington; J. Evans; J. Hatchard; and S. Hazard, Bath, 1798. 260–303.

Moretti, Franco. *Atlas of the European Novel*. London: Verso, 1998.

Motooka, Wendy. *The Age of Reasons: Quixotism, Sentimentalism and Political Economy in Eighteenth-Century Britain*. London: Routledge, 1998.

Mouffe, Chantal. "Hegemony and Ideology in Gramsci." *Gramsci and Marxist Theory*. Ed. Mouffe. London: Routledge and Kegan Paul, 1979. 168–204.

Nelles, William. "Omniscience for Atheists: Or, Jane Austen's Infallible Narrator." *Narrative* 14.2 (2006): 118–31.

Norton, Rictor. *Mistress of Udolpho: The Life of Ann Radcliffe*. London: Leicester UP, 1999.

Offer, Avner. "Farm Tenure and Land Values in England, c. 1750–1950." *Economic History Review* ns 44.1 (1991): 1–20.

Ogborn, Miles. *Spaces of Modernity: London's Geographies, 1680–1780*. New York: Guilford Press, 1998.

Oldenburg, Ray. *The Great Good Place*. 2nd ed. New York: Marlowe, 1999.

Olssen, Mark. *Michel Foucault: Materialism and Education*. Westport, CT: Greenwood Press, 1999.

"Our Households and Homes." *Englishwoman's Domestic Magazine* 15 (1873): 75–76.

*Oxford English Dictionary*. 2nd ed. 20 vols. Oxford: Clarendon Press, 1989.

Packham, Catherine. "The Physiology of Political Economy: Vitalism and Adam Smith's *Wealth of Nations*." *Journal of the History of Ideas* 63 (2002): 465–81.

Palmer, John. *Papers Relative to the Agreement by Government with Mr. Palmer for the Reform and Improvement of the Posts*. London: Cadell and Davies, 1797.

Parkes, Christopher. "*Joseph Andrews* and the Control of the Poor." *Studies in the Novel* 39.1 (2007): 17–30.

Pateman, Carole. *The Sexual Contract*. Stanford: Stanford UP, 1988.

Patmore, Coventry. *The Angel in the House*. 2 vols. London: Macmillan, 1863.

Paulson, Ronald. "Fielding, Hogarth, and Evil: Cruelty." *Henry Fielding (1707–1754): Novelist, Playwright, Journalist, Magistrate: A Double Anniversary Tribute*. Ed. Claude Rawson. Newark: U of Delaware P, 2008. 173–200.

———. *The Life of Henry Fielding: A Critical Biography.* Blackwell Critical Biographies. Oxford: Blackwell, 2000.

———. *Satire and the Novel in Eighteenth-Century England.* New Haven: Yale UP, 1967.

Pecora, Vincent P. *Households of the Soul.* Baltimore: Johns Hopkins UP, 1997.

Percy, Sholto, and Reuben Percy. *The Percy Anecdotes.* 20 vols. London: J. Cumberland, 1826.

Perry, Ruth. *Novel Relations: The Transformation of Kinship in English Literature and Culture, 1748–1818.* Cambridge: Cambridge UP, 2004.

Pitt, William. *An Address to the Landed Interest on the Deficiency of Habitations and Fuel for the Use of the Poor.* London: Elmsly and Bremner, 1797.

Pocock, J. G. A. *Virtue, Commerce, and History.* Cambridge: Cambridge UP, 1985.

Poovey, Mary. *Genres of the Credit Economy: Mediating Value in Eighteenth- and Nineteenth-Century Britain.* Chicago: U of Chicago P, 2008.

———. *Making a Social Body: British Cultural Formation 1830–1864.* Chicago: U of Chicago P, 1995.

———. *The Proper Lady and the Woman Writer: Ideology as Style in the Works of Mary Wollstonecraft, Mary Shelley, and Jane Austen.* Chicago: U of Chicago P, 1984.

———. *Uneven Developments: The Ideological Work of Gender in Mid-Victorian England.* Chicago: U of Chicago P, 1988.

Pope, Alexander. *The Dunciad.* Ed. James Sutherland. Vol. 5. Twickenham Edition of the Poems of Alexander Pope. 3rd ed. New Haven: Yale UP, 1963. 11 vols. 1961–69.

———. *The Rape of the Lock and Other Poems.* Ed. Geoffrey Tillotson. Vol. 2. Twickenham Edition of the Poems of Alexander Pope. 3rd ed. London: Methuen, 1962. 11 vols. 1961–69.

Pope, Alexander, and John Arbuthnot. *Memoirs of the Extraordinary Life, Works, and Discoveries of Martinus Scriblerus.* London: Hesperus: 2002.

Porter, Roy. *The Creation of the Modern World: The Untold Story of the British Enlightenment.* New York: Norton, 2000.

———. *English Society in the Eighteenth Century.* Harmondsworth, Middlesex: Penguin, 1982.

Potkay, Adam. *The Story of Joy: From the Bible to Late Romanticism.* Cambridge: Cambridge UP, 2007.

Pounds, N. J. G. *A History of the English Parish: The Culture of Religion from Augustine to Victoria.* Cambridge: Cambridge UP, 2000.

Pratt, Minnie Bruce. "Identity: Skin, Blood, Heart." *Yours in Struggle: Three Feminist Perspectives on Anti-Semitism and Racism.* Ed. Ellen Bulkin, Minnie Bruce Pratt, and Barbara Smith. New York: Long Haul Press, 1984. 11–63.

Pratt, Samuel Jackson. *Cottage Pictures; or, The Poor.* 3rd ed. London: Longman and Rees, 1803.

Radcliffe, Ann. *Gaston de Blondeville.* 4 vols. London: Henry Colburn, 1826.

———. *The Italian.* Ed. Frederick Garber. Oxford World's Classics. Oxford: Oxford UP, 1981.

———. *A Journey Made in the Summer of 1794, through Holland and the Western Frontier of Germany.* London: G. G. and J. Robinson, 1795.

———. *The Mysteries of Udolpho.* Ed. Bonamy Dobrée. Oxford World's Classics. Oxford: Oxford UP, 1966.

———. "On the Supernatural in Poetry." *New Monthly Magazine* 2nd ser., 16 (1826): 145–52.

———. *The Romance of the Forest.* Ed. Chloe Chard. Oxford: Oxford UP, 1986.

Randel, Fred V. "Wordsworth's Homecoming." *Studies in English Literature, 1500–1900* 17.4 (1977): 575–91.

Rapoport, Amos. "A Critical Look at the Concept 'Home.'" *The Home: Words, Interpretations, Meanings, and Environments.* Ed. David N. Benjamin. Ethnoscapes series. Aldershot: Avebury, 1995. 25–52.

Rawson, Claude, ed. *Henry Fielding (1707–1754): Novelist, Playwright, Journalist, Magistrate: A Double Anniversary Tribute.* Newark: U of Delaware P, 2008.

Ray, Gordon. *The Times English Dictionary.* London: HarperCollins, 2000.

Ricardo, David. *Principles of Political Economy and Taxation.* London: Dent, 1973.

Richards, Eric. *A History of the Highland Clearances.* 2 vols. London: Croom Helm, 1982.

Richardson, Alan. *Literature, Education, and Romanticism: Reading as Social Practice, 1780–1832.* Cambridge Studies in Romanticism. Cambridge: Cambridge UP, 1994.

Richardson, Samuel. *Pamela.* Ed. Peter Sabor. Penguin Classics. London: Penguin, 1985.

Rigby, Kate. "Ecstatic Dwelling: Perspectives on Place in European Romanticism." *Angelaki: Journal of the Theoretical Humanities* 9.2 (August 2004): 117–43.

Rivero, Albert J., ed. *Critical Essays on Henry Fielding.* Critical Essays on British Literature Series. New York: G. K. Hall, 1998.

Robertson, Fiona. *Legitimate Histories: Scott, Gothic, and the Authorities of Fiction.* Oxford: Clarendon Press, 1994.

Robinson, Howard. *The British Post Office: A History.* Princeton: Princeton UP, 1948.

Rogers, Deborah D., ed. *The Critical Response to Ann Radcliffe.* Westport, CT: Greenwood Press, 1994.

Rogers, Pat. "Fielding on Society, Crime, and the Law." *The Cambridge Companion to Henry Fielding.* Ed. Claude Rawson. Cambridge: Cambridge UP, 2007. 137–52.

Rose, George. *Observations on the Poor Laws.* 2nd ed. London: J. Hatchard, 1805.

Ruskin, John. *The Works of John Ruskin.* Ed. E. T. Cook and Alexander Wedderburn. 39 vols. London: George Allen, 1903–12.

Rybczynski, Witold. *Home: A Short History of an Idea.* New York: Viking, 1986.

Schillace, Brandy Lain. "'Temporary Failure of Mind': Déjà Vu and Epilepsy in Radcliffe's *The Mysteries of Udolpho.*" *Eighteenth-Century Studies* 42.2 (2009): 273–87.

Schmidgen, Wolfram. *Eighteenth-Century Fiction and the Law of Property.* Cambridge: Cambridge UP, 2002.

———. "Illegitimacy and Observation: The Bastard in the Eighteenth-Century Novel." *ELH* 69.1 (2002): 133–66.

———. "Picturing Property: Waverley and the common law." *Studies in the Novel* 29 (1997): 191–213.

Schmitt, Cannon. "Techniques of Terror, Technologies of Nationality: Ann Radcliffe's *The Italian.*" *ELH* 61.4 (1994): 853–76.

Schwartz, Bill. "An Englishman Abroad . . . and at Home: The Case of Paul Scott." *The Question of "Home."* Spec. issue of *New Formations* 17 (Summer 1992): 95–105.

Schwartz, Richard B. "Berkeley, Newtonian Space, and the Question of Evidence." *Probability, Time, and Space in Eighteenth Century Literature.* Ed. Paula Backscheider. Papers of the 1973–1976 Sessions of a Modern Language Association Group. New York: AMS Press, 1979. 259–73.

Scott, P. H. "The Politics of Sir Walter Scott." *Scott and His Influence: Papers of the Aberdeen Scott Conference, 1982.* Ed. J. H. Alexander and David Hewitt. Occasional Papers 6. Aberdeen: Association for Scottish Literary Studies, 1983. 208–17.

Scott, Walter. *The Bride of Lammermoor.* Ed. J. H. Alexander. Edinburgh Edition of the Waverley Novels. Vol. 7a. Edinburgh: Edinburgh UP, 1995.

———. *The Fortunes of Nigel.* Author's Edition of the Waverley Novels. Vol. 26. Edinburgh: Cadell, 1831.

———. *Ivanhoe.* Author's Edition of the Waverley Novels. Vols. 16–17. Edinburgh: Cadell, 1830.

———. *The Heart of Midlothian.* Ed. Tony Inglis. Penguin Classics. London: Penguin, 1994.

———. *The Lay of the Last Minstrel.* Ed. W. J. Alexander. Toronto: Copp Clark, 1901.

———. *Minstrelsy of the Scottish Border.* Ed. T. F. Henderson. 4 vols. Edinburgh. William Blackwood and Sons, 1902.

———. *The Miscellaneous Prose Works of Sir Walter Scott.* 6 vols. Edinburgh: Cadell, 1827.

———. *Peveril of the Peak.* Author's Edition of the Waverley Novels. Vols. 28–30. Edinburgh: Cadell, 1831.

———. "Prefatory Memoir to Mrs. Ann Radcliffe" *The Critical Response to Ann Radcliffe.* Ed. Deborah D. Rogers. Critical Responses in Arts and Letters. Westport, CT: Greenwood Press, 1994. 112–25.

———. *Rob Roy.* Author's Edition of the Waverley Novels. Vols. 7–8. Edinburgh: Cadell, 1832.

———. *Saint Ronan's Well.* Author's Edition of the Waverley Novels. Vols. 33–34. Edinburgh: Cadell, 1832.

———. *Saint Ronan's Well.* Ed. Mark Weinstein. Edinburgh Edition of the Waverley Novels. Vol. 16. Edinburgh: Edinburgh UP, 1995.

———. *The Tale of Old Mortality.* Ed. Peter Davidson and Jane Stevenson. Oxford World's Classics. Oxford: Oxford UP, 1993.

———. *The Tale of Old Mortality.* Ed. Douglas Mack. The Edinburgh Edition of the Waverley Novels. Vol. 4b. Edinburgh: Edinburgh UP, 1993.

———. *Waverley.* Ed. Andrew Hook. London: Penguin, 1972.

Shaftesbury, 3rd Earl of. *Characteristicks of Men, Manners, Opinions, Times.* 3 vols. London, 1711.

Shakespeare, William. *Hamlet. The Riverside Shakespeare.* Ed. Frank Kermode, G. Blakemore Evans, and J. J. M. Tobin. 2nd ed. Boston: Houghton Mifflin, 1997. 1182–1245.

———. *King Lear. The Riverside Shakespeare.* Ed. Frank Kermode, G. Blakemore Evans, and J. J. M. Tobin. 2nd ed. Boston: Houghton Mifflin, 1997. 1303–54.

Shaw, Harry. *The Forms of Historical Fiction: Sir Walter Scott and His Successors.* Ithaca: Cornell UP, 1983.

Sheffield, John Holroyd, 1st Earl of. *Observations on the Impolicy, Abuses, and False Interpretation of the Poor Laws.* London: J. Hatchard, 1818.

Shelley, Mary. "Roger Dodsworth, the Reanimated Englishman." *Collected Tales.* Ed. Charles E. Robinson. Baltimore: Johns Hopkins UP, 1990. 43–50.

Shelley, Percy Bysshe. *The Major Works.* Ed. Zachary Leader and Michael O'Neill. Oxford World's Classics. Oxford: Oxford UP, 2003.

Sherman, Sandra. *Imagining Poverty: Quantification and the Decline of Paternalism.* Columbus: Ohio State UP, 2001.

Simpson, David. *Wordsworth's Historical Imagination: The Poetry of Displacement.* New York: Methuen, 1987.

Sitter, John. "About Wit: Locke, Addison, Prior, and the Order of Things." *Rhetorics of Order/Ordering Rhetorics in English Neoclassical Literature.* Ed. J. Douglas Canfield and J. Paul Hunter. Newark: U of Delaware P, 1989. 137–57.

Skinner, Gillian. *Sensibility and Economics in the Novel, 1740–1800: The Price of a Tear.* Basingstoke: Macmillan, 1999.

Slack, Paul. *The English Poor Law, 1531–1782.* New Studies in Economic and Social History. Cambridge: Cambridge UP, 1995.

Smart, Barry. "The Politics of Truth and the Problem of Hegemony." *Foucault: A Critical Reader.* Ed. David Couzens Hoy. Oxford: Basil Blackwell, 1986. 157–73.

Smith, Adam. "A Letter to the Authors." *Edinburgh Review* 1.2 (August-December 1755): 63–79.

———. *The Wealth of Nations.* New York: Knopf, 1991.

Smith, Christopher J. P. *A Quest for Home: Reading Robert Southey.* Liverpool English Texts and Studies. Liverpool: Liverpool UP, 1997.

Smollett, Tobias. *The Expedition of Humphry Clinker.* Ed. Angus Ross. Penguin Classics. London: Penguin, 1967.

Snell, K. D. M. *Annals of the Labouring Poor: Social Change and Agrarian England, 1660–1900.* Cambridge Studies in Population, Economy and Society in Past Time. Cambridge: Cambridge UP, 1985.

Sokoll, Thomas. *Household and Family among the Poor: The Case of Two Essex Communities in the Late Eighteenth and Early Nineteenth Centuries.* Bochum: Universitätsverlag Brockmeyer, 1993.

Southey, Robert. *Letters from England by Don Manuel Alvarez Espriella.* 2 cols. 3rd American ed. Philadelphia: Benjamin Warner, 1818.

———. *Selected Shorter Poems, 1793–1810.* Ed. Lynda Pratt. London: Pickering and Chatto, 2004. The Pickering Masters. Vol. 5 of *Poetical Works 1793–1810,* 5 vols.

Spargo, Clifton R. "Begging the Question of Responsibility: The Vagrant Poor in Wordsworth's 'Beggars' and 'Resolution and Independence.'" *Studies in Romanticism* 39 (2000): 51–80.

Spedding, Patrick. "'The New Machine': Discovering the Limits of ECCO." *ELH* 44.4 (2011): 437–53.

Starbucks Corporation. "Frequently Asked Questions." starbuck.com. www.starbucks.com/customer/faq_qanda.asp?name=whitecup.

*The Statutes at Large Concerning the Provision for the Poor.* London: J. Baskett, 1741.

Steedman, Carolyn. "Servants and Their Relationship to the Unconscious." *Journal of British Studies* 42 (July 2003): 316–50.

Sterne, Laurence. *The Life and Opinions of Tristram Shandy, Gentleman.* Ed. Melvyn New and Joan New. Penguin Classics. London: Penguin, 1997.

Stirati, Antonella. *The Theory of Wages in Classical Economics: A Study of Adam Smith, David Ricardo and Their Contemporaries.* Trans. Joan Hall. Aldershot: Edward Elgar, 1994.

Stott, Anne. *Hannah More: The First Victorian.* Oxford: Oxford UP, 2003.

Sussman, Charlotte. "The Emptiness at the Heart of Midlothian: Nation, Narration, and Population." *Eighteenth-Century Fiction* 15.1 (2002): 103–26.

Tadmor, Naomi. *Family and Friends in Eighteenth-Century England: Household, Kinship and Patronage.* Cambridge: Cambridge UP, 2001.

Talfourd, Thomas Noon. "Memoir of the Life and Writings of Mrs. Radcliffe." *Gaston de Blondeville.* By Ann Radcliffe. 4 vols. London: Henry Colburn, 1826. 1:3–132.

Taylor, Geoffrey. *The Problem of Poverty: 1660–1834.* Seminar Studies in History. London: Longmans, Green, 1969.

Taylor, Jenny Bourne. "Re: Locations—From Bradford to Brighton." *The Question of "Home."* Spec. issue of *New Formations* 17 (Summer 1992): 86–94.

Taylor, John Tinnon. *Early Opposition to the English Novel.* New York: King's Crown Press, 1943.

Terry, Richard. "Akenside and the Controversy over Ridicule." *Mark Akenside: A Reassessment.* Ed. Robin Dix. Madison: Fairleigh Dickinson UP, 2000. 108–31.

Thompson, E. P. *The Making of the English Working Class.* New York: Vintage, 1966.

Thompson, Helen. "How *The Wanderer* Works: Reading Burney and Bourdieu." *ELH* 68 (2001): 965–89.

Thompson, James. *Models of Value: Eighteenth-Century Political Economy and the Novel.* Durham, NC: Duke UP, 1996.

*'Tis All a Cheat; or The Way of the World.* Northampton: R. Raikes and W. Dicey, 1720.

Tobin, Beth Fowkes. *Superintending the Poor: Charitable Ladies and Paternal Landlords in British Fiction, 1770–1860.* New Haven: Yale UP, 1993.

Todd, Janet. *The Sign of Angellica: Women, Writing, and Fiction, 1660–1800.* New York: Columbia UP, 1989.

Torfing, Jacob. *New Theories of Discourse: Laclau, Mouffe and Žižek.* Oxford: Blackwell, 1999.

Towner, John. *An Historical Geography of Recreation and Tourism in the Western World: 1540–1940.* Chichester: Wiley and Sons, 1996.

Townsend, Joseph. *Dissertation on the Poor Laws by a Well-Wisher to Mankind.* Reprint. Berkeley and Los Angeles: U of California P, 1971.

Trumbach, Randolph. *The Rise of the Egalitarian Family: Aristocratic Kinship and Domestic Relations in Eighteenth-Century England.* New York: Academic Press, 1978.

Trumpener, Katie. *Bardic Nationalism: The Romantic Novel and the British Empire.* Princeton: Princeton UP, 1997.

———. "National Character, Nationalist Plots: National Tale and Historical Novel in the Age of Waverley, 1806–1830." *ELH* 60.3 (1993): 685–731.

Trusler, John. *Modern Times, or, The Adventures of Gabriel Outcast.* 3 vols. 2nd ed. London: Printed for the author, 1785.

Turner, James. "Stephen Switzer and the Political Fallacy in Landscape Gardening History." *Eighteenth-Century Studies* 11.4 (1978): 489–96.

Ty, Eleanor. *Unsexed Revolutionaries: Five Women Novelists of the 1790s.* Toronto: U of Toronto P, 1993.

Vaggi, Gianni. *The Economics of François Quesnay.* Studies in Political Economy Series. London: Macmillan, 1987.

Valenze, Deborah D. *The First Industrial Woman.* Oxford: Oxford UP, 1995.

Vidler, Anthony. *The Architectural Uncanny: Essays in the Modern Unhomely.* Cambridge: MIT Press, 1992.

Wamwere, Koigi wa. *Negative Ethnicity: From Bias to Genocide*. New York: Seven Stories Press, 2003.

Warner, William Beatty. *Reading "Clarissa": The Struggles of Interpretation*. New Haven: Yale UP, 1979.

Waswo, Richard. "Story as Historiography in the Waverley Novels." *ELH* 47.2 (1980): 304–30.

Watson, Nicola. *Revolution and the Form of the British Novel, 1790–1825*. Oxford: Clarendon, 1994.

Watt, James. *Contesting the Gothic: Fiction, Genre, and Cultural Conflict, 1764–1832*. Cambridge: Cambridge UP, 1999.

Wayne, Don E. *Penshurst: The Semiotics of Place and the Poetics of History*. Madison: U of Wisconsin P, 1984.

Webb, Sidney, and Beatrice Webb. *English Local Government*. 11 vols. Hamden, CT: Archon, 1963.

———. *English Poor Law History. Part 1: The Old Poor Law*. Vol. 7 of Webb and Webb, *English Local Government*. Hamden, CT: Archon, 1963.

———. *The Parish and the County*. Vol. 1 of Webb and Webb, *English Local Government*. Hamden, CT: Archon, 1963.

Weber, Max. *Economy and Society: An Outline of Interpretive Sociology*. Ed. and trans. Guenther Roth and Claus Wittich. Berkeley and Los Angeles: U of California P, 1978.

———. *The Protestant Ethic and the "Spirit" of Capitalism and Other Writings*. Ed. and trans. Peter Baehr and Gordon C. Wells. Penguin Twentieth-Century Classics. London: Penguin, 2002.

Wedderburn, Alexander. Preface. *Edinburgh Review* 1.1 (January-July 1755): i–iv.

Williams, Peter. "Constituting Class and Gender: A Social History of the Home, 1700–1901." *Class and Space: The Making of Urban Society*. Ed. N. J. Thrift and Peter Williams. London: Routledge and Kegan Paul, 1987. 154–204.

Wilson, Edward. *Observations on the Present State of the Poor*. Reading: Smart and Cowslade, 1795.

Wilson, John. *The Isle of Palms, and Other Poems*. Edinburgh: John Ballantyne, 1812.

Wollstonecraft, Mary. *A Vindication of the Rights of Woman*. Ed. Carol H. Poston. Norton Critical Edition. 2nd ed. New York: Norton, 1988.

Wood, David Murukami, ed. *A Report on the Surveillance Society*. For the Information Commissioner by the Surveillance Studies Network. ico.gov.uk. www.ico.gov.uk/upload/documents/library/data_protection/practical_application/surveillance_society_full_report_2006.pdf.

Wood, John (of Bath). *Choir Gaure, Vulgarly Called Stonehenge*. Oxford, 1747.

Wood, John (Younger). *A Series of Plans for Cottages or Habitations of the Labourer*. New ed. London: I. and J. Taylor at the Architectural Library, 1792.

Woollacott, Angela. "'All This Is the Empire I Told Myself': Australian Women's Voyages 'Home' and the Articulation of Colonial Whiteness." *American Historical Review* 102.4 (1997): 1003–29.

Wordsworth, Dorothy, and William Wordsworth. *The Early Letters of William and Dorothy Wordsworth (1787–1805)*. Ed. Ernest de Selincourt. Oxford: Clarendon Press, 1935.

Wordsworth, William. *Home at Grasmere: Part First, Book First of The Recluse.* Ed. Beth Darlington. The Cornell Wordsworth. Ithaca: Cornell UP, 1977.

———. *Lyrical Ballads and Other Poems, 1797–1800.* Ed. James Butler and Karen Green. The Cornell Wordsworth. Ithaca: Cornell UP, 1993.

———. *Peter Bell.* Ed. John E. Jordan. The Cornell Wordsworth. Ithaca: Cornell UP, 1985.

———. *The Ruined Cottage and The Pedlar.* Ed. James A. Butler. The Cornell Wordsworth. Ithaca: Cornell UP, 1978.

———. *The Thirteen-Book "Prelude."* Ed. Mark L. Reed. 2 vols. The Cornell Wordsworth. Ithaca: Cornell UP, 1991.

Wycherley, William. *The Country Wife.* Ed. James Ogden. 2nd ed. New Mermaids. New York. Norton, 1991.

Young, Arthur. *The Example of France, A Warning to Britain.* 2nd ed. Bury St. Edmunds: J. Rackham, 1793.

———. *The Farmer's Tour through the East of England.* 4 vols. London, 1771.

———. *National Danger, and the Means of Safety.* London: W. Richardson, 1797.

———. *A Six Weeks Tour through the Southern Counties of England and Wales.* 3rd ed. London: W. Strahan et al., 1772.

Young, William. *Considerations on the Subject of Poor-Houses and Work-Houses, Their Pernicious Tendency . . . in a Letter to the Rt. Hon. W. Pitt.* London: John Stockdale, 1796.

———. *Observations Preliminary to a Proposed Amendment of the Poor Laws.* London: John Nichols, 1788.

Zangerl, Carl. "The Social Composition of the County Magistracy in England and Wales, 1831–1887." *Journal of British Studies* 11:1 (November 1971): 113–25.

Zirker, Malvin R. "General Introduction." *An Enquiry into the Causes of the Late Increase of Robbers and Related Writings.* Ed. Zirker. The Wesleyan Edition of the Works of Henry Fielding. Middletown, CT: Wesleyan UP, 1988. xvii–cxiv.

Žižek, Slavoj. *For They Know Not What They Do: Enjoyment as a Political Factor.* Phronesis series. London: Verso, 1991.

———. *The Plague of Fantasies.* London: Verso, 1997.

# Index